RACISM, THE BIBLE, and the AMERICAN DREAM

From Slavery to Obama

A Frank Discussion, from a Christian Perspective, on Racial Discrimination in America, and its effect on Life, Liberty, and the Pursuit of Happiness

RACISM,
THE BIBLE,
and the
AMERICAN DREAM

From Slavery to Obama

A Frank Discussion, from a Christian Perspective, on Racial Discrimination in America, and its effect on Life, Liberty, and the Pursuit of Happiness

Elreta Dodds

Press Toward The Mark Publications
Detroit Michigan

Racism, The Bible, and The American Dream

Copyright © 2011 Elreta Dodds
First Edition
Published by Press Toward The Mark Publications
P.O. Box 02099 Detroit, Michigan 48202
www.presstowardthemark.com

Scripture quotations marked KJV are taken from the Holy Bible , 1611 King James Version

Scripture quotations marked (NIV) are taken from the Holy Bible, New International Version®, NIV®, Copyright©1973, 1978, 1984 by Biblica, Inc.™ Used by permission of Zondervan, All rights reserved worldwide. www.zondervan.com

Scripture quotations from *THE MESSAGE*. Copyright © by Eugene H. Peterson 1993, 1994, 1995, 1996, 2000, 2001, 2002. Used by permission of NavPress Publishing Group.

Scripture quotations taken from the New American Standard Bible®, Copyright © 1960, 1962, 1963, 1968, 1971, 1972, 1973, 1975, 1977, 1995 by the Lockman Foundation Used by permission. www.Lockman.org

Scripture taken from the New King James Version. Copyright © 1982 by Thomas Nelson, Inc. Used by permission. All rights reserved.

Scripture quotations marked NLT are taken from the Holy Bible, New Living Translation, copyright 1996, 2004. Used by permission of Tyndale House Publishers, Inc., Wheaton, Illinois 60189. All rights reserved.

Scriptures marked as "(CEV)" are taken from the Contemporary English Version Copyright © 1995 by American Bible Society. Used by permission.

Scripture quotations marked (TNIV) are taken from the Holy Bible, Today's New International Version® TNIV, Copyright ©2001, 2005 by Biblica Inc.™ Used by permission of Zondervan. All rights reserved worldwide. www.zondervan.com

ISBN: 978-09660390-4-7

Library of Congress Control Number: 2010933980

Editor: Noreta Dennard, Detroit Michigan
Cover: Barb Gunia, Sans Serif Inc., Saline Michigan
Photo: Fox Portrait Studios, Eastpointe Michigan

PRINTED AND BOUND IN THE UNITED STATES OF AMERICA

In Dedication to all those, living or dead, who ever dared to speak out, or stand up, against any form of racism.

--Elreta Dodds

Acknowledgements...

A *Very Special Thanks* to Noreta Dennard, BA in Special Education, for her service as Copy Editor and for her detailed edit and critique of the book. She put her heart and soul into this project. *Special Thanks* to: Tenay Hankins for her edit and critique of the book, Allison Cross, Pastor of Fire and Rain Ministries of Muskegon Michigan for her work in fact checking the book; Dr. Jeffrey Alan Williams, Ph.D. in Human Services and Pastor of St. John Baptist Church of Smith's Creek Michigan, for his edit and critique of the Introduction and portions of chapter 5, his critique of the Epilogue, and for providing research materials on the Constitution, Affirmative Action, Civil Rights, Ethnicity, and Hurricane Katrina; Vickie Diane Archie, MA in Practical Theology, for her edit and critique of chapters 6 and 7, my pastor, Rev. Link Howard III, Pastor of Faith Christian Community Church of Port Huron Michigan, for his edit and critique of chapter 7 and his critique of the Epilogue; Martha Howard, First Lady of Faith Christian Community Church, for her critique of the Epilogue, Sualyn Holbrook, BA in Sociology and Christian Education, for giving me a copy of book, *The Covenant with Black America,* which became one of my research tools, and Barb Gunia of Sans Serif Incorporated, Saline Michigan, for her great work on the front and back covers.

Additional *Thanks,* in alphabetical order, to the following for helping with the decisions on the subtitle and front cover design: Vickie Diane Archie, Allen A. Dennard Jr., Noreta Dennard, Derek Grigsby, Tenay Hankins, Pastor Link Howard III, Pastor Anthony King, Pastor Jessica Totty, Pastor Kevin Totty, Minister Dwight White, Pastor Dr. Jeffrey A. Williams, Pastor Lydia Wright, and Shawntia Monique Wright. Additional *Thanks*, in alphabetical order, to the following for helping with the decision on the subtitle: Pastor Allison Cross, Allen Arthur Dennard Sr., Allena Octavia Dennard, Octavia Katrina Dodds, and Christian Ringo. Additional thanks in Alphabetical order, to the following for helping with the decision on the author photo: Noreta Dennard, Pastor Link Howard III, Martha Howard, and Dr. Jeffrey A. Williams.

A *Very Special Personal Thanks* to my mother, Octavia Katrina Dodds, who encouraged my desire as a child to write books, by buying me writing tablets (from what was then the Woolworth "5 & Dime store") at the time. I want to also thank her for making me learn, when I was a teenager, how to type (the correct way; without looking at the keyboard). And a *Very Special Personal Thanks* to my sister, Noreta Dennard, who is always willing to assist me in my writing projects, is always just as enthused about the projects as I am, and has not only edited my books but has oftentimes also produced and directed my plays. She is my "right arm." I can't thank both my mother and sister enough for their continued undying support and encouragement.

TABLE OF CONTENTS

CHAPTER 3
A HISTORY OF RACIAL DISCRIMINATION IN
AMERICA.............36

CHAPTER 4
THE CIVIL RIGHTS MOVEMENT IN AMERICA....61

CHAPTER 5
INSTITUTIONAL RACISM IN AMERICA...WHERE WE ARE TODAY....................78

CHAPTER 6
RACISM IN RELIGIONS AND IDEOLOGIES ASSOCIATED
WITH CHRISTIANITY.........181

CHAPTER 7
THE BIBICAL PERPECTIVE ON RACE AND RACISM...206

_____

APPENDIX: THE BASIC BELIEFS OF CHRISTIANITY...322

INTRODUCTION

The misuse of the Bible, of some, to justify prejudice and discrimination has been one of the main catalysts in the perpetuation of racism throughout the centuries, throughout the world, and throughout the history of the United States. The purpose of this work is threefold: to dispel any misconception of the Bible as a racist book in the hopes that those with this misconception will begin to think otherwise and thereupon embrace the Bible instead of rejecting it; to encourage those, who realize that racism exists in America but are apathetic towards this realization, to come to grips with the magnitude of the offense, let go of their apathy and speak out against racism when the opportunity arises, and to redirect, as many as possible, those who erroneously use the Bible as a weapon to justify racial hatred.

There is also a secondary aim of this book which is to better enlighten, overall, the reader about the seriousness of institutional racism against minorities that live in America but is either downplayed and/or not recognized by many of those who are not victims of it, or is altogether ignored by many of those who do indeed recognize it but, for one reason or another, look the other way.

It is understood and appreciated that throughout the centuries there have been numerous men and women from all walks of life and from all ethnic backgrounds, people of color as well as whites, who have spoken out, and stood up, against racial discrimination and oppression, many of whom gave up their own lives for the freedom and civil rights of others. This book is not intended to minimize any contribution that has been made, past or present, towards the establishment of a true racially equitable American society. But, contrary to popular belief, there is still much work to be done and therefore there is still much to be discussed. It's not an easy discussion, uncomfortable at best, but it is indeed, a necessary one; a crucial conversation. And although the issue of racism is often discussed as it pertains to social and civil issues; it is rarely discussed as it pertains to morality. In defense against the ideology that says the Bible condones racism; this book delves into the matter to reveal what the Scriptures actually teach regarding the issue.

In order to discuss what the Bible says and doesn't say about racism, racism must first be defined, a history of racism in America must be provided, racism that can be found in religious doctrine must be uncovered, and the institutional racism that is directed systematically and covertly at blacks and other minorities, that still exists today, must be exposed and challenged. This book therefore does just that. All of these preliminaries are discussed before getting to the meat of the matter: whether or not the Bible condones racism and racial discrimination. And in discussing these preliminaries in detail, the secondary purpose of better enlightening the reader about the continued existence of racism in America, is accomplished.

It must be emphasized that the term *racism* will be used for the most part to refer to racial discrimination, particularly racial discrimination against minorities. It should also be noted that the use of the word *minority* to refer to non-whites subliminally suggests that non-whites are "less than" since the word *minority* is derived from the word *minor* which is an adjective that means less in a quantitative way as well as less in significance or importance. However, because the use of the word *minority* has very much infiltrated American society when speaking of race relations and racial issues, and because at present there is no other word that has been coined to replace it; *minority* will be used within the pages of this book to refer to people who are classified as "non-white" but not as its definition pertains to significance or importance, but instead only as its definition pertains to numbers.

There is no doubt that certain liberties are always negatively affected when racism abounds, even in the minuteness of forms. And when liberties are negatively affected then the life and the pursuit of happiness of the targets of such racism are negatively affected as well. This brings us again to the reason for the secondary aim of this book and that is to aid in exposing the practices of institutional racism that saturate America so that in doing so, new voices will be encouraged to speak out against those practices.

When speaking of the history of racism in America one cannot help but to envision the Ku Klux Klan, lynch mobs, racial separation of public facilities and restaurants, the Civil Rights Movement, and the like. Many believe that since those extreme forms of racism do not exist in America today that racism, although still existing in some forms, is no longer the detriment to minorities that it once was. To give an example; there were a large portion of Americans who actually believed, upon the election of the first black President of the United States (President Barack Hussein Obama), that America had been catapulted into a post-racial era and that Obama's election as President proved that racism in America had been eradicated...overnight. However, many of those optimists now see that nothing could be farther from the truth.

The quests for money, power, and/or control have always been the main triggers that lead any one group of people to purpose towards dominating another group of people. Institutional racism (also referred to as systematic and/or structural racism) is an insidious form of racism in America that can still be as much of a detriment, quantitatively if not qualitatively, to minorities today just as was the historical racism in America that most are familiar with and don't deny. Because it is important to lay a foundation when expounding upon a topic, institutional racism is discussed quite heavily within these pages but only as a necessary component of the book's primary purpose. Still, institutional racism lurks beneath the shadows in every facet of American life and is so very pervasive that to discuss all of it in-depth would necessitate volumes.

It must be pointed out that when we use the term *institutional racism* what we are really referring to is *institutional discrimination* along with the underlying catalyst of racism that perpetuates that discrimination. *Institutional racism* is the term that has been coined to refer basically to the systematic and structural discrimination that pervades our social and civil institutions on a national scale. A more detailed description of the term is provided subsequently. Moreover, although other minorities besides blacks are focused upon in this book, the overall focus, as it pertains to racial discrimination against minorities, is on black Americans.

The book begins in the first chapter by defining what race is and what racism is. The different kinds of racism are discussed. Chapter 2 looks at how racism began and permeated in America. It looks at the advent of slavery, the Civil War, the casting of people into racial categories, and also takes a look at the Constitution of the United States in its relation to racial issues. Chapter 3 presents a history of racism and discrimination in America and is devoted mostly to a discussion of the Jim Crow era.

Chapter 4 goes on to focus on the history of the Civil Rights Movement and on pivotal events during that time. Chapter 5 takes a detailed look at institutional racism in America as it stands today. Chapter 6 looks at religious racism against minorities as it pertains to certain religions that are labeled as Christian but propagate racist teachings. The chapter also includes a discussion on the debate as to whether or not the Bible says blacks are cursed to be slaves. Chapter 7 defends the Bible against the belief that it teaches and/or condones racism or racial discrimination, and discusses the Bible's position on these matters. An Epilogue is thereafter provided. The book ends with an Appendix that explains the basic tenets of the Christian faith.

As stated earlier, the primary purpose of this book is to defend the Bible by debunking any viewpoint that accuses the Bible of teaching and/or supporting racism, and in doing so, points to the secondary purpose of shedding more light on the institutional racism against minorities that still flourishes in American society today. It is the hope, that along with the defense of the Bible in this area, the exposure of the sheer magnitude of what is persistent and ongoing institutional racism in America will help to pull those out of denial who actually think that racism in America is a thing of the past; will help to encourage those who have remained silent to say something against racist acts, particularly when racism and/or discrimination occurs within their circles; and will help to activate a cultural mindset toward the demise of racism in America once and for all.

Silence, whether due to fear of persecution, due to the fear of loss of privilege, or due to apathy, is indeed consent. On the other hand, silence, due to lack of knowledge is silence by design. There are those who work hard to convince the masses that racism in America is basically a thing of the past and that institutional racism has no real strong lasting effect on those who fall prey to it. Part of the tools they use in their strategy to minimize the racism that exists is to withhold the information that says otherwise. It is therefore by design that many Americans have been fooled into believing that there is no such thing as racism in America anymore, at least not to the extent to where it's worth discussing. But to the contrary, this is one of the many works that has been brought forth to help set the record straight on both counts, which are thus: count one...racism and discrimination against minorities is still very pervasive in America, and count two... no racism can be justified biblically because the Bible does not condone it. To these two ends this book endeavors to convince.

1.

RACE AND RACISM DEFINED

In order to begin our discussion we must first define what is meant by the term *race* and what racism is. This chapter defines race, talks about why people are put into racial categories, and identifies nine types of racism. Definitions and categories of race are different for different countries. We are particularly looking at what race means as it pertains to how it is defined in the United States.

WHAT RACE IS

For our purposes, "race" will be defined as a descriptive human category one fits into based on skin color, facial features, national origin, and/or ancestry. In America, the major deciding factor of one's racial identity has to do with whether or not one is considered to be white or non-white. Persons of color are categorized into several different "races" according to ancestry and national origin. A person of color is anyone who is considered not to be white and can include, but is not limited to, those who have been identified as African-Americans, Asian, Hispanic, Latino, Mexican, Native-Americans, and so forth. African-Americans are also referred to as black and white Americans are also referred to as Caucasian.

Americans are also often defined by their "ethnicity." Ethnicity has more to do with country and custom than with race. White Americans have many ethnic origins. Some white Americans are Irish, some are German, some are Polish, and the list goes on. Their ethnicity is defined by the country (and the customs of that country) in which their immediate ancestors came from. However, white Americans are hardly ever identified by their ethnic heritage and are simply referred to as Americans while Americans of color are usually identified in terms of their ethnicity and ancestral heritage.

There are many white people with various ethnic backgrounds but they are mostly looked at as white. Additionally, many black Americans have various ethnic backgrounds as well. There are black people with Native American ancestors, Cuban ancestors, Jamaican ancestors, Spanish ancestors, and even European ancestors. However, black Americans are usually only defined by their African ancestry even though the majority of black Americans were not born in Africa and have never been there.

WHY RACE IS

As expressed earlier, the annals of history, beginning with the earliest of antiquity, have taught us that one of man's most desired ambitions is to rule over others. To have rule or authority over another human being, in and of itself, is not necessarily wrong. A mother has authority over her child. An employer has authority over his employee. The government has authority over the people. However, often times, rulers and/or want-to-be rulers oppress those whom they rule or would like to rule. When this happens, these oppressive rulers inevitably develop a strong need to justify the oppression that they are imposing upon others. This strong need to justify the oppression develops because those who oppress others inherently know that it is basically wrong to do so.

Although the general belief is that God created the various races of mankind; the actuality is that God created the *human race* (human beings) with varying skin colors, facial features, hair texture, height, body mass, and so on. As discussed in detail in chapter 7, God identifies groups of people by nationality, not by what we term as *race*. But mankind has looked at the various differences of skin color, facial features, hair texture, and the like and has identified and categorized human beings based on these various physical differences. In America, *race* is what we call the category that people are fitted into when it comes to these various physical differences. "Race," as we know it, is therefore actually a creation of mankind resulting from the need that man has in general to rule, have power over, and at times oppress others.

Without emphasizing the physical differences of human beings, there can be no such thing as race, and without the idea or concept of race, there can be no foundation for racial supremacist thinking and consequently no rationalization to oppress others. Physical differences are what man has come to classify as racial differences. Supremacist thinking (the belief that one race of people is superior to another) results from the desire of one person or group of people to have ultimate power over another group of people. In order to justify the desire of such power, supremacists see the group of people that they desire power over as inferior. This view often times leads to an additional desire to totally annihilate the group of people that they see as inferior. Supremacist and racist thinking are basically the same, and many of those who embrace racist ideology often fall into the mindset of thinking that they are somehow on a similar level as God. God rules and is supreme. Therefore if they rule and convince themselves that they are supreme, then they assume a dangerous self-imposed god-like self-image. This god-like self-image gives them the sense that they are infallible and that their racism is justified.

In general, those who espouse racism never see themselves as belonging to what they deem as the inferior race. Instead, they always define the superior race as the race in which they themselves are categorized in. They are convinced that they are from a race of superior human beings.

A supremacist, a racist, or one who tends to discriminate against others based on the physical characteristics of those whom he or she is discriminating against, needs to be able to identify characteristics of other people that he or she believes is inferior and then group those people together in categories in order to comfortably label them as subhuman, undesirable, unintelligent, unworthy and so forth. They then convince themselves that these "unworthy" people deserve discriminatory treatment. This is why race is. Race is a necessary component of oppression. Oppression is an essential weapon of the power-hungry. And, oppression has a high probability of occurring any time one man rules another or desires to do so.

Consequently, whether or not one is more likely to experience racism and discrimination, depends on three factors, the first being what race he or she is identified as being part of. The second factor is the country he or she resides in, and the third factor is the racial category of people in that country who maintain control of the country as a group (the dominant group).

As stated earlier, with the creation of race comes the ability to categorize people into racial groups. In America this means that anyone who is not classified as white is classified as a "minority." The word "minority" was originally dubbed because it represented the fact that white people in America outnumbered all other racial groups. When compared to whites the non-white groups (when looked at individually) had lesser numbers and were therefore identified as minor in numbers to the white race's majority in numbers.

The word "minority" itself has a ring of inferiority. Although the word is used to connote less in size, the definition of it, as discussed in the Introduction, also means less in importance and/or value. Overall, race, as it pertains to skin color, facial features, and hair texture is a man-made way of categorizing human beings by appearance as a means by which the dominant group (the race of people that secures and/or maintains power and control over the non-dominant race) can establish control. In America, the non-dominant group is referred to as the "minority" group. The group being discriminated against must be placed into an identifiable category in order for racism and discrimination of the group as a whole to manifest in the first place. Hence, racial categorization is one of the tools used by the dominant, power-over group, to keep the non-dominant subjected group "in their place."

It should be noted that the dominant group of people is not always the group of people with the most numbers, but instead, with enough power to control. The dominant group in countries that exercise racial discrimination, whether institutionally or overtly, are often the group that is lesser in number. However, in America the dominant group (whites) is still the actual majority group numerically, while a third of the overall population is minorities. But things are changing. Statistics of live births in 2010 have indicated that close to half of the babies born in the United States are minorities. This trend was seen in 2008 when the Census Bureau reported that by 2050 non-whites will significantly outnumber whites and whites will numerically be in the minority.

The reason for this trend taking place has to do with the substantial number of Hispanic women of child-bearing age who are immigrating into America. One can only wonder whether or not whites will continue as the dominant group once the numbers reverse. But despite this numerical projection, white Americans are still the dominant group today and as the dominant group (as with any dominant group), they have power, as a whole, over all other racial groups through systematic and structural discrimination that we are referring to interchangeably as *institutional racism*. Institutional racism is very hard to see and its existence is often denied by members of the dominant group. But the very fact that there is a dominant racial group proves that racism abounds. In an ideal society, no one race of people would have dominance over another; all "races" would share equally in the benefits of that society without fear of discrimination, and all races would be treated equitably.

RACISM DEFINED

Racism, simply put, is the belief that one race of people is superior to another race of people. It is the belief that one person is better than another person by virtue of skin color, facial features, hair texture, or some other physical trait. As stated earlier, the person who thinks in this manner usually believes that the superior race is of the racial category in which he or she belongs. Because of America's recent history of enslaving blacks (the 1865 abolition of slavery was less than 200 years ago which means that the great grandparents of many black Americans were only a generation away from slavery themselves), the United States has had a significant problem in the area of race relations over the years. Racism in America has always been prevalent and a blemish to its reputation.

The terms *racism* and *racial discrimination* are often used interchangeably as are *racism* and *prejudice*. However, there are subtle differences. Racism is the flawed belief system that says one race of people is superior to another; hence, anyone who believes that one race of people is superior, in any capacity, is a racist. However, racial discrimination is not the belief itself but instead it is the inequitable treatment (be it overt or covert; conscious or subconscious) of those who are seen as inferior (resulting from racist beliefs) by those who see themselves as superior or somehow better. Racial discrimination in America against minorities is not always practiced actively and overtly but in today's time is more often practiced passively and covertly.

Racial discrimination, as a whole in today's America, is mostly practiced within a system of institutional racism (defined later) by the dominant group against minority groups, but it can also be practiced individually by persons in a minority group against other persons belonging to that same group or against persons from other minority groups or against persons from the dominant group.

Discrimination is the result of racism. Discrimination comes in many forms and has historically presented itself in America in the form of civil rights violations and infractions against the group of people that is seen as racially inferior by those in the dominant group. In 1966, the United Nations developed (and their members signed) what is referred to as *The International Convention on the Elimination of all forms of Racial Discrimination*. This Convention (an agreement between nations) contains 25 Articles that are divided into three parts. Part 1, Article 1 of the Convention defines racial discrimination as such:

> "any distinction, exclusion, restriction or preference based on race, colour, descent, or national or ethnic origin which has the purpose or effect of nullifying or impairing the recognition, enjoyment or exercise, on an equal footing, of human rights and fundamental freedoms in the political, economic, social, cultural or any other field of public life."[1]

Because the terms *racism* and *discrimination* are used interchangeably in American culture, the terms, for the purposes of our discussion, will be (as alluded to earlier) used interchangeably as well as one in the same.

---

[1] United Nations, *International Convention on the Elimination of all forms of Racism,* New York New York, 1966. Public Domain.

Racial Discrimination as defined above by the United Nations is considered an official definition.

Aside from defining racism and discrimination; prejudice must also be defined. Whereas the strict definition of racism is the belief in racial superiority and the strict definition of discrimination is the inequitable treatment of those who are looked at as inferior; prejudice is something altogether different. Theoretically, prejudice can be favorable or unfavorable; but for our purposes we will concentrate on the term as it applies to unfavorable prejudice. Prejudice, therefore, is the pre-judging of a person, in a negative way, before actually having some type of experience with that person that would justify the judgment. The pre-judgment is often due to attributing the same negative stereotypes to a person that have already been attributed to the group of people from which the person has been identified as belonging to by the one doing the judging. Stereotypes are unfounded objectionable qualities (which include but are not limited to behavioral characteristics) ascribed to a certain group of people. To stereotype a group of people is to assume that those who comprise the group are prone to act and behave in a certain way that is usually seen as negative to the person or persons ascribing the stereotype and also to the persons belonging to the group being stereotyped. Stereotyping leads to prejudice, which leads to "better than" supremacist thinking which leads to racial discrimination.

Prejudice, therefore, is the underlying thought process that often leads to what is termed *racism*. It is the thought process by which one human being thinks unfavorably about another human being or a group of people without justifiable cause. The unfavorable thought is usually due to some preconceived notion, stereotype, previous experience, fear, or similar reason. When one expresses prejudice they are prematurely expressing an opinion about another's character, abilities, and/or mindset. If the opinion is premature then it is unwarranted. The person has expressed an opinion about anther person without getting to know the person that they are expressing the opinion about. Although prejudice, when considering its overall definition, does not always lead to racism, racism is always preceded by prejudice.

In order for racial discrimination to flourish in any society whether overtly or covertly, actively or passively, there has to be a system in place which puts everyone in that society into racial categories. America is notorious for doing this. In any society, the presence of even just one minority group is undeniable proof that some form of racism exists in that society; otherwise, no one would be categorized as a minority. In his book "Diversity and Society," Joseph F. Healy defines minority groups as such:

6

"Minority status has more to do with the distribution of resources and power than with simple numbers."[2]

Healy goes on to base his definition on the distinctions first presented by Wagley and Harris in 1958 which identifies five characteristics that make up a minority group. According to Healy those characteristics are as follows:

> The members of the group experience a pattern of disadvantage or inequality. The members of the group share a visible trait or characteristic that differentiates them from other groups. The minority group is a self-conscious social unit. Membership in the group usually is determined at birth. Members tend to marry within the group.[3]

Therefore, our workable definition of a minority group is as such: a group of people that experience a pattern of disadvantage and/or inequality and share a visible trait or characteristic.

American scholars of race relations agree that there are basically two main types of racism: individual racism and institutional racism. We will look at both of these types of racism as well as ideological/scientific racism, reverse/reactionary racism, passive racism, active racism, horizontal racism, religious racism, and minority racism.

Individual racism

Individual racism is the belief by a person that certain individuals are inferior to other individuals due to race. It is the belief that people categorized under certain racial groups are superior to those categorized under certain other racial groups. It is the belief that certain races of people are undesirables and should not live in the same house, neighborhood, city, state, county, or country with a race of people that the particular individual deems superior. The individual racist usually sees the race that he or she is categorized under as the superior race. By deeming himself or herself

---

[2] Healy, Joseph F. *Diversity and Society, Race, Ethnicity, and Gender*, Pine Forge Press, Thousand Oaks California, copyright Sage Publications Inc. ,p. 6. Used by permission of the publisher.
[3] Healy, Joseph F. *Diversity and Society, Race, Ethnicity, and Gender*, Pine Forge Press, Thousand Oaks California, copyright Sage Publications Inc. ,p. 6. Used by permission of the publisher.

racially superior, the person who espouses individual racism believes that there is something about the "inferior" race of people that makes them such. That something is usually skin color. However, skin color is not the only biological variable that racists focus upon when pointing at what they think is inferior in other races. Facial features and hair texture are other biological traits that racists might point to as inferior. Social and cultural practices of a race of people or ethnic group might also be targeted by the racist as inferior.

A racist most always in some way or another practices the racism he or she believes in. It is difficult for a person to believe that another race of people is inferior and not act on it in some way. The racist might not overtly express his or her racism, but might instead express it in subtle ways or passive aggressively.

Institutional / structural / systematic racism

The phrase "institutional racism" was first coined by Stokely Carmichael and Charles Hamilton in their 1967 book *Black Power* and then further expounded upon by Louis Knowles and Kenneth Prewitt in their 1969 book *Institutional Racism in America*. In the book, Stokely and Hamilton are quoted as defining institutional racism as a second type of racism different from overt racism, in the following way:

> The second type is less overt, far more subtle, less identifiable in terms of specific individuals committing the acts. But it is no less destructive of human life. The second type originates in the operation of established and respected forces in the society, and thus receives far less public condemnation than the first type.[4]

Established and respected forces in society usually take form as organizations. The institutional organization is the operation of a certain system that provides a certain necessary human service. The structure of a social institution or system (say for example, health care) substantially affects the people who must live within the parameters of the rules of those institutions/organizations or who must depend on those institutions for increased quality of life. How the institution or system is structured plays a vital role as to whether or not all persons will be treated equally within the

---

[4] Reprinted with the permission of Simon and Schuster, Inc., from INSTITUIONAL RACISM IN AMERICA by Lois Knowles and Kenneth Prewitt. Copyright©1969 by Prentis-Hall, Inc. All rights reserved.

8

system of the institution in question. If the institution or system is structured in favor of a particular race then institutional racism emerges and the system therefore becomes flawed at the expense of a particular group of people. As indicated in the Introduction, when institutional racism is spoken of what is really being spoken of is institutional or systematic racial discrimination resulting from underlying racism. So, for our purposes when we speak specifically of institutional racism what we're basically speaking of is systematic racial discrimination that permeates in the structure of a social and/or societal institution.

Institutional racism comes about when the benefits of an institution serve one race of people better than it does another race of people. Institutional racism can only be imposed upon a race of people who have little or no power in the society in which they live.

There is no question that, in America, institutional racism overall is an injustice imposed upon blacks and other minority groups by the dominant group. This is not to say that white people are never victims of racism and that all white people knowingly contribute to this type of racism and it should be emphatically noted, as attested to in the Introduction, that there have been many white people who have vehemently fought against slavery, racism, and racial discrimination over the centuries even at the risk of great bodily harm or death. Despite this, racism, although not as overt as it once was, still exists in America to a considerable degree by way of institutional racism/discrimination which is perpetuated by an overall white establishment. In any society where there is systematic institutional racism, such discrimination positively benefits the dominant group (in America that would be whites) while negatively affecting the non-dominant groups (in America that would be blacks and other minorities). Some of the systems in which institutional racism flourish include, but are not limited to, medicine, education, the justice system, politics, employment, and housing. Opportunities in these systems (and any other social system in society) should be equitable and the services given to people through these systems should be evenly and fairly provided. But in countries where institutional racism abounds, this is simply not the case.

Active racism

Active racism is behavior or actions taken by a person or group of people with the express purpose of promoting supremacist ideologies and/or promoting racial discrimination against another person or group of people. Active racism is usually very blatant, but can also take place behind the scenes. The Ku Klux Klan[5] is an example of an organization that is actively racist against minorities.

Passive racism

Passive racism is when a person practices racial discrimination indirectly. It is when a person maintains certain racist beliefs and acts on those beliefs in a covert way. People who practice passive racism do not outwardly oppress a particular race of people but do so inconspicuously whether consciously or unconsciously as a result of their own engrained negative prejudices. To passively practice racial discrimination is to help to maintain, in a passive way, racial discriminatory practices against a certain racial group. It is also to see or to realize that racial discrimination has occurred in a certain situation and to keep silent about it, deny its existence, or to aid indirectly in promoting it. Those who engage in passive racism oftentimes benefit, in some way, from their passivity.

Scientific / ideological racism

Scientific racism is basically synonymous with ideological racism. Scientific racism is a belief that certain physical traits, that are generally characteristic of a certain "race" of people, directly determine the mental, physical, and intellectual capabilities along with the personality traits of that particular race. It is the idea that skin color directly affects a person's intelligence, personality, and the way he or she conducts himself or herself.[6]

Reverse / reactionary racism

Reverse racism and reactionary racism are used interchangeably. Reverse racism is when minorities express racist thoughts or perform racist acts against persons in the dominant group. In America, reverse racism would therefore be defined as a person of color expressing racist beliefs or performing racist acts against white people. The minority sees white people as the protagonists and initiators of racism overall and in response

---

[5] See Chapter 3

[6] In 1904, Ota Benga, a Pygmy from Africa was victimized by scientific racism by being placed in the Bronx Zoo in New York in order that Darwinism would be promoted. After much public outcry, he was eventually freed and sent to Virginia to assimilate into American society, but committed suicide by shooting himself in 1916 after his hopes of returning to Africa faded.

to this perception, they develop what they feel is justified racism against whites as a whole. They see the race that they are categorized in as a race that is superior to the white race. The term *reverse racism* has most notably been used, even by some within the American black community, to label the belief of those blacks who have expressed racist views against whites. Blacks who are reverse/reactionary racists also tend to believe that all white people are racists and that no white person can be trusted. Many blacks feel justified in expressing racist views against whites because of the racism that has been imposed upon blacks in America over the centuries and they therefore oftentimes don't even see the views of superiority that they expound as being racist. Some see reverse or reactionary racism as part of a defense mechanism some blacks have developed to feel like a legitimate human being in what they see as an overall racist society. Despite this, reverse racism is no more acceptable than white racism is against blacks and minorities.

Religious racism

Religious racism is the belief that says God has made one race of people superior to another. Of all the religious books that can be misused to support a misguided belief that one race is superior to another, there is no doubt that the Bible is the book most misused and misinterpreted when it comes to those who believe that God supports and condones racism. As is discussed in detail later in this book; the Mormons, the Klan, and those who follow the teachings of the Christian Identity movement (among others) are guilty of misinterpreting biblical scriptures in an effort to support their belief that whites are a superior people. Religious racism often leads to genocide and crimes against humanity; such as brutal slavery, systematic rape of women, and the establishment of concentration camps.

Minority racism

Minority racism is the belief of an individual (who belongs to a minority group), that the minority group that they belong to is superior to another minority group or other minority groups as a whole. In America minority groups include blacks, Jews, Arabs, Hispanics, Latinos, Koreans, Mexicans, Asians, Native Americans and others. There is often tension between these groups separate from any tensions between these groups and the dominant group. These tensions are oftentimes due to one group stereotyping another and acting on those stereotypes in some way.

Horizontal racism

Horizontal racism is similar to minority racism in that it is the belief of an individual (who belongs to a certain minority group) that the minority group that he or she belongs to is somehow inferior or superior to another minority group. With regards to feeling inferior, the individual has accepted (usually subconsciously but often consciously), as truth, the stereotypes that have been attributed to the minority group in which he or she belongs and they act on that acceptance. However, horizontal racism is also a belief by an individual (who belongs to a particular minority group) that certain people *that belong to that same minority group* are inferior or superior (e.g. better than, cleaner, more intelligent) in some way, (usually due to a variation of a certain physical characteristic), to others who belong to the same group. The difference here is that this particular form of racism is not only targeted towards people outside of the group, but that it is often also targeted towards people inside of the group as well.

CHAPTER SUMMATION

The quest for power and control leads to racism which ultimately leads to racial discrimination. Racism, in general, is defined as the belief that one race is superior to another. There are however, different categories of racism, which include but are not limited to individual, institutional, active, passive, scientific, religious, reverse, minority, and horizontal racism. Race itself is really a man-made schism cleverly created by those who wish to dominate and control people. As we shall see, race is not something God has created; it is something man has created. Once a society has established a dominant group (the group with the power), all other groups are considered *less than* in some way, thus setting the stage for racial discrimination. If one is discriminated against on a consistent basis within just one social system, then that person's quality of life is affected in some negative way which hinders or makes that person's pursuit of happiness all the more difficult. This simply should not be.

Since America was purportedly founded on Christian principles the question becomes whether or not racism is condoned by God. The Bible is the religious book that is used by many racists to justify and defend their bigoted beliefs. But their justification by using scripture is erroneous as we shall soon see. However, before getting to the main crux of the matter we must first take a look at the history of racial discrimination in America, how racism came to permeate America, the history and influence of the Civil Rights Movement in America, a detailed look at institutional racism in America today, and racism in religious doctrine. As discussed in detail in chapter 7, the Bible does not condone racism and since America was initially founded on Christian principles, every American citizen should have equal access to the American Dream of life, liberty, and the pursuit of happiness. But as we will see in examining things further, overt racism in times past and covert institutional racism in today's America, greatly hinders such equal access.

2.

THE RISE OF RACISM IN AMERICA

IT BEGAN WITH THE "INDIANS"

Racism in America began with the colonization of European settlers. Europeans began inhabiting the Americas shortly after Christopher Columbus made his voyage to the West in 1492. Christopher Columbus was born in the city of Genoa Italy in 1451 and lived to be 55 years of age. He was a sailor (specifically; a fifteenth century mariner explorer) and led four explorer sailing expeditions between 1492 and 1504. Between these years, Columbus made four voyages across the Atlantic Ocean with the purpose of finding a shorter route to the Far East in a quest for silks and spices. Instead, his first voyage led him and his crew, unbeknownst to him at the time, to an Island in the Bahamas[1] located off the shore of North America. There were people already living in the region. Columbus referred to the inhabitants as "Indians" since he thought that he was initially in India and that he had made it to the Asian continent. Today, we also refer to the "Indians" as Native Americans and the two identifiers are used interchangeably. Columbus and his men captured many Native Americans and sold them into slavery.

During his second trip, which took place between September 1493 and June of 1496, Columbus took sail in the hopes of finding gold and with the intent to enslave more Indians. This voyage consisted of 17 ships and 1500 men. During this voyage he began colonizing on the coast of Hispaniola. His third and fourth voyages brought him and his crewmen to Trinidad, Venezuela, Mexico, Honduras, Central America Panama, Jamaica, and the Dominican Republic. In the 1958 first edition of his book, *Jim Crow Guide*, Stetson Kennedy puts it the following way:

> When in 1492 Christopher Columbus opened the door to the white conquest of the Americas, there were nearly a million native Indians living in what is now the United States. Far from permitting this number to increase, the white man has vigorously pursued—both as individual enterprise and national policy—a

---

[1] Also referred to as the Caribbean Islands.

genocidal campaign expressly aimed, until quite recently, at the effective extermination of Indians from the continent. This campaign—consisting of relentless warfare, massacre, confinement, starvation, and neglect—was so successful that by 1923 less than a quarter of a million Indians remained in the U.S.A. Since then the pressures have been relaxed somewhat, permitting a certain increase in the Indian population, but with intensified efforts being made to exterminate Indian culture. By 1958 their number was still only half what it was upon the white man's arrival.[2]

Although the Europeans initially began enslaving Native Americans upon first arriving to the Americas, the Native Americans refused to be victims of captivity and enslavement and fought with fervor against the European occupiers who were attempting to exercise complete dominion over them. Thus began America's first attempt at "ethnic cleansing." In response to the Native Americans' unwillingness to subject themselves to slavery, the European colonialists, in essence, declared what could be considered as a genocidal war against them. The aim was to kill all of the Native Americans. There was also the prevalent fear among white men that Native American men and white women might eventually begin marrying one another. Because of this, the European men felt it was preferable to kill the Native Americans than to take the risk of intermarriage between Indian men and white women.

The Indians fought a gallant fight against European rule, but were eventually subjugated. They simply did not have the artillery and manpower with which to sustain their fighting power. However, they did have enough military strength to win the fight against the attempted genocide of their people. Their very existence today attests to the fact that America's first attempt at ethnic cleansing was not a successful one.

Ultimately, during the 1800s the white settlers (Europeans), who had by then taken over America, initiated agreements between themselves and the Indians. These agreements were known as peace treaties. Despite the making of these treaties, the "white man" continued to make war against the Native Americans. The settlers (or occupiers at this point) finally decided that it would be more cost effective to cease fire, portion off certain parts of the land, and designate those particular land portions for

---

[2] Kennedy, Stetson Jim Crow Guide, Florida Atlantic University Press, Boca Raton Florida, Third Printing 1992, p. 9, Used by permission of the rights holder, granted through copyright clearance center, www.copyright.com

the Indians. Although the Indians agreed to the treaties and although there is tribal sovereignty on the land reservations (meaning that the tribal laws of the Indians are separate from American laws and state laws); during the signing of these treaties in the nineteenth century, the Indians often signed under duress and large portions of land were bought from the Indians for little or nothing. These portions of land that the Indians were assigned to are now what are called reservations. Instead of integrating and living with the Native Americans, whites decided to separate themselves totally from them. Such separation is a type of apartheid.

Apartheid, simply put, is racial segregation. It is the practice of separating groups. America's apartheid of Native Americans still continues to this day. Native Americans, for the most part, still live on the reservations. In essence, this type of segregation between the races is what white supremacists want when it comes to blacks and Jews and what black nationalists want when it comes to whites. The fact that the Native Americans still live on reservations and are not really a part of American mainstream society is a constant reminder that racism, in its purist form, is still alive and well in America.

THE ADVENT OF AFRICAN SLAVERY IN AMERICA

After Christopher Columbus's voyage to America in 1492, European peoples began to colonize in the Caribbean Islands.[3] They treated the native Islanders violently. A great majority of the Islanders died, not only from the violence, but also from the diseases that the Europeans brought. The Europeans had brought with them convicted criminals from Europe that they had planned to use as slaves in the "New World." However, most of the prisoners died from tropical diseases. Because of this, the Europeans were left without anyone to work the mines and cultivate the tobacco crops. Consequently, it wasn't long before the Europeans began to look upon the African people as a great source of unpaid slave labor. The Portuguese had already proven how well productivity could expand with the use of African slave labor and it was also well known that Africans were not as likely to succumb to unfamiliar diseases. Furthermore, the Europeans were aware that Africa's West Coast was proliferated with chieftains eager to sell other Africans (who were

---

[3] Dodds, Elreta, *What The Bible Really says about Slavery*, Press Toward The Mark Publications, Detroit Michigan, copyright 2000, Third Printing. Much of this historical account is taken verbatim from this book written by this same author. Pgs. 47-48. Used by permission.

lawbreakers or prisoners of war) into the slave trade in return for firearms or other commodities.

The year 1532 marks the first time Africans were transported across the Atlantic for the purpose of enslavement. Some historians cite the date to be as early as 1502. The number of Africans forced across the Atlantic was small until the year 1630 when England, France, and Germany began to become active in the slave trade as a result of the increase of sugar plantations on the Caribbean Islands and in Brazil. This expanded what many blacks in America now refer to as the "African holocaust." The holocaust actually began with the Arab Islamic enslavement of African Christians (particularly from the North African regions) which took place from the fifth to the fifteenth century and has resurfaced in today's time as it pertains to the Northern Sudanese Arab-Islamic enslavement of the Southern Sudanese Christians.

In the early seventeenth century, America as well, began to take part in the atrocity of kidnapping and enslaving Africans. Because of ever-increasing plantations of tobacco and cotton, America filled her demand for African slaves as well. The first African slaves were brought to America in the year 1619. The slave trade continued to flourish because many slaves had to be replaced. During the 1600s and the 1700s most slaves did not survive life on the plantation past ten years. The food and water given the slaves were very little and fatalities due to exhaustion came quick.

During the late 1700s, the profits that the Europeans gained from slave trading began to wane when the prices for slaves increased three-fold because of the steady increase of slave traders set up along the west coast of Africa. Britain became the biggest in the slave trading business when it came to European control. However, as the economics of the slave trade began to dissipate so did the enthusiasm of continuing the trade. Some Europeans began to argue for the rights of the freedom and liberty of the slaves especially after America's war against Britain came to an end in 1783. Countries began abolishing the slave trade. In Holland the trade was abolished in 1814 and in France it was abolished in 1817. It should be emphasized that these countries began putting an end to the slave *trade* but not to slavery itself. In America slave trading was abolished in 1808. The abolishment of slave trading made it illegal to transport human "cargo" across the Atlantic. However, slaves were illegally smuggled across the Atlantic well into the late 1800s and slavery as a whole was not abolished in America until 1865 upon the ratification of the Thirteenth Constitutional Amendment.

Despite the abolishment of slavery in America, discrimination against blacks prevailed and Jim Crow[4] was eventually born, followed by widespread institutional racism that is practiced today.

The Civil War

In 1619 Virginia was the first colonial state to buy African slaves. The state initially bought twenty slaves at that time. Roughly a century and a half later, in 1776, the Declaration of Independence was signed into history. This Declaration liberated all thirteen American colonies from the control of Britain. A portion of the Declaration reads as follows:

> We hold these truths to be self-evident, that all men are created equal, that they are endowed by their Creator with certain unalienable Rights, that among these are Life, Liberty and the pursuit of Happiness. That to secure these rights, Governments are instituted among Men, deriving their just powers from the consent of the governed, That whenever any Form of Government becomes destructive of these ends, it is the Right of the People to alter or to abolish it, and to institute new Government, laying its foundation on such principles and organizing its powers in such form, as to them shall seem most likely to effect their Safety and Happiness.

Although the Declaration of Independence declared all men equal, black men and women were not treated equally or justly. In 1831 William Lloyd Garrison began publishing an anti-slavery newspaper which he called *The Liberator*. The Liberator became one of the most popular and renown anti-slavery editorial mechanisms of its day. Twenty years later, in 1851, *Uncle Tom's Cabin*, an anti-slavery novel written by Harriet Beecher Stowe, was published and had a significant effect in substantially reducing the tolerance of slavery in white society. Over a million copies of the book were sold in roughly twelve months and the novel generated so much support for the abolition of slavery that Abraham Lincoln has been allegedly quoted as crediting Stowe for the onset of the Civil War by remarking, "So this is the little lady that started this big war."

During this time, the anti-slavery states (northern states) slightly outnumbered the pro-slavery states (mostly southern states). Slaves had been brought into America in order to supply free labor for the booming cotton industry. Because most of the cotton grew in the South, the southern

---

[4] See Chapter Three

states financially benefited from the free labor of slavery and wanted no part in any kind of slavery reform or in the complete abolishment of it. As a result, the majority of the southern states began threatening to remove themselves from the Union (the combination of all states which make up the country as a whole). This was unacceptable. The northern states had no intentions of allowing the southern states to make themselves into a separate country.

The discourse between the southern states and the northern states quickly heightened which led to the Kansas Nebraska Act. This act gave the governing officials and the people of each state the opportunity to decide whether or not their state would support and allow the practice of slavery within its boundaries. Abraham Lincoln was President at the time and had plans to make slavery illegal. The southern states were aware of his plans. Consequently many southern states removed themselves from the Union. Interestingly, although Lincoln purposed to abolish slavery, his motives were in question. History tells us that Lincoln was interested in abolishing slavery, not necessarily for moral reasons, but instead, in an effort to keep the Union together. He did not want the South to become a separate entity. However, the North was such a powerful opponent of slavery that Lincoln had no choice but to address the issue of its possible abolishment.

Although Lincoln purposed to stop any further practice of slavery; he also wanted to send all former black slaves to Africa. However, to do so would have been financially unfeasible. Blacks were multiplying at a quick and steady pace.

During Lincoln's first months in office, he revoked the right that the states had to separate themselves from the Union. The states that were in favor of slavery (mostly southern states) formed an alliance between one another referring to themselves as the Confederate states. The remaining states were still referred to as the Union. Both sides began to prepare for war, particularly the Union states which began building protective forts in the advent of war. One of the forts built by the northern states was Fort Sumpter. In the spring of 1861, President Lincoln supplied weapons to this fort. The Confederates considered this act by Lincoln as a declaration of war. Consequently, during that same month, Confederate guerillas attacked the Fort. This battle marked the beginning of America's first and only Civil War. Robert E. Lee was the General for the Confederate Army and Ulysses S. Grant led the Union Army.

It took almost two years, but in 1862 the Confederate army conceded after a bloody Battle at Antietam in which the Union side won. Because of the immense bloodshed that resulted in the battle, Lincoln signed into effect The Emancipation Proclamation which basically entailed the issuance of two Executive orders. The first order would liberate all slaves by January 1, 1863 from any Confederate state that had not returned to the Union by that time. The second order identified the states to which the first order applied. Unfortunately the Proclamation was not a Congressional law but instead a presidential order. So there were many states that the Proclamation did not apply to. It did not apply to Union states and it did not apply to Union controlled southern states. The Union continued to win battles against the Confederates which led to four million slaves being set free by July of 1865. Despite this, fighting still continued because the Confederate army refused to give up. Lincoln promised the Confederate states that they could rejoin the Union if they put down their arms. On April 9, 1865, General Lee surrendered his Confederate Army. Although, by this time, mostly all slaves had been set free, a more permanent remedy was needed to guarantee that there would not be a resurgence of war. The Proclamation did not apply to the whole of the United States and therefore, slavery could futuristically rise up again if there were not a more powerful declaration in place to stop it. Slavery continued to exist here and there. The legal abolishment of slavery that applied to every state in America did not come about until the Thirteenth Amendment was ratified to the Constitution on December 18, 1865. But although slavery had been abolished and made illegal, overt racism and blatant disregard for the civil rights of black people and other minorities continued to take place with much of its effects still being fought against today.

The making of the United States Constitution

The United States Constitution was written seventy-three years before the onset of the Civil War. The laws of the Constitution apply to all states. The Constitution was originally written in 1787 and took effect in 1789 after it was accepted into practice in 1788. The Constitution is the document which encompasses the basic laws by which America is governed. Before the writing of the Constitution, the legal documents binding the states together (the states were also referred to as "colonies" at that time) were the Declaration of Independence of July 4, 1776 (which declared the states Independent of Great Britain) and the Articles of Confederation. The Articles were drafted in November of 1777 and submitted to the states for approval. In July 1778 enough states had given their approval for Congress to proceed with the steps needed to make the Articles operative. The Articles of Confederation was a document developed by Congress to establish a form of government agreeable to the states. The Articles were finally adopted in 1781.

Although the Articles instituted a formal set of rules that each state was obligated to adhere to, it did not thoroughly address, in detail, and sometimes not at all, many of the important governmental issues that needed to be addressed. The Articles established certain laws but did not provide a means whereby which to enforce those laws. Therefore, it was the prerogative of each state whether or not to abide by the laws which were set forth. This was a major drawback of the Articles.

With the inability of the Government to enforce the laws came the inability of the Government to enforce taxation. This plunged the Union into debt and impeded the Union's ability to be an equal player in foreign trade. The value of Union currency quickly diminished.

In 1785 commissioners from Maryland and Virginia met at President George Washington's home in order to resolve navigation and jurisdiction issues when it came to the Chesapeake, Potomac, and Pocomoke rivers which touched the borders of both states. The convening proved to be successful. During this meeting it was also decided that it would be good to have commissioners and representatives (delegates) from all thirteen states come together in a convention-like setting to discuss the issues regarding trade, taxation, and economy. Nine states agreed to have the convention.

The convention was scheduled to take place in September of 1786 in Annapolis Virginia, but only representatives from fives states showed up. Due to the small turn out, all of the state delegates who were in attendance decided that it was best not to attempt to make any major decisions with less than half of the states being represented. They therefore sent out a report urging all of the states to meet in Philadelphia in May of the following year. Congress agreed with the need for a convening and approved holding another convention. But this time, the entire Articles of Confederation would be looked at, not just the Articles that governed taxation and commerce.

Decidedly, in February of 1787, Congress sent word to the head of states that in May of that same year a group of delegates from each state would convene in Philadelphia for the "sole and express purpose of revising the Articles of Confederation." Only delegates from seven states were present. They were all wealthy white males. There were 55 delegates in all. They convened on May 25, 1787. At this meeting it was decided that a Constitution for all of the Union would be developed and implemented. This marked the first meeting of the drafting of the Constitution of the United States. By September of that same year a final draft had been developed. Thirty-nine delegates from twelve states agreed to sign the Constitution. It was necessary for nine states to ratify the Constitution before it could legally take effect and be made into law. In

June of 1788 the approval of the nine states was obtained which made the Constitution binding. Congress was notified of the ratification the following month and the new Constitution finally came into full operation after George Washington was sworn into office in April of 1789.

The Amendments to the Constitution

There have been twenty-seven Amendments to the Constitution, the first ten of which are collectively known as the "Bill of Rights." The Bill of Rights was approved by Congress in September of 1789 and formally approved by eleven states in 1791, which put all ten Amendments into legal effect. The Bill of Rights Amendments include the First Amendment which guarantees freedom of worship, speech, the press, and assembly; the Second Amendment which gives the right to bear arms; the Fourth Amendment which protects against unreasonable search and seizure; and the Fifth Amendment which protects against being tried twice for the same crime, being held for a capital or infamous crime without being charged for the specified crime, testifying against oneself, and being deprived of life, liberty, or property without due process of law.

Although the Fifth Amendment to the Bill of Rights protects against being deprived of life, liberty, and property; this did not aid in abolishing slavery. The Bill of Rights was not originally written for the rights of slaves nor was the Declaration of Independence, a portion of which declares, as we saw earlier, the following:

> We hold these truths to be self-evident, that all men are created equal, that they are endowed by their Creator with certain unalienable rights, that among these are life, liberty and the pursuit of happiness.

Initially, the Constitution (adopted by Congress in 1787, ten years following the Declaration of Independence) upheld slavery practices as evidenced by the following three Article Clauses:

Article 1, Section 2, Clause 3 reads,

> Representatives and direct taxes shall be apportioned among the several States which may be included within this Union, according to the respective numbers, which shall be determined by adding to the whole number of free persons, including those bound to service for a term

of years, and excluding Indians not taxed, three fifths of
all other persons.

The Constitution included slaves as being counted towards the number
of representatives that would be apportioned to a state, but only three-fifths
of each slave (excluding indentured servants;[5] those bound for only a
certain number of years) would be counted. Slaves were counted as only
three-fifths of a person.

Article 1, Section 9, Clause 1 reads:

> The Migration or importation of such persons as any of
> the States now existing shall think proper to admit, shall
> not be prohibited by the Congress prior to the Year one
> thousand eight hundred and eight, but a Tax or duty may
> be imposed on such Importation, not exceeding ten
> dollars for each Person.

The importation that the clause is referring to was human cargo (slaves)
"imported" to the states by way of the transatlantic slave trade. Congress
was concerned about making certain that the "cargo" was properly taxed.

Article 4, Section 2, Clause 3 reads,

> No person held to service or Labour in one State, under
> the laws thereof, escaping into another, shall, in
> consequence of any Law or regulation therein, be
> discharged from such service or labour, but shall be
> delivered up on Claim of the Party to whom such service
> or labour may be due.

This clause mandated the return of runaway slaves to their masters. All
three clauses, though subject to certain Amendments, have not been
deleted from the Constitution. They remain fixed in the document today.

---

[5] Indentured servants were basically immigrant whites, who by contract, worked
free for food and clothing for a certain amount of time; usually 3 to 7 years. They
were counted as whole people. The practice of indentured servitude quickly
dissipated in early America due to black slave labor.

- ### *The Thirteenth Amendment*

The Thirteenth Amendment addresses the issue of slavery and was added to the Constitution in order to permanently abolish the legality of slavery and prohibit its practice. It also makes involuntary servitude illegal, except in some cases, of those who have been convicted of a crime. The Amendment was initially written by two congressmen and one senator (James Ashly, James Wilson, and John Henderson). In January of 1865, Congress presented the proposed Amendment to state legislatures. In order to be put into law, the Thirteenth Amendment had to be ratified by no less than three fourths of all the states, which numbered thirty-six at the time. By December 6th of that same year twenty-seven states had ratified the proposed Amendment. The first section of the Thirteenth Amendment reads as follows:

> Neither slavery nor involuntary servitude, except as a punishment for crime whereof the party shall have been duly convicted, shall exist within the United States, or any place subject to their jurisdiction.

The second section reads,

> Congress shall have the power to enforce this article by appropriate legislation.

In order for an Amendment to become part of the Constitution, it must be ratified (formally approved and accepted) by three-quarters of the states. The first 27 states to ratify the Thirteenth Amendment (in order of ratification) were Illinois, Rhode Island, Michigan, Maryland, New York, Pennsylvania, West Virginia, Missouri, Maine, Kansas, Massachusetts, Virginia, Ohio, Indiana, Nevada, Louisiana, Minnesota, Wisconsin, Vermont, Tennessee, Arkansas, Connecticut, New Hampshire, South Carolina, Alabama, North Carolina, and Georgia. The states of Oregon, California, and Florida ratified by the end of December of that same year. Iowa and New Jersey ratified the Amendment in January of the following year. The state of Texas did not ratify until February of 1870, roughly four years after the Amendment was first ratified into law. The state of Delaware did not ratify until February 1901. The state of Kentucky did not ratify until March of 1976. And surprisingly, or maybe not so surprisingly, Mississippi did not ratify until March 16, of 1995, close to a century and a half later. Therefore, during the early nineties, the state of Mississippi condoned the enslavement of blacks.

The Thirteenth Amendment makes a distinction between slavery and involuntary servitude. Slavery is defined as forced labor obtained by physical restraint or threats of serious physical harm or forced labor by means of giving a person the impression that if they do not labor then they will be seriously harmed or physically restrained, or forced labor by means of threatened manipulation of the legal system against the person whom the labor is being forced upon. When the Amendment speaks of slavery, it is referring to the type of chattel slavery that was inflicted upon blacks during America's antebellum years.

Slavery (along with bonded labor, penal labor, prison labor, labor camp, trafficking) is a form of unfree labor. Unfree labor is defined as the practice of forcing people to work under the threat of making them destitute, under the threat of detainment, under threat of violence, and/or under the threat of death. If paid for his or her wages the pay is paltry or the person is paid in undesirable commodities. Sometimes a person is forced into unfree labor as a way to pay a debt. Another phrase that is often used when referring to unfree labor is *forced labor*.

On the other hand, involuntary servitude is the practice of forcefully compelling someone to work (whether paid or unpaid), for the benefit of oneself or for the benefit of someone else, by means of coercion. Coercion can take different forms. Coercion can be physical or psychological and can include the physical infliction of pain, verbal threats of physical or psychological harm, verbal intimidation, and/or verbal pressure of some kind. Any kind of overt or covert coercion that is used to compel a person to labor against their will is unethical and goes against that person's Thirteenth Amendment rights. In addition to physical and psychological coercion, coercion can also be broken down into predatory coercion, thought coercion (the attempt at altering the values and beliefs a person has), economic coercion, ideological coercion, disciplinary coercion, and religious coercion (i.e. forced conversions).

- **The Fourteenth Amendment**

Although the Thirteenth Amendment protects the general public from slavery, involuntary servitude, and in most instances unfree labor, additional Amendments had to be adopted and ratified in order to protect the civil rights of blacks. These additional Amendments are the Fourteenth and Fifteenth Amendments.

The proposal for the Fourteenth Amendment to the Constitution was made in June of 1866. The Amendment was ratified into the Constitution two years later in July of 1868. The Amendment was proposed and ratified in order to protect the human and civil rights of ex-slaves. The Fourteenth

25

Amendment is comprised of four sections, the first of which is most significant to our discussion. The first section of the Fourteenth Amendment reads as follows:

> All persons born or naturalized in the United States, and subject to the jurisdiction thereof, are citizens of the United States and of the State wherein they reside. No State shall make or enforce any law which shall abridge the privileges or immunities of citizens of the United States; nor shall any State deprive any person of life, liberty, or property, without due process of law; nor deny to any person within its jurisdiction the equal protection of the laws.

This Amendment is thought of as one of the most vital additions to the Constitution. It establishes due process of law and equal protection under the law for all Americans citizens, including black people and other minorities. One of the main reasons the Fourteenth Amendment was established is because black people, during the time, were not considered citizens of the United States. This was due to a decision that came about from the Dred Scott vs. Sandford court case.[6] The decision in the case denied blacks American citizenship and any privileges that came along with American citizenship. The fourth section of the Fourteenth Amendment reads as such:

---

[6] Dred Scott was John Emerson's slave. Emerson married a woman named Irene Marie Sanford. Emerson moved to Illinois, taking Scott with him. Illinois was a free state. After a stay in Illinois, Emerson moved his wife and Scott to Wisconsin, another free state. Scott met his wife there. Because of Scott's length of stay in the state of Illinois, he was legally eligible to apply for his freedom. But he did not do so. In December of 1843 Emerson died suddenly in the prime of life. When Scott tried to purchase his freedom three years later from Emerson's wife, she refused. Scott sued, citing Missouri's law that any slave that had ever been taken by their slave master to a free state was granted automatic freedom. After three trials and an appeal, the courts ruled, in 1850, that Scott was legally free. However, the Missouri Supreme court reversed the decision after Emerson's wife appealed a second time (turning her side of the case over to her brother-in-law, John Sanford). The ruling kept Scott in slave status which eventually led to the 1857 United States Supreme Court ruling (Dred Scott v. San[d]ford) that determined that blacks would not be allowed citizenship and that Congress could not make slavery illegal in certain territories. Many historians believe this ruling was a significant part of the slavery debate that played a part in leading up to the Civil War. The Thirteenth and Fourteenth Amendments to the Constitution overrode the ruling.

"The validity of the public debt of the United States, authorized by law, including debts incurred for payment of pensions and bounties for services in suppressing insurrection or rebellion, shall be questioned. But neither the United States nor any State shall assume or pay any debt or obligation incurred in aid of insurrection or rebellion against the United States, or any claim for the loss or emancipation of any slave; but all such debts, obligations and claims shall be held illegal and void."

This section of the Amendment basically exonerated the Government from owing any debts to the Confederate states for the cost of former slaves that had been emancipated by way of the Fourteenth Amendment.

The most significant aspects of the Fourteenth Amendment is that it included black people as among those defined as having national citizenship and made it illegal to deprive any person, including blacks, of "life, liberty, or property, without due process of law." The Amendment solidified the fact that blacks were no longer to be seen as subhuman but as equal to whites with the same rights. However, the majority of the southern states disregarded the Amendment by continuing to deny blacks the most basic of civil rights. And the United States Government did not intervene to uphold these rights until almost 100 years later.

- *The Fifteenth Amendment*

The Fifteenth Amendment was proposed by Congress in February of 1869 and was ratified on February 3, 1870. It reads as follows:

1 The right of citizens of the United States to vote shall not be denied or abridged by the United States or by any State on account of race, color, or previous condition of servitude.
2 The Congress shall have power to enforce this article by appropriate legislation

The Fifteenth Amendment to the United States Constitution enhanced the mandates of the Fourteenth Amendment by making it a violation of the Constitution for any state to deprive any citizen of his voting rights regardless of race or color.[7]

---

[7] Despite this Amendment to the Constitution, women were not allowed to vote until they won the right to vote in 1920 most notably through the efforts of Susan B. Anthony, Elizabeth Cady Stanton, and Lucy Stone, among others.

Despite its acceptance into the Constitution, Delaware did not ratify the Amendment until 1901, Oregon until 1959, California until 1962, Maryland until 1973, Kentucky until 1976, and Tennessee until 1997. This means that it wasn't until fairly recently that the states of Oregon, California, Maryland, Kentucky, and Tennessee agreed that it was unconstitutional to deprive black people of their voting rights.

After the ratification of the Fifteenth Amendment in 1870, blacks began holding elected offices and some even became members of state congress and of the House of Representatives. Black people also became judicial judges, state officers, and lieutenant governors.[8] But it wasn't long before whites, disgruntled at the idea of equal opportunity for blacks, began developing methods that would make it difficult for blacks to exercise their rights under this Amendment.

In an effort to discourage blacks from the polls, Southern states began to impose biased literary tests and poll taxes. The voting poll taxes were difficult for the majority of blacks to pay at the time. Many white southerners also used terrorist tactics against blacks to discourage them from voting and taking office. The emergence of the Ku Klux Klan[9] white terrorist organization was one noted result of this violence. Initially the Government stepped in to try to stop the assaults on blacks. However in 1877, the year Rutherford B. Hayes began his presidency, the Government ceased all efforts to stop the terrorism. In order to soothe the tempers of the south, Hayes withdrew Federal troop protection of blacks and did nothing to intercede when racial violence broke out at the polls. Many blacks were murdered at the polls and eventually the majority of the southern states prohibited blacks from voting. Any attempt by blacks to vote put them under threat of death. Because of the ongoing violent and discriminatory methods used against blacks in an effort to ensure that blacks wouldn't make it to the polls, blacks were basically disenfranchised from voting, and were also disenfranchised from holding political office. Things did not significantly begin to change until the Civil Rights Act of 1964 and the Voting Rights act of 1965 were passed.[10]

---

[8] This was part of what was called the Reconstruction Era. See chapter 3 for further discussion.

[9] See Chapter 3.

[10] Both Acts are discussed in chapter 4.

THE BIRTH OF "WHITE AMERICA" AND "BLACK AMERICA"

There continues to be such a strong racial divide between blacks and whites in America that the terms "white America" and "black America" have been coined by the media and the press. It is very common now to speak of the racial polarization in America between these two groups in those terms.

White America

America's earlier attempts to enslave and/or extinguish the Indians and the kidnapping and enslavement of Africans gave birth to what many black people refer to today as "white America." White America is a phrase that identifies and refers to the dominant racial group in America. As discussed in the previous chapter, the dominant racial group in America is the white race. The phrase "white America" is used to identify that segment of the American population (white people) that have power, privilege, and position, that overrides, in general, the power, privilege, and position of non-white American citizens. The most powerful operating structure in America is the United States Government which is controlled (even with Barack Obama as President) at top levels by whites (the Congress and the Senate are majority white). This is so because ultimately, any bill, if it is to be enacted, must be passed by Congress; and even if the President vetoes a bill, that veto can be overruled by a vote of Congress. Historically, America has basically been operated by white Americans.

Although there have been many individual white Americans (along with various organizations established and supported by whites) that have supported equal rights for minorities and have fought against various forms of racial discrimination, white America, as a whole, has had a history of turning a blind eye to civil rights infractions and discriminatory practices against minorities. This is not to minimize the effort of those whites who have cried out against racial injustices (the Civil War itself was a testimony to the distain many white northerners felt towards the inhumane system of slavery and their quest to put an end to it) but to point out the continued "power over" that white America possesses collectively and how that power has created a society rot with racial inequities.

During the attempted enslavement and then attempted genocide of the Native Americans along with the enslavement of Africans and blacks, the birth of White America emanated. When slavery was abolished in 1865 the majority of white Americans, including President Lincoln and even a great number of whites living in the free northern states, wanted Africans and blacks transported to Africa. However, it would have been too costly to do so. Therefore, blacks were forced to remain in a hostile land where whites, as a whole, saw them as undesirables. Blacks were in America to stay. And since southern states could also no longer enslave blacks to work the cotton fields, southern state governments began subjugating blacks in other ways, particularly by terrorizing them and denying them certain civil rights and civil liberties while the Federal Government stood by for nearly 100 years and allowed it to happen.

Black America

Black America is an outcome of white America. Black Americans have struggled over the centuries, after slavery was abolished, to define who they are. Although black America has assimilated into American society, this assimilation historically came with great resistance from white America. Unfortunately there is still a great racial divide between blacks and whites as evidenced most recently by the news media attention given to the subject of race since President Obama has been in office. Black Americans have developed a culture within American society that is different from the culture of the dominant group in such areas as music, political ideologies, leisure activities, and even religious worship. Black America still struggles to erase any racial inequities that continue to exist in America. Often to the dismay of white America, black America continues to speak against racial injustices and call for action against forms of racism that still exist within the country. Although warranted, the continued call for action unfortunately makes for an ongoing battle between the two groups as a whole. An annihilation of racial inequities would ultimately mean that the dominant group would have to give up its dominance. Groups who are accustomed to being in power never give up power easily.

Who's white and who's not

As indicated earlier, a system of racism cannot exist without categorizing which people belong to what race. During the early 1900s on into the 1960s, America went through great pains to categorize people into races. Different states had different legal definitions of race. Many of these definitions still exist on paper today.

After the Civil War and until the enactment of the Civil Rights Act of 1965,[11] white America was determined to keep "black America" (along with any other minority group) in subjection. As a result, whites labeled blacks according to the degree of black ancestry they had in their genealogy. American laws categorized anyone as "Negro" who had as little as one sixteenth "black blood"[12] or anyone who had discernable black facial characteristics. One-sixteenth means that the person being categorized as black had at least one great-great-grandparent who was black (i.e. one's father's father's father's father). This is four generations back. So a child could have a white looking mother and a white looking father, but if either parent had a black great-great grandparent then that child would be considered black in some respect (and so would his or her parents), even if the child looked white.

In the 1950s, census takers were instructed to categorize anyone as Negro who had any black ancestry even if they had white parentage as well. This was a change from twenty years before which mandated that people be categorized as black if they had one black parent, but if any less, then they would be categorized as Mulattoes. However Mulattoes weren't considered white and were discriminated against just the same.

The same distinctions made between black and white people were not necessarily made between white people and other people of color. A white American mixed with Indian blood was considered white as long as he or she was one fourth Indian or less. Furthermore, race was to be distinguished by the race of one's father (except, of course, for blacks when it came to a mixture of black and white). Consequently, if one's father was Chinese and the mother black, the person would be considered Chinese (two minorities). However, if one's father was white and the mother black, the person would be considered black. Apparently, more racism was therefore directed towards blacks than any other minority.

To understand better the enormity of America's history of racial categorization, we will need to take a look at how the states defined race through the late sixties. According to Stetson Kennedy, author of *Jim Crow Guide: The way it was*, the following is a sample of what some state laws imposed when it came to race: In Florida a black person was defined as anyone who had a sixteenth of "black blood." In Georgia, in order to be white, one could not have any trace or history (in facial features nor in ancestry) of African, Asian, and/or Native American

---

[11] See Chapter 3.

[12] There is no such thing as black blood or white blood. Blood is blood. But for the purposes of explaining the mindset of the time, the terminology "black blood" is being used.

ancestry. In Kentucky, one-fourth black blood was the measure. In Louisiana, a person with three-fourths black blood was identified as a Negro. A person with one black parent and one Mulatto parent was identified as a Griffe. A person with one black parent and one white parent was identified as a Mullato. A person with one-fourth black blood and three-fourths "white blood"[13] was identified as a Quadroon. And a person with one-eighth black blood and seven-eighths white blood was identified as an Octoroon.

Whether or not a person was identified as white had such an effect on a person's quality of life during those times, that court proceedings were often convened in order to determine a person's "whiteness." Not only were blood lines, ancestry, and physical appearance used to determine who was white and who wasn't but, according to Kennedy, other variables were used, including whether or not a person was known to associate with white people, whether or not a person was considered upper class, whether or not the person had white friends, and whether or not the person exercised the rights of white people, including voting rights and being able to go to certain places designated for whites only. These particular laws existed in 29 states and in 17 states interracial marriages were illegal. The Supreme Court did not declare laws against interracial marriages to be unconstitutional until 1967.

In the following quote, Ian Lopez, author of *White By Law*, describes race as a "social product" and discusses what he terms as its legal construction:

> Race is not, however, simply a matter of physical appearance and ancestry. Instead, it is primarily a function of the meanings given to these. On this level, too, law creates races. The statutes and cases that make up the laws of this country have directly contributed to defining the range of meanings without which notions of race could not exist.

Further along, Lopez goes on to say:

> Rather than simply shaping the social content of racial identity, however, the operation of law also creates the

---

[13] Kennedy, Stetson, *Jim Crow Guide; The Way it Was*, p. 50. As specified in the previous footnote, there is no such thing as black blood or white blood. Blood is blood. But for the purposes of explaining the mindset of the time, the terminology "black blood" is being used.

racial meanings that attach to features in a much more subtle and fundamental way: laws and legal decisions define which physical and ancestral traits codes as Black or White, and so on...[14]

From 1878 to 1944 the American judicial system was heavily involved in deciding which immigrants would be allowed citizenship and which immigrants would not. The decision whether or not to allow a person to become a citizen rested on the perceived race of the individual requesting citizenship. Court procedures were triggered when legislators disagreed on whether or not certain ethnic groups were white. Between 1878 and 1909, the courts decided that Mexicans were white but that Chinese, Hawaiian, Burmese, Japanese, and Native American peoples were not white. During that time the courts also decided that those who had parents with one parent being white and the other, Native American, were not white. The courts also decided during that time that people with one half white blood, one-fourth Japanese blood, and one fourth Chinese blood, were not white.

As time moved on, the courts were not as consistent with their decisions. In 1909 one American court decided that Asian Indians were *probably* not white and then in 1910 another court deemed them white. However, in 1917 a third court concluded they were not white and in 1919 yet another court decided Asian Indians were white. Then again in 1923 a fifth court decided that Asian Indians were not white. In 1909 and 1910 the courts concluded that Syrians were white, however, in 1913 and 1914 the courts decided that Syrians were not white. In 1915 the courts decided again that the Syrians were white. From 1909 to 1923 the courts were consistent in their decisions regarding racial categories of the Japanese, Filipinos, and Koreans. They were all deemed non-white.

From 1923 to 1924 the courts agreed that the Japanese, Asian Indians, Filipinos, and Afghan people were not white. However, in 1942 the courts decided that Arabs were not white only to reverse their decision in 1944, deeming them white.

Today, the United States Census Bureau and the Federal Office of Management and Budget (OMB) set the standards for racial and ethnic identification. As of the 2000 Census a person is considered white if they have origins from Europe, North Africa, or the Middle East. This would include, among others, Arabian, Jewish, German, and Polish peoples.

---

[14] Lopez, Ian F. Haney, *White by Law: The Legal Construction of Race*, New York University Press, New York and London, copyright 1996, pgs. 15-16. Used by permission of the publisher.

Persons identified as black or African-Americans are persons that have black African Ancestry. Haitians, Kenyans, and Nigerians are considered black. Those who have South and North Native American origins and have been accepted as a member of an Indian or Alaskan tribe are considered Native Americans or Alaskan Americans. Asians are identified as persons with origins from the Far East and can include but are not limited to the Chinese, Japanese, Koreans, Vietnamese, Filipinos, and persons from India. Then there are those who are considered to be Native Hawaiian or Pacific Islanders. Persons who have Spanish origins and are from Mexico, Puerto Rico, Cuba, Central America, or South America, are considered Hispanic, Latino, or Spanish. However, as of the 2010 census, Hispanics/Latinos were no longer considered to be a race. They are identified solely as an ethnic group.

The countries of Northern Africa are Algeria, Egypt, Libya, Morocco, Southern Sudan, Northern Sudan, Tunisia, and the Western Sahara. The majority of these countries are Muslim countries with a majority Arab population. In Northern Africa there are many people who are considered fair-skinned enough to be categorized as Caucasians. And despite the fact that many black Americans consider persons from the Middle East to be "people of color," America categorizes them as white. Most people from the Middle East are of Arabian or Jewish decent. It has been reported that some Arabs and some Egyptians are not pleased with the racial categories ascribed to them when they reach American soil.

Because of America's history of racial discrimination and inequities, there is no doubt that the quest to racially define a person is the result of America's initial underlying aim to implement and/or allow discrimination against a segment of its citizens.

CHAPTER SUMMATION

There is no doubt that America, as we know it now, has been built on a foundation of racism that began with an occupation of North America and an eventual take over of the land from the Native Americans. However, once it was realized that the Native Americans would not be enslaved without a fight and that European slaves easily succumbed to illnesses, white settlers (better described as occupiers) began to look elsewhere for slaves. They turned their attention to Africa and partook in one of the world's greatest atrocities against mankind; the kidnapping of Africans across the Atlantic into forced servitude.

Eventually the states became divided regarding the question of morality as it pertained to the enslavement of blacks and their gross mistreatment. The southern Confederate states were pro slavery while the northern Union states were against it. This led to the Civil War. The North won and slavery was abolished, but the seeds of racism had already been planted and it would take a hundred years before laws were put into affect to ensure the constitutional rights of black Americans as well as the rights of other persons of color and minorities. The following two chapters will take a further look at the history of discriminatory practices against people of color, specifically blacks, and will also examine the history of the Civil Rights Movement.

3.

A HISTORY OF RACIAL DISCRIMINATION IN AMERICA

Africans weren't the only people to be discriminated against by white America during the slavery era and post slavery civil rights era. The Chinese, Japanese, and poor European whites who had immigrated to America from other countries in order to try to make a better life for themselves faced racism and discrimination as well. In 1849, during what is known as the California gold rush, many of the Chinese migrated to America in search of gold. China had become impoverished which triggered a desire in many Chinese to come to America in the search of riches. At the time, foreigners were not prohibited from searching for the lucrative substance.

EARLY CHINESE IMMIGRANT DISCRIMINATION

The Chinese began to arrive in America in droves during the California gold rush. At first, when the gold was plentiful, Americans didn't mind that the Chinese had come to search for gold. Part of the reason Americans accepted the Chinese was due to the fact that the Chinese were given railroad and mining jobs and were paid less than what Americans would have been paid. America's economy was therefore strengthened not only by the onslaught of the free labor of slavery but also by the onslaught of the exploitation of the Chinese. Countless Chinese men worked the mines and the railroads. This was especially true in the early 1860s when the Central Pacific Railroad Company was at its hiring peak. At the time, this company was in charge of constructing the Transcontinental Railroad and had recruited many Chinese men to work the construction. Although the Chinese were getting much more in wages than they would have ever received in their homeland during that time, they were still making considerably less than what the average American would have made doing the same job.

Chinese men were referred to as "coolies" which was the equivalent to the derogatory term of "nigger" given to blacks. Although most of the Chinese men who had migrated to America did so voluntarily, there were many who had been trafficked in. They were kidnapped in China and brought across the waters to America against their will (much like Africans of that time). Once they got to America, they were forced to work for the railroads or the mines.

By 1850 the supply of gold began to decline. Consequently, racial tensions that were already present between white Americans and the Chinese escalated. Once gold began to become scarce along with a decreasing need for the railroad and mining labor force, racist organizations began fighting against Chinese immigration. As long as the United States could exploit the Chinese work force and as long as there was enough gold for everyone, the Chinese did not encounter the type of discrimination that would have hindered or prevented them from working the mines. But when resources became depleted, labor groups began threatening the Chinese with physical violence and eventually drove them from the railroads and the mines. As a result, the majority of the Chinese set up their own restaurants and laundering businesses, many of which proved successful. There was a post war decline in America's economy, overall, for several years after the Civil War ended in 1865. Many Americans blamed the economic decline on the Chinese. Consequently, the Government enacted what was called the Chinese Exclusion Act. This Act was put into law in 1882.

The Chinese Exclusion Act made it illegal for the Chinese to become United States citizens and also made it illegal for any additional Chinese to be granted immigration into America. The Act also made it difficult for the Chinese to leave the United States and reenter without certification which was very difficult to get. Violation of this Act was punishable by imprisonment or by deportation. The Act was renewed in 1892 and in 1902. The latter renewal included a revision that required every Chinese resident of America to obtain a certification that confirmed their residency. Deportation was the punishment for not having the certification. Senator George Frisbie Hoar was noted at the time for describing the Act as "the legalization of racial discrimination." This racism progressed into the early 1900s which resulted in the banning of all children of oriental heritage from attending white schools in some states.

Despite the racism and discrimination that the Chinese faced and despite the Chinese Exclusion Act, the Chinese continued to immigrate into the United States. Many of them were able to get past the barriers of the Act. San Francisco California was where most Chinese immigration initiated. In 1910 a detaining center for immigrants was created at Angel Island which is located in the San Francisco Bay. Thousands of Chinese were detained there from 1910 to 1940 and many of those who were allowed to enter the country were put in prison, beaten, and/or murdered.

In 1924 the Johnson Immigration Act was passed. This Act put further restrictions not only on the Chinese but on other Asian groups as well that wished to migrate to the United States. According to Stetson Kennedy,[1] the Johnson Immigration Act made "whiteness" the deciding factor as to whether or not an immigrant would be considered eligible to be allowed into the country. Armenians, Persians, and Syrians (Western Asia) were classified as white and were therefore allowed to enter into the country, while there was great debate as to whether or not people of Arab descent were "white enough."

Not only did the Johnson Immigration Act set the whiteness of one's skin as the standard by which foreigners could enter into the country but it established immigration quotas of various ethnic groups (usually of not more than 100 per group) and prohibited Chinese men who had already immigrated into America from bringing their Chinese wives into the country to be with them. No more than 100 Chinese were allowed to immigrate into the country at certain times. The fulfillment of this quota was sabotaged by the fact that whites who were born in China (and in India) were given first preference by the United States. According to Stetson, this, along with laws that were implemented against interracial marriages, forced a sizeable amount of Chinese men to live without intimate companionship.

In 1940 the National Act was adopted which finally gave American citizenship to persons, already living in the country, whose parents and ancestors were Chinese, Filipino, and/or Indian (but still did not allow for a less restrictive immigration of these ethnic groups until 1946 when Public Law 483 was implemented that extended citizenship rights to all the Chinese, Filipinos, Native Americans, and East Indians). However, with regard to the Filipinos, the Act clearly stated that the Filipinos that were given consideration were only those who were not considered to be half of one of the ethnic groups that were found "ineligible" (i.e. they could not be half Chinese or half Indian).

In 1943, due to the fact that the Chinese had become allies with America against Japan, Congress enacted the Chinese Exclusion Repeal Act which stopped the prohibition of Chinese immigration. It was legal again for the Chinese to enter the country. After nearly 30 years of serving as a Chinese holding center, Angel Island was finally dissolved as a place of Chinese detainment and was eventually converted into a State park. Although the Exclusion Act was repealed, the restrictions of the

---

[1] Author of *The Jim Crow Guide, The Way it Was,* Florida Atlantic University Press, Boca Raton, Third Printing, copyright ©1992

Immigration Act were not relaxed until the Immigration Act of 1965 was passed.

JIM CROW

"Jim Crow" was a phrase used to identify the overt discriminatory and racist practices imposed upon blacks beginning near the end of the nineteenth century. The phrase derived from the minstrel shows of the early 1800s, specifically originating from a song that used to be sung quite often by a white minstrel show entertainer named Thomas Dartmouth. His stage name was "Daddy Rice." Minstrel shows very often depicted blacks in negative ways. The negative depictions involved white men painting their faces black with charcoal paste and portraying blacks as slaphappy, obnoxious, and stupid. Jim Crow was the name of a character that Dartmouth sang about and portrayed. The character not only possessed all of the aforementioned negative traits, but was also a character that was depicted as inferior. Consequently, by the 1850s this racist stereotypical Jim Crow character had become an ingrained representation of black people in the minds of most white Americans.

The stage for the emergence of the Jim Crow phenomena was initially set with the adoption of the United States Constitution in 1789. The Constitution endorsed the mistreatment of blacks and other minorities in a number of ways. Black slaves were only to be counted as three-fifths of a person and Native Americans were not to be counted at all when it came to having representation in Congress. The Constitution also held that run-away-slaves were to be returned by force to the slave master they had run from, even if they had run from a slave state to a free state. The Supreme Court passed a law in 1857 which denied American citizenship to all black people of slave descent including those who had been born on American soil. In 1861 President James Buchanan, along with Congress, signed a joint resolution to the Constitution (the "first" Thirteenth Amendment) forbidding the enactment of any Amendment that would give any state the authority to interfere with the slave laws of any particular state in question (The Civil War began that same year). However, no more than two states ever ratified the Amendment. This Thirteenth Amendment was eventually dismissed and replaced with the 1865 Thirteenth Amendment that we are now familiar with which outlawed slavery.

After the end of the Civil war in April of 1865, blacks began to separate themselves from whites in an effort to be free of white oppression, especially in the southern states. However, southern whites were not willing to give up the power and rule they had over blacks. Whites, as a whole, therefore began instituting certain discriminatory laws against blacks. These laws were referred to as "the black codes."

The black code laws were passed mainly in southern states between the years of 1865 and 1867. These "codes" made it legal to openly discriminate against former slaves. The most oppressive of these codes made it difficult for blacks to live wherever they chose within the South and also made it difficult for them to comfortably migrate to the North. Congress stepped in and began passing legislation aimed at protecting the civil rights of black people at the time. This is the beginning of what was called Reconstruction.

Reconstruction and Redemption

Reconstruction was basically the period after the close of the Civil War in which the United States Government upheld the equality of black people. Reconstruction is said to have lasted from 1865 to 1877 (with some historians dating the start at 1863 with the enactment of the Emancipation Proclamation)[2]. During the period of Reconstruction, the southern states were occupied by military troops. The Republicans (labeled as radical at the time) controlled most of the state governments and pushed towards establishing the civil, political, and voting rights of blacks who had been freed. Civil rights acts were passed in 1866 and also in the early 1870s which allowed blacks to vote and even to run for office. Some of the acts that were passed were done so in order to enforce the acts that had already been passed. However, there was much opposition from whites, as a whole, but particularly in the South, when it came to protecting the civil rights of black people. The southern Democrats were at the forefront of this opposition.

At the beginning of 1873, white southern Democrats began to terrorize and kill freedmen (slaves who had been set free as a result of the passage of the Second Confiscation Act of 1862[3]) in an effort to discourage them from voting and running for political office. The Democrats referred to this movement as "Redemption." This Redemption movement of the Democrats led to the necessity of Congress using the military to enforce civil rights laws. The aim of the Democrats was to "redeem" the states from adhering to the rights of former slaves. By the year 1877, the influence of the Democrats had eventually made a substantial impact on

---

[2] See chapter 2

[3] The Act that freed the slaves of those who were found guilty of insurrection or treason against the Government, particularly Confederates who refused to surrender to the Union.

the states. Consequently, the majority of white voters in the nation no longer appreciated the use of the army to protect the civil rights of free blacks. As a result, Congress (and particularly the conservative white Democrats) became increasingly oppositional towards the idea of continuing the protection and began undermining any attempt to further fund military safeguards. In response, President Rutherford Hayes withdrew the troops from protecting the civil rights of blacks thus ending the period of Reconstruction. Although Reconstruction was dead, the period during Reconstruction along with the need for military enforcement, at the time, to enforce human and civil rights, became the main catalysts that ushered in the Fourteenth and Fifteenth Amendments[4] to the United States Constitution.

Segregation under Jim Crow

In 1883 the United States Supreme Court ruled against the Civil Rights Act of 1875 which had put certain measures in place to protect blacks against discriminatory and racist practices. This left the door wide open for states to pass discriminatory laws against black people. Although the Fourteenth Amendment had been ratified in 1868, many states ignored the Amendment when the Supreme Court ruled against this Act.

In 1890 the state of Louisiana passed Act 111 (the Separate Car Act) that disallowed the integration of blacks and whites on trains. Blacks and whites were to sit in separate railway cars. Although the accommodations were to be separate they were also to be of equal quality. However, there was a group of blacks and whites at the time that protested the segregation of railroad facilities and formed an organization to fight against "separate but equal." They named their organization the "Citizen's Committee to Test the Constitutionality of the Separate Car Act." Attorney Albion Tourgee took the case free of charge.

The Committee approached a man named Homer Plessy to help them with their cause. Plessy was one eighth black and was therefore considered an Octoroon.[5] Plessy looked white and agreed to ride the trains. The attempt of the Committee was to prove that there were too many gray areas when it came to keeping blacks separate from whites because many people who would be legally identified as black could also be physically identified as white and could "pass." They wanted to prove that separating the races was devoid of logic.

---

[4] See chapter 2
[5] See chapter 2

Despite the fact that Plessy looked white, he was deemed as black; so when he boarded the train on June 7, 1892 he was asked to sit in the car designated for persons of color. He refused and was arrested. Plessy took the case to court (Homer Adolph Plessy vs. the State of Louisiana) arguing that his constitutional rights under the Thirteenth and Fourteenth Amendments had been violated. The Judge who presided over the case was John Howard Ferguson. Ferguson ruled against Plessy. In response, Plessy appealed to Louisiana's Supreme Court. This court also ruled against Plessy. Plessy then appealed to the United States Supreme Court. Tourgee, along with his legal team which included James C. Walker and Samuel F. Phillips represented him. The case was heard on April 13, 1896.

The Supreme Court upheld the original decision leaving Plessy to plead guilty. He was made to pay a fine. The Supreme Court justified their decision to uphold Louisiana's Act 111 erroneously concluding that as long as the facilities were "equal" then there was no discrimination. They failed to realize that the very act of separating one race of people from another due to the fact that one race believes that the other race is not fit to share the same space, is a form of discrimination and racism. Furthermore, although the court deemed the railroad facilities as equal there was no question that other facilities such as public restrooms and the like were not equal and that the quality of facilities overall designated for blacks were substandard compared to those designated for whites.

The rulings in this case were the catalyst that spurred the practice of "separate but equal" which existed well into the 1960s and was only eradicated with the onset of the Civil Rights Movement[6] resulting in much bloodshed. The practice of "separate but equal" was finally abolished by the decision of Oliver Brown vs. Board of Education of Topeka in 1954, which is discussed below.

Education under Jim Crow: Brown vs. Board of Education

In the days of Jim Crow, in order for black people to prevail under the mentally and often times deadly oppressive system that Jim Crow rendered, they began to develop and establish colleges of their own so that blacks who were coming of age in the latter decades of the 1800s could further their education. Blacks were separated from whites at every level of education and it was black teachers who taught black pupils. At the end of the Civil War, less than 7% of blacks could read and write. Southern whites were vehemently opposed to blacks learning how to read

---

[6] See chapter 4.

and write. The opposition was so strong that southern states did not build public high schools for black children until the 1900s. By 1930, the literacy rate for blacks had increased to 77%. Not only were black children prevented from attending white schools but so were Native American and Mexican children.

Despite the increase in literacy that black people experienced during the 1930s, schools in at least 17 of America's states remained segregated into the early 1950s. The justification for this continued to be that although the schools were separate, they were equal. But they weren't. The schools that black children attended were of considerable lesser quality when compared to those that white children attended. White children did not have to walk as far to get to school as did black children. While white schools were located very close to where white children lived, many black children were forced to walk miles to black schools. Such was the case of Linda Brown. During the time of school segregation Linda, a black student who was in the third grade at the time living in Topeka Kansas with her father, had to walk a mile to get to her elementary school while a white elementary school sat just seven blocks away.

Linda's father, Oliver Brown, consequently attempted to enroll Linda into the white elementary school that was much closer to home. Linda was refused admittance. Mr. Brown did not give up and took the matter to McKinley Burnett, who was at the time, the president of the Topeka Chapter of the National Association for the Advancement of Colored People (NAACP).[7] Burnett gladly rallied to Mr. Brown's side. Burnett was able to encourage other black parents to become involved and in 1951 the Topeka branch of the NAACP asked for an injunction against the school segregation practices of the schools in Topeka. The case was heard at the Kansas U.S. District Court in June of that same year.

The NAACP argued that segregation caused black children to feel inferior because the ultimate message of segregation was that black children weren't good enough to be in the same classroom with white children and weren't good enough to play with, to associate with, and/or to be friends with white children. The court ultimately agreed with the NAACP on this issue and surprisingly wrote into their decision that segregation of school children due to racial bias is detrimental to "colored" children, triggers a sense of inferiority, and even impedes a

---

[7] A civil rights organization founded in 1909 by W.E.B. Dubois, Ida Wells, and others for the purpose of advocating for the rights of black Americans with a mission, as stated in 1911, "to promote equality of rights and eradicate caste or race prejudice among the citizens of the United States."

child's ability to learn when that child is the one receiving the message that he or she is inferior. However, despite the court's understanding of the psychologically debilitating effects of segregation, they ruled in favor of the Board of Education to keep the black students and white students of Topeka in separate schools because the Plessy vs. Ferguson ruling had never been overturned and was still in effect for the rest of the country.

But Brown and the NAACP didn't stop there. They appealed the lower court's decision to the United States Supreme Court in October of that same year (1951). The states of South Carolina, Virginia, and Delaware joined with the Topeka NAACP by submitting accounts similar to Linda's, and on May 17, 1954, the Supreme Court rendered its unanimous decision in favor of Brown and the NAACP citing that they believed that even if segregated schools were equal that minority children were still being deprived of "equal education opportunities" under the practice, that segregated schools are "inherently unequal," and that the plaintiffs in the case were being deprived of "equal protection under the law" which was a violation of the Fourteenth Amendment. Despite this victory for black students, the decision was only applicable as it pertained to segregated schools, not as it pertained to other public segregated facilities. It would take the onset of a bloody Civil Rights Movement to stop the overt racist practice of "separate but equal" and not only to stop it, but to enforce the decision handed down by the Supreme Court abolishing the practice in the education system.

The fight didn't end with the case of Linda Brown. In 1957 the all-white Central High School of Little Rock Arkansas denied the entrance of nine black teenagers who attempted to enroll into the school. The Arkansas state militia were called in but did nothing when whites spit on and intimidated the black teenagers that were trying to enter the school. The black students were threatened with being lynched and insulted with racial slurs. The militia had orders, despite the Supreme Court ruling three years earlier in the Brown case, not to prevent the white mob from trying to stop and discourage the black students from entering the school. Violence eventually broke out and black journalists were viciously attacked. Finally, after several days of television footage showing these black students being denied entrance and being mistreated, pressure from international sources prompted President Eisenhower to step in and do something. Eisenhower sent in Federal troops to protect the black students. The black students were finally allowed to enter the school but not without the protection of the United States Army. The incidents surrounding Central High School of Little Rock are discussed in more detail in the following chapter.

"Passing" under Jim Crow

During the Jim Crow era, roughly eight million "white" Americans were actually not white at all according to racial identification standards, but were either what was referred to as a mulatto, a griffe, a quadroon, or an octoroon. Any person labeled as such was considered "Negro" in one way or another and was regulated to a life void of certain fundamental civil rights. In order to live a better quality of life, there were those blacks who actually fit the definition of mullato, griffe, quadroon, or octoroon but looked white enough to "pass" as white. In other words, in order to live a better quality of life they hid the fact that they had black ancestry and portrayed themselves as "pure white" with no trace of "black blood." The advantages not only included social benefits but also included medical, financial, and employment benefits as well.

Many people who professed to be white were suspected of being some degree of black. Many of those who lived under a shadow of suspicion were hauled into court in order for there to be a determination as to whether or not they were truly white. Upon scrutiny of the court, many of those who were passing for white were identified as Negro. As a consequence they lost their jobs, their status in society, their homes, and much more. All of them were thereby subject to all of the racial discrimination that blacks were subject to at the time. Not only was a person negatively affected who had been discovered as passing, but his or her family and friends were negatively affected as well. The quality of life and societal privileges experienced by whites as opposed to the quality of life and discrimination experienced by blacks were so polarized that to refer to a white person as black, at the time, could have brought with it a lawsuit for slander.

Interracial marriage under Jim Crow

Interracial marriages (particularly marriages between blacks and whites) during the Jim Crow era in the United States were frowned upon and were illegal in the majority of the states. Interracial marriages (particularly when it came to the marriage of whites with blacks) was initially banned by the Thirteen colonies during colonial times beginning in 1664 when Maryland passed a law that made it illegal for white slave owners to marry their slaves (including white indentured servants). In 1690 these laws began to include marriages between whites and those blacks who had obtained their freedom. Thus the laws began to focus on race in lieu of focusing on social status. During the Civil War, debates surrounding the subject of interracial marriages became more plentiful resulting in the term "miscegenation" being coined. *Miscegenation* was a term used to refer to interracial marriages or interracial sexual unions, particularly between blacks and whites. The rising debate as to whether or not whites should be allowed to marry blacks became more prominent after slavery was legally abolished in 1865. State laws were passed that prohibited interracial marriages and interracial sexual intercourse. Consequently, miscegenation was deemed a felony.

Not only was it a felony for blacks and whites to marry one another or to have sexual intercourse with one another but it was also illegal for anyone to officiate the wedding of an interracial couple and those who dared to do so risked being charged with the "crime" of miscegenation themselves. Anti-miscegenation laws centered around who white people could and could not marry. Every anti-miscegenation law forbade the marriage of whites with any other racial group besides their own and particularly forbade whites to marry blacks. In 1908 the state of Oklahoma went even further and banned blacks from marrying *anyone* (even other persons of color) outside of their race.

Since America was initially purportedly founded on Christian principles, the morality or immorality of such laws had to be addressed. State lawmakers therefore began to justify laws prohibiting marriage between blacks and whites by focusing on a longstanding misinterpretation of the biblical account of the curse of Ham and his son Canaan (found in Genesis 9:18-27) as discussed in chapter 6. The misinterpretation erroneously categorized all black people as cursed to be the slaves of white people thus putting all blacks at a level of social status inferior to the social status of white people, in general, which fed into the false belief that blacks are inferior to whites on a human level. This false belief and biblical misinterpretation gave unrighteous justification to laws that banned interracial marriages.

Between the years 1691 (with the colony of Virginia being the first) and 1913 (with the state of Wyoming being the last) the following states passed anti-miscegenation laws (some of which were colonies at the time): Alabama, Arkansas, Arizona, California, Colorado, Delaware, Florida, Georgia, Idaho, Illinois, Indiana, Iowa, Kansas, Kentucky, Louisiana, Maine, Maryland, Massachusetts, Michigan, Mississippi, Missouri, Montana, Nebraska, Nevada, New Mexico, North Carolina, North Dakota, Ohio, Oklahoma, Oregon, Pennsylvania, Rhode Island, South Carolina, South Dakota, Tennessee, Texas, Utah, Virginia, Washington, West Virginia, and Wyoming. In all instances, black people were banned from marrying white people. Asians and Native Americans were also banned from marrying white people. Children of interracial marriages or unions were denied inheritance rights and white parents could have their children taken from them if they were found to be teaching their children against racial inequality and encouraging their children to accept miscegenation.

During Reconstruction, anti-miscegenation laws were repealed in the states of Alabama, Arkansas, Florida, Louisiana, South Carolina, and Texas making interracial marriage legal in those states only to be repealed by those same states during the influential Redemption movement led by radical Democrats that had set out to reverse the civil rights decisions implemented in favor of free blacks during Reconstruction.

In 1881 a black man named Tony Pace and a white woman named Mary Cox were living together as a couple in Alabama and were charged and convicted of fornication. They were both sentenced to two years in prison. They appealed all the way to the Supreme Court. As a result, after a two year legal battle, the Supreme Court denied the appeals, did not find the convictions of Pace and Cox to be a violation of the Fourteenth Amendment, and declared laws against interracial marriage to be constitutional. Moreover, the court also ruled all interracial marriages, and all interracial sexual unions, illegal and declared adultery and fornication a greater crime when committed between a man and a woman of different races than when committed between a man and a woman of the same race.

The Supreme Court did not overturn its decision in the Pace/Cox case until 1967 with its ruling of the Loving vs. Virginia case. In 1958 a white man named Richard Loving married a black woman named Mildred Jeter. The Lovings lived in Virginia but had been married in the District of Columbia which had no laws against interracial marriages. The state of Virginia, however, did have anti-miscegenation laws. After the Lovings were wed, they moved back to Virginia. Shortly afterwards, Virginia's circuit court charged the Lovings with violation of its anti-miscegenation laws and the couple was arrested in their bedroom. In January of 1959 the Lovings pleaded guilty in a court of law and both were given a 12 month jail term which the Judge Leon Bazile suspended on the stipulation that the Lovings would leave the state of Virginia never to return for a period of 25 years.

The Lovings moved to Washington D.C. and in 1963 appealed the Virginia court's earlier ruling. At the end of the appeal process in 1965 the same judge who had heard the original case also had the final say as to the appeal and did not reverse his decision.

The Lovings eventually took their case to the United States Supreme Court and in 1967 the Supreme Court ruled in favor of the Lovings citing the following:

47

Marriage is one of the 'basic civil rights of man,' fundamental to our very existence and survival. To deny this fundamental freedom on so unsupportable a basis as the racial classifications embodied in these statutes, classifications so directly subversive of the principle of equality at the heart of the Fourteenth Amendment, is surely to deprive all the State's citizens of liberty without due process of law. The Fourteenth Amendment requires that the freedom of choice to marry not be restricted by invidious racial discriminations. Under our Constitution, the freedom to marry, or not marry, a person of another race resides with the individual and cannot be infringed by the State. These convictions must be reversed. It is so ordered.[8]

After the United States Supreme Court declared anti-miscegenation laws unconstitutional, laws against interracial marriages that existed in sixteen remaining states were automatically abolished and made void. All of the other states besides the sixteen that had implemented anti-miscegenation laws, had at some time earlier, repealed their laws that banned interracial marriages. The sixteen states that held on to the laws and were forced to abolish the laws by means of the United States Supreme Court ruling of 1967 were: Alabama, Arkansas, Delaware, Florida, Georgia, Kentucky, Louisiana, Mississippi, Missouri, North Carolina, Oklahoma, South Carolina, Tennessee, Texas, Virginia, and West Virginia. Although the anti-miscegenation laws were automatically abolished, they were still on the books. The last remaining sixteen states finally took the laws off the books with South Carolina not officially doing so until 1998, and Alabama, not until the year 2000.

It has only been within the last forty years that laws against interracial marriages were banned in America and it was not until 2000 that the laws were permanently taken off the books in all states. It is therefore not a stretch to conclude that although there are no more laws against interracial marriages, there is still a strong mindset in America against such marital unions. Talk shows still feature discussions on interracial dating and marriage and many of those that lived through Loving vs. Virginia are still alive. Even though the laws against miscegenation were abolished, the mindset of many Americans had been strongly influenced against interracial marriages. During America's miscegenation struggle, many whites who claimed not to be prejudiced, still had (and still have to this

---

[8] Public Domain.

48

day) reservations if asked whether or not they would want their son or daughter to marry a black person. Those reservations might not necessarily exist because the person himself or herself is racist or prejudiced but might exist because they inherently know that a substantial amount of racism against persons of color still exists in America and they would not want their grandchildren to be subjected to it.

Although white America has accepted that there will be black people on the job working with them and have accepted that some whites have legitimate friendships with blacks, there is still an underlying message that exists in white America which says that whites marrying blacks is unacceptable, especially when it comes to black men marrying white women. There's no question that this underlying message stems from racism, but it may also have to do with the fact that a white woman or a white man who has black biological grandchildren is sure to be looked down upon (along with their grandchildren and the mother and father of those children) by a substantial portion of white people within their inner circles. There is also a certain amount of white privilege that comes along with being white (discussed in chapter 5) which won't be afforded a bi-racial grandchild. Since everyone wants what's best for his or her children and his or her grandchildren, it stands to reason that there are many white people, who although have nothing against black people, per se, certainly wouldn't want their son or daughter to marry a black person, because no one wants his or her child or grandchild to be disadvantaged in any way at all. They inherently know that racism against black people still continues to exist on many levels in America even if they don't openly admit it.

This is not to dismiss the fact that the same underlying message, that says that blacks marrying whites is unacceptable, exists in black America as well. The most prevalent reasons, however, for the underlying message in the two Americas are different (but not justifiably so). In black America, those who deem interracial marriages unacceptable do so because they feel interracial marriages symbolize what they feel is another underlying message that says black people are inferior as marriage partners even within their own race.[9] On the other hand, as it pertains to white America, it is speculated that one reason why whites who deem interracial marriages unacceptable, do so because, as stated earlier, they fear that their children (or grandchildren depending on who it is) may suffer persecution as a result of being bi-racial; but they also fear being ridiculed or ostracized themselves by other whites for having black children/grandchildren. This

---

[9] There are black Americans who believe that whites are inferior beings, but this is not the most prevalent reason for those in black America who are opposed to interracial marriages.

is not to say, however, that there aren't a number of these whites that actually believe that blacks are inferior to whites and because of this, believe that there should be no "race mixing."

In addition to the implementation of laws against interracial marriages in earlier times (particularly when it came to whites marrying blacks) it wasn't too long ago that a black man could easily fall victim to lynching by a white mob for merely looking at or speaking to a white woman. The lynching of black men and women by white mobs, without government intervention to put a stop to it, took place in America from 1883 to 1968. During this period, many black men were falsely accused of raping white women often resulting in black men being kidnapped and hung by white mobs. The message has always been that white women are off limits to black men which paralleled the anti-miscegenation laws of the same era. The mindset against interracial unions is still present in the United States and strong indication of its existence manifested with one particularly pivotal event in recent American history: the O.J. Simpson double murder trial verdict.

The O.J. Simpson double murder trial verdict

On June 12, 1994 Nicole Brown Simpson (ex-wife of American football hero, O.J. Simpson) and a friend of hers named Ronald Goldman, were murdered outside of Ms. Simpson's residence in Los Angeles California. Both victims were viciously stabbed to death. O.J. Simpson (Orenthal James Simpson), was charged with the murder. The marriage between the Simpsons was an interracial one. O.J. Simpson is black and Nicole Simpson was white.

The trial, which began in January of 1995, was televised and highly publicized. On October 3, 1995 O.J. Simpson was acquitted by a jury on all counts.[10] The jury found him not guilty. White America was outraged at the verdict while Black America celebrated. The outrage of white America at the verdict was so great that some blacks began to label the outcry as the "lynching of O.J. Simpson in the realm of public opinion." The feeling was that white America could not lynch Simpson literally, so they "lynched" him in other ways seriously impeding his quality of life on a social level. For several years following the 1995 acquittal, Simpson was blackballed in Hollywood, denigrated in the press, and ostracized within

---

[10] A wrongful death civil law suit was later brought against Simpson by Fred Goldman (Ronald Goldman's father) who eventually won the suit. In February of 1997, Simpson was found guilty of the wrongful death of Ronald Goldman and ordered to pay thirty-three million and a half dollars in damages.

his community. But this same outcry from white America was not apparent after Robert Blake, also a famous celebrity, was acquitted for the murder of his wife in 2005.

The Robert Blake murder trial verdict

In 2001, Bonnie Lee Bakley (a white woman), wife of Robert Blake, was found shot to death in the couple's car, which was parked around the corner from a restaurant that they had just patronized minutes prior. Mrs. Bakley had a gunshot wound to the head. Almost a year later, in 2002, Robert Blake was arrested for his wife's murder when Ronald Hambleton, a retired stuntman, accused Blake of having had approached him for hire to kill his wife. Blake is a white Hollywood celebrity best known for his role in the television series: Barretta. In March of 2005 Blake was acquitted by a jury of the murder charges as well as the charge of solicitation for murder. In November of that same year, his four children filed a civil law suit against him for the murder of their mother. Just as Simpson was found guilty of the wrongful death of Ron Goldman, Blake was found guilty of the wrongful death of his wife.

Although the scenarios are similar when looking at Simpson and Blake there is one very striking difference between the two cases: O.J. Simpson was persecuted in the court of public opinion after his acquittal whereas Blake was not. Not only had Blake not been subjected to the kind of criticism, media denigration, and social ostracism that Simpson had been subjected to, but on the night of Blake's acquittal many of his fans met him at Vitello's Italian restaurant to celebrate his victory while many of Simpson's fans had all but deserted him. The question therefore becomes: why the difference?

One can only speculate as to why one celebrity acquitted of murdering his wife was not vilified by white America while another celebrity acquitted of the same charges was. It is difficult not to assume that race had much to do with the double standard that was made between the two men. One could also point to the fact that black America celebrated the acquittal of O.J. Simpson while being relatively silent when it came to the acquittal of Blake. Some would however counter that Blake's trial wasn't publicized nearly to the extent in the media that Simpson's trial was which made for much of the frenzy surrounding Simpson's case. Moreover, at the time of Nicole Brown's murder it had only been 28 years since the Supreme Court abolished all anti-miscegenation laws. A generation had not yet passed. It is therefore safe to speculate, that more likely than not, anti-miscegenation sentiments still existed on the part of much of white America and that there are still a substantial number of white Americans who are not comfortable with the idea of blacks and whites marrying, particularly when it comes to black men marrying or having sexual unions with white women.[11] The constant media denigration of Simpson at the time left many blacks wondering whether or not Simpson would have experienced the same persecution in the court of public opinion and in the media had his wife been black.

This discussion of these two cases has been presented not in an effort to dismiss the possibility that both men might be guilty, but has been presented only in an effort to point out how underlying racism unfairly and unjustifiably breeds double standards in favor of whites.

Housing discrimination under Jim Crow

The first clause of the Civil Rights Act of 1866 deemed blacks as citizens of the United States and gave the same property rights access to blacks as it did whites. The clause reads as follows:

> Be it enacted by the Senate and House of Representatives of the United States of America in Congress assembled, That all persons born in the United States and not subject to any foreign power, excluding Indians not taxed, are hereby declared to be citizens of the United States; and such citizens, of every race and color, without regard to any previous condition of slavery or involuntary servitude, except as a punishment for crime whereof the party shall have been duly convicted, shall have the same right, in every State and Territory in the United States, to make and enforce contracts, to sue, be parties, and give evidence, to inherit, purchase, lease, sell, hold, and convey real and personal property, and to full and equal benefit of all laws and proceedings for the security of person and property, as is enjoyed by white citizens, and shall be subject to like punishment, pains, and penalties, and to none other, any law, statute, ordinance, regulation, or custom, to the contrary notwithstanding.

This clause of the Act clearly states that blacks were to be afforded the same opportunity for desirable housing and the like, as whites. But unfortunately this first Civil Rights Act was repealed in 1894. During the Jim Crow era white Americans could live anywhere they pleased.

---

[11] This is not to say that there aren't a substantial number of black Americans that are uncomfortable with interracial marriages as well.

However, racial zoning for minorities was put into place and blacks, as well as other minorities, could only live in certain places designated for them within the cities. Non-whites were designated to live in the less desirable parts of the city while whites lived in the better sections. Not only were black people forced to live in the worse areas of a city, but so were Chinese Americans among other minorities. Racial zoning created overcrowding in the segment of cities designated to minorities. Overcrowding of people in a living space creates substandard living resulting in ghettos and projects. For the Chinese this resulted in Chinese ghettos referred to as "Chinatowns." To further the point, blacks and whites could not live together unless the black person was domestically employed by the white person. Blacks and whites living together under any other circumstances brought a charge of disorderly conduct to both the black person and the white person living together. Whites could however, visit blacks in their homes.

In addition to denying blacks and other minorities the more desirable parts of the city in which to live, a practice called redlining also came into play when it came to housing discrimination against blacks as well as when it came to other services. Redlining[12] was the practice whereby white merchants, business owners, bankers, employers, mortgage representatives, housing authorities and the like, determined which segments of the population of a city would either be denied services and opportunities such as jobs, housing, loans, insurance, and so forth or if not denied these services then its residents be made to pay a higher cost for these services than whites were. The term *redlining* was coined by Chicago civil rights activists in the 1960s when referring to the actual practice of providers of services drawing a red line on a map (of the area in which they provided those services) during board meetings, and the like, in order to determine which areas of the city they would increase the cost of public services in. For the most part, the victims of redlining were black Americans. Unfortunately, redlining has not completely dissipated in today's American society.

THE KU KLUX KLAN

The Ku Klux Klan (KKK) is an American racist terrorist organization that has been in existence for over a century. The organization began in December 1865 through the efforts of six young Caucasian adult confederate veterans from Pulaski, Tennessee whose names were James R. Crowe, Calvin Jones, John D. Kennedy, John C. Lester, Frank O. McCord,

---

[12] See chapter 5

and Richard R. Reed. The Civil War had just ended about eight months prior to the emergence of the Klan and southerners were disgruntled about the outcome of the war. However, these six men began the Klan, not out of retaliation towards the abolition of slavery, but because of their desire to form a social club. The Klan was initially supposed to be no more than a new fraternity.

Once the idea to form a fraternity had solidified among them, the six men began meeting regularly in order to determine what they would name their new social club, how they would decide upon division of labor within the club, and what they would name their officers. In naming the club, Richard R. Reed, one of the six suggested to derive the name from the Greek word *kuklos* whose English derivative is *circle*. After some discussion, the men came up with non-word variations of the Greek word *kuklos* and eventually the term *Ku Klux Klan* was coined.

The six men wanted the name of their new order to sound mysterious and they wanted to make certain that the titles they gave their officers had no political or military inferences. Consequently, titles such as *Grand Cyclops* began to emerge which eventually led to titles such as *Imperial Wizard* and the like. The six decided that all those who would eventually join their order, and hold no particular position, would be called *ghouls*.

Eventually the six decided to disguise themselves in sheets and ride horses through the town of Pulaski during the night. The townspeople responded with unrest. Their unrest triggered more mischief on the part of the six and they began to add masks and pointed hats as part of their regalia. Just as in today's fraternities and sororities, initiation involved hazing and partaking in KKK rituals and ceremonies. In early 1866, the nightriders began to pay specific attention to blacks in the area. These night rides were especially intimidating to blacks, as the Klan soon discovered. Since blacks had very few rights during the time and were the focus of southern disgruntlement over the North's defeat of the South, they were easy targets for harassment, and the Klan began to harass them on a regular basis during these night rides. Verbal harassment eventually turned into violence. It is believed that the violence against blacks was never the original intent of the six. However, things got out of hand and the founders of the Klan lost control over the original intention of the Klan's formation. Splinter Klan groups were formed whose aim was to terrorize and intimidate blacks, Jews, and other minorities and non-Christians. The Klan also targeted southern unionists and northerners who had moved to the South. The Klan rode through the night masking their identities by wearing long white sheets that covered them from head to toe. They would cut out holes in the sheets for their eyes so that they could see. The Klan terrorized and murdered blacks and other minority groups by means of lynching, intimidation, and assault.

In April of 1867 Klansmen decided it was time to define their organization in terms of the philosophy it currently represented at the time which had developed into a quest to restore white supremacy by resisting Reconstruction. Consequently, propagating white supremacist views became their primary mission. By June of 1867 the Klan had murdered 197 people, mostly blacks and had assaulted an additional 548 persons. One of the Klan's main goals was to suppress the black vote. Near the end of 1868, two thousand people had been murdered and/or assaulted by the Klan in Louisiana alone, along with 200 black Republicans, as an intimidation tactic to discourage the black vote.

Because of the Klan's presence, federal troops continued to occupy the South in an effort to put a stop to the Klan's activities. By 1870 the Klan was completed eradicated under the presidential leadership of Ulysses S. Grant who fought the Klan through the enforcement of the Civil Rights Act of 1871 which lead to legal prosecution of Klan members. At its peak, this first Klan had grown to a membership of five hundred and fifty thousand.

However, in 1915 a second Ku Klux Klan was founded as the result of labor tensions that developed after the end of World War I. Veterans who were applying for jobs at the time often found themselves competing with European immigrants and blacks who had migrated from the South to the North. The Klan preached against blacks, Jews, and Catholics. They also victimized these groups of people by raiding their homes and lynching them along with burning crosses on their lawns and in the areas in which they lived.

In addition to post war competition in the job market between whites and other minorities, the film *The Birth of a Nation*[13] along with the conviction and mob lynching of Leo Frank[14] also helped to spur the resurrection of the Klan. The Klan began to teach that white people are God's chosen race of people and that Christianity is for the white man only. They went on to embrace what is called the *Christian Identity*

---

[13] See Chapter 5

[14] Leo Max Frank was a Jewish American living in Marietta Georgia who had been accused of raping and murdering a teenaged white girl in 1915. The trial was largely publicized. After Frank was convicted, new evidence arose that cast doubt on his guilt. As a result, Georgia's governor reduced his death sentence to life imprisonment. Shortly afterwards, on August 17, 1915 Frank was kidnapped from prison by roughly 26 white men, and lynched. Frank was 31 years old at the time.

Movement.[15] Despite its name, the movement has nothing to do with Christianity. Christian Identity began in 1940 when white supremacists identifying themselves as Christians decided to form their own churches with their main doctrine being racism. This second onslaught of the Klan had its peak membership in 1924 with approximately six million participants nation wide.

Klan membership began to dissipate in 1925 after the NAACP began complaining to Congress and particularly after civic groups began publicizing the names of the men hiding behind the sheets. Newspapers in the South also began printing articles against the Klan. Despite this, the Klan contributed substantially to the terrorization of blacks during the Civil Rights Movement of the 50s and 60s. Although its membership is considerably less than what it was in its hey-day, the Klan has never totally been disassembled and is still a force to be reckoned with in the continuing struggle against racism and racial discrimination in America.

The lynching of blacks and other minorities in America

One prominent example of the contemptible fallout that presented itself behind the abolition of slavery was the numerous lynching of black people by white mobs that began near the end of the 1800s and progressed on into the late 1960s, initially spurred on by the Klan. According to a curriculum unit outline written by Robert A. Gibson, there were 4,730 people who were lynched by white mobs between the years of 1882 and 1951. Roughly 73% of the people lynched during this time where black while 27% percent were white.[16] Italian-Americans, Native Americans, and Mexicans were also the victims of lynching. However, with the surge of Jim Crow, the majority of those lynched were blacks and the majority of the lynching that took place was in the South.

According to historian, Leon F. Litwack, an additional 11 years brings the total to approximately 4,742 black men and women that were lynched in the southern states from the late 1800s to 1968. Angry white mobs would gather and drag incarcerated blacks out of jail or from their homes as a result of questionable allegations of murder, rape and the like and even resulting from the smallest of reasons (e.g. suspicious behavior, talking to a white woman). The Government allowed these terrorist and murderous acts

---

[15] See Chapter 6

[16] Gibson, Robert A., *The Negro Holocaust: Lynching and Race Riots in the United States,* 1880-1950, Yale-New Haven Teachers Institute, Yale Station, New Haven Connecticut, 1979 Volume II. Factual information taken from website address: http://www.yale.edu/ynhti/curriculum/units/1979/2/79.02.04.x.html

to take place without substantial interference until the 60s. Less than one percent of those involved in the murder and lynching of blacks and other minorities during this period were ever brought to trial despite the fact that many of them were photographed carrying out these murders. Any black who was alleged to have committed a crime against a white person or who was alleged to have insulted a white person was in danger of being lynched, particularly in the South. Because of the continued threat of violence, intimidation, and the lingering practice of discrimination, many blacks from the South migrated to the North looking for a better life. Segregation was not prevalent in the North and lynching in the North was mostly unheard of. Several thousand black American men and women made this journey from the South to the North between the years of 1910 and 1940. So many blacks made this pilgrimage that the occurrence is referred to historically as the Great Migration.

From 1883 to 1960, photographs of much of the lynching were taken. Many of these photographs were made into postcards and sent to whites (by whites) all over the country as souvenirs and keepsakes. The making and mailing of postcards of black men and women being lynched became an American phenomenon and many whites who supported the lynching would send the postcards to their family and friends. In 1908 Time Magazine condemned the postcards and the U.S. Post Master General refused to mail them. However, the distribution of the postcards did not stop until 1960 and no doubt there are some in America today who are still holding onto them as a macabre memento of their own racist ideologies.

In February of 2000, sixty of these postcards of photographed lynching were exhibited at the Roth Horowitz gallery in New York. James Allen, a white man, who lived in Atlanta, had spent fifteen years collecting the photographs in order to eventually exhibit them to make people more aware of the history of the stark injustices that had been levied against black people in American in earlier times. Because many of the families who had the postcards considered them to be keepsakes and souvenirs, Allen was forced to offer money for the cards, many of which he paid up to an excess of thirty thousand dollars.

It wasn't until 1946, after the end of World War II, that the Government finally stepped in and began fighting against the public mob lynching of blacks. The Justice Department was successful in convicting, Tom Crews, a man guilty of participating in a lynching. But he was only given a sentence of one year in jail and made to pay a one thousand dollar fine. However, there was another lynching that occurred in 1946 that followed; and this particular event (the lynching of four blacks; two men and two women near Atlanta Georgia) made headlines. The Federal Bureau of Investigation (FBI), at long last, went after the criminals. Although no one was ever convicted for the crime, the involvement of the FBI alone gave the message that those who set out to lynch people would themselves be subject to prosecution.

Finally, lynching was no longer being tolerated by the Government. This marked the beginning of the end of mass mob lynching but lynching would still continue to occur, carried out by small groups of perpetrators, at least once per year after that on into the late sixties.

Despite the fact that the Government stepped in to make lynching a federal offence, the final act of the lynching of blacks did not occur until 1981. On March 20, 1981, Michael Donald, a nineteen year old black man was attacked at random (in Mobile Alabama) by two members of the Ku Klux Klan and lynched. This was done as retaliation against blacks when the results of a trial ended in a hung jury in which a black man, named Josephus Anderson, was accused of murdering a white police officer. Henry Hays and James Cole were arrested and convicted for the lynching. Bennie Hays was also arrested but died before the trial began. Although the murder of Donald was the last recorded lynching in the United States, there have been two other subsequent hate crime murders against blacks since then similar to a lynching; the 1998 truck dragging death of a 49-year old black man, named James Bryd, who was decapitated during the dragging and the 2008 truck dragging death of a 24-year old black man named Brandon McClelland. Both men were murdered in Texas by white men. The McClelland incident received little press.

In 2005 the United States Senate apologized, through Senate Resolution 39, for failing to take action sooner against the lynching of blacks. The Resolution is referred to as the "Resolution Recognizing the Passage of United States Senate Resolution 39 and Honoring Doria Lee Johnson. Segments of the Resolution read as follows:

> WHEREAS on June 13, 2005, the United States Senate took a historic step by approving Resolution 39 which called for the lawmakers to apologize to lynching victims, survivors, and their descendants; and
> WHEREAS Resolution 39 represents the first time the Senate has apologized for the nation's treatment of African-Americans; and
> WHEREAS, Resolution 39 specifically expresses remorse for the failure of the United States Government to outlaw a crime that took the lives of at least 4,742 people, most of them African American men, from 1882 to 1968; and

WHEREAS, lynching occurred in all but four states in the contiguous United States and less than 1 percent of the perpetrators were brought to justice; and

WHEREAS historically, powerful southern Senators blocked federal anti-lynching legislation for decades despite the fact that the U.S. House of Representatives three times passed measures to make lynching a federal offense, more than 200 anti-lynching bills were introduced in the first half of the 20th Century and seven Presidents between 1890 and 1952 petitioned Congress to take action against lynching: and

WHEREAS the effort to pass Resolution 39 was lead by Senators George Allen (R-Va) and Mary Landrieu (D-La) who obtained the support of 78 additional Senators who joined the resolution as co-sponsors; and

WHEREAS, Resolution 39 was passed in large part because lynching survivors and the descendants of victims would not let the brutal crimes be forgotten and insisted that the United States Senate acknowledge and apologize for their predecessor's failure to take action to stop lynching; and

WHEREAS, as the great-great granddaughter of lynching victim Anthony P. Crawford, who was brutally murdered in 1916 in Abbeville, South Carolina, Doria Dee Johnson and her family were invited to Washington, D.C. to witness the Senate's voice vote for Resolution 39; and

WHEREAS Doria Dee Johnson, a lifelong Evanston resident, is one of the individuals who fought for the passage of Resolution 39 as a member of the United States Senate Steering Committee for the Anti-Lynching Apology;...[17]

The Resolution was ratified on June 13, 2005. The next day, the Washington Post published an article written by staff writer Avis Thomas-Lester entitled, "A Senate Apology for History on Lynching." Lester indicated that out of the total number of 100 Senators, 20 hadn't signed on as co-sponsors and many Senators were absent from the floor during this historic occasion although they had signed on in support of the Resolution. She noted that Trent Lott and Thad Cochran (Mississippi republicans)

---

[17] Government document. Public Domain.

hadn't co-sponsored the Resolution. Mississippi had the highest number of lynching incidences in America's history. The article also indicated that in times past when this issue was previously brought to the Senate floor, there were senators who basically argued (1930s) that the lynching, particularly of black men, should continue in order to reduce the perceived threat that black men were to white women.

CHAPTER SUMMATION

Although there has been, within the last three centuries, injustices pitted against other minorities as well, the history of the violence against blacks in the form of physical assaults and lynching have made historical hostilities against blacks in America particularly egregious. The North's Civil War victory was just the beginning of the continued strenuous efforts to guarantee equal rights for black people living in America. Even with Grant's win of the war and the Declaration of Independence's proclamation, roughly a century earlier, that all men are created equal, the quest for the civil rights of every American became an uphill battle. Although the Thirteenth and Fourteenth Amendments were added to the Constitution permanently abolishing slavery and giving all persons equal protection under the law respectively, blacks were still to suffer through blatant Jim Crow discrimination at the hands of racist state laws in front of a backdrop of an apathetic government.

There is no question that the overt racism and discrimination that blacks suffered at the hands of white America before and during the Jim Crow era had a direct affect on the ability, of those who were the target of such oppression, to pursue and obtain the fruits of the American Dream. Blacks lived in a constant state of threat of death particularly in the South and were denied the total integration into American society as a whole which hindered their ability to gain the same financial, educational, and career successes as their white counterparts. There was no improvement of this situation until many brave black men and women and other minorities, along with many brave white men and women as well, began to cry out against the atrocities of racial discrimination leading to a resistance against bigotry and the murder of innocent blacks, culminating into the Civil Rights Movement of the 50s and 60s led by Rev. Dr. Martin Luther King Jr. which paved the way to the slow death of Jim Crow, lynching, and overt discriminatory practices against blacks and other minorities.

4.

THE CIVIL RIGHTS MOVEMENT

THE CIVIL RIGHTS MOVEMENT IN AMERICA

The American Civil Rights Movement began in 1954 with the case of Brown vs. Board of Education and is said to have ended with the implementation of the Voting Rights Act of 1965. As discussed in the previous chapter, in the case of Brown vs. Board of Education, the Supreme Court not only declared segregation unconstitutional but overrode the "separate but equal" ruling that came as a result of the Plessy vs. Ferguson court ruling of 1896, also discussed in the previous chapter. The Brown vs. Board of Education thus was the catalyst that began the fight for blacks to be given the right to go to school with white children and it fueled a Civil Rights Movement that would last for eleven years.

The Emmett Till Murder

Although, since the onset of the Klan, blacks had been terrorized by lynching, brutalities, rapes, and the like, that went unchecked by the Federal Government and state governments, it wasn't until the brutal murder of Emmett Till that blacks began to systematically fight back. Emmett Till (born July 25, 1941), arrived in Mississippi from Chicago at the age of fourteen on August 21, 1955 to visit with his uncle for the summer. Three days later, while in Mississippi, he and a few of his friends were at a local store (Bryant's Grocery and Meat Market owned by Roy Bryant and his wife, Carolyn). Although he had been warned by his mother to be careful how he spoke to white people in the South, Emmett had no understanding of the magnitude of southern prejudices and discrimination at the time. So, allegedly, on a dare from his friends, Emmett flirted with Ms. Bryant in the store. According to historical reports, his words to her were "bye, baby" as she was leaving.

Not long afterwards Emmett was kidnapped by Mr. and Mrs. Bryant. Emmett was murdered and his body (which was discovered three days later) was thrown into the Tallahatchie River. He had been shot, one of his eyes had been gouged out, his forehead was crushed in, and barbed wire was around his neck. Emmett had been disfigured beyond recognition. Upon the insistence of his mother, Emmett's funeral was open casket.

Emmett's mother wanted the whole world to see what had been done to her teenaged boy. The whole world took notice and the black community in America began to demand justice.

Rev. Dr. Martin Luther King Jr.

In the same year that Emmett Till had been murdered, civil rights activist, Dr. Martin Luther King Jr., became the central figure in the Montgomery Bus Boycott. King has the distinction of being the most legendary civil rights activist in the history of America. King was born in Atlanta Georgia on January 15, 1929 to Martin Luther King Sr. and Alberta Williams King. King had a Christian upbringing. His father was the pastor of Ebenezer Baptist Church located in Atlanta Georgia. King eventually took over the pastorate after his father's death in 1960. In 1948 King received a Bachelor of Arts degree in Sociology from Morehouse College. In 1951 he received a Bachelor of Divinity degree from Pennsylvania's Crozer Theological Seminary and from there earned a Doctorate in Philosophy in Systematic Theology from Boston University in 1955. He was also the recipient of twenty Honorary Doctorates from various colleges nationally and internationally. In 1954 King became the pastor of the Dexter Avenue Baptist Church located in Montgomery Alabama. During this time he was a member of the Executive committee of the NAACP.[1] In 1957 King became the president of the Southern Leadership Conference. He was the author of five books and at age 35 he became the youngest person ever to have received the Nobel Peace Prize. He received the prize for his non-violent struggles against racism, discrimination, and civil rights infractions.

King began championing the cause for civil rights of black Americans in 1955 when he became one of the key organizers of the Montgomery Bus Boycott. From there he was instrumental in the organization of several non-violent protest movements; most notably the 1963 March on Washington where he preached his famous "I Have a Dream" speech and the 1965 marches from Selma to Montgomery.

In the latter years, just before his assassination, King began to focus on poverty issues and the Vietnam War. King was adamantly opposed to the war and began to speak out against it. He organized another march on Washington in early 1968 in an effort to galvanize aid for the poor. But this march did not get the same support from civil rights leaders as did the March on Washington five years prior. Shortly after the 1968 March on Washington, King became involved with the concerns of the black

---

[1] See chapter 3

sanitation workers who worked for the city of Memphis Tennessee. He flew to Memphis to speak at a rally that was to take place on April 3rd of that same year. He made his speech at the Mason Temple Church of God in Christ. During the rally events, King stayed at the Lorraine Motel in Memphis. On the evening of April 4, 1968, King was shot as he stood on the balcony of the motel. He was rushed to the hospital and died an hour later.

The Montgomery Bus Boycott

The Montgomery Bus Boycott resulted in a Supreme Court ruling that declared segregation of bus passengers a violation of the United States Constitution. Before the ruling, blacks who used the public bus transportation in Montgomery were made to sit in the back rows of the bus while white people sat in the front rows. If a bus was full, this meant that there were two middle rows in which there was a row of white people and then a row of black people behind that row. If a white person boarded a full bus then all of the black people in the middle "black row" would have to get up and let the white person sit down, starting a new row for the whites. And even though there were empty seats in the new row, the blacks that got up would have to stand because blacks were not allowed to sit by whites. Conversely, if a black person entered the bus when it was full, it was understood that they would automatically stand. White people were not mandated to give up their seats for blacks.

The boycott was organized by King and other black leaders of the Montgomery community after Rosa Parks, a black woman, refused to give up her seat to a white man and was consequently arrested and put behind bars. Parks was arrested on December 1, 1955. The boycott began four days later. During the boycott, blacks did not ride the buses. They car-pooled, walked, and rode bikes to where they had to go. The boycott lasted a little over a year. The effect of blacks not riding the bus devastated the public bus company by depleting its revenues to 35% of what it was garnering before the boycott. The Montgomery Bus company was forced to desegregate as a result of considerable revenues that were lost coupled with a 1956 Supreme Court Decision that upheld an earlier decision that year that was handed down by the Federal District Court which had determined the unconstitutionality of racially segregating bus passengers.

Two years later in 1957 the incidents that occurred at Central High School located in Little Rock Arkansas (discussed briefly in the previous chapter) were to be the catalysts that mobilized the country into the desegregation of the public school system.

Little Rock Central High

The United States Supreme Court declared segregation of public schools unconstitutional in 1954. Consequently, white public schools were forced to begin establishing plans to desegregate. Little Rock Central High School (Little Rock Arkansas) personnel developed plans to desegregate by the year 1957. The date for integration was set for September 3rd of that year; the first day of school after summer break. Nine black students[2] were registered to begin classes. Segregationists planned a protest and the Governor of Arkansas, Orval Faubus, supported the protest and ordered the National Guard to prevent the black students from entering the school. When the black students arrived for class, the Guard prohibited them from going in. This made national headlines. President Dwight Eisenhower contacted Governor Faubus to discourage him from these actions.

Due to judicial pressure from Judge Ronald Davies of the Federal District Court, the Governor withdrew the Guard on September 20th. However, hundreds of segregationist protesters surrounded the school three days later on the 23rd as school personnel again attempted integration. The police were deployed this time and managed to escort the black students out of the school (away from the awareness of the protesters) who had already been inside. But the protestors began to riot as soon as they discovered that the students were inside. As a safety precaution, the police escorted the students out of the school.

The next day, September 24th, per a request from Little Rock's Mayor, Woodrow Mann, asking for Federal troops to be sent to protect the students, President Eisenhower dispatched the 101st Airborne Division of the United States Army to the school and also sent 10,000 (ten thousand) National Guardsmen. This time the Guard was federalized and by order of the President was sent to protect the students and enforce the integration effort instead of to prevent it. On Wednesday, September 25th, the students entered the school safely and began their studies. However, they were the target of racial attacks throughout the school year which included being spit on, being verbally abused, and being constantly terrified and intimidated as they walked through the halls of Little Rock Central High. The school board continued to fight against the integration and in an effort to do so, closed the school completely down at the end of the school year. All students were forced to register for classes elsewhere for the upcoming school year. The majority of the white students began attending white private schools in the area. The school board was eventually pressured by

---

[2] Thelma Mothershed, Minnijean Brown, Elizabeth Eckford, Gloria Ray, Jefferson Thomas, Melba Pattillo, Terrance Roberts, Carlotta Walls, Ernest Green

federal authorities to reopen the school. Central High was reopened in 1958 to integration.

The Woolworths lunch counter sit-ins

Woolworths was a retail chain drugstore founded by Frank Woolworth. The first of these chain stores was built in 1878 in Lancaster Pennsylvania. In 1879 the store name was changed from Woolworth 5cent store to Woolworth 5 & 10 (which the public referred to as "Woolworth five and dime"). Over time, the Woolworth chain became known as Woolworths, had grown to 3000 stores nationwide, and had become a cultural landmark in America during the early 1900s through the mid 1900s. The Woolworths stores stocked affordable retail merchandise and also provided lunch counter/soda fountain food service.[3] Many southern restaurants and eateries were segregated during the time. Woolworths was no exception.

On January 31, 1960, a black college student named Joseph McNeill sat at the lunch counter at Woolworths in Greensboro North Carolina and was refused service. By sitting at the counter, McNeill was protesting segregation state law. The policy at this particular store was that blacks were not to be served (even though they were allowed to work behind the counter). The next day McNeill returned with three of his college friends (David Richmond, Franklin McCain, and Ezell Blair) and the four of them sat at the counter. They were not served. They stayed at the lunch counter until it closed. Before long, others, black and white, protesting segregation, joined them at the counter. Within two weeks there were anti-segregation food counter sit-ins in thirty cities and eleven states. Many protestors had drinks dumped on them, were burned with cigarettes, had mustard and ketchup poured into their hair and the like. However, those who sat-in refused to budge. By December of 1960 over 70,000 people had participated in sit-ins in over 100 cities and 20 states around the country. Overall 3,600 protesters were arrested and put in jail while 187 students were expelled. National attention given to the sit-ins eventually helped to change the tide and within six months there were 26 southern cities that had desegregated their lunch counters. Protestors also conducted wade-ins at segregated beaches, read-ins at segregated libraries, and even pray-ins at segregated white churches, all of which proved to be helpful in exposing and eliminating blatant discrimination. By 1963 lunch counters across America were integrated but not without the infamous incident in

---

[3] Woolworths eventually went out of business. The name of the firm was changed to Venator Group in 1997 and then to Footlocker in 2001.

Birmingham Alabama in which college students, in an attempt to integrate the counters there, were met with police dogs and fire hoses. Martin Luther King Jr. was intricately involved with the Birmingham Alabama protest. He along with several students were arrested and jailed. Although sit-ins had been successful in various areas, there were still segments of the South that refused integration of any kind until forced to do so by the implementation of the 1964 Civil Rights Act. All in all, roughly 50,000 black and white men and women had participated in the sit-ins with 2,000 of those having had been arrested at some point.

The Freedom Riders

In 1960 the United States Supreme Court declared segregation of interstate public facilities to be illegal. This ruling resulted from the Boynton vs. Virginia case.[4] The Court cited that segregation in such instances was a direct violation of the Interstate Commerce Act which regulated the railroads and forbade "undue or unreasonable preference" and "personal discrimination." This meant that there could no more be separate black and white waiting rooms, drinking fountains, bathrooms, and the like in bus stations and train stations. Although the law against this type of segregation had been passed, many southern states ignored the law and continued practicing such segregation. Black people in the South began to test the ruling by riding public transportation through the South. Despite the United States Supreme Court decision making segregation of public transportation illegal, those who tested the law were often attacked by angry white mobs set on keeping things the way they were. Eventually, those who dared to challenge the system would be called Freedom Riders.

The Freedom Riders were organized by the Congress for Racial Equality (CORE) which was a civil rights organization founded in 1942 by an interracial group of concerned citizens. In 1947 CORE organized a civil rights protest that involved sending eight black men and eight white men to ride buses through four states (Kentucky, North Carolina, Tennessee, and Virginia). These 16 men would sit next to one another interracially

---

[4] In 1958 Bruce Boynton, a black Howard University law student, was traveling from Washington to Alabama on a Trailways bus. The driver stopped at a diner in Virginia. Boynton sat in the white section of the diner and upon being asked to leave the area, refused. He was arrested and fined. He sued the state of Virginia citing violation of the Interstate Commerce Act. The case went all the way to the Supreme Court of the United States and in 1960, the Supreme Court reversed the decisions of the lower courts in favor of Boynton declaring that he had indeed be discriminated against unconstitutionally in consideration of the Interstate Commerce Act.

(whites and blacks sitting beside one another) on the buses, which at the time was against the law in those states. The men were arrested several times and jailed but no violence came out of it. The Freedom Rides of 1961 were organized by CORE for a similar purpose, and, as in 1947, the Freedom Riders were comprised of both blacks and whites.

The first journey of the Freedom Riders that were organized in 1961 took place on May 14th of that same year when a group of blacks loaded onto a Greyhound bus in Washington D.C. with the intent of riding the bus to New Orleans. However, when they got to Alabama they were confronted by an angry white mob who fired-bombed one of the buses and beat the riders with baseball bats, iron pipes, and chains as they fled the bus. The mob also attacked the riders of a second bus by entering the bus and beating them. Many of the riders had to be hospitalized. The Freedom Riders were arrested for unlawful assembly and for violating certain Jim Crow laws that were still on the books in the South. This did not dissuade the Freedom Riders and three days later replacement riders were sent to travel from Nashville to Mississippi. They were arrested and jailed. Then on May 21st the Riders boarded a bus in order to travel from Birmingham Alabama to Montgomery Alabama. They were beaten by an angry white mob without intervention from the police. Again, many of them had to be hospitalized. The Ku Klux Klan was the main catalyst behind the formulation of the mobs. The Greyhound and Trailways bus companies were the companies mostly used for the rides. However, there was so much violence along the paths that the bus drivers began to become afraid to drive the buses.

White Freedom Riders were often beaten more severely by the Klan than were black Freedom Riders but all were severely beaten. Despite the danger and the violence, the Freedom Riders persisted and in May 28, 1961 after arriving in Jackson Mississippi many of the Freedom Riders, over three hundred in all, were arrested. The authorities purposely overcrowded the jails with the Freedom riders. Many of the Freedom Riders were sorely mistreated while in jail. They were stripped to their underwear and placed in Maximum security. While incarcerated they were also deprived of mattresses, toothbrushes, sheets, and window screens. Consequently the cells became filled with mosquitoes that fed on them.

John F. Kennedy was President of the United States during the time of the Freedom Rides. He initially faulted the Freedom Riders for making trouble and attempted to discourage freedom riding, despite the fact that segregation of public transportation was illegal. Finally, through the insistence of Robert Kennedy (President Kennedy's brother) the Interstate Commerce Commission issued a new ruling forbidding segregation in public transportation. A new law came into effect in November of 1961.

This time all of the segregation signs designating "white only" and "colored only" were removed from all areas of bus stations and terminals including the lobbies, restrooms, and drinking fountains.

James Meredith and the University of Mississippi

As stated earlier, even though the United States Supreme Court had declared school segregation unconstitutional, the majority of colleges and universities continued to practice segregation by not admitting blacks. In 1961 a black man named James Meredith applied to the University of Mississippi. Meredith was 29 years old at the time. Meredith had spent two years at Jackson State College (located in Jackson Mississippi) which was and still is identified as a black university (the college eventually gained university status). Meredith wanted to transfer from Jackson College to the University of Mississippi but his application was rejected. University of Mississippi school officials cited the lack of backing from University of Mississippi alumni and the non participation of Jackson State College with the Southern Association of Secondary Schools as the reasons for Meredith's entry disqualification. In May of that same year, Meredith sued the University of Mississippi for discrimination. The law suit accused the University of rejecting Meredith as a student because of his race.

Although the Federal District Court rejected Meredith's lawsuit, Meredith won his case through the United States Court of Appeals which declared that "Meredith had been rejected solely because he was a Negro." The following year, as a result of this decision, the Federal District Court ordered the University of Mississippi to allow Meredith to attend classes. The Governor of Mississippi at the time, Ross Barnett, publicly, through television and the news media, opposed Meredith's fight to be admitted into the all-white university. When Meredith attempted to register on September 20, 1962, the Governor stopped him from doing so. Meredith did not give up and returned to the campus within a week accompanied by the Chief Federal Marshall and an attorney. But Meredith was once again stopped. Eventually the situation unfolded into a major standoff. On September 30th, President Kennedy discharged troops and Federal Marshals.

Meredith, by aid of Federal authorities, was able to secretly spend the night in one of the halls on campus. When it was discovered that Meredith was somewhere on campus, over a thousand angry white students gathered together to protest his being there. But although army troops had been dispatched to the area, only the Marshals and State troopers were actually dispatched to the scene. They were outnumbered by the crowd and were not able to control it. The protesters became violent and in the end many people had been injured and two people killed. Meredith eventually graduated from the University of Mississippi in 1963 with a Bachelor of Arts degree in political science but he had to be protected by Marshals every day he went to class.

Sixteenth Street Baptist Church

On September 15, 1963, members of the Ku Klux Klan (reportedly, Thomas Blanton, Herman Cash, Robert Chambliss, and Bob Cherry) bombed the Sixteenth Street Baptist church (a church that was attended by blacks) located in Birmingham Alabama. The men allegedly used 19 sticks of dynamite in order to set off the time delayed blast. The bombing was in response to the overall fight for integration by those who opposed segregation laws, specifically in response to the steps that had been taken by activists to integrate public schools and universities. The church was first established in 1873 as the "First Colored Baptist Church of Birmingham" and had progressed through the years to become an icon of civil rights activism in the Birmingham black community at the time. The bomb had been planted in the basement of the church and the blast occurred at 10:22 on that Sunday morning. Twenty-six children were in the process of entering the basement just before the bomb went off. Four of those children were killed in the explosion; 22 other people were injured.

The bombing backfired as to the anti-integration political statement it was meant to make and instead a national outcry ensued. The young girls that were murdered in the blast were Addie Mae Collins (14 years old), Denise McNair (11 years old), Carole Robinson (14 years old), and Cynthia Wesley (14 years old). Violence erupted after the wake of the incident with two more youths being killed that day. Johnny Robinson (a black youth, 16 years of age) was gunned down by police after throwing rocks at two white people in a car and Virgil Ware (a black youth, 13 years of age) was gunned down by two white teenaged boys while he was riding his bike.

Robert Chambliss was convicted of the murders of the four young girls in 1978 and died in prison in 1985. Thomas Blanton was convicted in 2001 and Bobby Frank Cherry in 2002. Cherry died in prison in 2004. Herman Cash died in 1994. He was never charged.

The 1963 March on Washington for Jobs and Freedom

On August 28, 1963 one of the most famous marches in history took place at the Capital of Washington D.C. It was called the "March on

Washington for Jobs and Freedom." The March was the fifth organized march in American history at the time. Preceding it was the 1894 Coxey's Army March, the 1913 Women's Suffrage March, the 1925 Ku Klux Klan March, and the 1932 Bonus Army March, each garnering an estimated crowd of five-hundred, five thousand, thirty-five thousand and twenty thousand respectively. The 1963 March on Washington for Jobs and Freedom garnered an unprecedented two hundred and fifty thousand people. The composition of march attendees was roughly eighty percent black and twenty percent white.

Although the organizers of the march agreed that the main purpose was to protest civil rights infractions against black Americans, the organizers disagreed as to the specifics of the purpose of the march. There was conflict as to whether or not the march should focus on President Kennedy's slowness to support and endorse civil rights issues, whether or not the focus should be on the positive show of support from Kennedy with his recent introduction of the civil rights bill, or whether or not the focus should be on ongoing civil rights concerns that the bill had not addressed. The official statement from the march organizers was that the event was implemented in order to give support to the new bill; however there was some criticism of the insufficiency of the bill, voiced during the march, particularly by John Lewis during his speech.

Despite inner disparities regarding the purpose of the march, the march came to be known as the primary symbol of the American Civil Rights Movement with Martin Luther King's "I Have a Dream" speech being the pivotal point of that symbolism. The speech that King made at the march is world renown as one of the most moving speeches ever made. Two of the most notable parts of his speech included his quoting of the segment of the Declaration of Independence which declares that all men are created equal and his "dream" that one day his children would not be judged by their color, but by the "content of their character."

The 1963 March on Washington was one of the main forces that triggered the enactment of the Civil Rights Act of 1964. The Act was also triggered by the culmination of civil rights struggles during that era and by the assassination of President Kennedy on November 22, 1963.

The Civil Rights Act of 1964

In June of 1963, President Kennedy, five months before his assassination, sent a civil rights bill to Congress in order to pass an Act which, if passed, would make it illegal on a national level for a business establishment to refuse service to a minority and would also give greater securities to minorities with regard to the vote. However, there was some criticism of the bill from black activist leaders because the bill did not address police brutality and racial discrimination when it came to privatized employment.

Kennedy began to take the steps that would be needed to pass the bill but he was assassinated in November of that same year before the bill could pass. Vice President Lyndon Johnson was sworn in as president shortly after Kennedy was assassinated. Johnson aggressively took strides, in the form of strong public endorsement of the bill, to make certain that the bill was passed. On February 10, 1964 the bill was passed by the House of Representatives and moved to the Senate for the final vote. Despite the attempt of many of the southern Senators to block the bill, the bill was passed by a Senate vote of 73 to 27 and was finally signed into law by President Johnson on June 2, 1964. The introduction to the Act reads as follows:

An Act to enforce the constitutional right to vote, to confer jurisdiction upon the district courts of the United States to provide injunctive relief against discrimination in public accommodations, to authorize the Attorney General to institute suits to protect constitutional rights in public facilities and public education, to extend the Commission on Civil Rights, to prevent discrimination in federally assisted programs, to establish a Commission on Equal Employment Opportunity, and for other purposes. Be it enacted by the Senate and House of Representatives of the United States of America in Congress assembled, That this Act may be cited as the "Civil Rights Act of 1964."

Title Two, Section 201 (a) of the Act declares the following:

All Persons shall be entitled to the full and equal enjoyment of the goods, services, facilities, and privileges, advantages, and accommodations of any place of public accommodation, as defined in this section, without discrimination or segregation on the ground of race, color, religion, or national origin.

Title Four, Section 401 items a and b made it illegal to deny any minority admission into public schools based on race, color, religion, or national origin. These sections of the Act specifically state the following:

(b) "Desegregation" means the assignment of students to public schools and within such schools without regard to their race, color, religion, or national origin, but "desegregation" shall not mean the assignment of students to public schools in order to overcome racial imbalance.

(c) "Public school" means any elementary or secondary educational institution, and "public college" means any institution of higher education or any technical or vocational school above the secondary school level, provided that such public school or public college is operated by a State, subdivision of a State, or governmental agency within a State, or operated wholly or predominantly from or through the use of governmental funds or property, or funds or property derived from a governmental source.

Despite the ratification of this Act, civil rights liberties continued to be grossly violated, which prompted President Johnson to issue Executive Order 11246 (a supplement order to Kennedy's Executive order to 10925 which established the President's Committee on Equal Employment Opportunity). Executive Order 11246 introduced the concept of Affirmative Action, which is discussed in the following chapter.

The 1965 Selma Marches

The Selma Marches were a culmination of three specific marches that took place in the city of Selma Alabama in 1965. The marches centered on the acquisition of fair voting rights for minorities and were organized by Amelia Boynton. These marches involved many high level civil rights leaders. During this time, blacks were deterred from voting by intimidation and violence that was hurled at them from the Ku Klux Klan at the voting polls. Blacks were also deterred from voting by the implementation of unfair literacy tests that were imposed.

Boynton, along with her family had organized a voter's registration task force for blacks living in the city. The task force was unsuccessful because of the resistance they encountered from hate groups, the courts, and public officials. Eventually, the Boynton family solicited the help of Dr. Martin Luther King Jr. .

Despite the Civil Rights Act that was enacted a year earlier, blacks were attacked, beaten, and arrested in Selma when they attempted to go into movie theaters and certain eateries. They were also arrested and jailed when attempting to register to vote.

King had begun addressing the issue through his Southern Christian Leadership Conference (SCLC) organization and in January of 1965 the

72

Selma Voting Rights Movement began. A court injunction had been imposed the year before by Judge James Hare upon the city of Selma making it illegal for groups of three or more who were associated with the SCLC to gather together. In February of 1965, Jimmie Lee Jackson, a young black man in his early twenties, was shot by police in Marion County during a civil rights protest event. In response, the SCLC organized a protest march. It was planned that marchers would walk from the city of Selma to the city of Montgomery. The march was to take place on March 7, 1965 and was to begin on Highway 80. Roughly 600 marchers commenced the long walk that day.

George Wallace was the Governor of Alabama during this time. He deemed the march a threat to the safety of the citizens of Alabama and called in the state troops. The marchers had only walked six blocks when they were attacked by the troopers and by police. Many of the marchers were beaten with bull whips and bully clubs, including Amelia Boynton, who almost died from her injuries. The mayhem of this march was shown nationally because the media was also there to film and photograph the event. Seventeen marchers were hospitalized as a result of the attacks. Because of the brutality of the attacks on the marchers, the number of marchers that had to be hospitalized, and the fact that the day of the March was on a Sunday, this first Selma March eventually came to be known as "Bloody Sunday."

King organized another march two days after Bloody Sunday. Again, the plan was for marchers to walk from Selma to the city of Montgomery Alabama. However, Judge Frank Johnson issued a restraining order forcing King to turn back the marchers. A prayer vigil was therefore held instead which symbolized a "ceremonial" march. Later on that evening, James Reeb, a white minister and supporter of the march, was physically attacked and beaten (along with two others) by anti-march protestors. Reeb died two days later. After the death of Reeb, Judge Johnson reversed his decision and allowed the march to take place. Consequently, a third march commenced on the 21st of that same month. It took three days for the marchers to finally reach Montgomery. When the marchers reached their destination they celebrated with a concert that included Sammy Davis Jr. and Harry Belefonte. The following day, on the 25th, King delivered a speech at the state Capital. This third march took place without incident.

Malcolm X

Malcolm X was born in Omaha Nebraska on May 19, 1925 to Earl and Louise Little. Malcolm X is considered by many to be second to Dr.

Martin Luther King Jr. in the civil rights struggle of the twentieth century when it comes to equal rights for black Americans. Malcolm's birth name was Malcolm Little. Malcolm's father, Earl Little, was an advocate of civil rights during his day and was found dead in 1931 near trolley tracks in Lansing Michigan where the family had moved to a couple of years earlier. Malcolm, as well as others in the black community always believed that his father was killed by white supremacists. Malcolm's mother, Louise Little, eventually began to suffer from mental illness and was committed to a mental institution where she stayed for roughly 26 years. As a young man, Malcolm began to involve himself in criminal activities and was arrested in 1945 for burglary. He was paroled in 1952. While in prison, he was introduced to the Nation of Islam, a religion that taught racial separatism and black supremacy.

Malcolm X eventually met the leader of the Nation of Islam, Elijah Muhammad. The two men formed a bond and eventually, Malcolm X became minister of the Nation's Mosque in New York, giving him substantial status in the Nation. Malcolm spoke on the street corners of New York against racism and discrimination and became world renown as a leader in the Civil Rights Movement while moving up through the ranks of his new found religion. However, his messages promoted violence against whites and also promoted the religion of the Nation of Islam.

Although Malcolm's message was significantly different from King's when it came to the methods that each man felt should be used to move blacks towards equality (King's message was a non-violent one while Malcolm's message was equality "by any means necessary"), Malcolm had an irrefutable influential effect on the Civil Rights Movement but his contribution to the movement was marred by the supremacist teachings of the Nation of Islam along with infightings within the Nation. Malcolm X was assassinated in 1965 by members of the Nation of Islam after rejecting their supremacist teachings and after publicly criticizing Elijah Muhammad.

The Voting Rights Act of 1965

The Voting Rights Act of 1965 was enacted in order to enforce the Fifteenth Amendment which made it a violation of the Constitution for any state to deprive any citizen of his or her voting rights regardless of race or color. The Act itself did not federalize the right to vote but instead prohibited discriminatory practices that many states put into effect in an effort to deprive black Americans the right to vote.

The Voting Rights Act prohibited the practice of implementing prerequisites to voting that were clearly discriminatory against blacks.

Before the Voting Rights Act of 1965 was enacted, literacy tests were given in order to qualify or disqualify voters. It soon became apparent that many blacks who were able to read were not passed on the test while many whites who were not able to read were passed. The Voting Rights Act of 1965 did away with these tests. Most of this disenfranchisement of the black vote was exercised within the southern states. Section 2 of the Voting Rights Act of 1965 reads:

> No voting qualification or prerequisite to voting, or standard, practice, or procedure shall be imposed or applied by any State or political subdivision to deny or abridge the right of any citizen of the United States to vote on account of race or color.

Section 3b documents the Attorney General's duty to monitor the states' adherence to the Act and to investigate any infraction of the Act. It reads:

> If in a proceeding instituted by the Attorney General under any statute to enforce the guarantees of the fifteenth amendment in any State or political subdivision the court finds that a test or device has been used for the purpose or with the effect of denying or abridging the right of any citizen of the United States to vote on account of race or color, it shall suspend the use of tests and devices in such State or political subdivisions as the court shall determine is appropriate and for such period as it deems necessary.

Section 4c defines "test or devise" as the following:

> The phrase "test or device" shall mean any requirement that a person as a prerequisite for voting or registration for voting (1) demonstrate the ability to read, write, understand, or interpret any matter, (2) demonstrate any educational achievement or his knowledge of any particular subject, (3) possess good moral character, or (4) prove his qualifications by the voucher of registered voters or members of any other class.

Section 10d of the Act made it illegal for states to deny a person the right to vote for failure to pay a poll tax. Poll taxes were implemented by many states as a way to discourage people of color from voting. Many blacks at the time simply did not have the money to pay the tax. Sub-clauses (a) and (b) of Section 11 of the Act protected persons against the voting process being unfairly rigged and also against threats and intimidation. The clauses read as follows:

> (a)No person acting under color of law shall fail or refuse to permit any person to vote who is entitled to vote under any provision of this Act or is otherwise qualified to vote, or willfully fail or refuse to tabulate, count, and report such person's vote.

> (b)No person, whether acting under color of law or otherwise, shall intimidate, threaten, or coerce, or attempt to intimidate, threaten, or coerce any person for voting or attempting to vote, or intimidate, threaten, or coerce, or attempt to intimidate, threaten, or coerce any person for urging or aiding any person to vote or attempt to vote, or intimidate, threaten, or coerce any person for exercising any powers or duties under section 3(a), 6, 8, 9, 10, or 12(e).

This Voting Rights Act was approved on August 6, 1965. Black voters could no longer be deterred from the voting booths by use of poll taxation, literacy tests, and intimidation without such a practice being in violation of the law.

CHAPTER SUMMATION

As one can see, there has been a long hard struggle towards securing the rights of people of color in America, particularly the rights of black people. It was not until the United States Government began to be seen internationally as not doing enough for the plight of blacks that the Government finally stepped in, under Kennedy, to begin to look at changing the laws to protect the fundamental civil liberties of black Americans and other people of color living in the United States. With much bloodshed and the loss of hundreds of lives, the United States Government began to gradually, if not reluctantly, address the issue of racial discrimination head on. As discussed in the previous chapter, the Thirteenth Amendment permanently abolish slavery, the Fourteenth Amendment mandated due process of law and gave all persons equal protection under the law, and the Fifteenth Amendment made it against the law for any state to deprive men of voting rights. However, as we have seen in this chapter, it was not until the Civil Rights Act of 1964 and the Voting Rights Act of 1965, that these Amendments, as well as other Acts that were implemented to protect the rights of minorities, began being adhered to.

Our examination of the Civil Rights Movement in this chapter has focused upon those events in American history that have been most noted as significant occurrences that helped to change the tide of racism. It is by no means a complete list of events nor is it a complete list of the injustices that were imposed upon black Americans and other minorities during those tenuous years. Despite this, our look into the historicity of the Civil Rights Movement, along with our earlier examination of America's history of overt racism and inhumane oppression against blacks in particular, reveals enough information about these historical occurrences to make it almost impossible for even the most naïve of persons to minimize the cruelty of the era.

The most optimistic of persons would be hard pressed to deny that the racial prejudices and the discriminatory acts that triggered the necessity for the Civil Rights Movement have not been totally annihilated. Racism in America has simply reinvented itself. It has gone from being blatantly callous to insidiously inconspicuous. Racism against people of color in America now exists in a form that is more difficult to detect but that is still very hurtful to those on the receiving end of it. Although not as blatant as racism in times past, this modern-day racism still has substantial power to negatively affect, in many devastating ways, a person's quality of life who falls prey to it, which has a direct correlation, overall, as to whether or not the American Dream, at its fullest potential in relation to the drive and candor of any American in question, is equally assessable to every United States citizen. In today's time, racism in America is systematic and structural resulting ultimately in institutional racism.[5] The following chapter will take a look at institutional racism that is present in America today.

---

[5] The three descriptions are used interchangeably. See Chapter 1.

5.

INSTITUTIONAL RACISM IN AMERICA...WHERE WE ARE TODAY

INSTITUTIONAL RACISM IN POLITICS

The vote

The definition of the word *suffrage* means the right to vote. Since most adult Americans have this right, the United States defines itself as a nation with universal suffrage. However, there was a time in American history where all of its citizens were not given the right to vote, particularly blacks, women, and Native Americans.

In the latter part of the 1700s, only white men (who were not Catholics or Quakers) that owned property were allowed to vote. Everyone else, including Jews and women, was denied this right. In the mid 1800s, Mexican Americans had to pass certain English literacy requirements and they also had to own property before being given the right to vote. These requirements were used as a means to discourage or disqualify them from voting. Those that did pass were met with violence.

Before the onset of the Civil War there were only a few northern states that allowed free black men to vote. Enslaved black men and women as well as white women were not allowed to vote in any state. During this time neither the Constitution nor the Federal Government offered any protection against this type of discrimination. Therefore, voting power belonged almost exclusively to white men.

The end of the Civil War came in 1865. Not long afterwards, the Military Reconstruction Act of 1867 was instituted. The Act allowed for the southern Confederate states to reenter the Union and join the northern states under one flag but only upon the condition that the Confederates allow all men, black and white, to have equal voting rights.

In 1870 the Fifteenth Amendment was ratified and specifically stated that the right to vote shall not be denied based on "race, color, or previous condition of servitude."[1] The Fifteenth Amendment was ratified as a way

---

[1] It should be noted that women were not allowed to vote no matter what their racial identity was until the ratification of the Nineteenth Amendment in 1920.

to prevent discrimination at the polls. Not only was the Fifteenth Amendment ratified, but Congress also enacted the Enforcement Act in that same year. This Act served to make criminal any attempt to violate a person's right to vote and served to invoke certain criminal penalties for any such violation. And for a while, it worked. In the southern states, thousands of black people registered to vote. Black people also became political candidates and many of them were elected to serve in local offices as well as in Federal and state offices (even in the Confederate states). This is what is referred to as the Reconstruction Era.[2] However, a large number of whites did not like the fact that black people, who were once slaves, could vote and even run as political candidates in elections. As a result, many of the terrorist organizations at the time, including the Ku Klux Klan[3] began to use violence and intimidation against blacks (and those who supported the rights of blacks) in order to discourage the enforcement of the Fifteenth Amendment. Eventually the Government allowed this terrorist climate to reign which resulted in whites regaining control of the legislative activities of southern states.

In addition to the aforementioned, southern states often times disregarded the Fifteenth Amendment by creating local and unwritten laws that circumvented its mandates. As discussed in the previous chapter, examples of the tactics used to disqualify unwanted voters or unwanted political candidates were the implementation of voting poll taxes, literacy tests, and similar discriminatory strategies. It was not until the enactment of the 1957 Civil Rights Act that things began to change. This Act led to the establishment of a Civil Rights Department in which the Attorney General was given the authority to counteract any unfair voting regulation being imposed upon blacks or other minorities. The activities of this Department led to provisions against discriminatory voting practices. These provisions were included into the 1964 Civil Rights Act.

But despite the implementation of the Fifteenth Amendment, the enforcement of that Amendment, the 1957 and 1964 Civil Rights Acts, and the fact that the Constitution declares that voting rights cannot be denied because of race, color, or servitude;[4] there are still serious flaws in the American voting system today that many Americans are not keenly aware of.

First, not every adult American citizen has the right to vote. In some states, persons who have been convicted of a felony permanently lose their

---

[2] See Chapter 3
[3] See Chapter 3
[4] These Constitutional rights did not include the right of women to vote. The Nineteenth Amendment of 1920 finally gave women the vote.

right to vote even after their release (only the states of Maine and Vermont allow federal prisoners to vote while they are serving their time). Also, many states will not allow people to vote who have been declared mentally unsound in some way. The latter would include a wide range of people who suffer from certain mental illnesses and those who are cognitively challenged. In disallowing the vote to those who have been deemed mentally ill or incompetent the assumption is that the mentally ill can at no time make a sound judgment. However, in order to cast a vote, it only takes a decision of personal preference and an ability to read the ballot and follow directions.

The problem with disallowing the vote to those who have been convicted of a felony is that to do so not only goes against the notion of reform (once a convicted felon is released from prison) but also ignores the fact there are many people who have been innocently convicted. Those who are innocently convicted not only have been wrongfully disenfranchised of their right to vote but, depending on the state they lived in before their incarceration, are also consequently wrongfully disenfranchised of their right to vote after they've been released. These facts become even more disturbing when we look at the disproportionate number of minorities who are convicted and sent to prison as opposed to the number of whites.

Since there is an unquestionable and substantial overrepresentation of black people serving prison time in the United States as a result of structural/institutional racism of the judicial system (discussed later on in this chapter) then what follows as one of the results of this overrepresentation is the disenfranchisement of the vote for that same overrepresented population. Overrepresentation of minorities in the penal system translates into an overrepresentation of minorities that are denied the vote.[5] We will also see, later on in this chapter, that mental health professionals have a greater tendency, to a higher degree, to diagnose blacks as having mental illnesses than they do in diagnosing whites as

---

[5]Not only are convicted felons denied the vote in most states (and in many states the vote is reestablished for released felons but only under certain conditions) but aliens (who have not yet acquired American citizenship) and American nationals are also denied the right to vote even though they live in America and are expected to pay taxes. Aliens are those who have immigrated to America from other countries often in quest of establishing a better economic life for themselves and their families or because of some type of political or religious persecution that they are escaping from. In general, nationals are those who are natives of territory which is under United States possession. Some nationals are citizens, others are subjects. Those nationals who are not citizens are still legally protected by the U.S. but do not have all of the political privileges that U.S. citizens have.

having mental illnesses who present with the same psychological symptoms. This is an additional factor that leads to a disproportionate number of blacks (when compared to whites) denied the vote in America.

As stated earlier, in all but two states, convicted felons are denied the right to vote while still serving time and because there is a disproportionate number of blacks in prison as compared to whites; this disenfranchisement of voting rights for prisoners becomes a race equity issue. The denial of voting rights to prisoners automatically lends itself to institutional racism, since, as we will see, there is an overrepresentation of blacks doing hard time. But even though the right to vote is a serious issue as it pertains to institutional/systematic racism, there is a particular system in the elections and voting arena, due to its covert inconspicuousness, that is more suspect and questionable than the denial of certain people's right to vote, and that suspect and questionable system is the Electoral College.

The Electoral College

Many Americans believe that when they vote in a presidential election that they are voting directly for the presidential candidate of their choice. However, nothing could be farther from the truth. Instead, when each American electorate (any citizen of the United States who has the right to vote) votes in a presidential election, they are actually voting for the electors that represent that candidate, not the candidate himself or herself. Then, about five weeks later, the electors in each state are the ones who actually vote directly for the presidential candidate.

The irony of all of this is that not only don't most people realize that when they cast their vote they are casting a vote for the electors and not directly for the presidential candidate of their choice, but most Americans have no idea who these electors are (only Maine and Nebraska select electors by popular vote). In many states the names of the electors do not appear on the ballot and in those states in which the electors' names do appear, the names are in fine print.

The fact that the electors' names do not appear on many state ballots or appear only in fine print brings suspicion to the process as a whole. It is almost as if state governments want to make sure not to remind the voters that they are, in actuality, voting for the electors; not for the presidential candidate. If the public were to be reminded then the public might begin to demand to know who these people are, how they are selected, and whether or not the racial, gender, and age makeup of the Electoral College is representative of each individual state and the nation as a whole.

There are a total of 538 people that comprise the Electoral College. This number is derived by allotting each state the same number of electors as that state has senators and state representatives. All in all there are 100 senators and 435 state representatives nationwide which makes up Congress overall. When adding the 3 electors that have been provided to the District of Columbia through the enactment of the Twenty-third Amendment, the total national allotment for the number of electors under the Constitution equals 538.

Each elector has pledged to vote for the candidate of the party that they have been chosen to represent. The only person that the Constitution bans from serving as an elector is anyone who holds "an office of trust or profit under the United States." This ban does not include state officials and/or legislators. There are no age, residency, or citizenship requirements that are mandated in order to serve as an elector. However, in practice, electors are nominated at State Party conventions or by vote of a party's state committee. Electors are often times people who are personal friends of a presidential candidate, persons who have some kind of political affiliation with the presidential candidate, state elected officials, party leaders, and the like. This ultimately means that the average every-day American citizen is not likely to be nominated as an elector.

This brings us to another flaw in the system. Proponents of the Electoral College argue that the process was initially established (via the United States Constitution of 1787) as a means to prevent a larger state (at the time there were only 13) from electing one of their "favorite sons." The majority of the American citizens resided in the larger states and the fear was that a direct voting system would ensure that "good ol' boys" running for president would therefore always be elected from the larger states and the smaller states wouldn't have much of a chance.

This type of thinking was spurred on by the fact that there was really no way to get all of the information necessary about each candidate to each person in each state. There was no television, no radio, no telephones, and no Internet; and therefore people would be more inclined to vote for candidates who were natives of the states in which they lived; people that they knew or at least were keenly aware of.

Proponents of the Electoral College argue that the Electoral College was mainly adapted so that the smaller states would feel more at ease in joining the Union and also so that smaller states could maintain fair representation when it came to presidential elections. In other words, the Electoral College was established to prevent cronyism from having a significant effect in the outcome of presidential elections. But the disabling of the "'good ol' boy network" by means of the Electoral College (if indeed the "network" was ever truly disabled) in earlier years only manifested in later years in party officials nominating their "favorite sons" into the Electoral College, which was the very thing that the Electoral College was established to fight against.

The actual original reason for the Electoral College is twofold. Aside from the reason mentioned above, the most prevailing reason is that the founding fathers were afraid that if given the opportunity of a direct vote, the voting public would be likely, without intent, to put a tyrant or a shyster in office. It was felt that the general public was not intellectually adept enough to know who to vote for and who not to vote for, that the public would be manipulated by a scoundrel running for president, and that the public wouldn't have wits enough to see through any misleading political rhetoric coming from a candidate. The founding fathers simply did not trust the American people to make the "right choice" when it came to the vote for president. So, it was felt that an Electoral College was needed to make the right choice for them.

However, some believe that there was a more insidious reason behind the establishment of the Electoral College; that being that it was used as a way in which the slave states at the time would have a disproportionate increase of Congressional representation. In his Spring 2001 issue of Colorlines magazine, Executive Editor Bob Wing is quoted as saying the following:

> At the demand of James Madison and other Virginia slaveholders, this pro-slavery allocation of Congresspersons also became the basis for allocation of votes in the Electoral College. It is a dirty little secret that the Electoral College was rigged up for the express purpose of translating the disproportionate Congressional power of the slaveholders into undue influence over the election of the presidency. Virginia slaveholders proceeded to hold the presidency for 32 of the Constitution's first 36 years.

> Since slavery was abolished, the new justification for the Electoral College is that it allows smaller states to retain some impact on elections. And so it does—to the benefit of conservative white Republican states. As Harvard law professor Lani Guinier reports, in Wyoming, one Electoral College vote corresponds to 71,000 voters, while in large-population states (where the votes of people of color are more numerous) the ratio is one

electoral vote to over 200,000 voters. So much for one person, one vote.[6]

Some today would say that Wing's argument is now a mute one since the United States has now elected its first black president by means of this very same Electoral College. But the election of President Barack Obama does not negate the argument that the Electoral College is a significant player in a systematically discriminatory political field. It's just that this time around, the institutional discriminatory set up was outdone by the overwhelming support of Mr. Obama not only in black America but in white America as well. President Obama received 43% of the white vote. This was an unprecedented percentage of white votes for a black candidate. But such a percentage is what was needed to get past the race inequity of the Electoral College system. The institutional racism within America's world of politics still exists despite the fact that a black man now sits in the White House. The Electoral College gives evidence of this, particularly when looking at who the people are that serve in the College. Very few minorities serve in this College and it has proven very difficult to find out just exactly who these 538 people are and what the actual racial make up of the College is.

A presidential candidate needs at least half the Electoral College vote plus one to win the presidency. This calculates to at least 270 electoral votes (one half of 538 equals 269, plus one is 270).

Opponents of the Electoral College have cited many problems that come along with this type of voting system. The main problem with the electoral voting system is that it is a "winner take all" procedure. For example, California has 55 electoral votes. If a presidential candidate receives the majority popular (electorate)[7] vote in California *even if it's only by one vote*, the candidate will get *all* 55 electoral votes. The ratio of California electoral votes given to each presidential candidate in this example (one candidate gets none while the other candidate gets all) does not represent the ratio of popular votes both candidates actually received. Thus, the candidate who received the 55 electoral votes in our example clearly received a disproportionate number of those votes. This makes it very possible for a candidate to lose the nationwide popular vote but still win the electoral vote because one candidate could have a marginal

---

[6] Wing, Bob.,*"White Power in Election 2000,"* Colorlines: The National News Magazine on Race and Politics, Spring 2001, copyright ©2001, online www.colorlines.com/article.php?ID=127&p=2 Used by permission of the publisher

[7] The vote of the people, not the Electoral College vote.

popular vote majority in states that have a large number of electoral votes while the opposing candidate wins the popular vote in states that have a lesser number of electoral votes. This is exactly what happened in the year 2000 when George Bush and Al Gore ran. Bush lost the popular vote but won the electoral vote. Gore won the popular vote but lost the electoral. Bush therefore won the presidency although *the people* voted for Gore.

When looking even deeper, one must take into account that it is also possible for two presidential candidates to tie at 269 electoral votes or for more than two candidates to receive electoral votes (someone else besides the Republican and the Democratic candidates that are running). If, for instance, four candidates received electoral votes then the three with the most votes would be considered. If more than two candidates received electoral votes but none of the candidates received the mandatory electoral vote of half plus one, the decision would then go to the congressional House of Representatives. The House of Representatives is one part of Congress; the part that is composed of the 438 state representatives, (while the Senate is the other part; composed of the 100 state senators overall).

In instances where there are more than three candidates with electoral votes, the House would only vote on the three candidates that received the majority of electoral votes and if there were two candidates who tied within that three, then the House would vote on just those two candidates. Each state could only submit one vote from the House (which means that the representatives of each state would have to come to an agreement on which candidate to vote for). Since there are 50 states altogether, a majority of 26 votes or above would be needed to win the presidency. Since the District of Columbia is not a state (if it were considered a state then America would have 51 states instead of 50), it has one representative but that representative cannot vote on the floor. The District of Columbia has no senatorial representation at all. Therefore all the people living in the District of Columbia would be automatically disenfranchised (a bill was passed by the Senate in February of 2009 to rectify this; however the bill became stalled after a proposed amendment was added to it). When taking into account non-Hispanic whites, nearly 70% of the people living in the District of Columbia are minorities, with blacks making up 54%.

There is also the possibility that there was no candidate that received the majority of electoral votes. If this were to happen then the House of Representatives would vote for the three candidates with the most votes and the Senate would vote for the two candidates for Vice President who had the most electoral votes. The Vice Presidential candidate who wins this vote would become the Vice President Elect. If by January 20th the House could not come to a majority vote as to who would serve as President, then the Vice President Elect would act as President until the

House could come to a decision. Still, there's a possibility that the House, for some reason, may not be able to come to a decision as it pertains to voting in the Vice President Elect. If this were the case, then the Senate would make the decision as to who to elect for Vice President. Since there are 100 U.S. Senators,[8] a majority vote of at least 51 Senate votes would be needed to vote a candidate in as Vice President. But once again, it is possible that there could be a tie between candidates (50 votes each). If this were to happen, the acting President would appoint a Vice President pending an approval from Congress. There is a presidential line of succession for situations which would call for an acting President. The line of succession is documented in the Constitution. The first five successors are as follows: Vice President, Speaker of the House, President Pro Tempore of the Senate, Secretary of State, and Secretary of Treasury.

This is a complicated system that need not be. When a presidential candidate wins the presidency without the majority of the popular vote, he is referred to as the "minority president." The eradication of the Electoral College voting system would substantially decrease any probability of a minority president being voted into office because it would substantially decrease a tie in the first place. Additionally, the possibility of the District of Columbia being deprived the voting power of senate representation would be substantially diminished.

All the electors of a state are pledged to vote for whichever candidate wins the majority popular vote in their state, even if they have a preference for another candidate. This is why many voters will not vote third party because third party candidates never get enough popular votes to win all of the electoral votes in any given state. The only thing that voting for a third party candidate can do is skew the popular vote in favor of one of the top two contenders (Republican or Democrat). This brings us to additional problems cited by the opponents of the Electoral College, the first being that the electoral vote forces the voting public into a two-party race. It is difficult for another party to emerge.

The second major problem of the electoral voting system is that there is always a possibility that an elector, although pledged to vote for the

---

[8] There is only one black Senator. The Senate is over 90% white. There are, conflicting reports as to how many blacks and other minorities are in the House of the current Congress (111th). The general calculation is that there are 332 to 335 whites, 39 to 42 blacks, 25 to 27 Hispanics, and 5 to 6 Asians. Blacks are underrepresented in the House at roughly making up 13% of the population but only 9.5% of the House. Asians are also underrepresented making up roughly 4.6% of the population but only roughly 1% of the House. Hispanics are also underrepresented making up roughly 15.8% of the population but only roughly 6% of the House.

candidate with the most popular votes, decides instead to vote for the candidate of his or her own personal choice. An elector who does this is referred to as a "faithless elector." Furthermore, in only 26 states are electors bound by law or by pledge to vote for the candidate that has the majority vote in their state. In the other 24 states the electors are not obligated. In other words, although these electors are supposed to vote for whoever wins the majority vote in their state, they can vote for whoever they want to vote for regardless as to how the majority of the people in their state voted and they can do this legally without fear of any criminal prosecution.

Throughout the annals of history, since the Electoral College was implemented by the founding fathers, there have been a total of 156 faithless electors who did not vote for the candidate that won the majority vote in their state.

Just to cite some examples, in the year 2000, Barbara Lett-Simmons, a Democrat elector for the District of Columbia, abstained from voting. She was expected to cast her vote for Al Gore but refused to cast any vote at all. Although her abstention did not affect the outcome of the presidency it spoke volumes as to the power the electors have. In 1968 Dr. Lloyd W. Bailey, who was a North Carolina Republican elector cast his vote for third party candidate George Wallace who had already received 46 electoral votes and was known for supporting segregation of the races and discriminatory practices against blacks. In the 1960 election of President John F. Kennedy, there were 14 electors who refused to vote for him because of his support for the civil rights of black people. These 14 electors voted for Harry Byrd instead, who was a Senator from Virginia. In 1948, Preston Parks, a Tennessee Democrat voted for third party candidate Strom Thurman. Thurman was another candidate who, at the time, expressed discriminatory views against blacks. It should be noted that Thurman received 39 electoral votes all coming from the southern states of Louisiana, Alabama, Mississippi, and South Carolina even though he garnered no more than 3% of the popular vote. This is another testimony to the unfair power of the electoral voting system. And in 1836, twenty-three electors from the state of Virginia refused to cast their votes for Richard M. Johnson who was the Democratic Party's Vice President Nominee. They refused to cast their votes because of an allegation that Johnson had, at some time in his life, lived with a black woman. The Senate ended up making the decision as to who would be Vice President and voted for Johnson.

There is always some concern that an elector will go against his or her pledge due to some racial or prejudicial way of thinking of that particular elector. A great concern, when it comes to the question of fairness regarding the electoral voting system, is whether or not the system is racially discriminatory. When looking at the overall picture of how such a system undermines the direct voting power of black Americans, there is little doubt that the system lends itself to political institutional racism. Consider the following excerpts from an article written by Attorney Matthew Hoffman published online in 1999 by "The Nation" magazine:

> The problem lies in the winner-take-all method that forty-eight of the fifty states use to select presidential electors, those shadowy figures whom our Constitution entrusts with the task of choosing the President. Because voting in U.S. presidential elections is sharply polarized along racial lines, this system prevents African-American voters in many states from choosing even a single elector. And that isn't simply undemocratic—it might be illegal.
>
> To understand the problem, consider what happened in Alabama in the 1992 election. George Bush won the state handily with 47.9 percentage of the vote, claiming all nine of its electoral votes. But exit polls indicated that 91 percent of African-American voters in Alabama—who make up roughly two-ninths of the state's electorate—voted for Bill Clinton. Despite this overwhelming level of support, Clinton, with only 30 percent of the white vote, didn't secure a single electoral vote in Alabama. African-American voters might just as well have stayed home.[9]

The Fact that Barack Obama won the presidency in 2008 does not mean that structural racism does not exist within the voting system; it simply means that in 2008, the popularity of the candidate outweighed the racism of the system, which is a rarity. As stated earlier, President Obama garnered 43% of the white vote which significantly aided him in obtaining the amount of electoral votes he needed overall to win the presidency. It was the power of the white vote that got him in office coupled with the black vote. But any voting system that gives more voting power to any one

---

[9] Hoffman, Matthew; *"Electoral College Dropouts,"* Reprinted with permission from the June 17, 1999 issue of The Nation. Portion's of each week's Nation magazine can be accessed at http://www.thenation.com.
http://www.thenation.com. http://www.thenation/article/electoral-college-dropouts

group of people, whether done intentionally or not, is a system that needs to be changed. Bob Wing agrees with Hoffman's take on the problem and is quoted as saying the following in a year 2000 article he wrote published online by Colorlines magazine:

> The Electoral College negates the votes of almost half of all people of color. For example, 53 percent of all blacks live in the Southern states, where this year, as usual, they voted over 90 percent Democratic. However, white Republicans out-voted them in every Southern state (and every border state except Maryland). As a result, every single Southern Electoral College vote was awarded to Bush. While nationally, whites voted 54-42 for Bush, Southern whites, as usual, gave over 70 percent of their votes to him. They thus completely erased the massive Southern black and Latino and Native American vote for Gore in that region.

> Since Electoral College votes go entirely to whichever candidate wins the plurality in each state, whether that plurality be by one vote or one million votes, the result was the same as if blacks and other people of color in the South had not voted at all. Similarly negated were the votes of the millions of Native Americans and Latino voters who live in overwhelmingly white Republican states like Arizona, Nevada, Oklahoma, Utah, the Dakotas, Montana—and Texas. The tyranny of the white majority prevails.[10]

In addition to the racial disparity of the electoral voting system, the system also causes a person's vote in one state to outweigh the vote of another person in another state. For example the population of the state of Wyoming is roughly 500,000 while the state of Texas has over 24 million people residing there. Wyoming has been assigned 3 electoral votes while Texas has been assigned 34 electoral votes. Therefore, when we do the math, there is one electoral vote for every 167,000 Wyoming-state residents whereas in the state of Texas there is one electoral vote for

---

[10] Wing, Bob, *White Power in Election 2000*, spring 2001, *Colorlines: News for Action* Online Magazine, copyright © 2001, Used by permission of the publisher. http://www.colorlines.com/article.php?ID=127&p=2

roughly every 729,000 people. This means that a person who resides in the state of Wyoming has more voting power than a person who resides in the state of Texas because an individual vote in Wyoming counts 4 times as much in the Electoral College as does an individual vote in Texas. However, this advantage has little impact on the black population who live in Wyoming because the percentage of blacks living there is only 1% (one percent) compared to a 96% population of whites.

Because of the weight of votes that the Electoral College creates, there are many who argue that the Electoral College actually helps to give minorities more of an advantage in the voting system. However, this argument begins to sour when looking at percentages of the black population for states with the highest number of Electoral College electors and states with the fewest. The state of California has 55 Electoral College electors; which is the highest of any state (the second highest is Texas coming in at 34). But black people make up only 6.3% of California's population. The overwhelming majority of the population is white (including non-Hispanic whites and white Hispanics). Texas has a black population of 11.5% which is still at the low end. So the two states with the greatest electoral voting power have a fairly low percentage of blacks living in those states.

On the other hand, in the District of Columbia, blacks outnumber whites at an astonishing 54%. Although the District of Columbia is not a state, it is a viable part of America. Despite this, the District of Columbia has only 3 electoral votes and has no voting representation in the United States Senate and only one voting delegate in the House who is limited to only voting in House committees. To add to this, D.C. residents were not allowed to vote in presidential elections until the 1961 ratification of the Twenty-third Amendment. Ultimately then, the state with the greatest electoral voting power (California) has a considerably low black population and the district with the highest percentage of blacks living within its borders (D.C.) has the lowest number of electors (along with Wyoming, Vermont, Alaska, Delaware, Montana, South Dakota, North Dakota), was refused the vote until 1961, and has no voting representation in Congress.

To bring the point home further, according to a 2001 Internet article written by Gary Parish entitled, "The Electoral College: Source of Inequality and Social Justice in America," because of the resulting inequities of the Electoral College voting system, the value of a vote cast by a white person is 6% higher than a vote cast by a black person, 10% higher than a vote cast by a Hispanic person, 9% higher than a vote cast by Jewish person, 3% higher than a vote cast by an Asian person, and 11% higher than a vote cast by an immigrant.

The United Nations has declared that the United States, by use of the Electoral College, violates Article 21 of the United Nations Declaration of Human Rights, which guarantees universal and equal suffrage. The UN has listed the United States to be in non-compliance with this article along with other countries such as Afghanistan, Iraq, Iran, China, and North Korea. Examples of countries that are listed as being in compliance are Russia, France, Germany, Japan, Italy, and Brazil. When it comes to fairness in American voting practices, the United States is no better than many third world countries. Each individual vote should hold just as much weight as any other individual vote, but in America, this is not the case, and this disparity does indeed cut across racial lines.

With evidence that the Electoral College gives higher value to a vote cast by a white American as opposed to American minorities, one wonders how President Barack Obama won the presidential election of 2008, since he is black. He won because white men as well as white youths significantly supported him as did the majority of blacks and Hispanics. As stated earlier, however, this does not bring credence to the argument of some that the Electoral College is a racially fair system; this just means that with any system of institutional or structural racism, there is always someone who will beat the system. But a system in which a certain segment of the population has to beat it in order to succeed in it, should not be a system that is tolerated.

The United States Congress

The United States Congress is the legislative entity that makes laws in America. This means that those who serve in the United States Congress are very important people. They are the very people that decide what laws the American people are to abide by. Article 1 and Section 1 of the United States Constitution reads,

> All legislative Powers herein granted shall be vested in a Congress of the United States, which shall consist of a Senate and House of Representatives.

As mentioned earlier, the United States Senate is composed of one hundred members, two for each of the 50 states. The United States House of Representatives is composed of 435 members. Because the Senate is a smaller body of the Congress with just as much voting power as the House and because Senators serve 6 years while House Representatives only serve two, the Senate is considered more elite that the House of Representatives.

91

Although each state has two U.S. congressional senators, the number of House representatives that are apportioned to a state is based on the population of that state. House representatives are also referred to as state congressional representatives. Each senator and each House representative has one vote. All votes hold equal weight.

U.S. House Representatives as well as senators are voted in by state popular election. But senators and representatives can also be appointed by a governor if a Senate or House seat is vacated mid-term for some reason. The system has been designed so that a third of the senate seats come up for reelection every two years along with the House. Therefore, there is a "new" Congress every two years. One third of senate seats are up for re-election every two years along with the House.

When laws are made, the proposed bill must first "go through Congress" to be voted on by the Senate and the House. The main function of Congress is to make laws. Congress (the House and the Senate) is convened once a year in January. Article 1 and Section 7 of the Constitution reads,

> Every Bill which shall have passed the House of
> Representatives and the Senate, shall, before it becomes
> a Law, be presented to the President of the United States.

The proposed bill, if it passes through Congress, is presented to the President. The President can either approve or veto (disapprove) the bill. If the President approves the bill, he signs it and once he signs it; it is the Law. If the President vetoes the bill this means that he or she has rejected it (with written objections) and once it is rejected it is sent back to the House or to the Senate, whichever part of Congress it originated from. The bill is reconsidered by the Congress and eventually voted on again upon revision. But this time around, it takes two thirds of the House along with two thirds of the Senate to override the President's veto of a bill. This means that Congress has the power to override the Presidential rejection of a bill and pass it into Law themselves. The bill must get two thirds of the vote from both the House and the Senate to be passed into law after a veto from the President; if this two thirds vote is not present, the bill doesn't pass into Law. Governors can also veto state bills.

When looking at how laws are made, it is evident that Congress has more power than the President to pass a bill into law. And although Governors also have the power to veto a bill, state congresses also have more power than their governors do to pass a bill into state law.

Because of the law-making power of the United States Congress, it is important that minorities are well represented in both parts of Congress.

But they are not. There is only one black U.S. senator out of one hundred. And blacks, Hispanics, and Asians are underrepresented in the House. As we've seen earlier, blacks represent about 9.5% of the House but roughly 13% of the population of the United States, and it gets even sketchier when looking at Asian and Hispanic representation in the House. This brings to question whether or not laws that are being passed are adequately and equitably taking into consideration the concerns of minorities, particularly blacks. The under-representation of blacks and other minorities in the U.S. Congress brings scrutiny to the legislative process as a whole despite the fact that there is now a black President in the White House. The President must still answer to Congress.

Office of the Governor

The governor's role is a powerful one because he or she runs the state in similar fashion as the president runs the country. The governor acts, so to speak, as the president of the state that he or she governs. Just as the President signs bills into federal law or vetoes those bills, the governor also signs state bills into law or vetoes them. Governors run the state. Each state has its own state senate and state house of representatives which function similarly to the United States Senate and House.

Governors (as well as the President), have the power to execute Executive Orders for the state over which they reside. Essentially, an Executive Order is a decree that can only be made by a governor or the President which declares that a certain change be made or that a certain action be taken. With the power of an Executive order a governor can reorganize executive branch agencies, establish commissions and the like, declare a state of emergency or end it, and so forth. The military can also be deployed to a state by Executive Order. Executive Orders are not supposed to be used to usurp a state or federal law in any way; however, there have been instances where governors (and presidents) have abused their power of authority when it comes to exercising their right to issue an Executive Order.

An example of such an abuse of power was the issuing of Executive order 9066 by President Theodore Roosevelt in February 1942 which resulted in 120,000 Japanese and Japanese Americans (along with 11,000 German Americans and 3,000 Italian Americans) being sent to internment camps during World War II. And when it comes to Executive order abuses by the Governor's Office, one of the most flagrant examples of a governor abusing his or her power of authority was when, in 1957, Governor George Wallace issued an Executive Order prohibiting the integration of the city of Birmingham Alabama's public schools. His Executive Order defied the

93

Supreme Court's recent ruling of integration at the time and was consequently met with President John Kennedy's federalization and deployment of Alabama's National Guard to make certain that black children were allowed into the schools.

When considering the aforementioned, there is no question that the office of Governor is one of the most powerful political positions to be in and only rivals that of the Vice President. Governors are in prime positions to be considered as qualified to run for President.

There have only been four black governors in all of American history thus far. Pinkny Benton Stewart Pinchback was the first. After resigning as a captain in the Union Army during the Civil War, (he resigned because of the racism that infiltrated the army against the black soldiers), Pinchback moved to New Orleans and there he began a political career during the Reconstruction Era.[11] He eventually became one of the state Senators of Louisiana and from there became Senate President Pro Tempore. From there he became acting Lieutenant Governor when Lieutenant Governor Oscar Gunn (another black first) died and then went on to become sitting Governor when Governor Henry Clay Warmoth had to step aside (per Louisiana law at the time) while going through impeachment charges. Pinchback became Governor of Louisiana on December 9, 1872. Warmoth was not impeached and resumed the seat on January 14, 1873 after the charges against him were dismissed. Pinchback had served as governor for just 35 days and not without receiving several hate mail letters and threats against his life from all across the country. Interestingly, Pinchback didn't look black. He looked white but was considered black because his mother was biracial. She had been a former slave. Pinchback's father was his mother's former slave master, William Pinchback. William Pinchback was white. Pinchback's parents lived together as man and wife.

It was not until 118 years later that a second black governor emerged. Lawrence Douglas Wilder was voted in as Governor of Virginia in 1990 and served one four-year term. Then, it was not until twenty-seven years later before there would be another black governor after Wilder. On January 4, 2007 Deval Patrick was voted in as Governor of the state of Massachusetts, making him the first black person to ever serve in that capacity in that state. Shortly afterwards, in March of 2007, then Lieutenant Governor David Alexander Paterson, a black man, became Governor of the state of New York after Governor Eliot Spitzer resigned.

---

[11] See Chapter 3

Office of the President of the United States

In November of 2008 Barack Hussein Obama was voted into the office of the presidency. He is the first black person ever to be voted in as the President of the United States.[12] Although this was a monumental event, the voting in of a black man as President of the United States raised many issues and gave credence to the longstanding notion that America still has a long way to go when it comes to the elimination of racism against minorities. While initially many hailed President Obama's victory as evidence that America was entering into what was deemed a "post-racial America," it soon became apparent that closing the great racial divide in America is still an uphill battle. One must remember that while 43% of the white vote went to Obama, 57% of the white vote didn't. This is a sizeable amount of whites that did not vote for Obama and there is a portion of them that are not pleased that a black man is in the White House and that a black woman is First Lady; and they have made their displeasure known. As a matter of fact, the election of Barack Obama into the presidency has helped to uncover many strong racist sentiments that still exist in America.

When taking into account certain reactions of many white Americans to Obama's presidency, one is hard pressed to deny that the United States is no closer to a post-racial America than it was before Obama became President. One reason why such a denial would be difficult to uphold is due to the death threats made against President Obama during his campaign and after he became President. The death threats against Obama, particularly those during his campaign, were unprecedented. According to a Newswatch Magazine[13] article written by Modupe Ongunbayo in November of 2008, Obama received close to 200 death threats shortly after he was elected President. These threats mainly came from white supremacist groups in the form of emails and website rhetoric. Ongunbayo indicated that the Secret Service requested the aid of the Federal Bureau of Investigation to probe into the threats. The article named three white supremacist websites in particular where the threats were emanating from

---

[12] Some would disagree and argue that there were earlier "black" presidents but that they did not look black so no-one questioned their race. The men in question are Thomas Jefferson, Andrew Jackson, Abraham Lincoln, Warren Harding, and Calvin Coolidge. If indeed these men were of African descent, there would still be no arguing that Obama is most definitely the first black president to be voted into the Office of the Presidency who *looks* black.

[13] Ongunbayo, Modupe, article: *Death Threats against Oba*ma, Newswatch, online magazine, Sunday November 23, 2008, http://www.newswatchngr.com/index.php?=com_content&task=view&id=297&item=41option / www.newswatch.com

and indicated that there were still several sites posing threats besides the three sites specifically mentioned. The article also cited the state of Oklahoma in particular as where white nationalists passed out propaganda pitted against Obama and even posted this propaganda on residential mailboxes. The Ku Klux Klan (KKK) was mentioned as being a catalyst behind many of these events, even to the extent where there were two men with ties to the KKK who were arrested in Tennessee after it was discovered that they had plans to "incapacitate 88 blacks including Obama." There were even reports of certain southern states threatening to remove themselves from the United States Union.

Although there were a plethora of death threats against Obama when he took presidential office, the number of these threats pale in comparison to the number of death threats President Obama received during his campaign. It is reported that President Obama received at least five hundred death threats during his campaign in 2007. This number of death threats hurled towards a presidential candidate running for office was a first in American history. In May of 2007 Barack Obama received full Secret Service protection while running for office. It has never been necessary, in the history of American presidential elections, for any other candidate to receive this type of protection so early in the race. There is no question that President Obama had received these death threats solely due to the color of his skin.

Aside from the death threats, President Obama has had to endure a great deal of racially motivated mockery. In December of 2008, Paul Shanklin, a white comedian known for writing satirical songs that mock political figures, released an album (compact disc) entitled "We Hate the USA." Included on the album was a parody song (mocking then President Elect Barack Obama and political activist Al Sharpton) entitled, "Barack, the Magic Negro." The title itself is offensive to blacks specifically because of the use of the word "Negro." There are 41 parody tracks on the CD and "Barack the Magic Negro" is the only song in which the title specifies race. The lyrics of the song are offensive in that they accuse Obama of not being "authentically" black because he is not from the "hood" and makes Sharpton out to be a raving lunatic because he lost the presidency to an "unauthentic" black man. Limbaugh was the first to play the song on the air. In July of 2008 Shanklin released a Utube video entitled, "Obama Osama." In the video, the face of Obama was superimposed onto the headdress and attire of Osama Bin Laden; the underlying message being that Obama is a type of Osama Bin Laden. It was not only extremely inappropriate for a presidential candidate of the United States to be parodied with the most wanted terrorist in the world but it was also particularly dangerous to do so in Obama's case, in light of the hundreds of death threats that he received during his campaign and continues to receive during his presidency.

In one of the most controversial media attacks on Obama; the New York Post, printed a cartoon in February of 2009 that depicted two white police officers shooting and killing a chimpanzee. In the cartoon, one police officer says to the other (after the chimp has been shot down and is depicted as dead), "they'll have to find someone else to write the next stimulus bill." At the time, President Obama was in the middle of preparing the stimulus bill to present to Congress. One would be hard pressed not to think that the Post was indirectly referring to Obama as the chimp. Depicting blacks as monkeys and chimps was very common during the Jim Crow era and therefore to do so now is extremely offensive to the black community. Moreover, the chimp had been shot dead in the cartoon which gave a dangerous message since President Obama was indirectly referred to as the chimp. Certainly the New York Post knew this.

The Post is the oldest running daily newspaper in the country, established in 1801. The Post was around through slavery, the Civil War, Jim Crow, and the Civil rights era. There's no doubt therefore that the Post knew what they were doing. The Post however, made no apologies to President Obama and to black America. Instead the Editor-in-Chief attempted to justify the mockery as harmless parody. Al Sharpton expressed his concern about the racial overtones during a television news interview the following day after the cartoon was printed. He expressed the sentiments of black America but the New York Post didn't seem to be listening. Despite the racial overtones of the cartoon and what seemed to be an attack on the President, the bigger tragedy was the insensitivity the Post had when it came to the 55 year-old woman (Charla Nash) who had been severely mauled by a chimpanzee the day before (of which the cartoon stems). The chimpanzee bit off both of Ms. Nash's hands and bit into her face so severely that it ripped parts of it off. Ms. Nash barely survived and is facially disfigured and blinded from the incident. Not only did the New York Post seem to be oblivious to the fact that the cartoon was dangerously suggestive with regard to the President, but the Post also apparently thought it was acceptable to parody the actual tragic event of a woman who lost both hands, was blinded, and disfigured by means of a chimpanzee attack.

Aside from the President having been depicted as a chimpanzee, First Lady Michelle Obama has also been put under similar attack. In March of 2010, Walt Baker, CEO of the Tennessee Hospitality Association forwarded an email to his constituents that compared the First Lady to a chimp. The email was leaked to the media and he was fired.

Making mockery of the President is bad enough, but never before has a First Lady of the White House been so blatantly disrespected as has Michelle Obama. In 2009 and part of 2010, the very first picture that one came across when visiting the Google™ Internet image search engine when searching for Internet photos of Michelle Obama was a picture of a monkey's face interposed upon hers. After some public outcry, Google™ apologized for the picture but still continued to show it. After further public outcry, Google™ moved the picture from the first page of the search. As of early September 2010, the picture was on the 9th page of the image-search (the order of the pictures change often). It was no longer the very first image one saw of Michelle Obama when searching images of her on Google™, but it was still there. Further into the search, as of early September 2010, there was another image of First Lady Michelle Obama found on Google™ in which she was depicted strung up by the wrists on a tree wearing a red dress and the Ku Klux Klan had surrounded her and was branding her bare back where they'd torn off that part of her dress. No other First Lady has ever had to endure such sadistic images of herself. It would have been considered unconscionable. But when it comes to Michelle Obama, the first black woman to become First Lady, it is considered freedom of speech. Clearly this image is unarguably racist. There was also an image depicting a mock Playboy Magazine cover in which Michelle Obama's face was interposed upon a scantily clad model.

When it comes to mocking the First Lady, some might argue that previous First Ladies (particularly Barbara Bush and Laura Bush) have also been the victims of defacement on Internet sites. Although abhorrent, their defacement have no racial overtones and neither of them are depicted as being hung on a tree, stripped, branded, and about to be whipped.

Some would also argue that many presidents in the past have been parodied, mocked, and highly criticized and therefore it shouldn't be any different with Obama. However, President Obama is the only president in the history of the United States wherein the color of his skin has been the theme of the mockery. There was no song written entitled, "Bush the Magic White man." And although previous presidents may have been compared to monkeys at some point or another, white America is not straddled with the experience of experiencing Jim Crow discrimination first hand that included portraying them in such a light, while historically, black America is. Obama has been the first President Elect as well as the first President of the United States ever to be hung in effigy by United States citizens.[14] In October of 2008 he was hung in effigy in Kentucky by

---

[14] Sarah Palin was also hung in effigy that year. She was the first United States Vice Presidential candidate to ever be hung in effigy by United States citizens.

two white college students. The students claimed that they did so as a Halloween prank. And in January of 2010 President Obama was hung in effigy outside a storefront in Plains Georgia by means of a large black doll on a noose with the President's name pasted on it.

In addition to the aforementioned, President Obama has been the target of an insurmountable amount of criticism from the media, specifically from television news shows and radio right-wing talk shows, particularly during his first five months in office. It took the sudden death of Michael Jackson to put the constant barrage of editorial criticism on hold, and then, only momentarily. The Pew Research Center for the People and the Press took a poll in April of 2009 and discovered that Fox News (a major global television network) was the number one answer given from those who were asked as to which television news stations were too critical of Obama.

In looking even deeper into the media's reaction to a black man winning the presidency, one must take into consideration Rush Limbaugh, a radio host described as a conservative political commentator who hosts a program of his own entitled, "The Rush Limbaugh Show." During the airing of his shows, it has been reported that Limbaugh often makes racially inflammatory remarks. Although there are many white Americans who are appalled by the remarks that he makes, there are a substantial number of white Americans that support Limbaugh and his radio program.

In January of 2009 Limbaugh was quoted as saying that he hopes President Obama "fails." Later he explained that he meant he hoped that certain of his policies fail and not the man himself. However, there were those who found his sincerity questionable due to a history of on-air remarks he has made that many consider racist. Eight months after Limbaugh stated that he hopes President Obama fails, Congressman Joe Wilson blurted out "He lies!" during the Presidential address at a point in the message in which President Obama was giving reassurances that the health bill did not include insuring illegal immigrants. This was an unprecedented disrespect of the President by a member of Congress.

In addition, 2009 was the year that the Tea Party Movement emerged as the result of protests against President Obama's health care reform and certain recovery Acts that he was able to get passed into law. The Tea Party Movement quickly grew to 250,000 members nationwide. Some members of the Party blatantly held up signs with messages that were considered by both blacks and whites (including many in the white media) to be racist and depicted the President in ways that many felt were racist. One particular sign that caught the nation's eye was a sign that superimposed a picture of Obama's face on the body of an African witch doctor. However, the leaders of the Tea Party did not do anything significant to curb these racist acts until Mark Williams (leader of the Tea Party Express) wrote, in July of 2010, a satirical fictional letter on his blog mocking black people. The fictional letter was from black people to Abraham Lincoln and it read, "We coloreds have taken a vote and decided that we don't cotton to the whole emancipation thing. Freedom means having to work for real, think for ourselves and take consequences along with the rewards. That is just far too much to ask of us colored people." Williams was removed from his post but not until the NAACP became involved and pointed out publicly that his "letter" was indeed racist along with many other acts of certain Tea Partiers. Most of America, whites as well as minorities, agreed that Tea Party leaders needed to curb the actions of those members who were prone to making racist statements and to sending racist messages.

Jimmy Carter, former President, put political correctness aside and called it as he saw it when he said the following during an interview on September 15, 2009, with Brian Williams of NBC:

> I think an overwhelming portion of the intensely demonstrated animosity toward President Barack Obama is based on the fact that this is a black man; that he is African-American. I live in the South and I've seen the South come a long way, and I've seen the rest of the country that shared the South's attitude towards minorities at that particular time, particularly African-Americans. And that racism inclination still exists. And I think it's bubbled up to the surface because of a belief among many white people, and not just in the South but around the country, that African-Americans are not qualified to lead this great country. It's an abominable circumstance and grieves me and concerns me very deeply.

In taking into account the unprecedented death threats against President Obama along with the unprecedented hangings in effigy, lyrical mocking, constant criticism from the media during his first year in office, the indirect depiction of Obama as a chimpanzee shot down by the police in the New York Post, and the sadistic imagery against his wife that no other First Lady has had to endure, it would be difficult to deny that much of what Jimmy Carter said, rings true. It does appear that just by virtue of the fact that Barack Obama is the first black president, he has the burden (even though not many admit it) of proving that a black man can successfully run the country. The presidents before him never had the burden of proving

100

that white men could successfully run the country. It has always been automatically assumed that they can.

In addition to what has become a prevailing onslaught of racial remarks against President Obama and his wife was the initial quest by a segment of white America to prove that Barack Hussein Obama, is not really black. Obama's father was from the African country of Kenya and unquestionably black. Obama's mother was white. While white supremacists have no doubt that President Obama is black, other segments of white society are quick to say that Obama is not really America's first black president because he is "50% white." Some have even labeled him as Caucasian. Then there are those that say that he is ethnically Arab and that he has some black in him, but that the black that he has in him is insignificant to the amount of white and Arab blood that he possesses. For them, the depiction of a black man as president of the United States is an oxymoron, which puts them in a dilemma. They must either deny his presidency or deny his race. There's no doubt that Obama is indeed President of the United States; so, instead of accepting that the President of the United States is indeed black, they try to convince themselves and others that he's not really all that black, or that he's only black to a point, or that he's not really black at all. After all, a black man can't really run the country, can he?

To insist that President Obama is really white or that he is not really black is to deny that President Obama is indeed black. He, himself has identified himself as "African-American." It is therefore apparent that Obama considers himself black. Besides this, he looks black. Today we use the term "biracial" to describe a person who has one black parent and one white parent, but if forced to identify a biracial American as either black or white; the majority of Americans would opt for the former. Hence, most Americans would identify President Obama as black (African-American) just by looks alone. Despite the fact that he is biracial, in the days of Jim Crow, Obama would have been black enough to be subject to all of the discrimination and racism that Jim Crow had to offer. Unless he had been able to pass for white (and he wouldn't have, looking as he does) Obama would not have been exempt from the shackles of Jim Crow simply because his mother was white. There would have been no question about Obama's blackness had he lived as a young man during those times. Therefore, there should be no question about it now. But amazingly there is.

When taking the presidency into account, the more accurate test as to whether or not America is on the verge of becoming post-racial does not have as much to do with the fact that a black man was finally voted into the Presidential office but instead whether or not it will take another two hundred years to vote another black person in.

INSTITUTIONAL RACISM IN LAW ENFORCEMENT AND THE JUDICIAL SYSTEM

Racial Profiling

Racial profiling is mostly associated with law enforcement. It occurs when a person has been stopped by the police or detained by legal authorities because he or she is suspected, because of his or her race, of possibly engaging in a criminal activity. Other factors might include the age of the person and the type of clothes the person was wearing at the time he or she was stopped or detained as well as the type of car he or she was driving. Another factor that is used, at times, is a person's presumed socio-economic status. A person can be racially profiled anywhere; while driving, while trying to board a plane, even while simply walking down the street.

The majority of victims of racial profiling are minorities with black people being the most victimized by it. In his book, "Driving while Black," Kenneth Meeks puts it the following way:

> It's generally targeted [racial profiling] more toward young black American men and women than any other racial group, although Asians, Hispanics, and even young whites with long hair and a hip-hop flair about them get profiled more every day. It doesn't matter if there is "probable cause" or not in many instances. A police officer or a security guard or anyone in a role of authority can detain and question people...[15]

According to an October 2008 study (on racism and the Los Angeles Police) conducted by Ian Ayres and Jonathan Borowsky,[16] black drivers were stopped by police 3,400 more times that white drivers while Hispanic drivers were stopped 360 times more than whites. Additionally, it was

---

[15] Meeks, Kenneth, *Driving While Black*, Broadway Books, New York, NY, copyright ©2000 p.5. Fair use per permission of the publisher.
[16] Ayres, Ian and Jonathan Borowsky, *A Study of Racially Disparate Outcomes in the Los Angeles Police Department*, written for the ACLU, October 27, 2008 (taken from an Internet article by TChris entitled *Racial Profiling in the LAPD*, Talk Left, the Politics of Crime, Internet site, Section Civil Liberties, http://www.talkleft.com/story/2008/10/27/14266/187

found that blacks were frisked 127% more than whites while Hispanics were frisked 43% more than whites. The most egregious discovery was that whites were 43% more likely than blacks and 31% more likely than Hispanics to have a weapon when frisked, indicating that blacks and Hispanics were frisked unjustly at a substantially much higher rate than whites.

Louisiana is no stranger to racial profiling either. In an August 2008 report presented by the Louisiana ACLU,[17] statistics indicate that in certain areas of New Orleans, blacks are nearly 3 to 4 times more likely to be arrested than whites.[18]

In looking at the examples cited when it comes to the Los Angeles and Louisiana Police Departments, it's not a stretch to assume that similar discriminatory practices are prevalent in other states and cities around the country as well.

Racial profiling has been rampant in America for many years. It is an old and persistent phenomenon. In 1992 an elderly white woman was allegedly attacked in her home in Oneonta New York. She had indicated that her attacker was a black man. She had also indicated that the man cut himself on the hand while attacking her. Therefore, police stopped every black man that they came across to take a look at his hands for any sign of a cut. Any knick or bruise on any black man's hands at the time would have made him suspect and he would have probably been taken into custody for questioning.

In 1999 the famed actor Danny Glover filed a formal complaint with the Taxi Commission of New York City because of the many times he had been passed up by Taxi cab drivers on the streets of New York only to witness those same drivers pick up white customers just a few feet beyond where he was standing.

Interstate 95 in New Jersey is notorious for being a thoroughfare by which black motorists are stopped constantly because there is suspicion that they may be transporting drugs. And if a black man is driving a luxury car on that particular Interstate, chances increase substantially that he will be pulled over.

According to the ACLU, the selling and possession of drugs by whites and blacks are statistically proportionate to the percentage of each group living in the United States. Whites are 70% of the population while blacks

---

[17] American Civil Liberties Union
[18] www. Aclu.org, ACLU *Releases Report on Racial Profiling in Louisiana* http://www.aclu.org/racialjustice/racialprofiling/36358prs20080806.html

are roughly 13% of the population.[19] Accordingly, research indicates that 70% of the population who are using and/or selling drugs is white while 13% is black. However, law enforcement, along with the general population, are under the false impression that blacks use and sell more illegal drugs than do whites. Belief in this erroneous impression fuels the injustice of racial profiling.

One of the most blatant examples of racial profiling that occurred in American history was that which resulted from the 1942 Executive Order 9066 (mentioned earlier) in which at least 120,000 Japanese Americans were harassed by the authorities, made to follow curfews, stripped of their property, put under arrest, and ultimately sent to prison camps for no other reason than the fact that they were Japanese. At the time, America was in the middle of World War II in which the Japanese were being fought against.

A similar occurrence happened as a result of the attack on America which took place on September 11, 2001 when the Twin Towers in New York City were toppled by terrorists who flew airplanes into both buildings. Over 3,000 lives were lost. Afterwards, it was discovered that Osama Bin Laden of Afghanistan, leader of the Taliban (a hardcore fundamentalist Islamic religious group) was responsible. Bin Laden gladly took responsibility and voiced his distain for the United States. Almost immediately, Arab Americans became the victims of racial profiling. Authorities began detaining any Arab American who was suspected of having even the remoteness of ties with identified terrorists. Arab men were routinely taken from their homes, interrogated and detained for months, without due process of law. It should be noted that although Arab Americans are categorized as white, they are not viewed as white by the overall society and are instead viewed ethnically as Arabs.

There were even those in other minority groups who, although having had at some point been a victim of racial profiling themselves, believed that the profiling of Arab Americans was justified. There were incidences when Arab Americans or anyone who appeared to be an Arab was refused flight on planes because the other passengers boarding the plane didn't want to fly with them. Instead of denying flight to those who refused to fly with an Arab American, most airlines, at the time, went along with denying flight to the person being profiled. This same type of fervor that had risen up against Arab Americans was similar to the racism and discrimination that Japanese Americans experienced on American soil in the early 40s. This is not to disavow the U.S. Government's responsibility

---

[19] It has been projected that by year 2050 half the people residing in the United States will be people of color.

to fight terrorism within its borders, which could mean the investigation of certain persons; but there is a difference between having significant probable cause to suspect someone and holding someone suspect simply because he or she fits a racial profile.

When questioning the integrity of racial profiling, we have but to look at the case of Timothy McVeigh. Timothy James McVeigh, a white male, was born in April of 1968 and was executed by the Federal Government on June 11, 2001 for bombing the Alfred P. Murrah Federal Building located in Oklahoma City, Oklahoma. The bombing took place on April 19, 1995 and was considered the worse act of terrorism, at the time, on American soil before the terrorist acts of 9-11. McVeigh was an army veteran, former member of the National Rifle Association, and had been bullied when he was in school as a kid. McVeigh was highly intrigued with guns and had a growing antagonistic attitude towards the U.S. Government. McVeigh was 26 years old when he bombed the Federal building. McVeigh was also known to read white supremacist literature. The point here is this: although McVeigh had committed the worse act of terrorism on American soil (before the 9-11 attacks), the racial profiling of white men who had a similar profile as McVeigh, never took place to the extent that it did when it came to the detainment of the Japanese and to the profiling of Arab Americans. Young white men, who were army veterans and members of the NRA with an intrigue towards guns and a tendency to read white supremacist literature, were never rounded up and interrogated. They were not subjected to the type of racial profiling that Arab Americans were subjected to six and a half years later. The double standard speaks loud and clear.

Racial profiling while shopping is another area in which minorities are often targeted. In an online article written for the University of Pittsburg University Times in October of 2007, Kimberly Barlow[20] refers to a study conducted by Shaun L. Gabbidon[21] and George Higgins[22] on retail racial profiling. The study took place in Philadelphia. In the study, retail racial profiling manifested itself in a delay to serve minorities when they enter a store as well as in the belief of retailers and employees of retailers that minorities are more likely to shoplift, resulting in closer store monitoring of minorities, as opposed to whites. The study shows that blacks are no

---

[20] Barlow, Kimberly L., *Retail Racism Studied*, University of Pittsburg, University Times, Volume 40, number 5, October 25, 2007
http://mac10.umc.pitt.edu/u/FMPro?-db=ustory&-lay=a&-format=d.html&storyid=7788&-Find
[21] Professor of Criminal Justice at Penn State University.
[22] University of Louisville.

more likely to shoplift than whites are but are much more likely to be suspected of either shoplifting or thought of as having a higher likelihood than whites to shoplift. With this suspicion comes an increased focus on minority shoppers, which leads to more arrests of minority shoplifters as opposed to white shoplifters, consequently feeding into the stereotype. The study also shows that minorities who are victims of retail racial profiling rarely report the incident because they have accepted the "normalcy" of such profiling. This kind of mindset only helps to fuel such profiling. To add to this, the research revealed that although 59% of retail profiling of minorities was done by whites, that 24% of the profilers were black, 11% were Asian, and 5% were Hispanic. This tells us that 40% of those who are guilty of the retail racial profiling of minorities, are minorities themselves which points to an apparent infiltration of racism in American society that is so pervasive that even minorities have been socialized to believe the racial stereotypes of other minority groups as well as those of the group that they themselves belong to.

Not only are blacks and other minorities profiled while driving and while shopping but minorities, especially black women and Hispanics, are also profiled while flying, particularly by U.S. customs agents when returning from Jamaica. Some of the most profound cases of racial profiling have occurred at Customs and in 1999 a class action suit was brought against U.S. Customs citing the discriminatory, humiliating, and harassing treatment of at least 90 black women. Black women were being searched twice as much as white women and white men were being searched a third less than blacks. Overall, during the search, the women were often made to strip naked while officers inserted their fingers into the women's rectums and vaginal areas looking for evidence of narcotics contraband. Many of the women were also made to take laxatives since some criminals who transport drugs into the country do so by ingesting packets of cocaine.

- ***The case of Janneral Denson***

Particularly disturbing was the detainment and strip search of Janneral Denson, a black woman, who was six months pregnant when she was pulled aside, in 1997, to be searched. The search escalated to the point where the agents watched her use the bathroom. After a while Mrs. Denson refused to cooperate any longer which resulted in Custom agents handcuffing her and transporting her to Jackson Memorial Hospital in Miami where she was handcuffed to the bed and given a sonogram. The sonogram proved that she was not carrying any drugs. However, the Customs agents still persisted with their inhumane actions by continuing to have her handcuffed to the hospital bed and forcing her to take a laxative for a further examination of the contents of her stomach. Kenneth Meeks continues the account as follows:

> "The United States Customs Service, Denson told Congress, gave a pregnant woman a laxative and would not release her until she passed three clear stool samples. It wasn't until the next day that she was driven back to Fort Lauderdale Airport and released from custody. For the next two days she suffered from severe diarrhea and incredible pain. She told Congress that soon she began bleeding. Eight days later she was rushed to the hospital, where doctors performed an emergency cesarean. Her son, Jordan, was born weighing three pounds, four ounces. He was placed in prenatal intensive care for over a month." [23]

After being chained (handcuffed) to a hospital bed for nearly two days and forced to take laxatives, Mrs. Denson was finally released. There was no evidence of drugs in her system. She had been given no mercy at all in regards to her pregnancy. In May of 1999 Mrs. Densen testified during a hearing, resulting from an investigation of the U.S. Customs Service Passenger Inspection Operations, in which she described her painful ordeal. There is no question that due to the heinous treatment she received by Customs that her baby was born prematurely. No one yet knows what the long term effects her ordeal will have on her child.

After the class action suit and a number of individual lawsuits came to a close, certain changes were made by Customs in order to curtail the intrusiveness of the searches. The changes included implementing the use of body scanners latex breathalyzers, mobile digital X-ray equipment, and passenger service representative programs. However, this only makes the search more tolerable but does nothing to address the profiling that leads to the disproportionate number of black women being searched when reentering the country.

Airline passengers began to sue Customs for discriminatory searches. U.S. Senator Richard J. Durbin asked the United States General Accounting Office (GAO) for a review of Customs' policies and procedures. The GAO reviewed their policies and procedures and

---

[23] Meeks, Kenneth, *Driving While Black*, Broadway Books, New York, NY, copyright 2000, p.120. Fair use by permission of the publisher.

submitted a report, dated March 17, 2000. The GAO is quoted below with regard to the differences the office found when it came to selecting black women for search.

> Generally, searched passengers of particular races and gender were more likely than other passengers to be subjected to more intrusive types of personal searches (being strip-searched or x-rayed) after being subjected to frisks or pat downs. However, in some cases, those types of passengers who were more likely to be subjected to more intrusive personal searches were not as likely to be found carrying contraband. Specifically White men and women and Black women were more likely than Black men and Hispanic men and women to be strip-searched rather than patted down or frisked, but they were less likely to be found carrying contraband. The most pronounced difference occurred with Black women who were U.S. citizens. They were 9 times more likely than White women who were U.S. citizens to be x-rayed after being frisked or patted down in fiscal year 1998. But on the basis of x-ray results, Black women who were U.S. citizens were less than half as likely to be found carrying contraband as White women who were U.S. citizens were. Some patterns of selecting passengers for more intrusive searches indicated that these more intrusive searches sometimes resulted in certain types of passengers being selected for such searches at rates that were not consistent with the rates of finding contraband.[24]

Due to GOA findings that revealed black women were subjected to more intrusive searches (including ex-rays) as opposed to white women, Customs reported that they began collecting more complete and accurate data and began better monitoring of personal search data. Customs also developed a Passenger Data Analysis Team, revised their personal search handbook, retrained their personnel, and implemented increased

---

[24] (United States General Accounting Office), Washington D.C. 20458, A report to the Honorable Richard J. Durbin of the United States Senate, March 17, 2000 from the United States General Accounting Office, U.S. Customs Service: *Better Targeting of Airline Passengers for Personal Searches could produce Better Results*, p.2 Government Document. Public Domain.
http://www.gao.gov/new.items/gg00038.pdf

management oversight. However, no further investigation has been done to determine whether or not Customs has made any significant improvement in their discriminatory intrusive search practices.

According to the ACLU, in 2002, the Senate debated the "good faith exemption" clause in the Andean Trade Promotion and Drug Eradication Act that allows Customs agents to get away with illegal searches of persons such as what was done to Mrs. Denson, simply by saying that their motives were true. However, under current law, Customs are already protected from liability by "qualified immunity."

Overall, police brutality and misconduct against minorities continues to be a problem in America. In 1998 Amnesty International became involved, which resulted in a 150 page report by Amnesty exposing the human rights violations against minorities that plagued America then and that continue to plague America now.

- *2010 Arizona Immigration Law*

The country of Mexico borders the states of Arizona, California, New Mexico, and Texas. The citizens of Mexico are referred to as Mexicans in the same way that American citizens are referred to as Americans. The difference is that Mexico is not the "melting pot" that America is. According to the United States Central Intelligence Agency (CIA), 91% of the people who live in Mexico are of Amerindian and/or Spanish heritage and 92% of Mexican's population speak only Spanish. Only 9% of Mexico's population is white and there is 1% other. Persons who have prevalent Spanish ancestry are referred to as Hispanic. Therefore the majority of Mexicans are Hispanic.

Along with Mexicans who enter into the United States legally, there are thousands of Mexicans that continue to enter the United States illegally on a yearly basis through 42 cities that rest along the borders of Arizona, California, New Mexico, and Texas. While approximately 5 million Mexicans are in the country via the proper channels, roughly 7 million Mexicans reside in the United States illegally. These illegal crossings often times result in criminal activity on the part of both the Mexicans who are immigrating illegally and the Americans who are illegally hiring immigrants for services. Arizona officials have indicated that violent border crimes have risen sharply due to the upsurge of Mexicans who are crossing the border into Arizona illegally.

In an effort to address Arizona's illegal influx and much of the criminality that occurs along Arizona's border as a result, Arizona's Senate Bill 1070 was signed into law in April of 2010. The Bill includes a new Article (Article 8) entitled, "Enforcement of Immigration Laws."

Many believe that portions of the new Article, particularly Section 2, Article B, clause B, create an atmosphere that will overtly allow for racial profiling abuses. Section 2, Article B, clause B reads as follows:

> For any lawful contact made by a law enforcement official or a law enforcement agency of this state or a law enforcement official or a law enforcement agency of a county, city, town, or other political subdivision of this state in the enforcement of any other law or ordinance of a county, city, or town, of this state where reasonable suspicion exists that the person is an alien and is unlawfully present in the United States, A reasonable attempt shall be made, when practicable, to determine the immigration status of the person, except if the determination may hinder or obstruct an investigation. Any person who is arrested shall have the person's immigration status determined before the person is released. The person's immigration status shall be verified with the federal government pursuant to 8 United States code section 1373 (c).

> A Law Enforcement official or agency of this state or a county, city, town, or other political subdivision of this state may not consider race, color or national origin in implementing the requirements of this subsection except to the extent permitted by the United States or Arizona Constitution. A person is presumed to not be an alien who is unlawfully present in the United States if the person provides to the Law Enforcement officer or agency any of the following:
> 1. A valid Arizona driver's license.
> 2. A valid Arizona nonoperating identification license.
> 3. A valid tribal enrollment card or other form of valid identification.
> 4. If the entity requires proof of legal presence in the United States before issuance, any valid United States federal, state, or local government issued identification.

Arizona state officials believe that their law enforcement officers and officials will be able to carry out the mandate of the Law without succumbing to the temptation of racial profiling. But most of the country, including the President of the United States, has voiced strong opposition to the Act. When considering the rising racial tensions in America that have manifested since Obama was voted into office as President, America's overall history of discrimination against minorities, the racism that still exists today in the form of institutional and systematic discrimination, and the fact that racial profiling is still a problem all across America, some would argue that it is naïve for anyone to think that such a law will not lead to racial profiling abuses.

The Law states that a law enforcement official may not "consider race, color, or national origin in implementing the requirements." However, the overwhelming majority of Mexicans are Hispanic, to the degree that many use the identifiers interchangeably. This means that, non-Hispanic persons will not as readily be looked upon with suspicion as will Hispanic persons. To underline the point; if a police officer pulls a black Arizonian over for speeding and discovers that the driver mistakenly left his driver's license at home; more than likely the officer will not suspect the driver of being an illegal alien, since the population of blacks living in Mexico is less than one percent. However, if that same officer pulls a Hispanic Arizonian over for speeding and discovers that the driver mistakenly left his driver's license at home; the officer then has reason to suspect, according to the new Law, that the driver could be an illegal alien; not because he is without his driver's license, although the law states that this would be the reason, but because he is without his driver's license *and* he is Hispanic. The fact that he is Hispanic will cause the suspicion, not the fact that he is without a license. If the fact that he is without a license is what will cause suspicion then it should also cause suspicion when it comes to the black driver since the black person was without his license too. We can safely surmise, however, that unless the black person spoke with a Spanish accent, he would not be under suspicion of being an illegal alien.

The Law also states that race, color, or national origin cannot be considered "except to the extent permitted by the United States or Arizona Constitution." Here we have a statement that virtually says that race, color, or national origin *can be* considered if permitted by the United States or Arizona Constitution. But there is no explanation as to what circumstances would trigger the exception. It is left up to speculation. Not only this, but for the Law to state that race, color, or national origin cannot be considered and then for it to state that it can, but only under certain conditions and then not list in detail what those conditions are, is double talk.

The Law states that the authorities must have "reasonable suspicion" that the person is an alien and unlawfully present in the United States in order to proceed in acting upon that suspicion. The problem is, however, that "reasonable suspicion" prior to proceeding to act upon that suspicion, is not defined in the Law. The concern that the opponents of this law has is that all Hispanics living in Arizona will fall under "reasonable suspicion" just by virtue of the fact that they are Hispanic, and because of this, they will need to make sure to carry identification with them at all times in case they are stopped and questioned. This means they must carry identification when walking, or jogging, or riding the bus, or just when being out in society in general. Non-Hispanic persons living in Arizona will be able to walk the streets without fear of retribution if they are stopped for any reason and they are not carrying some form of identification that proves their citizenship; but Hispanics who are in the country legally will feel compelled to carry some form of identification that proves they are American citizens just in case they are stopped because they know that if they are stopped, then according to the law, they could automatically be arrested and thrown in jail if they cannot readily prove their citizenship on the spot. One would therefore be hard-pressed to argue against the position that President Obama has taken on this issue and that is that this kind of law lends itself to racial profiling. There is no question that something must be done to curtail the criminal activity that Arizona is experiencing due to the influx of illegal immigrants gaining entry into the country through their state. Collaborating with the Government to develop strategies to better secure the border is a better option than implementing a law that will lead to racial profiling abuses.

Because of the signing of the bill into law, the Justice Department of the Federal Government, specifically the United States of America, brought suit against the state of Arizona, specifically Arizona state Governor Janice K. Brewer by bringing forth a civil action lawsuit for injunction of the Act. Clause 4 under the Introduction subheading of the lawsuit reads as follows:

> S.B. 1070 pursues only one goal – "attrition" – and ignores the many other objectives that Congress has established for the federal immigration system. And even in pursuing attrition, S.B. 1070 disrupts federal enforcement priorities and resources that focus on aliens who pose a threat to national security or public safety. If allowed to go into effect, S.B. 1070's mandatory enforcement scheme will conflict with and undermine the federal government's careful balance of immigration enforcement priorities and objectives. For example, it will impose significant and counterproductive burdens on the federal agencies charged with enforcing the national immigration scheme, diverting resources and

attention from the dangerous aliens who the federal government targets as its top enforcement priority. It will cause the detention and harassment of authorized visitors, immigrants, and citizens who do not have or carry identification documents specified by the statute, or who otherwise will be swept into the ambit of S.B. 1070's "attrition through enforcement" approach. It will conflict with longstanding federal law governing the registration, smuggling, and employment of aliens. It will altogether ignore humanitarian concerns, such as the protections available under federal law for an alien who has a well-founded fear of persecution or who has been the victim of a natural disaster. And it will interfere with vital foreign policy and national security interests by disrupting the United State's relationship with Mexico and other countries. [25]

The lawsuit speaks for itself. The Government intervened to stop a state from imposing a law that is believed will ultimately lead to overt racist acts against certain citizens of that state. Judge Susan Bolton issued a preliminary injunction against the Law that blocked many controversial aspects of the Law including the clause that gave law enforcement the legal go-ahead to stop a person on "reasonable suspicion." Arizona Governor Jan Brewer appealed the ruling and indicated that she is ready to fight the ruling all the way up to the Supreme Court.

The Criminal Justice System

There is no question that there is racial discrimination against minorities in the criminal justice system. As stated earlier, black Americans only make up 13% of the United States population which is a very small percentage of a whole. However, according to a 2007 report published by the American Sociological Association, although racial injustices in the criminal justice system have declined over the last 50 years or so; the problem of judicial racial disparities and discrimination against minorities still substantially exists in America.

---

[25] United States of America, Plaintiff v State of Arizona; and Janice K. Brewer, Governor of the State of Arizona, in her Official Capacity; case 2:10-cv-10413-NVW Document 1 Filed 07-06-10, pgs. 2-3. Government document. Public Domain.

According to the report, blacks are significantly more likely to be arrested for violent crimes than are whites who commit those same crimes. The ASA reports that the group most affected by the disparities of justice in America's legal system is young black men who live in low income neighborhoods and inner cities. In particular, the policies that developed in the '80s and '90s as a result on the war on drugs have specifically affected young black men in a very negative way.

There is a mandatory prison sentence of five years for those who are caught with five grams or more of crack cocaine in their possession. However, possession of the same amount of the same drug in powder form does not yield a mandatory five-year prison sentence. As a matter of fact, in order for a person to be sentenced to five years in prison for possessing the powdered form of cocaine, they must have up to 100 times the amount it takes to be convicted and sentenced to prison for possession of crack cocaine.

Statistically, when it comes to drug possession, blacks who use and/or sell cocaine have a higher tendency towards possession of crack cocaine (when compared to whites who use and/or sell cocaine) and most live in inner city neighborhoods. Whites who use or sell cocaine have a higher tendency towards powdered cocaine (when compared to blacks) and live in affluent neighborhoods. The law itself therefore automatically places blacks who use or sell cocaine at a disproportionately higher probability of being incarcerated for drug possession than whites who use or sell the same drug in the same quantity or higher quantities.

The Government implemented such a law in the mid-80s under the belief that crack cocaine is more powerful that powdered cocaine. It has recently been determined that there is no concrete evidence that crack cocaine is more addictive than its counterpart. Despite the fact that it was thought that crack cocaine was more dangerous than the powdered form; the Government was also aware that crack cocaine is mostly sold and used in black neighborhoods while powdered cocaine is mostly sold and used in white neighborhoods. This is not to, in any way, support the use of cocaine, but to point out the difference made in the law that unquestionably creates a form of structural racism in the justice system when it comes to "the war on drugs."

According to the 1997 Bureau of Justice Statistics, black American men have a one in four chance of being convicted of a crime and sent to prison as compared to white American men who have a one in twenty-three chance of the same. Although black Americans comprise only 15% of all the illegal drug users in the United States as opposed to 72% of American whites, the statistics revealed that 37% of those who are arrested for illegal use or possession of drugs are black. This means that twice as many blacks are arrested for this type of criminal behavior than are whites even though whites are by far the greatest offenders. According to an American Sociological Association (ASA) report, at the end of 2004, things hadn't gotten much better. Roughly 8% of black men between the ages of 25 and 29 were incarcerated as compared to only 1.2% of white men and 2.5% of Hispanic men who used or sold drugs.

These statistics give credence to a much earlier report submitted by the United States Sentencing Commission which found in 1990 that a higher percentage of whites were able to get reduced sentences from plea bargaining than were blacks and Latinos.

When alleged perpetrators plea bargain, they plead guilty or "no contest" to the crime they've been charged with (even though many of them are actually innocent) in hopes for a reduced sentence. Often times they plead guilty when they are innocent. America's adage that says persons are innocent *until* proven guilty is a statement that when looked at closely assumes the guilt of the accused because of the subliminal suggestion that the person is actually guilty but just hasn't been proven guilty yet and *until* he can be proven guilty, he's innocent. A more appropriate rendering, therefore, would be that an accused person is innocent *unless* proven guilty. The language of the latter gives the better psychological edge of innocence while the former statement already has the person convicted, in a manner of speaking. It is no wonder that the United States has overcrowding in prisons. The subliminal cultural mentality from the onset of an allegation or charge says that the accused is guilty.

Cases that are plea-bargained never go to trial. In 1991, the San Jose Mercury News, as part of a study, examined nearly a million judiciary cases. It was found that whites who had no prior record were statistically more likely to be successful in having federal charges against them reduced than blacks and Latinos were who had no prior record.

Those conducting the study discovered that conscious overt racism wasn't necessarily the culprit but that an ingrained subconscious racism resulting from fears triggered by stereotypical beliefs was. The main point here is that the study gave evidence that race can indeed be a factor in whether or not justice is delivered equitably. The research reveals that there is overwhelming data that shows that the underlying problem in the overrepresentation of minorities in the prison system stems from discrimination in the judicial process.

According to the American Sociological Association (ASA), in 2001 roughly 16% of black men, as opposed to only roughly 2% of white men were or had been incarcerated in state or federal prisons. And black men made up 41% percent of all prisoners as compared to 34% of white inmates and 19% of Hispanic inmates. The ASA reports that in the later part of 2007 "about 1 in 3 black males, 1 in 6 Hispanic males, and 1 in 17 white males are expected to go to prison during their lifetime."[26] This is a huge disparity when considering that black people, as a whole, make up a very small portion of the population. Because of America's ingrained racial prejudices, young black men are the most targeted when it comes to discrimination in the criminal justice system. For them, just walking down the street in the "wrong" neighborhood could lead to arrest. This not only negatively affects the lives of young black men but there is also a residual negative affect that young black women experience as well. Many of these men are fathers, husbands, and brothers. Not only is the life of the one arrested disrupted when he is sentenced to prison but so is the life of his immediate family members.

In 2002, it was determined that black youths between the ages of 10 and 17 years of age are twice as likely to be arrested as opposed to white youths of the same age. This statistic is even more staggering when taking into account that white youths outnumber black youths in America by 44%. In addition, black youths going through the juvenile system for the same crimes as white youths, are 31% more likely to end up in the adult penal system for those crimes than are white youth. Research indicates most of the racial discrimination that occurs within America's criminal justice system occurs at the juvenile level in regards to minorities.

- ## *The Jena 6*

One of the most recent examples in American history that gives testimony to the fact that black youths are treated much more harshly by the judicial system than white youths are for the same or similar crimes is the case referred to colloquially as "The Jena 6."

Jena is a city in Louisiana in which 85% of the residents are white and roughly 12% are black. Jena is a very small city with a population of under 3,000. There is a tree in the vicinity of Jena High school. It was an unspoken rule that only white students could gather under this tree. On August 31, 2006, Kenneth Purvis, a black student, asked a faculty member if he could sit under the tree. The faculty member told him that he could sit wherever he wanted to sit. Purvis and a group of his friends (white and black) sat under the tree. The following day there were three nooses hung on the tree. The nooses had been hung by white students. The three white

---

[26] *Race, Ethnicity, and the Criminal Justice System*, American Sociological Association, Department of Research and Development, http://www.asanet.org/galleries/Research/ASARaceCrime.pdf p.17, Fair use.

youths were identified and the Principal decided to expel them but he was overruled by the LaSalle Parish School Board; the white youths were instead suspended for three days. Many of the black students protested the decision not to expel the three white youths. They protested by gathering other black students and sitting, as a group, under the tree. On November 30th of that same year the Academic Building of the school was set on fire. The arsonist has never been caught.

On the night of the fire, another black student named Robert Bailey attended a party with some of his friends. He was physically attacked by a group of white students at the party. The white students used beer bottles in the attack. Although there was a group of white students that attacked Bailey, only one of those students was arrested and charged. The charge was simple battery and the student received probation. Two days after Bailey was attacked at the party, he and two of his friends were at a convenience store. One of the white youths who had attacked Bailey at the party was also there with his friends. A confrontation ensued between the two groups and one of the white youths reportedly pulled out a sawed-off shot gun. The three black youths managed to take the shotgun away from the white youth. They took the gun to the police station. Instead of seeing the taking of the gun as self defense, the Jena police opted to see it as stealing and charged Bailey for theft. The white youth was never charged.

On December 4, 2006, a student named Justin Barker reportedly teased Bailey at school about Bailey having had been beaten up. Bailey and five other black youths physically attacked Barker. No weapons were used but Barker was reportedly beaten unconscious and ended up in the hospital with a concussion, a swollen eye and bruises to the face. He was released three hours later. The next day six black students were arrested and eventually charged with attempted murder, one of which faced up to 22 years in prison. Those arrested were Carwin Jones, Jesse Ray Beard, Bryant Purvis, Robert Bailey, Theo Shaw, and Mychal Bell. Mychal Bell was initially convicted of aggravated battery but his conviction was overturned when it was proven that his rights were violated in being tried as an adult. The charges were later reduced to simple battery as were the charges for the remaining black students when in 2009 (after a huge outcry from black America, a march on Jena by thousands of black activists protesting against the charges that were levied against the black youths, and a two and a half year legal battle), they were allowed to plead no contest to a simple battery charge and put on probation for a year. There was also a financial settlement agreed upon by the families.

The reason why there was such a huge outcry from black America in regards to this case was because when a black student (Robert Bailey) was beaten by a group of white youths that attacked him with beer bottles and one of which eventually pulled a shotgun on him, only one of the white youths was charged and he was not charged with attempted murder but with simple battery. However, when a white student (Justin Barker) was attacked by black students, all of the black students involved (not just one) were arrested and charged but not with simple battery like the white student was, but instead with attempted murder.

The racial inequities as it pertains to the charges brought forth and the sentencing in this case, couldn't be any clearer. And in order for the black youths to have received the same treatment in the court system as the white youths did, black activists from all over the country had to step in and say something; otherwise, the six black youths would have still been in prison for the same crime that white youths committed who were walking free. These types of racial inequities and double standards persist on an ongoing basis not only in America's juvenile justice system, but in its justice system overall.

- ▪ *The death penalty and sentencing*

One of the most heinous forms of institutional racism prevalent in the American justice system is the tendency for blacks to be sentenced to death at a higher rate than whites. Although black Americans comprise only 13% of people living in America they currently make up an astounding 50% of the total United States prison population and an even more astounding 40% of all prisoners who are awaiting execution on death row. Furthermore, one third of all adult black men who are in their twenties are either in jail, in prison, or under correctional supervision. This has a devastating effect on the black family in general.

A study conducted in the state of Georgia during the 1970s revealed that there was a substantially higher probability of blacks being sentenced to death, who had been convicted of murdering whites than there was when it came to whites who had been convicted of murdering blacks. The study also showed that killing a white person increased the perpetrator's chance of being sentenced to death four times as much when compared to the probability of a person being sentenced to death for murdering a black person. According to an article by the ACLU dated February of 2003 and entitled, "Race and the Death Penalty from the American Civil Liberties Union," these results coincide with studies conducted in 2003 at the University of Maryland in which data suggested that alleged perpetrators of murder have a higher probability of being sentenced to death if the victim is white. Just one year earlier, national statistics showed that as of October 2002 only 12 white convicted perpetrators of murder were sentenced to death when the person who had been murdered was black as opposed to 178 blacks convicted of murder who were sentenced to death when the person they had allegedly murdered was white. The underlying message from this is that white people are more valuable than black people. Such racism in the American system must be done away with.

To further add to these racial disparities, the majority of people who are awaiting execution do not have the finances to obtain private attorneys and are consequently forced to be represented by public defenders. Most court appointed public defenders have very high caseloads and are not able to give as much time to individual cases as a hired attorney would be. Therefore, persons on death row usually have had less quality representation than persons who committed the same crime but are not on death row. The majority of those on death row could not afford to hire an attorney.

The ACLU also reports that 80% of all cases that involve death sentences are cases in which the murder victim was white even though white murder victims only account for 50% of the total number of murder cases yearly in the United States. There are 38 states that allow for capital punishment and 98% of the prosecutors in these states are white. This fact increases the probability that blacks who are convicted of murder will be substantially more likely to be sentenced to death as opposed to whites who are convicted of murder due to the sheer existence of institutional/structural racism that has become an innate part of American society whether consciously acknowledged or not.

According to the ACLU, research overwhelmingly shows that a black person who murders a white person is substantially more likely to be sentenced to death as opposed to a black person who murders another black person, a white person who murders a white person, or a white person who murders a black person. Not only is there overwhelming proof that there is unequal justice on a state by state level when it comes to the judicial system and capital punishment, but since the implementation of DNA testing, it has been proven that a staggering and disturbing number of people awaiting execution on death row have actually been innocent of the crime they've been accused of. Many were exonerated after years of declaring their innocence; a declaration that initially fell on deaf ears and an institutionalized racially discriminatory justice system.

Moreover, when it comes to sentences, aside from death sentencing, it has been found that black people convicted of crimes are given longer sentences, on average, than white people who are convicted of the same crimes. In the National Urban League's publication of "The State of Black America 2009," a list of crimes and the average number of months blacks and whites are sentenced for those crimes are listed in what the authors of the book refer to as the *Equality Index of Black America*. The list spans the years 1999 to 2007. The sentencing disparities are listed for the year 2004 which is the most recent listing.

The Index reveals that black men were sentenced to 256 months on average for murder while white men were sentenced to 232 months; black men were sentenced to 101 months on average for robbery while white men were sentenced to 88 months; black men were sentenced to 51 months on average for aggravated assault while white men were sentenced to 42 months; black men were sentenced to 47 months on average for burglary while white men where sentenced to 44 months; black men were sentenced to 47 months on average for other violent crimes while white men were sentenced to 43 months; black men were sentenced to 23 months on average for larceny while white men were sentenced to 21 months; and black men were sentenced to 23 months on average for drug possession while white men were sentenced to 22 months. The research did find that white men were sentenced to 3 more months on average than black men for drug trafficking and to 2 more months on average for fraud than black men were sentenced. It also found that black men were sentenced, on average, 6 months less than white men for sexual assault. But these exceptions are still not enough to balance out the overall disparity of sentencing that exists between black and white men.

The index also revealed that black women were sentenced to 231 months on average overall while white women were sentenced to 152 months, and black women were sentenced to 80 months on average for robbery while white women were sentenced to 55 months. However there was roughly an equal amount of sentencing when examining lesser crimes and sentencing between blacks and whites in the female prison population with black women having a slight edge. The problem in disparity of sentencing mainly lies with the fact that black men, according to the most recent figures that are available, are given longer sentences than white men are for a sizeable number of the same crimes and that specifically, both black men and women are given much longer sentences for murder than white men and women are.

THE INSTITUTIONAL RACISM OF HOLLYWOOD

Early film making

There is no question that America's film industry has been discriminatory against minorities since its inception in the late 1800s. The "movies" were off and running after Thomas Edison's invention of the large-screen film projector which he presented to the public in 1896. For the most part, the overwhelming majority of films was financed by whites and, in general, did not depict minorities in a positive light until the 1960s. The first film to be released that had an all-black cast was "The Pullman Porter" which was produced in 1910. This film was produced through the Foster Photoplay Company followed by "The Railroad Porter, produced in 1912 and "The Fall Guy," produced in 1913. All three black films were categorized as silent shorts. The Foster Photoplay company was owned and operated by William Foster, who was America's first black movie producer. His aim was to produce black film comedies that did not degrade blacks. Foster was eager to uplift the image of black America through his motion pictures.

White film makers of the time depicted black people as lazy, shiftless, stupid, and easily frightened. Foster fought against these stereotypical depictions by producing black films that portrayed black people in a more positive light, depicting the black middle-class lifestyle of the North that was absent from films produced by whites. Although Foster was initially successful as a film maker he began to have cash flow problems and it was difficult for him to find distribution. Consequently, his company folded in 1916. The NAACP was very vocal during that time against two films in particular produced by white production companies that portrayed blacks negatively. Those two films were *The Nigger*, released in 1914 and *The Birth of a Nation*, released in 1915.

The Birth of a Nation

The making of *The Birth of a Nation* was prompted by increasing opportunities for southern blacks to make a living in the growing industrial culture of the North. However, many southern whites, who wanted to keep blacks economically oppressed in the South, did not appreciate the fact that blacks could migrate to the North and become financially independent. As a result, lynching of blacks multiplied. In the *Birth of a Nation,* the Ku Klux Klan terrorizes blacks as a way of keeping them "in line." One particular scene depicts the Klan prohibiting blacks from voting. Two separate scenes depict white women fleeing from black men who are attempting to rape them. And then in one of the final scenes the Ku Klux Klan hunts down one of the black men and lynches him. *The Birth of a Nation* encouraged a resurgence of membership into the Klan. The movie was endorsed by President Woodrow Wilson at the time and was designed to stir up the racial hatred that many whites of that day already had against black people. *The Birth of a Nation* was the first American movie "blockbuster" and the showing of it created many challenges between blacks who rallied for civil rights and whites who wanted the rights of blacks to continue to be blocked.

Despite the fact that *The Birth of a Nation* not only encouraged Klan membership at the time of its original showing but continues to encourage Klan membership today, portrayed black men as sexual brutes, and encouraged mob lynching of black men, it was voted as one of the top 100 American films of all time in 1998 by the American Film Institute. It came in 44th. Before that, the film was voted into the National Film Registry[27] in 1993 and is also listed at number 133 in the 2010 TSPDT[28] list of the top 1000 Greatest Movies of all times. The inclusion of *Birth of a Nation* into the top 100 American films caused great controversy. Of course, many black Americans were justifiably appalled that such a racist film would be voted in as one of the greatest films of all time. It is akin to Adolph Hitler's "Mein Kampf"[29] being voted in as one of the greatest literary works of all time. To do so would be an insult to Jews all over the world and therefore such a thing would probably never be considered. But when it comes to avoiding what would be insulting to black America; white America often times misses the mark, or just doesn't care. It is disturbing to many black Americans that a film that applauds racism, lynching, and terrorism against a race of people would be applauded to such an extent.

Oscar Micheaux

Oscar Micheaux was born in Metropolis Illinois on January 2, 1884 and died in Charlotte North Carolina in 1951. He is considered the father of black movie making. During his lifetime, Micheaux produced over forty films between 1919 and 1940. In his youth he worked as a coal miner and eventually became a homesteader and wrote a novel which he entitled, "Homesteader." After failed attempts to get his novel made into a movie, he studied the art of film making and in 1918 established his own movie production and book publishing companies. Micheaux soon became the most prevalent black movie producer in what was called the "race movies." The "race movies" were movies produced mainly by blacks targeted at a black audience. They were independent films that were made in an effort to challenge the racial discrimination in the Hollywood film

---

[27] A National registry made up of a board that preserves what they consider to be important films. The Library of Congress keeps the preserved films.

[28] The list is developed resulting from the favorite movie picks of over two thousand filmmakers and movie critiques.

[29] Adolph Hitler was the head of the National Socialists German Worker's Party (more commonly known as the Nazi party) from 1921 until his death in 1945. Hitler was responsible for the killing of six million Jews in an attempt to annihilate the Jewish race. Hitler expressed his disdain for the Jews in this book, "Mein Kampf" (translated, "My Struggle"). The book was published in 1925.

industry and the stereotypical depiction of blacks that was prevalent in white produced movies.

Micheaux was a social activist and considered to be somewhat radical because he addressed controversial topics through his films; topics which included interracial relationships and blacks passing as whites among other unsettling themes at the time. The second film, produced in 1920, was entitled *Within our Gates* and defied the racist message that saturated *Birth of a Nation.*

The year 1928 saw the onset of sound films ("talkies") which led to blacks getting more opportunities to appear in movie roles than previously. However, most of the roles available for blacks were those of singers and dancers and the stereotypes were still maintained. Micheaux struggled to keep his independent film company operating. He experienced an abundance of financial problems in trying to keep his business afloat. It was difficult for Micheaux to obtain distribution, so he did most of his marketing and distribution himself by traveling from city to city to meet with theater owners and exhibitors. Despite his perseverance, Micheaux was forced into bankruptcy in 1928. However, in 1929 Micheaux collaborated with Leo Brecher and Frank Schiffman who were white theater owners. Brecher and Schiffman had enough clout and money to help Micheaux continue making films by backing him financially. In 1931 Micheaux released his first talking film.

Black independent films stayed alive for a while but the white major film studios monopolized the industry well into the 1940s and the increase in black roles in white films, no matter how stereotypical and minimal the parts, triggered the decline of black independent films at the time.

"Blaxploitation" films

The blaxploitation period is said to have lasted from 1970 to 1974. The term "blaxploitation" is used because white-owned movie distribution companies did not begin distributing black films until black producers began making films in which sex, money, and drugs, became the main theme. Furthermore, there were at least 100 black films during the four-year blaxploitation era of the 70s but more than 80% of these films were under the control of white movie executives or financiers. Some would argue that blaxploitation films still exist today.

During the 1950s and 60s Sidney Poitier was one of the few black actors who played roles that did not feed into black stereotypes. However, there were no feature Hollywood films that had been directed by a black person until 1969 when Gordon Parks directed *The Learning Tree* produced by Warner Brothers. *The Learning Tree* recounts the coming of age of Gordon Parks in 1920s Kansas. The film was not exploitive and has many positive messages. At the time Kenny Hyman, a studio-head at Warner Brothers, was determined to break down some of the racial discrimination in Hollywood by insisting that Warner Brothers put up the money for a black man to direct one of their feature films. Hyman wanted Gordon Parks to be that man and Hyman eventually got what he wanted. Once Hyman opened the door, many other studio execs saw no reason to keep the door closed any longer. Warner Brothers backed the production of *The Learning Tree* for three million dollars. The film not only had a black director but also had a black producer, a black musical score composer, and even a black cameraman, all of which were a first. However, since white distribution companies would generally only distribute black movies where sex, drugs, and money were the main themes, black directors and producers felt compelled to comply which led to such blaxpoitation films as *Shaft*, produced by Gordon Parks in 1971, and *Superfly*, which was produced by his son in the following year.

Unfortunately, the blaxploitation films of the 70s helped to usher in a new set of black stereotypes that revolved around sex, drugs, and money. Business was booming. But in the early eighties, blaxploitation films began to lose momentum due to the onset of what then became the latest marketing strategy; the "saturation marketing" of new films which catapulted films like *Raiders of the Lost Ark* into legendary status. During this time, under 10% of all the American movies being produced on the big screen had blacks and Hispanics in major roles.

In 1981 less than 10% of the films that were released portrayed blacks in a major role, and more often than not, any major movie role given to a black actor was a role alongside a white leading actor. Hollywood's employment discrimination has not only taken place in front of the camera, but has taken place behind it as well. It was this kind of imbalance that prompted Warrington Hudlin to establish and become the president of a non-profit black filmmaking organization. He named his organization the *Black Filmmaking Foundation* (BFF). BFF was founded in 1978 and headquartered in New York. The foundation financially assisted black filmmakers by administering grants to black independents.

It should be noted that blacks were not the only minorities negatively depicted in films produced by whites. Almost any minority was portrayed stereotypically, including Asians and Native Americans.

As if employment discrimination, lack of distribution, and the history of minority stereotyping wasn't enough, Hollywood has also had an overt history of turning a blind eye to the artistic achievement of blacks and other minorities in Hollywood, especially when it has come to the Academy Awards.

Oscar isn't color blind

The Academy Awards is an annual American filmmaking awards ceremony whereby actors, directors, cinematographers, special effects personnel, and a host of others are given an Oscar award for being voted as most outstanding in their category of expertise where filmmaking is concerned. The awards are granted by the Academy of Motion Picture Arts and Sciences. The "Oscar" is a golden statue of a man that stands about a foot and a half in height. It is the most coveted award in Hollywood. Hollywood began its Academy Awards ceremony in 1928 to award outstanding achievement for the previous year. The Academy Awards event is nationally and internationally televised every year.

The term "Hollywood" has become the standard reference when speaking of the American film industry overall. It is no secret that the Hollywood film industry has overlooked granting Oscar awards to many deserving minority film artists over the decades. Most institutional racism is difficult to detect, but Hollywood-racism is not only overt but conducts itself comfortably in plain view with little challenge. This is partly due to the fact that Hollywood is a society unto itself, separate from mainstream American society.

When considering the number of award categories, the number of nominees under those categories, and the years that the awards have existed, we will be able to get a good idea of the sheer enormity of the racial discrimination that exists in the Hollywood film industry.

There are 24 award categories. The categories are: best picture, best director, best actor, best actress, best supporting actor, best supporting actress, best original screenplay, best adapted screenplay, best foreign film, best animated feature, best original score, best original song, best art director, best cinematography, best costume design, best make-up, best documentary feature, best sound mixing, best sound editing, best visual effects, best film editing, best short film-animation, best short film-live action, and best documentary short subject.

There are 5 nominees for each category with few exceptions. Therefore, there are roughly 120 nominees for each award ceremony. As of this writing, it has been 82 years since the first awards. When multiplying the number of yearly nominees by the number of 82 years we are looking at approximately 9,800 film artists that have been nominated for an award over the years with roughly 1,968 of them having won the Oscar; only of which 26 were black (approximately just 1.3%).

Hattie McDaniel was the first black American to win an Academy Award. She won for best supporting actress in 1940 for her portrayal as "Mammy" in the movie, "Gone with the Wind." Since then only four black

125

actors have won for best actor, one black actress for best actress, four black actors for best supporting, and three additional black actresses for best supporting (four altogether with McDaniel). It must be noted that there has been some recent concern expressed among blacks regarding the roles that black actresses have won for which include comedic, sexually promiscuous, and domestically violent roles along with the stereotypical role of "Mammy" that was played by McDaniel. Some feel that the Academy's tendency to award black actresses for negative roles plays into the overall stereotyping of black women.[30]

When it comes to music, eight black composers have won for best original song, and only one black composer has ever won for best original movie score. For sound, only two blacks have ever won with a third win for best achievement in sound mixing.

In looking at special awards; James Baskett (the first black male actor to receive an academy award) was given an honorary award in 1947 for his portrayal of Uncle Remus in the 1946 racially controversial movie, *Song of the South,* and Sidney Poitier was given an honorary lifetime achievement award in 2002. To date, Poitier is the only black film star to have received this award. Additionally only one black writer has ever won for best adapted screenplay and only one black producer for best documentary short subject (who shared the Oscar with his collaborative producer).

To put things in perspective, no black screen artists were awarded the Oscar until 1940 which was twelve years after the inception of the awards. Then it took another 23 years (1963) for it to happen again with Sidney Poitier taking the best actor Oscar home with his portrayal in *Lilies of the Field.* This was the first time that any black actor or actress had been recognized by the Academy for best actor/actress in a leading role, which is only second to best picture and best director in award status recognition. It took another 38 years before the award would again be granted to a black actor or actress for best performer in a leading role.

As of this writing, the Oscar has never been awarded to a black American for the following categories: best director of a major motion picture, best original screenplay, best documentary feature, best animated feature, best art director, best cinematography, best costume design, best make-up, best sound editing, best visual effects, best film editing, best short film-animation, and best short film-live action.

---

[30]However, Hollywood cannot be totally to blame for this because the Hip Hop and Rap music industry created and controlled mostly by blacks constantly portrays black women as sexually promiscuous and in sexually degrading ways.

Hollywood has also fallen short when it has come to awarding the Oscar to other minorities besides blacks. Only two Asians have won for best actor, the first was Yul Brynner[31] winning in 1957. No Asian film artist has ever won for best actress. Two Asian actresses have won for best supporting. Overall, Asians have won the Oscar only 33 times which puts them at close to two percent of all those who have ever won. They are recognized more than blacks; but not significantly. The difference is that Asians have won in more categories including art direction, cinematography, and best costume. However, no Asian has ever won for best picture or best director.

Hispanics have only been awarded the Oscar 26 times beginning with Jose Ferrer who won for best actor in 1956. Only two additional Hispanic film artists have won for best actor since then and only one Hispanic film artist has won for best actress. Only one Hispanic film artist has won for best supporting actress along with only one Hispanic film star for best supporting actor. Hispanics have also been recognized in more categories, however, no Hispanic has ever won for best picture, or best director.

It is unarguable that there have been a sizeable amount of minorities in film making throughout the history of Hollywood; particularly black actors and actresses. However, when looking at black Americans, Asians, and Hispanics, only roughly 3 percent of minorities have been recognized by the Academy for their film-industry talents. The small percentage of minorities who have won Academy Awards and the length of time that it has taken the Academy to grant those awards can only be attributed to discrimination that lies within the film industry, which still exists in a prevalent way, to this day, despite the strides that Hollywood has made to recognize more minorities in recent years. And even with the Academy Award wins that blacks have been given, some would vehemently argue that many of those awards were given for roles that perpetrate black stereotypes.

THE INSTITUTIONAL RACISM OF BEAUTY

"Lookism"

There are many factors in this world that can give a person power. There is money, fame, status, and more. Beauty, although not normally spoken of as a factor that generates personal power for the person who possesses it, is a factor nonetheless. Unfortunately, the way a person looks and how

---

[31] Yul Brynner was born in Russia. Certain areas of Russia are considered to lie in Asia while other areas are considered to lie in Europe.

society at large views the appearance of someone can significantly affect the many aspects of that person's life. There are certain jobs that only those who are looked upon in society as beautiful will be considered for and certain careers cater specifically to people who are seen as attractive.

There's no doubt that beauty is power. Studies have shown that teachers tend to be more attentive to the children in the classroom that are the most attractive. Attractiveness is often the determining factor as to whether or not a person is hired, fired, treated respectfully, and the list goes on.

In her book "Survival of the Prettiest," Nancy Etcoff coins the word *lookism*. She basically defines this term as "beauty prejudice" and theorizes that beauty prejudice is a different prejudice from racism or sexism in the fact that often times racism and sexism is manifested on a conscious level whereas lookism is not. Most people are not aware when they are exercising their own prejudices according to their own perception of another's beauty.

According to Etcoff, studies show that, when it comes to how women see men, beauty can be usurped by status. In other words, women are more attracted to an average looking man who has status and prestige, than to a man who is very attractive but has no status. However, the same does not work for a woman, as Etcoff points out in the following quote:

> Anthropologist John Marshall Townsend showed people pictures of men and women who ranged from great-looking to below average and who were described as training to be in either low, medium, or high-paying professions (waiter, teacher, or doctor). They were asked whether this was a person they might like to have a cup of coffee with, date, have sex with, or even marry. Not surprisingly, women preferred the best-looking man with the most money. But below him, average-looking or even unattractive doctors received the same ratings as very attractive teachers. Status compensated for looks. This was not true when men evaluated women. Unattractive women were not preferred, no matter what their status.[32] [33]

---

[32] Etcoff, Nancy, *Survival of the Prettiest: The Science of Beauty*, First Anchor Books Edition, Division of Random House Inc, July 2000, New York; copyright 1999, p. 79, Fair use per permission of the publisher.

[33] *'They were asked whether this was a person they might like to have a cup of coffee with, date, have sex with...'* By using this quote, the author is not advocating sex before marriage.

Based on the preceding quote, we can assume that beauty trumps all other assets that a woman might possess including talent and intelligence when it comes to a man's selection of a mate.

Etcoff goes on to explain that lookism is very much prevalent in the workplace. Attractive men are more likely to be promoted and given raises. They are also more likely to be selected for the job in a hiring process. The same applies to attractive women; but there are times that attractiveness can play against a woman in the workplace. In her research, Etcoff contends that there was one study in which the data indicated that beautiful women were less likely to be made partners in law firms and be selected for managerial positions. However, as a whole, both men and women who rated high on good looks fared much better in the workplace when it came to position and status.

Etcoff makes distinctions between attractive people, plain or average looking people (which is the majority of people), and unattractive people. She found that, there is great prejudice against people who are considered by most people as being unattractive, particularly against women who are considered to be unattractive. Not only is it more difficult for women who are considered unattractive to find employment and to compete successfully for better salaries when compared to women who are seen as either attractive or average looking, but it is also more difficult for women who are considered unattractive to find a marriage partner, especially a marriage partner that is suitable enough to properly provide for her.

With all this said, there is no question that America's standard of beauty has a profound negative affect on those who live in America and don't fit the standard. The areas that are affected, which include livelihood, financial stability, and the probability of promotion, are important aspects of a person's life. If one's livelihood, financial stability, and/or potential for promotion or success are impeded merely by one's looks, then beauty standards can significantly contribute to institutional racism.

Although Etcoff theorizes that beauty prejudice is different from racism, there are plausible arguments to the contrary. Beauty prejudice in America is not really that much different from racial prejudice because much of what is deemed beautiful or not beautiful has a lot to do with physical "racial" characteristics.

Institutional beauty-racism/prejudice is the discriminatory result of a society's standardized beauty that identifies certain physical characteristics of one group of people as more attractive when compared to the physical characteristics of another group of people. The characteristics that are most prone to come under the scrutiny of this kind of racism are skin color, hair texture, eye color, eye shape, nose structure, and lip contour.

Hair

According to Etcoff's studies, flawless skin tops the list for the most desirable physical characteristic. Healthy radiant hair comes in at a strong second.

The problem is, for the last four centuries or so, America's definition of healthy radiant hair has not included the course texture of hair that the majority of black people possess. During the slavery era, African women were made to cover their heads with rags or scarves because overall, the slave masters at the time, felt that the course texture of African hair was substandard when compared to straight or wavy hair more characteristic of Europeans. As time progressed, black Americans began to believe this very same thing. Black women were and still are particularly affected by the mindset that says course hair is substandard.

In 1920 Walter Sammons of Philadelphia Pennsylvania, a black man, invented and patented what is today referred to as the straightening comb. The straightening comb was created for the express purpose of straightening course hair (the type of hair that most black people have) by way of heat. Sammons described the straightening comb as an "improved" comb that helps to better comb out the "kinks" in course hair. Basically the devise was a hot iron made in the shape of a comb. The comb could either be heated in an encased iron ring or directly over fire. After it was heated to a certain temperature it was used to comb through the hair in order to straighten it. It is still used today.

There were certain problems with the straightening comb or "hot comb," as colloquially referred to. First, the more course and kinky the hair, the more heat had to be applied in order to straighten ("press") the hair. For some, this would eventually take the hair out. The only other option that was available to straighten course hair was to chemically relax the hair. The "hair relaxer" for black people was invented by Garrett Morgan, a black man (born in 1877) who founded the G.A. Morgan Hair Refining Company in 1913. But relaxers also had a tendency to take the hair out, especially those that contained lye (which was the case during the earlier years of the invention). Many black people's hair could not "hold" a press or "take" a relaxer (now most commonly referred to as a "perm"). The courser the hair, the quicker the hair would revert back to its natural state, when pressed, even if the hair got just a little wet (e.g. sweat). This meant that an overabundance of heat or a relaxer had to be applied to very course hair in order to straighten it. For many, this would do nothing but eventually damage the hair and keep it from growing. In many instances, the hair would fall out. This was particularly distressing to many black

130

females that found that their hair could not hold a press or a perm. These particular black females were often times regulated to wearing wigs.

Before the "afro" (the wearing of black hair in its natural state by simply lifting it up via a comb) came into style in the mid 1960s (largely due to the bravery of actress Cecily Tyson who was one of the first to wear her hair in its natural state), black women who visited the beauty parlors to get their hair pressed would make certain not to leave the parlor between the time their hair was washed and pressed (or relaxed). This was because it was an understood embarrassment for them if the rest of society were to see their hair in its natural state. If they left the parlor before their hair was completed being straightened (say, to go to the corner store), they made certain to cover their hair with a scarf or something similar. It was understood among black females that it was taboo for them to show their hair as God had naturally created it. Not only was it taboo to allow the greater society to see the natural state of their hair but black women were discouraged from wearing their hair in its natural state in front of other black people as well, and especially in front of black men. It was not allowed and was seen the same as being caught with your pants down.

Although black men were not as affected as black women were by the strong messages that had been passed down through the years which said that course kinky hair was substandard when compared to straight wavy hair; before the onset of the "afro" in the 1960s, it was just as taboo for black men to let their hair grow too much if they were not going to press it or perm it. Before the 60s a black person was deemed unkempt if he or she showed too much of the natural texture of his or her hair. However, black men had the advantage of cutting their hair, as opposed to black women, and therefore were not as pressured to perm or press their hair as were black women. But this doesn't mean that black men were not affected at all. Both black men and women were equally affected by what was, and still is, considered in black America as the beauty of "good hair."

"Good hair" is a colloquialism used in black America that refers to hair that some black people have that is naturally wavy, void of "kinks" and "naps," and is but slightly course. "Good hair" is hair that is closer in texture to the hair of white people. It is finely textured wavy hair. A black man or woman who has "good hair" is usually seen by other black Americans (but not necessarily by white Americans) as being more attractive than those blacks who do not have "good hair." Not only do many blacks see other blacks with "good hair" as more attractive but they often times also see them as a more desirable candidate for a mate in the hopes that their offspring will inherit the "good hair."

The problem with referring to a certain texture of hair as "good" implies that any texture of hair that is radically different from what is called good, is bad. If a person sees a certain hair texture as bad then they are ultimately seeing that particular hair texture as undesirable, substandard, and/or inferior. Unfortunately many black people developed this way of thinking about the course texture of African hair as a direct result from the racist messages passed down through generations that says that the kinky course texture of black hair in general is ugly and substandard. Television commercials that advertise hair products are particularly notorious for feeding into this bias. And even though, from the emergence of the afro to the current time, there have been a select segment of black Americans that have stepped out to wear their hair as God made it; void of pressing, perms, relaxing, and/or weaving; in general this has not been the case. The message that continues to be accepted overall in the black community is that the natural texture of black hair is too course and needs to be "fixed" and that long flowing silky hair is the preferred look as opposed to afros, locks,[34] and braids.[35] This is not to say that there is anything "wrong" with perming, pressing, and weaving; but just to emphasize that there's nothing "wrong" with the natural look either.

Skin color

There is little argument against the fact that the color of one's skin has a great deal to do with how one is treated in American society. Although things have increasingly improved over the last century or so when it comes to prejudices regarding skin color, there is still much progress still to be made.

Unfortunately, racism, discrimination, and prejudice when it comes to skin color can be summed up in one statement; the darker the color of a person's skin, the more likely the person is to experience some form of racism and/or discrimination.[36] The discrimination reveals itself in many ways, including mate-selection disparities according to skin color. Women

---

[34] Strands of hair are twisted. Left uncombed, hair begins to "lock" or to grow into itself creating ropes of hair that continue to grow becoming more elongated as time passes. With many black women, locking their hair is the only way that their hair will grow long.

[35] In 1 Timothy 2:9 Paul instructs women not to wear braided hair. The passage reads, "I also want women to dress modestly, with decency and propriety, not with braided hair or gold or pearls or expensive clothes..." It should be noted that theologians have indicated that during those times there was an over-extravagancy given to braided hair. Paul was basically referring to this over-extravagancy when it came to braided hair and was not referring to simply-styled braided hair.

[36] It should be noted that within the culture of white America, very pale skin is considered unattractive. White America therefore embraces the tanned look.

are particularly affected by societal skin color preferences in societies where many races of people compose the society at large. Etcoff puts it the following way:

> Racial differences will swamp any subtle differences among women due to age or fecundity or parity. And of course in multiracial societies a man's desire for a lighter-skinned woman may have little to do with his beauty detectors and much to do with his status aspirations or his racism. When black women in South Africa in the 1970s suffered an epidemic of a severe skin disorder called ochronosis because of their excessive skin bleaching, this was not caused by their overzealous attempts to look nubile, but by their desire to have lighter skin in a society where rights and privileges were tied to skin color." [37]

Etcoff had earlier acknowledged the tendency for men to choose lighter-skinned women in the mate selection process and indicated that V.S Ramachandran, a neuroscientist, has suggested that this type of favor towards lighter-skinned women, that men exhibit when selecting a mate, might have something to do with an innate tendency towards selecting a woman who more easily shows tell-tale signs of sickness or disease; the rationalization being that sickness and disease is better revealed on lighter-skinned individuals. Ramachandran continued to suggest that due to the fact that certain diseases are easier seen on lighter-skinned women than on darker-skinned women, men are better able to determine whether or not a lighter-skinned woman is suitable reproductively. If there are no outward signs of sickness then she looks to be suitable, and thus men are more likely to select lighter-skinned women as mates. However, Ramachandran simply made a suggestion. There is no proof that confirms Ramachandran's hypothesis.

Since Ramachandran only suggests, and does not prove his theory that men, as a whole, prefer lighter-skinned women due to subconscious attempts at selecting the "fittest" woman for child bearing, Etcoff goes on to expound upon the fact that in multiracial societies a man who has a light-skinned woman on his arm automatically gains more status than a man who has a dark-skinned woman on his arm. In other words,

---

[37] Etcoff, Nancy, *Survival of the Prettiest: The Science of Beauty*, First Anchor Books Edition, Division of Random House Inc, July 2000, New York; copyright 1999, p. 106, Fair use per permission of the publisher.

multiracial societies applaud men who select lighter-skinned women as mates. The propensity for the unspoken nod of approval from other men and society as a whole is much higher for those men who select lighter-skinned women as opposed to darker-skinned women. It doesn't appear that this selection has anything to do with the discerning of a woman's reproductive prowess but instead, has simply to do with preference. Etcoff backs up her claim by citing the outbreak of women suffering from ochronosis in the 70s in South Africa (previous quote) which was a direct result from women bleaching their skin to a lighter color in an effort to be afforded the same privileges as those women in the same country who were lighter-skinned.

It appears that light-skinned women are simply seen as more beautiful than dark-skinned women because society says they are. Although, in America, it is now politically incorrect to publicly state one's propensity toward the selection of lighter-skinned women for a mate, a job, or whatever other positive thing there is to get, the propensity still exists. It not only exists, in general, across racial lines, but it also exists *inside* racial lines as well.

Dark-skinned men have also had their share of discrimination thrown at them when it comes to the color of their skin in the mate selection process. It is said that women want men who are "tall, dark, and handsome," but there is a limit as to how dark is considered handsome. Not only have many white women in America been discouraged by their families and friends from marrying black men but there are many black women in America who have been discouraged by their families and friends from marrying black men who are "too dark." The fear of those doing the discouraging in the former scenario is that the white women will have children who will have visible signs of blackness and the fear of those doing the discouraging in the latter scenario is that the black women will have children, especially girls, that are "too dark" in a society that caters more to lighter-skinned women thus limiting her chances of finding a mate and excluding her from certain career opportunities.

While, within black America, very dark-skinned black men can be seen as undesirable by black baby boomers hoping to marry off their daughters who don't want their daughters marrying a man who is "too dark," black women looking for a mate, on the whole, find dark-skinned African-American men no less appealing than brown-skinned or light-skinned black men. However, very dark-skinned black women are, in general, seen as less desirable by black men as well as by black parents hoping to marry off their sons who want light-skinned grandchildren.

This lookism in the form of skin color prejudice within black America itself has raged on throughout the post antebellum years and has unfortunately done much to pit black men and women against one another. And although there has been a cooling of this kind of thought, the residual effects still linger especially when it comes to the plight of the very dark-skinned black woman. Not only does she live in white America where men in general prefer white and lighter-skinned women, but she also lives in black America, where the same preference towards lighter-skinned black American women is often expressed within her own group.

Fears that trigger a white woman's friends or relatives into discouraging her from marrying a black man (or a white man from marrying a black woman) or fears that trigger a black woman's friends or relatives into discouraging her from marrying a dark-skinned black man (or a black man from marrying a dark-skinned black woman) might not have as much to do with being prejudiced as it does with not wanting their loved one to be placed in a position whereby they too, along with their children, will begin to feel the sting of individual and institutional racism (or in the case of black women, their darker-skinned children will feel the sting of lookism not only from white America but from black America as well). Many white Americans have a tendency to deny that racism still exists in the United States until they are faced with the possibility of having bi-racial grandchildren.

American society's preference for whites and lighter-skinned blacks has not only been evident in films (take the movie King Kong,[38] for instance) but has been particularly evident in certain television mediums and programs. Although, today blacks and other minorities are now seen in television commercials, the ratio of black people and other minorities to white people in television commercials is still staggeringly imbalanced in favor of whites. Discrimination also still exists when it comes to national television news anchoring and reporting. There remains a certain "look" that producers are searching for. Dark-skinned black women are rarely seen in this medium, if at all. Brown-skinned and light-skinned black women are on the rise in television media but are still seen sparingly as opposed to their white counterparts.

---

[38] The movie *King Kong* was first made in 1933, then again in 1976 and 2005. The two earlier versions depicted black African tribal chiefs attempting to trade multiple numbers of black women from their tribe for one white woman to sacrifice to a monster guerrilla; the messages being that white women are more valuable, that they are more beautiful, and that it takes multiple black women to equal one white woman. In all three versions the monster is so intrigued with the beauty of the white woman that he decides to take care of her as opposed to accepting her as a sacrifice like he did all the black women before her. This kind of message, weather overt or covert, clearly falls into the category of institutional racism of beauty standards.

In addition to the disparaging small number of dark-skinned black women seen in the area of television media, the disparity becomes even more pronounced when looking at the supermodel industry. The international runway is blatantly lacking in black models. In the Fall 2008 edition of the Ebony Fashion Fair Magazine, Ginger Scott wrote an article entitled *Fade to Black: The Disappearance of the Black Model* in which she focused upon the growing trend in the fashion modeling industry to exclude black women from the catwalk. She indicates that not only have black models been affected in the industry by what some are calling overt racism, but that black designers have also been affected as well. Scott reveals that the fashion industry has come under a cloud of sharp criticism due to the many allegations of racial inequity as well as the industry's limited view of what constitutes beauty. She defends her position by suggesting that in browsing through any major fashion magazine the consumer will soon realize that models of color are scarce. Scott reveals that the issue has become so magnified that the concern over models that are anorexic has taken a back seat to the problems of racial discrimination in the industry.

There is no doubt about it; international fashion shows rarely include more than one or two men and women of color (including Asians and Hispanics); the message being that people of color, for the most part, are not really beautiful enough for the runway. And although strides have been made in the past few decades or so to include blacks and other people of color in areas of television media; there is still great room for improvement. Moreover, "the look" that television producers want when pursuing hopefuls to fill news anchor spots and the like often does not include a black look. But aside from all of this; no event has been more the poster child for what it means to promote a discriminatory view of beauty than the Miss America Pageant has been.

"There she is..."

The Miss America Pageant had its roots in 1921. It began, in the fall of that year, as a National Beauty Contest that took place in Atlantic City. Eight women Contestants competed to be selected as America's most beautiful bathing beauty. Margaret Gorman, a white sixteen year old teenager that looked like the famed movie starlet Mary Pickford, won this first Pageant.

From 1921 to 1982, all of the women who won the Pageant were white. However, it should be noted that Bess Meyerson was the first Jewish woman to be crowned the title in 1945.

It was noticeably evident that black women were not welcome to compete in the Pageant. Not only was it noticeably evident but initially, and for many years afterwards, the Pageant contracts specifically indicated that all the contestants had to be white.

In response to the obvious racism that the Pageant represented, J. Morris Anderson produced the first Miss Black America Pageant in 1968. The Pageant was held in Philadelphia Pennsylvania on August 17th of that year. This was black America's answer to Miss America and a protest to the Pageant's exclusion of black women. In excluding black women, or any woman of color for that matter, from the Miss America Pageant, white America was essentially saying that white women were more beautiful than black women (and all other women as well) and were therefore more deserving of the adoration, esteem, and financial benefits of the Pageant than were black women.

Eventually, certain sponsors began to pull their support away from the Miss America Pageant because of the undeniable discriminatory practices that came along with the Pageant. This opened the door for a black woman to compete and in 1970 Cheryl Brown became the first black contestant to compete in the Pageant. From 1970 to 1980 only ten black women competed in the Pageant. In 1980 a black woman finally made it to the top five. Her name was Lencola Sullivan. She was from Arkansas. Finally, in 1983, Vanessa Williams, at twenty-three years old, became the first black woman to be crowned Miss America. It took 62 years for Pageant officials, along with white America as a whole, to finally decide that black women are no less beautiful than white women.

Williams was paid up to $125,000 in fees during her first year as Miss America. This was quite a bit of money in 1983 and still is today. Unfortunately Williams also received death threats and hate mail, something that had never happened in the history of the Pageant. There was also great concern in the black community that Williams did not look "black enough." In other words, it was felt that Pageant officials had purposely selected a black woman who had more the look and physical features of a white woman. The indirect message was that darker-skinned black women who have more defined African facial features and course hair were not as attractive as lighter-skinned black women who have European facial features and straight or wavy hair.

In July of 1984 Vanessa Williams became the center of scandal when she told the press that Penthouse would be publishing nude photos of her in their magazine. She had allowed the photos to be taken of her earlier in her life, reportedly to earn extra money at the time. Penthouse got hold to the photos. When the Pageant officials became aware of the scandal they gave Williams three days to resign. She was to give up her title. Her runner up would consequently be crowned by default. Although Williams would be allowed to keep the scholarship and money that she had won, she was the first Miss America ever to be asked to give up her crown. Suzette Charles, a black woman, was the runner up and was given the crown. It should be pointed out that Ms. Charles is light-skinned and many would consider her easily to be mistaken for white.

There were and still are great benefits to winning the Miss America Pageant. Those benefits include scholarships, modeling contracts, being booked on talk shows, being asked to be a part of pivotal political events and so on. It has been said that the Pageant is the largest independent international organization to offer scholarships for women. As a whole, the Pageant has been said to be able to change a woman's life significantly for the better. Despite this, concerns not only of racism but also of sexism have followed the Pageant's history.

Racial barriers within the Pageant have decreased somewhat since Vanessa Williams' win in 1984. Since then there have been six other black women who have been crowned Miss America; two are light-skinned (Kimberly Aiken and Erika Harold), three are brown-skinned (Debbye Turner, Marjorie Vincent, Caressa Cameron), and only one would be considered dark-skinned by some (Ericka Dunlap who won the crown in 2004). Some would describe Aiken, Harold, and Cameron as having European facial features.

It appears that the Miss America Pageant officials (along with Miss USA Pageant officials)[39] had began attempting to be more inclusive, but the United States as a whole still has a long way to go when it comes to the issue of beauty standards and the effects that such standards have on black America and minorities in general.

INSTITUTIONAL RACISM IN THE HEALTH CARE SYSTEM

There is a long history of racial disparity in America when it comes to equal health care opportunities. This disparity comes from an abominable seed planted in the era before the Civil War in which "mad scientist" experiments were conducted on black slaves. These "experiments" were carried out against the will of the slaves that were victimized by these atrocities. The experiments included injecting black slaves with the small pox virus, dousing blacks with boiling water in order to test whether or not doing so could cure pneumonia, and putting blacks in ovens in order to determine whether or not certain medical potions would help in aiding human beings to withstand burning heat. Harriet Washington, author of

---

[39] The Miss USA Pageant was similar to the Miss America Pageant.

"Medical Apartheid: The Dark History of Medical Experimentation of Black Americans from Colonial Times to the Present," gives a comprehensive history of the horrific medical experiments that blacks have been involuntarily subjected to throughout the centuries that most people know little about. Among the many accounts she gives, Washington makes mention of one particular surgeon (James Marion Sims) during the slavery era who, in an attempt to cure vesicovaginal fistula,[40] performed heinous "medical experiments" on young black female slaves in which he would make incisions into their vaginal area while they were fully conscious. Despite his house of horrors, he was celebrated internationally for what was thought to have been his discovery of a cure. Similarly, such inhumane "experiments" were conducted on Jews in the German Nazi Concentration camps (1933-1939). Although we often times hear about such atrocities committed against the Jews during the Jewish Holocaust, we rarely hear about similar atrocities that were committed against black people during the slavery era.

Blacks were not only used in medical experiments without their knowledge before the advent of the Civil War, but afterwards as well. One of the most infamous of these medical experiments is what is now known as the Tuskegee Syphilis study. In 1932, six-hundred black men were encouraged by the United States Public Health Service to become part of a medical study. The Government knew that roughly four-hundred of these men had contracted the venereal disease of syphilis, which was the reason that they were chosen for the study. The remaining two-hundred men did not have syphilis. The men who had been diagnosed with syphilis were not told that they had the disease. Instead, all 600 men were given the erroneous information that they had "bad blood." However, what the Government was really doing was observing the long term effects that non-treatment of the disease would have on the men who were infected by it. In order to make certain that these men would continue to participate in the study, the Public Health Department gave them free food, burial insurance, and free transportation to and from the hospital where the study was taking place. Most of the men were very poor and had very little education. Therefore the incentives used to bait them worked.

---

[40] A fistula is an abnormal passageway between two organs. A vesicovaginal fistula is an abnormal duct or abscess that develops between the bladder (the urinary tract) and vagina more commonly as a result of violent rape, prolonged labor during childbirth, a tumor, or an error made during a hysterectomy procedure. The irregularity of the duct causes a great deal of uncontrolled urination and quite a bit of embarrassment for the sufferer.

It was not until 1972, long after it was discovered that penicillin could be used to cure syphilis,[41] that the infected men who survived, were finally told that they had syphilis and that they had unknowingly been part of an experiment. This has been the longest time in recorded history (40 years in all) that medical treatment has been purposely withheld from unsuspecting participants in a study for the purpose of experimentation.

The health care system in America is still riddled with racial inequities. Statistics reveal that black newborn babies are more likely to weigh significantly less than white newborn babies and are twice as likely to die within a year after being born than are white babies.

Black American males are seven times more likely to die young when compared to the death rate of young white American males. Upon first becoming aware of this fact there are those who would argue that the reason for this phenomenon is because homicide rates are higher in black communities than in white communities. But when looking deeper into the matter one soon discovers that this conclusion is not all encompassing. According to a 2001 article written by Cara Fauci for the Boston College Third World Law Journal, the following must also be considered:

> When statistical data is examined in various cause of death categories it becomes readily apparent that the higher premature death rate for African Americans is not simply a ramification of a higher incidence of homicide within African American communities. For example, African-American men have 100% more deaths due to diabetes, 92.6% more deaths due to cerebral vascular disorders, 88.4% more deaths from cirrhosis of the liver, and 81.8% more deaths due to pulmonary infectious diseases than European-American males. Additionally, African Americans are more likely than European Americans to contract and suffer from certain diseases such as tuberculosis, asthma, heart disease, cervical cancer, astute respiratory disease, appendicitis, hernia, pneumonia, influenza, and hypertension. In summary, when statistical information such as birth weight, infant mortality, life expectancy, and the likelihood of contracting certain diseases is examined, it becomes readily apparent that

---

[41] The medical benefits of penicillin were recognized in 1928 and its commercial use began ten years afterwards.

the status of African American health is lower than the status of European American health."[42]

Fauci cites the reason for much of the above disparities to be the lack of available health care for black Americans. She reminds us that in America, access to health care is not a fundamental right but instead it is a privilege. Only those who have health care benefits through employment, retirement, or self-pay have access to health care. All others do not. Therefore access to health care not only depends on whether or not one is working but whether or not health care is a part of the job benefit if one is working. Health care benefits are rarely included in the package of a minimum wage job. Blacks are disproportionately poor in America. Poor people usually only qualify for minimum wage jobs. Since minimum wage jobs do not normally provide health insurance, a disproportionate number of black people in America are hence without health insurance. Many blacks do not even qualify to receive Medicaid benefits.

Since a sizeable number of blacks lack health insurance as opposed to whites, blacks are substantially less likely to visit a doctor on a regular basis for routine check ups than whites are. This of course, leads to undetected and untreated illnesses. Moreover, private hospitals have a history of significantly limiting the number of admissions allowed for lower class patients as compared with the allowable number for middle class and upper class patients. This reduced admittance of poor people is due to the fact that most lower-income citizens lack adequate health insurance.[43]

Hospitals also have a history of practicing what is commonly called "patient dumping." Patient dumping is when private hospitals transfer economically underprivileged patients to other health care facilities. In

---

[42] Fauci, Cara A., *Racism and Health Care in America: Legal Responses to Racial Disparities in the Allocation of Kidneys*, Boston College Third World Law 2000-2001 Journal, Volume 21, pages 35-68, Student Publications. Copyright©2001 by Boston College Law School, Reprinted from 21 B.C. Third World L.J. 37 (2001) http://www.bc.edu/bc_org/avp/law/lwsch/journals/bctwj/21_1/02_TXT.htm (page 3 of 12 when viewed from on-line) p. 37 from Journal source. Used by Permission of the publisher.

[43] President Obama's health care bill was recently passed into law which prohibits insurance companies from denying coverage to children who have pre-existing illnesses and also provides coverage for adults with high risk pre-existing illnesses. By 2014 subsidies will be provided for the purchase of health care. Health care will be provided to the needy and most all employers will be mandated to provide their employees with health care coverage or otherwise be subject to penalties.

other words, private hospital personnel transfer the patient elsewhere, thereby in reality, refusing to treat the patient. Private hospitals have a long history of transferring blacks to public hospitals, especially low income blacks. To combat these occurrences, Congress passed legislation in 1986 that would make the practice of patient dumping illegal. This legislation was called the Emergency Medical Treatment and Active Labor Act (EMTALA). This Act still exists today. However, it has many loopholes and is not readily enforced. Therefore, the problem of patient dumping, although not as overt as it once was, still occurs.

Access to prescription drugs is another area of health care in which discrimination against blacks is practiced. In her article, Fauci points out that studies show that doctors are less apt to prescribe medication for blacks than they are for whites. Fauci cites a 1994 article printed in the New England Journal of medicine which exposed the fact that black people, who were at the time infected with the human immunodeficiency virus (HIV), were less likely to be prescribed the necessary pharmaceutical drugs that they needed to prolong their lives than were whites who had contracted the same virus. This disparity existed even after income and medical insurance factors were controlled for. Black people with HIV, who had the same medical benefits and insurance as whites were not receiving the same health care. Blacks were receiving a lesser quality of care than their white counterparts, for no apparent reason. When looking at the ills that America has faced when it comes to its racial problems, there is no question that the color of the patient's skin in these cases had a huge effect on the quality of care the patient received in the treatment of HIV/AIDs.

Not only have there been vast discrepancies between the health care treatment of black and white Americans when it comes to the AIDs virus, but Fauci describes similar disparities between blacks and whites when it comes to other diseases as well. Fauci also reports that black Americans are not as likely to receive needed invasive treatments for certain maladies as are white Americans. She cites that for every 100 white men that are treated by way of coronary angiography, only 50 black men are given this same life-saving treatment. Additionally, roughly only 35 black men are afforded coronary artery bypass surgery for every 100 white men that are afforded the same life-saving operation. Fauci also points out that studies indicate that there is a tendency for health care professionals not to treat the diseases of pneumonia, glaucoma, and kidney failure as aggressively when treating black Americans who suffer from these diseases as they do when treating white Americans who suffer from these same diseases; and this is even so when both parties have the same or similar health insurance benefits.

Fauci goes on to reveal that the Journal of the American Medical Association has reported that black women are less likely to receive cesarean section operations during childbirth as compared to white women, even when the complications are the same as the childbirth complications experienced by white women and even when they have the same medical benefits as white women. This alarming fact endangers the health and wellbeing of the next generation of American black children right from the point of birth.

Moreover, Fauci points out that not only are life-saving treatments more likely to be withheld from blacks as opposed to whites, but that surgeries which result in handicapping the patient are more likely to be performed on blacks than on whites. These types of surgeries include amputations and bilateral orchiectomies (surgery to remove the testicles; the last medical resort for men suffering from prostate cancer). Fauci concluded that the percentage of these types of operations are higher for blacks because black people are less likely to be properly diagnosed early enough to treat illnesses before they progress to a state in which such aggressive treatment is necessary.

Not only are there health care disparities when it comes to treating blacks and whites for physical ailments but there are also discriminatory disparities when it comes to mental health care as well. Fauci reports that, when psychotherapy would prove beneficial, black Americans are not as likely to be referred as are whites, and if they are referred, the probability is much higher for blacks than for whites that they will be referred to an inexperienced therapist. There is also a greater probability that the therapy sessions that blacks participate in will be shorter in length.

Despite all of her research, Fauci's main purpose for writing her article centers around discriminatory practices when it comes to black Americans receiving kidney transplants. Human beings are born with two kidneys. The kidney is a human organ that cleans the blood. Urine is a result of that cleansing. Without the kidneys, the human body would be poisoned by internal waste and would eventually die. Chronic kidney failure (renal failure) is the consistent inability of the kidneys to clean the blood. There are only two ways to treat kidney failure; by dialysis or by means of a kidney transplant.

Fauci reports that there is a higher percentage of patient satisfaction with the treatment of kidney transplants than with the treatment of dialysis. However, there is a shortage of kidneys that are available for transplant in the United States.

The first kidney transplant was performed in 1954 and in 1984 the National Organ Transplant Act was implemented. By means of this Act, the Federal Government developed the Organ Procurement and

Transportation Network which was established, through the United Network for Organ Sharing (UNOS), to match persons willing to donate their kidneys with persons in need of one. One of the core functions of these agencies is to obtain kidneys from the specific region where the agency is. These agencies give the organs to patients who live in the geographic location of the agency. If there is no one in the area in need of a kidney transplant, then other areas will be considered. However, where a patient lives has a great bearing on whether or not the patient will receive a needed kidney. Each individual agency that is a part of UNOS has a list of people waiting for a kidney. Each agency also has its own guidelines when making a decision as to who receives a kidney. These guidelines are the determining factors as to whether or not a person will be placed on a waiting list for a kidney.

Fauci's article reveals that research has shown that black Americans suffer from chronic kidney failure at a higher rate than do white Americans. She indicates that although black people make up only "12%"[44] of the United States population, they make up 34% of the population that suffers from chronic kidney failure. Fauci states that only 22% of African-Americans who need kidney transplants receive kidneys while 74% of white Americans who need kidney transplants receive kidneys. The reasons cited for the causes of this kind of disparity are firstly; blacks do not donate kidneys nearly as much as whites do. Many believe that this lag in kidney donation from the black community is partly due to what some deem as a strong distrust that many black people have of the medical field. When taking into account what has already been discussed when it comes to disparities in medical treatment between blacks and whites, we can see that this distrust in not unwarranted.

Secondly, there is a distinct possibility, although it cannot be readily proven, that doctors are not as likely to place blacks on the kidney recipients list as they are to place whites. Thirdly, UNOS agencies did not pair donors with recipients unless there was a close antigen match between the two. But such a match between blacks and whites is low. However, it has now been discovered that such a match is not absolutely necessary for a successful transplant since there are now drugs on the market that will counteract the body's rejection of a transplant. So, the fact that kidney donations come more from whites than from blacks should not be a determining factor as to who is to be considered for a transplant.

In 1984 the Organ Procurement and Transportation Network was mandated by cause of the National Organ Transplant Act of 1984 to make all organ transplant opportunities equitable to all races. Despite this, black

---

[44] Since her article was written the population has risen to roughly 13%.

Americans still receive fewer life-saving kidney transplants than do white Americans.

In looking further at the underlying racism that exists in America's health care system, we will turn to *The Covenant*, published in 2006 by The Smiley Group Incorporated, with an Introduction by Tavis Smiley. The following are just some of the facts that *The Covenant* reveals when it comes to the health care of black Americans: although black Americans suffer significantly more from high blood pressure than whites do, white Americans are more likely to be treated for the disease. Blacks who are infected with the HIV virus have a seven percent higher death rate resulting from the virus than white Americans do. Black Americans who suffer from cancer have a 30% higher death rate from the disease than white Americans do who suffer from cancer and also, blacks who suffer from diabetes are 27% more likely to die from the disease than whites are who have been diagnosed with diabetes. Moreover, the mortality rate for blacks who die due to asthma is three times higher than the mortality rate of whites who die from the disease.

Much of the above disparities have to do with a combination of three things, those being: the health insurance crisis within the black community, the fact that 32% of all black Americans do not have a general physician or regular doctor, and the fear of doctors and hospitals that many blacks experience due to the historical exploits and criminal behavior of the health industry when it comes to the medical treatment or medical non-treatment that blacks have or haven't received over the years. To add to this, the 2009 Equality Index of Black America[45] documented that as of the latest research (2007) 19.5% of black people do not have health insurance while 10.4% of whites do not have it and that the percentage of black people from ages 18 to 64 who don't have a "usual source of health insurance" was 25.4% with whites at 13.7%.

In addition to the existence of racial disparities when it comes to how America tends to the physical health care of black Americans and other minorities as opposed to how it tends to the physical health care of whites; racial disparities, as mentioned before, are also being made in the mental health field as well, particularly when it comes to diagnosing mental illnesses; specifically schizophrenia. An article, written in 2005 by Staff Writer Shankar Vedantam, for the Washington Post entitled, "Racial Disparities found in Pinpointing Mental Illness," gives a clear view of this problem by documenting the work of John Zeber who analyzed and studied, for the U.S. Department of Veteran Affairs, data specific to

---

[45] King, Martin Luther (Foreword), National Urban League, The State of Black America 2009, copyright 2009, p.31

medical costs and the quality of medical treatment. Vedantam is quoted as saying:

> John Zeber recently examined one of the nation's largest databases of psychiatric cases to evaluate how doctors diagnose schizophrenia, a disorder that often portends years of powerful brain-altering drugs, social ostracism and forced hospitalizations.
>
> Although schizophrenia has been shown to affect all ethnic groups at the same rate, the scientist found that blacks in the United States were more than four times as likely to be diagnosed with the disorder as whites. Hispanics were more than three times as likely to be diagnosed as whites.
>
> Zeber, who studies quality, cost and access issues for the U.S. Department of Veterans Affairs, found that differences in wealth, drug addiction and other variables could not explain the disparity in diagnoses: "The only factor that was truly important was race."
>
> The analysis of 134,523 mentally ill patients in a VA registry is by far the largest national sample to show broad ethnic disparities in the diagnosis of serious mental disorders in the United States. The data confirm the fears of experts who have warned for years that minorities are more likely to be misdiagnosed as having serious psychiatric problems..."[46]

Vedantam goes on to quote Zeber as saying in a 2004 report:

> Race appears to matter and still appears to adversely pervade the clinical encounter, whether consciously or not.[47]

---

[46] From the Washington Post © June 28, 2005. The Washington Post. All rights reserved. Used by permission and protected by the Copyright Laws of the United States. The printing, copying, redistribution or retransmission of the Material without express written permission is prohibited. Vedantam, Shankar., Staff writer, *Racial Disparities found in Pinpointing Mental Illness.*
[47] Ibid.

In order to understand the sheer seriousness of such a misdiagnosis, we have to take a look at what schizophrenia actually is. Schizophrenia is a biological disorder that affects the brain which significantly impairs the thinking process and consequently adversely affects behavior. It is a disease of the mind. The symptoms of schizophrenia include, but are not limited to the following: psychotic events (delusions, particularly paranoid, grandiose, and/or persecutory delusions, and/or sensory hallucinations [hearing, smelling, and/or seeing things that aren't there]), disorganized speech, bizarre behavior (resulting from bizarre delusions and/or hallucinations), disorganized thinking, flattened affect (person is expressionless, stares into space), and/or catatonia (chronic rigid posture resistant to movement). The Fourth Edition of the Diagnostic and Statistical Manual of Mental Disorders defines schizophrenia as follows:

> The individual with Schizophrenia may display inappropriate affect (e.g. smiling, laughing, or a silly facial expression in the absence of an appropriate stimulus), which is one of the defining features of the Disorganized Type. Anhedonia is common and is manifested by a loss of interest or pleasure. Dysphoric mood may take the form of depression, anxiety, or anger. There may be disturbances in sleep pattern (e.g. sleeping during the day and nighttime activity or restlessness). The individual may show lack of interest in eating or may refuse food as a consequence of delusional beliefs. Often there are abnormalities of psychomotor activity (e.g., pacing, rocking, or apathetic immobility). Difficulty in concentration, attention, and memory is frequently evident. A majority of individuals with Schizophrenia have poor insight regarding the fact that they have a psychotic illness. Evidence suggests that poor insight is a manifestation of the illness itself rather than a coping strategy.[48]

Unfortunately, the diagnosis of mental illness in American society brings with it a certain stigma, particularly if one is diagnosed as being schizophrenic, bipolar, or depressed. There's no doubt that a diagnosis of

---

[48] Reprinted with Permission from the Diagnostic and Statistical Manual of Mental Disorders, Fourth Edition, Text Revision, (copyright 2000) American Psychiatric Association, p. 304.

schizophrenia places a person in a certain category. The diagnosis itself gives the impression that the person suffering with such an illness will not be able to function normally in society. If then, blacks are being misdiagnosed with the illness at a significantly high rate and the illness itself is known to plunge its victims into a denial of its existence then those blacks who are misdiagnosed who resist the diagnosis won't be looked at as credible. Furthermore, treatment for schizophrenia includes psychotropic medication that can have devastating physical side effects which add to the dysfunctional look of the disease. The injustice therefore in misdiagnosing someone with the disease is far reaching indeed and can lead to additional prejudicial treatment including difficulty finding employment and, as discussed earlier, disenfranchisement of the right to vote.

Overall, the misdiagnosis of a psychological illness will significantly disrupt a person's life. In addition, purposely withholding medical treatment from a group of people can and does cause permanent disability and premature death to those that the treatment has been withheld from. When it comes to the American Dream, the state of one's health can have a significant effect on the potential one has to live comfortably. Living the American dream not only means having certain material possessions but it also means being free and content. One's happiness has a lot to do with one's quality of life. Most people would trade any amount of money to live a pain free healthy life. If therefore, there is racism in the health care sector of American society then life, liberty, and the pursuit of happiness is stopped short for those who are negatively affected by the racial disparities affecting health care availability and practices.

ENVIRONMENTAL INSTITUTIONAL RACISM

Environmental institutional/structural racism occurs when man-made rules and regulations pertaining to the environment negatively affect neighborhoods, communities, and/or cities in which minorities make up the majority of the population. Regulations regarding pollution are usually at the forefront of the controversy when looking at environmental racism. However, there can be other factors that contribute to man-made environmental conditions that are designed in such a way as to threaten the health and/or well-being of those who live within the parameters of the environmental hazard.

When looking at the results of a 2007 study conducted by the United Church of Christ Commission for Racial Justice (CRJ), it was revealed that decisions as to where to put toxic and hazardous waste sites have much to do with the race of the people living in the proposed site. Locations where

148

the population is largely composed of minorities are given first consideration for the development and implementation of these dangerous sites. Robert D. Bullard, Paul Mohai, and Robin Saha[49] wrote the study. In her 2007 article "What Color is Toxic Waste," Sandy Sorensen says the following:

> The 2007 study was authored by Robert D. Bullard, director of the Environmental Justice Resource Center at Clark Atlanta University; Paul Mohai, professor at University of Michigan's School of Natural Resources and Environment, Robin Saha, assistant professor of environmental studies at the University of Montana; and Beverly Wright, sociologist and founding director of UCC-related Dillard University's Deep South Center for Environmental Justice. According to the study, people of color comprise the majority of the population living near the nation's commercial hazardous waste facilities. Researchers found that for Latinos/as, African Americans and Asian/Pacific Islanders, major disparities in the location of hazardous waste facilities exist in the majority of the Environmental Protection Agency's regions. The findings are particularly troubling, because they indicate that those environmental protections that do exist on the books are not equally enforced.[50]

The study is a twenty-year follow-up to an initial study conducted by CRJ which resulted in the publishing of a report entitled, "Toxic Waste and Race in the United States." The 2007 follow-up study found the same racial inequities when it came to landfills and toxic waste sites as did the 1987 study; that race plays a major part in where the facilities will be located and that laws designed to curtail the environmental institutional racism of toxic dumping in minority communities are barely enforced, if at all.

Although, when defining environmental racism, the main focus is pollution disposal, it is fitting to add to the equation any environmental

---

[49] Clark Atlanta University Environmental Justice Resource Center Director, Natural Resources and Environment Professor, University of Michigan, and University of Montana Environmental Studies assistant professor, respectively.

[50] Sorensen, Sandy, *What Color is Toxic Waste?* Internet Article, United Church of Christ, http://www.ucc.org/ucnews/octnov07/what-color-is-toxic-waste.html, October – November 2007, October 1, 2007 p. 4. Used by permission of the author.

factor that would cause harm to the health and well-being of a particular group of people. Therefore, not only can pollution be an environmental substance that is dangerous to people but so can any condition that poses a threat to environmental safety. With this said, one of the most egregious examples of environmental institutional racism in recent history centers around the aftermath of Hurricane Katrina and how a lack of preparation for this particular hurricane devastated an entire city populated mostly by blacks.

Hurricane Katrina

A hurricane is a swirling storm that usually has its beginning over a warm sea and travels across an ocean. With it come rain, thunder, and lighting. It is a sea cyclone, of sorts, that develops and carries with it tons of water as it moves.

Hurricanes are divided into categories depending on the miles per hour of wind speed that they produce. A category 1 Hurricane produces wind speeds between 75 to 95 miles per hour and is considered weak. A category 2 hurricane produces wind speeds between 96 to 110 miles per hour and is considered moderate. A category 3 hurricane produces wind speeds between 111 to 130 miles per hour and is considered strong. A category 4 hurricane produces wind speeds between 131-155 miles per hour and is considered very strong. And a category 5 hurricane produces wind speeds between 156 to 200 miles per hour (and sometimes over 200 miles per hour) and is considered devastating. Most damage by hurricanes is not caused by the winds but is caused by the flooding that the winds produce.

On August 29, 2005, Hurricane Katrina struck the gulf Coast early morning. New Orleans Louisiana was the hardest hit resulting in eighty percent (80%) of the city being flooded under water. New Orleans is ten feet below sea level. The hurricane began its formation as a category 1 over the Bahamas on August 23, 2005 and eventually moved through Alabama, Florida, and Georgia, before reaching New Orleans. Hurricane Katrina also affected Kentucky and Ohio because of the flooding of the Mississippi River.

Although Hurricane Katrina became a category 5 the day before it hit Louisiana, by the time it reached land in New Orleans it was a strong category 3, some say a 4. What actually caused such great devastation of New Orleans sending it under water was the "breaking" of the levees[51]. There were 53 levee breaches in the levee system that was federally

---

[51] An embankment built to sustain flood waters.

designed to keep hurricane flood waters out of New Orleans. As a result of this breach of levees, along with inadequate floodwalls, the city was severely flooded causing the deaths of 1,577 Louisiana state residents while 2 people died in Alabama, 14 people died in Florida, 2 people died in Georgia, 1 person died in Kentucky, 238 people died in Mississippi, and 2 people died in Ohio. Altogether 1,836 people died as a result of Hurricane Katrina while 705 people are still missing. It was the third deadliest Hurricane in American history costing 81 billion dollars in damages.

- *Levee history*

A levee is a man-made embankment that runs parallel to rivers or other large bodies of water for the purpose of preventing the overflow of water onto the mainland. Levees are made to prevent flooding and are composed of slabs that can range in height from 13 to 25 feet.

In 1927 heavy rains caused the Mississippi River to flood which breached levee systems at the time. The levees designed to protect New Orleans were dynamited before the flood waters reached the city in order to divert the water and prevent the flooding of the city. Most of the flood water was consequently diverted from the city of New Orleans. At the time, the city of New Orleans was wealthier than its surrounding parishes. In 1965 Hurricane Betsy devastated the city of New Orleans. The levees were breached and flood waters poured into the city. 164,000 homes were flooded and the ninth ward was particularly devastated triggering some to believe that the levees were once again intentionally dynamited but this time in order to divert waters from the wealthier French Quarters and flood the poorer parts of New Orleans that had become densely populated with blacks. After the devastation, city officials began reconstruction of the levees but the job was never completed.

- *Details and implications*

In 2005 there were 500,000 residents in New Orleans, two-thirds of which were black with nearly 30% of its residents living below the poverty line. Before the Katrina catastrophe, the state of Louisiana ranked 49th in health care service for children; one spot from being at the bottom of the list. A month after the disaster, nearly half of New Orleans' residents had no medical insurance and were arriving in droves to the hospitals to be treated for breathing difficulties associated with chronic exposure to mold. Suicides, post Katrina, had risen to three times its rate pre-Katrina.

151

President Bush initially blamed New Orleans Mayor Ray Nagin for the poor response to the Katrina disaster. However, the people of New Orleans pointed the finger at the Federal Government. One of the main problems was that at certain critical moments, officials were confused about who was in charge. An article in the September 2005 issue of Time Magazine questioned the actions of four people when it came to the systems failure regarding Katrina; Mayor Ray Nagin, Governor Kathleen Babineaux Blanco, Federal Emergency Management Agency (FEMA) Director Michael Brown, and Secretary of Homeland Security, Michael Chertoff.

The article claims that Ray Nagin was the person responsible for the preparation of a timely and organized evacuation. Nagin did abide by the evacuation plan but because of the vast number of poor people that lived in the city, the plan did not adequately fit the needs of the people. Furthermore, and most importantly, it was estimated that even with the best of evacuation plans, 100,000 people would not have been able to easily leave because they did not have transportation. The Superdome was supposed to be a last place of refuge. But there was also an unreasonable expectation that those taking refuge in the Superdome would bring an ample amount of food and water to hold them for at least the majority of the week. However, if the 100,000 people didn't have the means to leave the city before the hurricane struck, then it stands to reason that they certainly would not have had the means to carry the necessary food, water, toiletries, and other supplies that it would take to survive in the Superdome for a week.

The article also indicated that the Superdome had been used as a place of refuge in 1998 when hurricane George struck. At that time 14,000 people descended upon the stadium. The result was shear pandemonium and theft. The article also noted that 80% of New Orleans residents did indeed leave the city and their success in doing so was largely due to Nagin's implementation of an interstate freeway plan that redirected driving paths. On the other hand, there were buses available to take stranded residents to the Superdome but not to take them out of the city. Furthermore, when the storm finally hit, communication systems went awry. Radios, phones, and cell phones were not working for at least two days.

The year prior, in 2004, FEMA funded a study in order to determine how New Orleans would be affected by a category 5 hurricane. They did this by computer simulation. However, the information that the study revealed was ignored, including the fact that 127,000 people in New Orleans did not have their own personal means of transportation and hundreds were homeless and disabled. These issues became barriers to evacuation during the aftermath of Hurricane Katrina.

On Friday, August 26, 2005, before Hurricane Katrina struck, Governor Blanco declared a state of emergency in Louisiana. On August 27th, she asked President Bush to declare a Federal state of emergency in Louisiana. The emergency was declared and the Department of Homeland Security (DHS) along with FEMA were given the full authority to respond. The following day at 9:30 in the morning, Mayor Nagin mandated the evacuation of New Orleans because it was determined that the levees would not hold up.

Later on that evening roughly 30,000 New Orleans residents took refuge in the city's Superdome expecting to sit-out the hurricane. There was no more than 36-hours worth of food in the Superdome. However, residents did not expect the city to be plunged under water and both the Superdome and Convention Center became death traps when there was no way to get out of the city.

Monday August 29th the levees breached and the flood waters came pouring in. Max Mayfield, National Hurricane Center Director advised and warned the White House about the potential devastation. A portion of the roof came off of the Superdome. The Governor reported that the people in the Superdome were okay and that there were several more hours of storm to go through. People who were still in New Orleans heard explosions the morning of the storm. It was the levees breaking. The explosive sounds were so loud that many residents of New Orleans who heard the explosive sounds believed that the levees were being purposely blown apart. However, most believed that the explosive sounds were the result of the levees breaking.

By midday on the 29th, 80% of New Orleans was under water. Brown finally gave permission for 1,000 DHS employees to be sent to Louisiana but he gave them two days to arrive there. Governor Blanco desperately called the President again for help later on that night. The President did not respond until two days later and the National Guard troops did not arrive in Louisiana until August 31st.

Eighty Thousand people were trapped inside the city. Governor Blanco called the White House again earlier that morning and insisted on speaking to the President. She was finally routed to him and asked him for any and all help that he could give. Residents trapped in the city began to wade through the water to try to get to the Superdome. Some of the water flood levels were eight feet or higher. People were wading in water that was up to their necks. In many places the water had risen to 20 feet. To add to the misery, it was also very hot; at least 95 degrees. The United States Coast Guard began to rescue people who were stranded on the roofs. Hundreds of them were taken to the Superdome. By the third day of the aftermath, roughly 20,000 to 30,000 people began to converge on the Convention

Center. But there was no food or water there. People in New Orleans were dying.

By September 1st there were still no orders or commands being given. No one was taking charge. Mayor Nagin issued a "desperate SOS" to the Federal Government. Michael Brown sent resources to the Center. On September 2nd, the President and the Federal Government began to respond. Buses were dispatched to the city for rescue but not until September 5th, seven days into the aftermath. On September 13th President Bush admitted that the response to Hurricane Katrina was seriously flawed on all levels of Government. He took full responsibility.

During the time the evacuees were stranded at the Superdome the situation was dire. The water soon stopped running and the toilets overflowed and backed up. People were not able to bathe or change clothes; nor were they able to take care of fundamental hygiene necessities like brushing their teeth. Many of the teenaged girls and young women found themselves having to endure menstrual periods without the availability of feminine hygiene products. No one had anticipated that it would be almost a week until any help arrived. Life at the Superdome became what many have referred to as a living hell.

Rumors began to circulate across America that gang members were running rampant within the Superdome and Convention Center killing people and raping women and small children, when in actuality, four died in the Superdome reportedly of natural causes, one overdosed on drugs, and one committed suicide by jumping to his death. At the Convention Center, another four people were found dead, with only one death attributed to foul play. Although these statistics are still very disturbing (one can't help but wonder whether or not the condition of having to endure the environment of the Superdome contributed to the four natural deaths and suicide); this is a far cry from the multiple murders and rapes that were being reported. This is not to say that there were no rapes since such a crime is often not reported, but upon investigation there was no evidence that rapes had taken place. There was also no evidence that murders had taken place in the Superdome.

As discussed earlier, there was a very slow Federal response to the Hurricane Katrina catastrophe. The response, in and of itself, was a catastrophe. According to Spike Lee's documentary of the event[52], Mayor Nagin asked for reinforcement troops and Greyhound buses in order to transport stranded residents out of New Orleans, but the President did not respond until days later. Nagin indicated that the reason why it took so

---

[52] Lee, Spike, Director: *When the Levees Broke,* Documentary Film, copyright © 2006.

long to get appropriate help into the city was due to the discrepancies between the Government and the state of Louisiana as to who had the authority to do something. The Federal Government did not want to overstep the rights of the state. Nagin felt that the Governor was hesitant to make the necessary calls to the Government but the Governor indicated that she called the President several times at the onset but was not getting the responses that she needed to get. In the meantime, without food and water, or a means to escape, people were dying.

The Government had been warned about the possibility of Hurricane Katrina causing ruinous damage, but did nothing. There was no massive airdrop of food or water 5 days into the ordeal.

According to Lee's documentary, those being rescued were taken to the Superdome, the Convention Center, or the expressway ramps. There's a bridge that extends across the bank of the Mississippi River to New Orleans through the suburb of Gretna. Seventy-five percent of the Gretna's residents are white while the remaining 35% are black. Gretna was affected by the hurricane but not nearly as severely as New Orleans. The residents of Gretna were still able to stay in their homes. Some victims of the hurricane were on the bridge for five days. The people on the bridge were mostly poor people and blacks. No water or food was available on the bridge and there were no toilet facilities. There was also no way to get needed prescription medication and there was no protection from the sun.

According to Lee's documentary as well as an article written by Journalist Carol Kopp entitled, "The Bridge to Gretna,"[53] after three days from the time Katrina struck, the people on the bridge became desperate and began walking across the bridge in order to get out of town. Six thousand of those people were put on buses assisted by the Gretna police. The bridge was one of the few pathways out but this particular way out meant passing through the city of Gretna. The following day thousands more residents, along with some tourists that had been in a hotel for four days without electricity or running water, began walking across the bridge. But this time the Gretna police met the group with guns. The Gretna police had blocked off the bridge and were not allowing people to walk through Gretna in order to get out of New Orleans. Gretna police along with their squad cars were lined up across the bridge to create a blockade. As the evacuees approached, the police fired shotgun blasts into the air as a warning for the evacuees not to approach. According to Lee's

---

[53] Kopp, Carol, The *Bridge to Gretna: Why did Police block desperate Refugees from New Orleans,* Gretna Louisiana December 18, 2005 copyright MMV, CBS World Wide Incorporated, CBS News/60 Minutes website. http://www.cbsnews.com/stories/2005/12/15/60minutes/main1129440.shtml

documentary the police had orders to shoot to kill and referred to the evacuees as "thugs."

People were trapped in New Orleans with no food, water, or shelter, and with decomposing bodies strewn all over. The unsanitary conditions were deplorable and health hazards were unimaginable. Anyone would have been desperate to get out.

It has been reported that the officials and community of Gretna did not want the citizens of New Orleans crossing their community in order to leave the city so they blocked, via the police, one of the few pathways out of the city. According to Kopp's article, Chief of Police, Author Lawson was quoted by CBS News as justifying the blockade by saying the city of Gretna needed to be protected. By saying this, Lawson put the evacuees on the same level as criminals.

The majority of the people trying to leave the bridge were black while the majority of the officers preventing them from doing so and threatening their lives if they tried, where white. The majority of people living in Gretna were white. Blacks were in danger of being shot by the police because the white community of Gretna looked upon these desperate blacks as possible looters. As a result of not being able to walk to safety, there were some who set up camp on the bridge; but Gretna officers eventually drove by in squad cars pointing their guns and ordered them off the bridge.

The incident on the bridge can be compared with the incident that blacks experienced on the levees in 1927 during the flooding of the Mississippi River which produced the same devastating results as Hurricane Katrina. Roughly 10,000 people, mostly black, had to be rescued from the countryside where the waters ran because certain parts of the levees were initially dynamited in order to redirect the flooding to the poorer parts of the area. These 10,000 people were taken to a portion of the levee and forced to stay on a portion of high ground that was at the crown of the levee bordering the city of Greenville. They were provided blankets and they put together make-shift tents, but there was no food, water, or clean sanitation and authorities did not allow them to leave for days for fear that these blacks would leave Louisiana altogether and by doing so deplete the cropping and farming labor force that Louisiana had come to rely on. History repeated itself with the onslaught of Hurricane Katrina.

During a one-hour special NBC television program dedicated to a Hurricane Katrina disaster relief effort that was aired five days after the onslaught of the disaster (September 3rd), rapper Kanye West made the following remarks "they've given them permission to go down and shoot us...George Bush doesn't care about black people." The last half of the statement is questionable but the first half is undeniable. The police were indeed given permission to shoot people who were trying to leave New Orleans via the bridge on foot. The majority of those people were black.

West also made reference to two stories that appeared in *Yahoo!News* online newspaper on August 30th, a day after New Orleans flooded. One clip had a picture of a white woman and a white man wading in chest-deep water. The woman was carrying bread and another item. They both had knapsacks strapped to their backs. The narrative under the photograph read, "two residents wade through chest-deep water after finding bread and soda from a local grocery store after Hurricane Katrina came through the area in New Orleans, Louisiana."

Another clip had a picture of a black man wading through the same chest-deep water. He was carrying what appeared to be a boxed food item in one hand a huge garbage bag in the other. But the narrative under this photograph read as follows, "a young man walks through chest deep flood water after looting a grocery store in New Orleans on Tuesday, Aug. 30, 2005. Flood waters continue to rise in New Orleans after Hurricane Katrina did extensive damage when it hit." This kind of thing is indisputably racist. The two white residents were seen as simply trying to survive and they were excused while the black man who was simply trying to survive as well was portrayed as a criminal by being labeled a looter. The only difference was skin color. Moreover, when looking at Gretna's reaction to the tragedy one would be hard pressed not to speculate that Gretna's fears were fueled by racial bias and had the people on the bridge been mostly white that the fear of looting may not have been present and the people may have been allowed to cross into safety instead of being made to stay in a situation where lives were being threatened because the necessities to sustain life were absent.

On August 31st Lieutenant General Russel Honore was assigned to be the commander of the Joint Task Force Katrina and was to organize military relief. Honore made the soldiers put down their weapons, told them that they were on a rescue mission (not a shoot to kill mission), and went on to evacuate the 25,000 people who were at the Convention Center. The Convention Center was evacuated by September 3rd. Henore and his troops also continued the search and rescue mission throughout the majority of the New Orleans area and part of Mississippi. He brought with him an army convoy of food and supplies. He was hailed a hero because he was a major influence that helped turn around the hostile attitudes against the victims of Katrina. However, there were still problems that emerged with the army's handling of the victims.

Although Lieutenant Honore helped to change attitudes and emphasized to the army and the world that the purpose of their mission was to rescue people, the rescue itself still brought with it serious concerns and criticisms. According to some of the victims that appeared in Lee's documentary; the army separated men from women in their evacuation of the Superdome and the Convention Center. Many people were ordered to get on the buses without knowing where their family and friends were in the midst of the crowd. The army did not inform the evacuees where they were going. And the evacuees were not informed where they were until they got to the destination. Hundreds of the evacuees were taken to the Baton Rouge Convention Center and the Houston Astrodome that served as shelters until they were flown out to other states. Several evacuees were taken to places like Oklahoma and Utah where they had no friends or family. The evacuation separated family members scattering them many distances from one another in various states. Hundreds of children were separated from their parents. Evacuees were dispersed in 49 states with one-way tickets. Some black people likened their treatment to America's treatment of African slaves when families were torn apart in similar fashion.

FEMA subsidized hotel rooms for the evacuees for 3 months but after the three months were over, the evacuees were on their own. Many of them didn't have the money to continue paying for their stay and they had no place to return to in New Orleans. The city had been destroyed and it would take months to rebuild. For many, experiencing the aftermath of Hurricane Katrina was worse than going through the Hurricane itself. Suicide rates and post traumatic stress syndrome rose significantly among Katrina survivors.

The Core of Engineers became responsible for moving debris from New Orleans. They didn't begin moving the debris until February 2006; four months after the tragedy. During the tragedy, people had not only died of drowning but hundreds died of heat strokes, dehydration, complications due to not having their prescription medications, and many who carried oxygen tanks with them died of complications from not having enough oxygen with them. Six months after the catastrophe, all of the homes had not yet been searched and search crews were still finding bodies in homes. FEMA was responsible for the in-home search for dead bodies. FEMA workers were to spray-paint doors with markings as to whether or not homes had bodies in them. Often times they got it wrong and family members would come back to their homes with markings indicating that there were no dead bodies inside only to walk in and tragically find a dead relative in a decomposed state. Once the floods subsided it could be seen that dead and badly decomposed bodies were littered all over the city of New Orleans. It took two months to drain the water from the city and begin clean-up efforts.

To add insult to injury, the state of Louisiana is very rich in natural resources such as oil and natural gas. Its wetlands are particularly important because they act as a storm buffer and help to purify the water. All types of fish, land animals, and birds live in and migrate to the wetlands creating thousands of jobs and billions of revenue dollars (this is why the 2010 BP oil spill has been so devastating to the region).

Louisiana produces 25% of the nation's natural gas and 20% of its oil. Louisiana's oil and gas are passed along to several states for profit, but at the time of Hurricane Katrina, Louisiana was not benefiting at all financially from the production and industrialization of these natural resources. Louisiana was not getting any percentage of the financial revenue. Whereas states such as Texas, New Mexico, Wyoming, Colorado, and Alaska were getting a piece of their own pie when it came to reaping a financial benefit from the utilization of their natural resources, Louisiana was not.

Because of this disparity, Governor Blanco sued the Government in May of 2006 and eventually made some significant inroads as a result of the lawsuit. In August of 2006, not too long after the initiation of the lawsuit, the Domenici-Landrieu Gulf of Mexico Energy Security Act was passed. Thirty-seven percent of offshore revenues would now go to the state of Louisiana along with other Gulf coast states. The disparaging news in all of this is that it took the devastation of Hurricane Katrina to make this happen and correct this egregious wrong. And although millions of dollars have been poured into the reconstruction and repair of the levees there is still warranted concern that not enough has been done to make certain that the levees and flood walls can withstand a category 5.

What makes the events of Hurricane Katrina an example of environmental racism is the fact that the devastation that this hurricane caused could have been avoided if the levees had been refurbished to withstand the waters. However, the Government, although aware that the strength of the levees was insufficient and that the non-restructuring of the levees would cause great ruin should a category 3, 4, or 5 hurricane hit, did nothing. Ultimately, it was the poor work on the levees that led to the terrible aftermath of Hurricane Katrina, not the hurricane itself. The tragedy could have been avoided by strengthening the levees.

One cannot help but wonder as to whether or not this apparent lack of interest in strengthening the levees was due to the shifting of wealth between 1927 and 2005, and the knowledge that in 1965 the worse of the flooding that resulted from Hurricane Betsy devastated the inner city but not the wealthy areas. It was already common knowledge that the waters would divert away from the wealthy segment of Louisiana just as the waters did in 1965 since not much had been done since then to better strengthen the levees. The Government knew, along with many Louisiana state officials and residents that the outskirts (the suburbs where most of the whites lived) were already protected from flooding and that the city of New Orleans, where mostly blacks lived, was left wide open.

INSTITUTIONAL RACISM IN THE FOSTER CARE SYSTEM

The child welfare system in America has many facets nationwide. The Department of Human and Social Services is the federal agency charged by statute to ensure protection of children in assuring that children in America are safe from abuse and neglect within their own families. Child protective services (the component of the Department of Human and Social services that investigates alleged abuse and neglect) has legal authority to petition the court to remove any child from a home environment that has been deemed by the Department as putting the child at risk of harm, whether environmentally, medically, physically, emotionally, and in some states; educationally.

Although the intentions of Social Services and the child welfare system (governed by child protection laws) are noble and although there have been many children removed from potentially dangerous home environments, there are a substantial number of children who would have been better off in the long run if they had never been removed from their home in the first place.

Great strides have been taken, in many states, within the last few years to decrease the number of children coming into care, but there still remains the disturbing trend in the system to remove children of color at an alarmingly substantially higher rate than white children even though the rate of abuse and/or neglect is no different for either group.

In 2006, the Joint Center for Political and Economic Studies Health Policy Institute published a report written by Ernestine F. Jones, entitled, "Public Policies and Practices in Child Welfare Systems that affect Life Options for Children of Color."[54] This report details the racial disparities and discrimination that exists in America's child welfare system. The Center cited a statistical report submitted by the Federal Interagency Forum on Child and Family Statistics. The report reveals that in 2003 there were 73 million minors (persons under the age of 18) living in America

---

[54] Jones, Ernestine F., *Public Policies and Practices in Child Welfare Systems that Affect Life Options for Children of Color*, Joint Center for Political and Economic Studies, Washington D.C., www.joingcenters.org, copyright 2006, http://www.jointcenter.org/hpi/files/manual/public%20Policies%20andPercent20P ractices%20inPercent20Child%20Welfare.pdf

and of those 73 million minors, roughly half a million had been removed from their homes by the child welfare system due to substantiated abuse and/or neglect. This means that suspected abuse or neglect was reported to the Department of Social Services[55] and the Department consequently investigated and came to the conclusion that there was enough preponderance of evidence of child abuse or neglect and risk of continued abuse and/or neglect to warrant petitioning the court for removal of the children from the home.

Statistics cited by the Black Administrators in Child Welfare Inc., (BACW) indicate that in 2004, there were 518,000 children in America's foster care system with the average age being 10 years old and the average time in care being 30 months.

According to a fact sheet entitled, "Racial Disproportionality in the Child Welfare System" published by the Jim Casey Youth Opportunities Initiative[56] in 2003, black children comprise roughly 20% of all the children in the United States but they represent approximately 40% of the children in the United States who have been removed from their homes and placed into the foster care system. This is alarming when compared to the statistics of removal for white children. The fact sheet indicates that white children make up 64% of the children living in America, which is a considerably higher number than black children. Despite this, white children represent only 31% of the children in America that have been removed from their homes and placed into the foster care system. Statistics from the Federal Interagency Forum supports this statistic indicating that although black children make up only one-fifth of the children living in the United States, they represent two-fifths of the children who have been placed into the foster care system, which means that black children account for twice the number of children in the system even though black people as a whole only make up approximately 13 % of the entire U.S. population.[57]

The Fact Sheet also cites some of the reasons for the disproportionality of children of color in care; one of which has to do with the difficulty mandated reporters and many who work within the system have in distinguishing poverty from neglect. Statistically, blacks live in poverty at

---

[55] There is a Department of Human/Social Services for each state although referred to differently in many states.

[56] Jim Casey Youth Opportunities Initiative, Racial Disproportionality in the Child Welfare System, copyright 2003, St. Louis Missouri, data for the Fact Sheet comes from Dorothy Roberts, Racial Disproportionality in the U.S. Child Welfare System, Annie E. Casey Foundation, 2002, Jennifer Clark, unpublished paper, 2002; CWLA, Child Abuse and Neglect: A Look at the States, 2000.

[57] Some estimates are now at roughly 15%.

a much higher rate than whites which automatically makes blacks more vulnerable to the child protection system. According to the National Poverty Center,[58] in 2008, 24.7% of blacks lived in poverty, 23.2% of Hispanics lived in poverty, and 11.6% of Asians lived in poverty while only 8.6% of whites lived in poverty. Persons on assistance are twice as likely to have a child protective services investigation substantiated as opposed to people who are not receiving monetary assistance from the government.

The overrepresentation of children of color in the foster care system is staggering. Latino children are overrepresented in 6 states, Native Americans are overrepresented in 24 states, and black children are overrepresented in 46 states. White children are not overrepresented. This disparity becomes even more vivid when looking at the breakdown of the disparity reflected in certain states that were focused on in the Joint Center Report.

According to the Report, when looking at the states of California, Florida, Georgia, Illinois, Maryland, and New York, the following statistics for year 2000 were prevalent: In California, black children made up only 7.5% of the population of children in that state while white children made up 34%. However, black children represented the same percentage of children in care (31%) as did white children. In Florida, black children made up 21.2% of the population of children while white children made up 55.4%. However, black children represented 47.1% of the children in foster care while white children represented 3% less than that. In Georgia, black children made up 34.4% of the population of children while white children made up 55.5%. However, black children represented over half of the population of children in the foster care system at 59% while white children made up less than half at 37.3%. In Illinois, black children made up just 18.7% of the population of children as compared to white children who made up over half in that state at 59.2%. However, black children represented an astounding 73.5% of the children in foster care while white children only represented 21.3%. In Maryland, black children represented 32.2% of that state's population of children while white children made up 55.9%. But again, black children represented an overwhelming 76.8% of children in foster care while white children only represented 21.3%. Finally, in New York, black children made up 19.3% of the population of children while white children made up 54.6%. However, black children represented 3.5% more children in the

---

[58] National Poverty Center, *Poverty in the United States Frequently Asked Questions,* The University of Michigan, Gerald R. Ford School of Public Policy, copyright, 2006 Regents of the University of Michigan, http://www.npc.umich.edu/poverty/

foster care system than did white children (blacks at 43.5% while whites were at 40.6%).

According to a 2009 Policy Brief provided by Casey Family Programs, entitled, "Disproportionality: The Overrepresentation of Children of Color in the Foster Care System," children of color constitute less than half of the child population of the United states at 42% but more than half of the children in foster care by 57%. Of the 42% of children of color that are in care in the United States, an astounding 33.9% are black with the population of black children at only 15.1% (a reduction from 2003).

One of the most unsettling discoveries in regards to the disparity issue when it comes to children in the foster care system is the fact that black parents and/or caregivers do not abuse their children or the children that they are caring for, at any greater frequency than white parents/caretakers do. According to the Joint Center report, the disparities that exist in the foster care system begin at the point of a protective services investigation. Black families are more likely to be investigated than are white families for the same alleged offenses, especially when the allegations have to do with emotional abuse, mental abuse/injury, drug use, alcohol use, neglect, death of a child, and/or a bad injury to a child.

The Joint Center study found that some of the reasons for these racial disparities are directly related to disparities when it comes to health care treatment. The Center cited a 2002 report written by Smedly, Stith and Nelson entitled, "Unequal Treatment, What Health care Providers need to know about Racial and Ethnic Disparities in Health care." The report revealed that it was determined that children of minorities are significantly less likely to receive appropriate health care as compared to children of whites even if the parents/caretakers of both do not differ in the ability they have to provide health care to their children. If then, blacks have a more difficult time getting their children the proper medical treatment solely based on the color of their skin and despite whether or not they have the means in which to do so, then black families are automatically more likely to be investigated for medical neglect of their children than are white families and therefore, are consequently more likely to have their children removed from their homes due to medical neglect.

The Joint Center study also revealed that doctors have a tendency to judge black parents much more harshly and prejudicially than they do white parents. Among a plethora of stereotypes, doctors often see blacks as not as smart as white people, as more prone to be non-compliant with health care advice than white people, and as more prone towards drug addiction than white people. It was found that these types of perceptions were basically unfounded and a result of racial bias. This kind of stereotyping often leads to more protective service complaints against black parents than complaints against white parents. There is often no concrete reason for the suspicion of child neglect or abuse aside from what the doctor may have conjured up in his (or her) own mind as a result of his discriminatory thinking that he or she might not even be aware of.

In a study conducted in the year 2000 by Johnson-Reid and Barth, as cited by the Joint Center report, it was found that there is a negative correlation between the foster care system and the juvenile justice system when it comes to the future of children who have been in foster care, specifically when children are in care due to some form of abuse. Unfortunately, a substantial number of children who have experienced the foster care system end up in jail or in prison as adults. They also often end up homeless. Johnson-Reid and Barth also found through their research that in many states, the majority of felony crimes committed were committed by adults who had once been in the foster care system.

As we saw earlier, further racial disparities exist when looking at the juvenile justice system. When it comes to the juvenile justice system, structural and systematic racism exists and is particularly evident when looking at certain stages in the process of legally declaring a minor a delinquent and bringing that minor into the system of juvenile correction. According to the Joint Center report, black youths are significantly more likely to be arrested and detained than white youths are for the same alleged offense. Black youths are also more likely to be charged, adjudicated a delinquent, be tried as an adult, and imprisoned significantly more than white youths are for the same alleged crimes. Research also shows that not only are black youths, who have been adjudicated as delinquents, more likely to be incarcerated than are white youths for the same crimes, but they are also more likely to be subjected to stricter sentencing.

With what has been said, there is no argument that a black child in America has a substantially greater probability of being brought into the foster care system and ending up in jail than a white child in America has, simply by virtue of being black.

Professionals in the field have begun to realize that there are unfair disparities made between families of color and white families and have begun to address the issue. It is believed that the problem not only has to do with racial bias but that it also has to do with systemic discrimination and that there is also a problem with the structure of the child welfare system itself. It is believed this is so because it has been determined that blacks who work within the system have been just as guilty as whites who work within the system of producing the disparities. The discrimination has become institutionalized to a point where the system itself is the catalyst for the racial inequities that exist within it.

Removal from the home is an extremely traumatic event for a child and most children do not fully recover from the emotional devastation of the event. Children should therefore only be removed from the home if it is absolutely necessary to their safety and wellbeing. Race, should never be a factor, intentionally or unintentionally.

In order to counteract the overrepresentation of children of color in America's child welfare system, certain organizations have stepped up to the plate. Included among the organizations heading the list are the Black Administrators in Child Welfare Inc. (BACW), the Joint Center Health Policy Institute (HPI), the Joint Center for Political and Economic Studies, and the Casey Alliance for Racial Equality (which consists of the Annie E. Casey Foundation, the Marguerite Casey Foundation, the Casey Family Programs, the Casey Family Services, the Jim Casey Employment Initiative, and the Center for the Study of Social Policy). Methodologies that have been implemented to address the problem include the redesign of the child welfare system as a whole which encompasses new approaches such as the restructuring of child placement procedures.

Despite the steps that are being made to combat the institutional racism that exists within America's child welfare system, there is still a long road ahead towards eradicating the overrepresentation of children of color within the system completely.

INSTITUTIONAL RACISM IN THE HOUSING MARKET

Although the Fair Housing Act has made discriminatory housing illegal; inequities still abound behind the scenes. Realtors have been notorious in using certain strategies to steer blacks away from white neighborhoods (often erroneously reporting that a property is no longer on the market when it is, or quoting a price for a home that exceeds what it is going for on the market and so forth) and many whites, when surveyed, are very vocal about not wanting to live in neighborhoods where the majority of the residents are black. Moreover, many are vocal about not wanting blacks to move into the neighborhoods that they reside in.[59]

Whites who do decide to move into black neighborhoods are not under any pressure to prove themselves worthy of being there. Neither are they under any pressure to prove that they are worthy of being in white

---

[59] In July of 2010 it was reported in the Detroit News as well as other news sources that black residents of Eastpointe Michigan (a suburb of Detroit composed mostly of white residents) received racially motivated threats in the mail demanding that they leave the neighborhood or be killed. The threats were brought to the attention of the local police and the FBI.

neighborhoods. However, it is the opposite for blacks. Blacks who move into white neighborhoods are often times put under an unspoken microscope and although it is not ever overtly stated, it is understood by both the whites in the neighborhood and the blacks that move in that the blacks must prove themselves worthy to be there.

White Flight

White flight occurs when whites begin moving out of neighborhoods that blacks begin to move into. It has been estimated that once blacks begin making up 15% of a neighborhood population that is majority white, many white people begin leaving that neighborhood. Many of them begin leaving because they are afraid their property values will decrease. Ironically, the onslaught of a sudden move of numerous people from a neighborhood does cause property values to decrease. So a self-fulfilling prophecy comes to pass. The value of the property goes down, not because black people are less valuable themselves, but because any sudden mass exodus from a neighborhood means a sudden rash of empty houses and a sudden rash of empty houses translates into a buyers market of which the real estate industry takes advantage of once the snowball effect begins. Real estate agencies have even been known to create this snowball effect themselves by purposely buying a house in an all white neighborhood, then selling the house to a black family for a lesser price which would often times cause white panic in the neighborhood causing the whites to flee, in turn creating a drop in property value for that neighborhood. The real estate agents would then sell the properties to other blacks for much higher prices (although the values had actually deceased), thereby making more in commissions than they would if they had sold to whites. This practice is called blockbusting and was a very popular practice until changes in housing laws prevented its continuation. The practice of blockbusting disappeared by the 80s but white flight is still a common occurrence today.

Because white flight is still a common occurrence, when a neighborhood that used to be majority white becomes majority black, property values have already decreased at the onset of the change. Therefore it is very easy for houses in one area of a community that is majority white to have higher property values than houses in another area of that same community in which mostly black people live. This kind of racial inequity that stems from individual racism and grows into institutional racism in the real estate market does, most definitely, put a housing barrier between blacks and the American Dream that is not there for whites in the sense that a black person can own the same kind of home as a white person with the same dimensions and number of square feet, but the value of the black person's home will probably be less than the value of the white person's home unless the black person lives in the same neighborhood as the white person and white flight has not yet begun to take place.

Predatory Lending

Predatory lending has taken place when banks lend unfair or inequitable mortgage loans to customers or lend loans to customers who do not meet the qualifications of being able to pay the loan back successfully.

Sub-prime lending is when a financial institution lends money to a borrower (who doesn't qualify for a loan at a prime lending rate because of a low credit score) at a higher interest rate in order to offset any possible risk of non-reimbursement from the borrower. It is one of the main causes that contributed to the housing market crisis of 2008 that has translated into thousands of foreclosed homes across America.

In 2006 the National Community Reinvestment Coalition published research results which gave data indicating that middle and upper class blacks who actually qualified for a prime loan were given sub-prime loans instead at double the occurrence that sub-prime loans were given to whites who had the same economic background. A lower interest rate yields a higher percentage of the monthly mortgage payment that is deducted from the principle owed on the house. Conversely, a higher interest rate would result in a lower percentage of the monthly payment going towards the principle and a lot more money going to the banks. During the hey-day of this type of lending, the sub-prime loans that were given to blacks created an imbalance between black and white homeowners overall when it came to the net wealth that was generated from owning a house. It has been estimated that because of this inequity the median net wealth of white homeowners was three times greater than that of black homeowners overall before the housing crash of 2008.[60]

---

[60] This information is taken from an online resource entitled *Predatory Lending and the Mortgage Crisis: A Modern Example of Structural Racism.*
http://www.eraseracismny.org/html/library/housing/resources/published_reports/P redatory_lending_mortgage_crisis.pdf which was referenced from Wilhelmina A. Leigh and Danielle Ruff, Joint Center for Political and Economic Studies #1, *African American and Homeownership, Separate and Unequal*, 1940 to 2006 (November 2007)

Redlining

Many discriminatory practices have emerged throughout America's history as a result of racial tensions and injustices manifested from the slavery era. Redlining is one of these practices which, when implemented, has a direct negative effect on the livelihood and quality of life of those who are the victims of it.

As discussed briefly in Chapter 3, the term *redlining* was first coined in the sixties and refers to the practice of disallowing or inflating mortgages and insurances for persons who live in certain areas. More often than not, the areas in which the mortgages and insurances are disallowed or substantially inflated are neighborhoods and cities where blacks and other minorities are the majority of the population. Not only has redlining occurred when it comes to housing but practices still exist today whereby minorities who live in urban areas are made to pay higher prices for the same services offered in suburban areas.

When the practice first began, real estate and insurance companies would literally draw a red line on a map in order to indicate to employees and other business owners which areas they would deny services and opportunities to. Although mortgages and insurances were on the top of the list when it came to denials of monetary loans and medical care coverage respectively, other services that were redlined included basic banking, health care access, and job opportunities. Moreover, certain major businesses would not place their retail chains inside the borders of urban cities where the majority of minorities reside.

Although redlining is not as prevalent in America as it once was, the practice still exists. Redlining is particularly evident today when looking at current car insurance rates for inner city America as compared to car insurance rates for suburban America. Instead of going strictly by the driving record of the consumer, car insurance companies are getting away with charging higher rates to people with good driving records who happen to live in certain areas (modern-day redlining). Suburban America pays substantially less in car insurance than do those who live in the urban inner cities and the majority of people who live in the inner cities are blacks and other minorities. Car insurance companies set prices according to zip codes and one car insurance company in particular was alleged to have set discriminatory prices according to education and occupation.[61]

---

[61] In 2006 GEICO was filed suit upon by Cohen, Milstein, Hausfeld and Toll PLLC and Nicholas Kaster & Anderson alleging that the company was discriminating against black Americans by setting higher insurance prices for blacks as compared to the prices they set for white consumers. The discrimination

To cite an example; the people of the city of Detroit continue to suffer this type of targeted discrimination emanating from the car insurance companies. In 2009 Detroit was identified as the 12th largest populated city in the United States with an estimated 821,792 people living within the city. Seventy percent of Detroit's population is black, which is a decrease from 80.1 % in 2006. But seventy percent is a good-sized majority. There is redlining taking place in the city of Detroit particularly when it comes to car insurance estimates. Detroiters (despite individual driving records and whether or not an insurance holder's car has ever been stolen or vandalized) are forced to pay three times more for car insurance coverage than those who live in the suburban outskirts. The only way Detroiters can get around the high insurance rates is to carry an exorbitantly high deductible. This is modern-day redlining. It is a discriminatory practice that has come to the attention of the city officials. But the practice has not been done away with and as of early 2010, 50% of the people residing in Detroit were unemployed (according to city officials). This means that a great majority of Detroiters cannot afford reasonable insurance premiums, let alone inflated ones. Not being able to pay inflated insurance prices leads many to risk driving without insurance particularly in cities like Detroit where public transportation is unreliable and there is no mass transit. It's a vicious cycle. Driving without insurance often leads to suspended licenses and the inability to drive a car negatively affects one's ability to get to work or to look for a job especially in cities where public transportation is unreliable and there is no mass transit. The cumulative effect of inflated insurance prices can be devastating for those who cannot afford insurance and can even lead to jail time for those caught driving out of desperation on a suspended license due to not having insurance.

Redlining creates a snowball effect. One inopportune situation leads to another and before long the very livelihood of the person caught in its snare is often at stake. Redlining is a racially discriminatory system that often times goes undetected. Detroit Michigan is not the only city in

---

tactics allegedly used had to do with making education the determinant as to the amount that would be charged. Reportedly and allegedly, customers who possessed only a high school diploma or less were identified as high risk and charged more for insurance premiums as compared to customers who had college or advanced degrees. Allegedly, GEICO was aware of the statistics. The percentage of blacks who possess college and advanced degrees is almost half that of the percentage of whites (17% as compared to 30% in 2005) who possess the same which would make the practice of setting prices according to education, discriminatory. There is no available proof that a person with a college degree is any better a driver than a person without a degree.

American where redlining is an issue. In almost every major city where blacks and/or minorities make up the majority of the population, there is some form of redlining.

INSTUTIONAL RACISM IN EDUCATION

Despite the fact that the Supreme Court rendered school "separate but equal" practices unconstitutional,[62] thereby making segregation practices in public schools illegal, most major universities during the time of Jim Crow[63] rarely accepted blacks or Jews into their educational system. This along with similar practices when it came to hiring blacks into professional jobs triggered the implementation of what is now the much debated Affirmative Action process.[64] One is also left to wonder whether or not separate and *unequal* practices still exist in the United States when it comes to minorities and education. Just by looking at observational data alone one could easily conclude that inner city public schools that service the majority of black elementary, junior high, and high school students in America are substantially inferior, on a significant level when it comes to physical environment as compared to the private and public schools that service the majority of white American students who are in the same grades. The physical environment of urban schools in America as compared to the physical environment of suburban schools are oftentimes significantly substandard with leaky toilets contributing to unsanitary bathroom conditions, pest control problems, overcrowding in the classrooms, lack of supplies, text book shortages, unhealthy lunches, the lack of air conditioned classrooms in the summer, asbestos endangerment, leaking roofs, falling plaster, and the like.

Jonathan Kozol has been writing about the discrepancies between inner-city public schools and suburban public schools since 1991. For years he has traveled the country to investigate the school environment disparities between black children and white children. From 2000 to 2005, Kozol visited sixty schools in eleven states over a period of five years (2000-2005). What he found was troubling, to say the least. Kozol's first book which was published in 1991 is entitled, "Savage Inequalities" and his second book (2005) is entitled, "The Shame of the Nation: The Restoration of Apartheid schooling in America." The titles of Kozol's books speak for themselves. In Kozol's "The Shame of the Nation," he is quoted as saying the following pertaining to one of the urban schools that

---

[62] See Chapter 3.
[63] See Chapter 3.
[64] Discussed later in this chapter.

he visited (the conditions of which resembled the majority of the urban schools that he visited):

> Fremont High School, as court papers document has "15 fewer bathrooms than the law requires." Of the limited number of bathrooms that are working in the school, "only one or two...are open and unlocked for girls to use." Long lines of girls are "waiting to use the bathrooms," which are generally "unclean' and 'lack basic supplies," including toilet paper. Some of the classrooms "do not have air-conditioning," so that the students "become red-faced and unable to concentrate" during the "extreme heat of summer." The rats observed by children in their elementary schools proliferate at Fremont High as well. "Rats in eleven...classrooms," maintenance records of the school report. "Rat droppings" are recorded "in bins and drawers" of the high school's kitchen. "Hamburger buns" are being "eaten off [the] bread-delivery rack," school records note. No matter how many times I read these tawdry details in court filings and depositions, I'm always surprised again to learn how often these unsanitary physical conditions are permitted to continue in a public school even after media accounts describe them vividly.[65]

This type of environment unquestionably makes it more difficult for one to learn in than an environment that is free of rats, roaches, unsanitary bathroom conditions, and sweltering heat. Children in urban public schools (which are for the most part, black children and other children of color), in general do not start on the same playing field as white children because of the substandard physical school conditions that are commonplace in inner-city schools all throughout America. This makes for a type of "separate and unequal" pre-college educational environment in America in which a substantial number of black children are attending environmentally substandard public schools while a substantial number of white children attend "state-of-the-art" suburban schools. It's difficult to

---

[65]Kozol, Jonathan. *The Shame of the Nation: The Restoration of Apartheid Schooling in America*, Three Rivers Press, an imprint of the Crown Publishing Group, a division of Random House, Inc., New York, 2005, p.177, Fair Use by permission of the publisher.

learn when one is dodging roaches, constantly wiping sweat, and trying not to go to the bathroom because the toilets are backed up. It goes without saying that children who are forced to learn in such unacceptable environments may find it more difficult to concentrate on their studies as opposed to the children of those privileged enough to attend schools that are environmentally sound and conducive to learning. The latter depiction does not normally describe inner-city schools but instead describes schools which cater to white children and schools set in suburbia away from children of color.

It has come to a point in America that it is almost impossible to find a "good-paying job" without a college degree. If then, the playing field is uneven in the elementary, junior high, and high school level when it comes to the disparity of environmental school conditions, then it is logical to conclude that because of the physical environments of the schools that minorities are made to endure, getting through school is more difficult for minorities which means that grade point averages can be negatively affected which means that getting accepted into college is more difficult which ultimately affects future employability. When taking into consideration this "snowball effect" one can hardly ignore the reality that the institutional racism of the educational system, as it relates to the physical environment of the inner-city school, can have a profound negative effect on the employability of children of color once they become adults.

INSTITUTIONAL RACISM IN THE WORKPLACE

During the fight for the civil rights of minorities in the sixties, it became evident that discriminatory hiring practices against blacks and other minorities as well as discrimination in the workplace was rampant across America. Something needed to be done to even the playing field and to decrease the trend towards significant minority under-representation. In order to take measures against discriminatory hiring practices and discriminatory practices within the workplace (such as discriminatory practices that affect promotions, merit pay, and the like) certain actions began to be taken. These actions included what is now known as Affirmative Action, the establishment of the Equal Employment Opportunity Commission, and the enactment of the Equal Opportunity Act all of which are discussed next along with the counteractive effects of what are referred to as the "glass ceiling" and "white privilege" phenomena.

Affirmative Action

Affirmative Action is a series of Executive Orders, orders, and policies developed since the early sixties to ensure that minorities and women are given the same job opportunities in the workplace as white men are. Over time, the definition expanded to include race equity when it comes to college admissions and opportunity for academic advancement. Affirmative Action began as a phrase coined by President John F. Kennedy in 1961 who by Executive Order 10925, mandated Federal contractors to "take affirmative action to ensure that applicants are treated equally without regard to race, color, religion, sex, or national origin."[66] The first three introductory statements of the Executive Order read as such:

> WHEREAS discrimination because of race, creed, color, or national origin is contrary to the Constitutional principles and policies of the United States; and 13 CFR 1960 Supp.
>
> WHEREAS it is the plain and positive obligation of the United States Government to promote and ensure equal opportunity for all qualified persons, without regard to race, creed, color, or national origin, employed or seeking employment with the Federal Government and on government contracts; and
>
> WHEREAS it is the policy of the executive branch of the Government to encourage by positive measures equal opportunity for all qualified persons within the Government...[67]

Three years later the Civil Rights Act of 1964 was signed into law. Part of that Act prohibited employers from discriminating. The Equal Employment Opportunity Commission (EEOC) was also established during that year. The following year, in 1965, President Lyndon B.

---

[66] The History of Affirmative Action Policies, Americans for a Fair Chance, Washington D.C. http://www.inmotionmagazine.com/aahist.html, published in *In Motion Magazine*, October 12, 2003. Online resource. Fair use.

[67] President John F. Kennedy, Executive Order 10925, 1961, taken from Internet resource http://www.thecre.com/fedlaw/legal6/eo10925.htm Government document. Public Domain.

Johnson expanded upon Kennedy's Order by issuing Executive Order 11246 which required affirmative action of all government contractors to ensure the hiring of minorities and to ensure that equal employment opportunities would be given to minorities. In 1967 Johnson added to this via an Amendment to his earlier order. The Amendment mandated that federal contractors were also to guarantee that women would be given fair opportunity for employment as well as minorities.

In 1970 President Richard Nixon added an order to the previous executive orders. Nixon's order addressed the "underutilization" of minorities in the federal contractual workforce and put in steps to reverse this trend. Nixon revised the order a year later to include women. In 1979 the Supreme Court ruled, in a case involving the United Steel Workers of America, that if there was reason to believe that inequities were being practiced due to race then the factor of race could be brought in as an additional consideration when hiring and promoting employees as long as doing so did not jeopardize the employment rights of white employees.

By 1985 there were efforts being made by some of President Ronald Reagan's constituents to do away with Johnson's Executive Order 11246 that was established in 1965. But this attempt at repeal was unsuccessful at the time. In 1986 the Supreme Court again voted to resolve and correct the discrimination that was being placed upon minorities by the steel unions. The court also established barriers for any further discrimination by allowing race to be a factor in certain employee decisions when it came to minority racial equities. In 1987 the Supreme Court ruled similarly in another court case involving the Transportation Agency of Santa Clara County California in which it was deemed that women and minorities were significantly underrepresented in the workplace and therefore consideration of race and gender, in order to decrease discrimination, could be considered when hiring.

In 1995 the Equal Opportunity Act was put into law by Congress. The Act prohibits discrimination on the basis of race, gender, religious beliefs, and other factors. The Act forbids indirect discrimination as well as direct discrimination in the workplace, schools and colleges, clubs, local governments, and in any business that provides goods and services. In light of this Act, the University of California has done away with its Affirmative Action policies as has Universities in Washington and Michigan. But in 1995, the Glass Ceiling Commission released a report which uncovered the fact that the ingrained discriminatory practices still persisted to exist, despite the Act, and therefore suggested that Corporate America continue to use Affirmative Action as a way to fight what had become a form of discrimination that was not easily seen; an

174

institutionalized structural form of employment and education discrimination against minorities and women.

The Glass Ceiling

The "Glass Ceiling" is a phrase that was coined in the eighties and refers to a workplace environment in which executive opportunities are denied to women and minorities. The metaphor is used as such; the hopeful executive candidate who is a minority or woman can look up and see the next level but doesn't realize that, for them, they are looking through a clear glass ceiling invisible to the naked eye and that once they begin reaching for the next level they eventually bump into the glass and finally realize that it is there. The glass symbolizes the institutional racism and sexism that creates barriers for promotion and advancement for women and minorities.

The Glass Ceiling Commission was established by Congress in 1991 and was created in order to study the trend in America that promotes white men to the top of the executive corporate ladder (a phenomenon seen in public and private industry) while putting up invisible barriers to prevent women and minorities from reaching those same levels. The Commission researched, studied, and published their findings between 1991 and 1996 and was composed of twenty-one Commissioners. In his introduction to the Commission's fact-finding report of 1995, Robert Reich, Secretary of Labor at the time, was Chairman of the Commission. He wrote:

> Thanks to the leadership and vision of Secretary Elizabeth Dole—and that of her able successor, Secretary Lynn Martin—the Department of Labor became closely involved in identifying and publicizing the glass ceiling problem, issuing a Report on the Glass Ceiling Initiative in 1991. Senator Robert Dole, who introduced the Glass Ceiling Act in 1991 praised Martin's report noting that it "confirms what many of us have suspected all along—the existence of invisible artificial barriers blocking women and minorities from advancing up the corporate ladder to management and executive positions." For this Senator the issue boils down to "ensuring equal access and equal opportunity."[68]

---

[68] Glass Ceiling Commission, *Good for Business: Making full use of the Nation's Human Capital, The Environmental Scan,* A Fact-Finding Report of the Glass

In this report it was determined that 97% of the top corporate executives in America were white men. It was also determined that minorities who did make it to the top, were compensated less in wages than were their white counterparts. There has been little improvement since the 90s. In 2003, reports from the United States Census Bureau showed that women still make roughly 25% less than men do for doing the same job and for possessing the same skill sets. And recent reports from the Ethnic Majority[69] indicate that black Americans in particular (as opposed to other minorities) are compensated 21% less in wages than their white counterparts who do the same job and have the same educational background.

In the Executive Summary portion of the report it was documented that there are three main barriers that prevent racial and gender promotional equity in the workplace, which are: societal barriers, internal structural barriers, and governmental barriers.

Societal barriers can include a conscious or unconscious use of stereotyping and racial/gender bias. Internal structural barriers often embrace recruitment efforts that exclude women and minorities, produce an office environment that tends to make minorities and women feel uncomfortable and not part of the social office network, excludes minorities and women from the office "pipeline" that channels information through the corporation, agency, or department about certain promotional opportunities that have come about (this exclusion of minorities often comes in the form of racially motivated nepotism, cronyism, and the "good ol' boys" network), promotes the tendency not to include minorities and women on committees, task forces, and the like that would make them more visible and give them more opportunity to advance, and also promotes the tendency to expect more from the job performance of minorities and women than that of white men when it comes to promotions.

The old adage in black America that says that blacks have to work twice as hard as whites do to prove that they are on the same level of competency and proficiency at their jobs as whites are, was proven true by the Commission. Additionally, governmental barriers also include inconsistent legal enforcement of laws against discrimination in the workforce. When taking the aforementioned into consideration, it can be

---

Ceiling Commission, Washington D.D. 1995. Government document. Public Domain.

[69] The Ethnic Majority is the name of a website (www. EthnicMajority.com) that was found by Clifford Tong in 2002. Tong is the CEO of Diverse Strategies, a management consulting firm.

safely assumed that more often than not, minorities who break the glass ceiling often find themselves being set up to fail or sabotaged in their work efforts, not only by those under their authority but often times by the Executives above them as well.

White Privilege

The phrase "white privilege" was first coined in a 1988 essay written by Dr. Peggy McIntosh[70] entitled, White Privilege and Male Privilege: A Personal Account of Coming to see Correspondences through Work in Women's Studies." Dr. McIntosh is white and is famously quoted as saying the following in her essay:

> I think whites are carefully taught not to recognize white privilege, as males are taught not to recognize male privilege. So I have begun in an untutored way to ask what it is like to have white privilege. I have begun to see white privilege as an invisible package of unearned assets that I can count on cashing in each day, but about which I was "meant" to remain oblivious. White privilege is an invisible weightless knapsack of special provisions, maps, passports, codebooks, visas, clothes, tools, and blank checks.[71]

The special provisions, maps, passports, and etc. that Dr. McIntosh refers to are figurative descriptions of societal privileges. Dr. McIntosh goes on to identify what she refers to as some of the "daily effects" that she experiences that come about as a result of the automatic invisible and unspoken privileges she has as a result of being white that minorities do not have. Her list is autobiographical. She compared herself only with black American female colleagues who worked with her in the same building at the time. Some of the 46 daily advantages that she identifies as connected chiefly, though not exclusively with her race, are as follows in her own words:

---

[70] Associate Director of the Wellesley Center for Women.

[71] McIntosh, Peggy. Taken from her essay entitled, *White Privilege and Male Privilege: A Personal Account of Coming to see Correspondences through Work in Women's Studies.* Center for Research on Women, Wellesley College, MA, copyright ©1988. p. 1, Used by permission of the author.

- If I should need to move, I can be pretty sure of renting or purchasing housing in an area which I can afford and in which I would want to live.
- I can be reasonably sure that my neighbors in such a location will be neutral or pleasant to me.
- I can go shopping alone most of the time, fairly well assured that I will not be followed or harassed by store detectives.
- I can turn on the television or open to the front page of the paper and see people of my race widely and positively represented.
- I can be sure that my children will be given curricular materials that testify to the existence of their race.
- Whether I use checks, credit cards, or cash, I can count on my skin color not to work against the appearance that I am financially reliable.
- I did not have to educate our children to be aware of systematic racism for their own daily physical protection.
- I can speak in public to a powerful male group without putting my race on trial.
- I can do well in a challenging situation without being called a credit to my race.
- I am never asked to speak for all the people of my racial group.
- I can be reasonably sure that if I ask to talk to "the person in charge," I will be facing a person of my race.
- If a traffic cop pulls me over or if the IRS audits my tax return, I can be sure I haven't been singled out because of my race.
- I can be pretty sure that an argument with a colleague of another race is more likely to jeopardize her chances for advancement than to jeopardize mine.
- I can be fairly sure that if I argue for the promotion of a person of another race, or a program centering on race, this is not likely to cost me heavily within my present setting, even if my colleagues disagree with me.
- If I declare there is a racial issue at hand, or there isn't a racial issue at hand, my race will lend me more credibility for either position than a person of color will have.

- I can worry about racism without being seen as self-interested or self-seeking.
- If my day, week, or year is going badly, I need not ask of each negative episode or situation whether it has racial overtones.
- I can think over many options, social, political, imaginative, or professional, without asking whether a person of my race would be accepted or allowed to do what I want to do.
- I can be sure that if I need legal or medical help, my race will not work against me.
- If I have low credibility as a leader, I can be sure that my race is not the problem.[72]

Much of what Dr. McIntosh lists supports the discussion regarding institutional/systematic racism that has been discussed already in this chapter. Dr. McIntosh boldly shed light on the subject of the great advantage whites have in American society just by being white.

This white privilege is present in every area of everyday living and particularly manifests itself in the workplace, law enforcement, judicial settings, hospitals, schools, and colleges. It even manifests itself when it comes to the debate as to whether or not the Confederate Flag should be allowed to be flown or as to whether or not its image should be made available for purchase by those who want to display it (e.g. some states allow motorists to purchase the image of the Confederate flag for personalized license plates). Black America sees the Confederate flag in the same way the Jews see the swastika: as a sign of racial oppression. In the eyes of most black people, the Confederate flag represents the cruel and brutal enslavement of Africans; but despite this, white America retains the privilege to publicly wave this flag and place its image on various items, including stamps and license plates.

We can even see white privilege when looking at the media coverage of missing persons. Television airwaves are loaded with questionable imbalances when it comes to minority representation. To justify this statement one only has to look closely at certain programming and at what is deemed as news worthy events. Missing white children and missing

---

[72] McIntosh, Peggy. Taken from her essay entitled, *White Privilege and Male Privilege: A Personal Account of Coming to see Correspondences through Work in Women's Studies.* Center for Research on Women, Wellesley College, MA, copyright © 1988. Used by permission of the author.

white adults are often covered in the national television news media for months on end until the missing person, or unfortunately, the missing person's body is found. Not only are white children, who are missing, more likely to receive national television coverage in order that they might be found but their pictures are more likely to be distributed on milk cartons, billboards and the like than are black children and other minority children who are missing. There are no statistics here; just simple observation. Consistent media coverage is rarely given to minority children and adults who are missing, particularly blacks. As a matter of fact, such coverage is so rarely given to blacks that it's easy to wonder whether there are any blacks missing.

Although white privilege is present in every area of everyday living, it is very insidious and not easily seen nor readily recognized particularly by those who enjoy its benefits.

White privilege is the first cousin to racial discrimination. Where there is white privilege there is sure to be discrimination lurking closely in the shadows (e.g. the glass ceiling phenomenon is a type of racism in and of itself). This is why those who speak of eliminating Affirmative Action should not speak of doing so unless they also speak of eliminating white privilege and glass ceilings. Otherwise, Affirmative Action, although not the most perfect system is one of the few, if not the only, check-and-balance that minorities have to fight against systematic racism in the workplace and in the universities and colleges as well.

CHAPTER SUMMATION

Although many facets of institutional racism have been discussed; what has been covered is only a segment of the racial discrimination that exists in America pivoted against blacks and other minorities. Much of this discrimination is subtle, but it's there.

We've specifically looked at institutional racism when it comes to the vote, the election of politicians, law enforcement, the judicial system, Hollywood, beauty standards, the health care system, the environment as a whole, the foster care system, housing, schools and education, and the workplace. The riveting fact is that any experience that a minority might have in being the target of racism, within any of these institutions that has been discussed (or within any institution that has not been discussed for that matter), has the potential to considerably negatively affect that person for the rest of his or her life. But it doesn't stop here. Now that we have taken a detailed look as to what racism and discrimination is, its history in America, and racism in its current form, we are ready to examine a very troubling side to all of this indeed...racism in religion.

6.

Racism in Religions and Ideologies Associated with Christianity

One of the most troubling forms of racism that looms across America aside from institutional/systematic racism is religious racism. Religious racism[1] can be found in the pages of certain religious books or can be the result of the misinterpretation of religious doctrine. In this chapter we will take a look at two particular religions that identify themselves with Christianity (the Christian Identity movement and the Mormons) that currently promote racism or have promoted racism in the past. A detailed description of the doctrines and beliefs of true orthodox Christianity is provided in the Appendix.

Since this book is aimed at dispelling the belief that the Bible condones racism, we are taking a look at the Christian Identity Movement and Mormonism (although there are additional religions besides these two that condone racism or have done so in the past) in order to argue against the particular racist doctrines that both religions have a history of propagating that have been inaccurately tied to orthodox Christianity. We will also be debunking a false teaching that has survived throughout the ages which says that black people are biblically cursed to be the slaves and we will be looking at the phenomena of the "white church" and the "black church."

THE CHRISTIAN IDENTITY MOVEMENT

Christian Identity began in 1940 when white supremacists identifying themselves as Christians decided to form their own churches. Their doctrine teaches racism. Members of the movement (not limited to but including the Ku Klux Klan) see themselves as descendants of the nation of Israel due to the fact that the northern kingdom of Israel was defeated by the Assyrians around 722 B.C.

Christian Identity is a white racist extremist religious movement that fosters white supremacist views. The progression of militia groups that exist throughout the United States has been triggered by the religious teachings of Christian Identity (oftentimes simply referred to as Identity).

---

[1] See Chapter 1.

Each state in America has active Identity organizations. And other white supremacy groups such as the Aryan Nations and the Ku Klux Klan embrace the religious doctrine that Identity promotes.

General teachings of Christian Identity

Identity teaches that people of the "white race" (specifically white people with Anglo-Saxon, Celtic, or German ancestry) are really God's chosen people whom the Bible speaks of and that they, not the Jews, are the true Israelites. It teaches that Adam was the father of the white race only and that Christianity is only for white people. Those who embrace Identity believe that white people are "the lost sheep of the House of Israel" and tend to involve themselves in political agendas that express and support a very strong anti-government way of thinking. They also believe that the Jews and any person of color are out to annihilate white people and that the Jews are literally the product of a sexual union that they say took place between Eve and the devil himself. They believe that the serpent (the devil) that tricked eve in the Garden of Eden was a "Negro."

In addition, Identity movement participants say that people of color, are the "beasts of the fields" spoken of in the book of Genesis. They believe that people of color are on the same levels as animals. They teach what they call the "purity of the white race." Interracial marriages are therefore vehemently discouraged because for Identity, preserving the "purity" of the white race is of the highest priority.

According to Christian apologetic author Richard Abanes, Christian Identity followers basically believe that Adam and Eve were not actually the first two human beings but they were instead the first two *white* human beings (whom they refer to as Aryans), that the Israelites of the Old Testament were not Jewish but were instead white, and that all white people today have come from them, that all other people who are not white are an entirely different species of being and are pre-Adamic (meaning that they existed before Adam and Eve), that the Jewish people are actually descendants of Satan himself, that Jesus was not Jewish but instead he was white, and that Armageddon[2] will be a race war between the Caucasian race and all other races.

Aside from the above, the most grievous doctrine that Christian Identity teaches is that Jesus Christ is the Savior of the white race only and that everyone else has been born into spiritual damnation and destruction simply because they're not white.

---

[2] Revelation 16:14-16 coupled with Revelation 19:11-21, see your Bible

Specific teachings of Christian Identity

The foundation of the teachings of the Identity movement is set in its members' misrepresentation and misinterpretation of the biblical creation account. They believe that all non-white people are not descendants of Adam and Eve but are instead descendants of a group of people, who have no souls, whom they believe, were created before Adam and Eve. They teach that these pre-Adamic people are spiritually inferior to the white race that they say came from Adam and Eve. They go on to say that "race-mixing" was the original sin in the Garden of Eden and that God caused a flood (Genesis chapters 6 and 7)[3] to cover the earth because of this so-called sin of race-mixing. Since they believe that people of color are beasts, they combine this particular part of their racist theology with the passage of Scripture located in Leviticus 20:15-16. The commands cited in the passage were part of those commands given to the Israelites during the dispensation of the Law in which God commanded that certain actions be met with capital punishment. The passage reads:

> [15]If a man has sexual relations with an animal, he must be put to death, and you must kill the animal. [16]If a woman approaches an animal to have sexual relations with it, kill both the woman and the animal. They must be put to death; their blood will be on their own heads." (NIV)

Since those in the Identity movement believe that people of color are beasts and since God commanded (during the Dispensation of the Law[4])

---

[3] See your Bible.

[4]Most Christian theologians believe that there are seven dispensations (time periods) to which the Bible refers: The dispensations of Innocence, Conscious, Human government, Promise, the Law, Grace, and Kingdom. We are now living in the dispensation of Grace; the period during Christ's ministry on earth and after his resurrection. There are different God-ordained rules for the different time periods. For instance, in the book of Leviticus, God's Law declared that an adulterer and an adulteress must be put to death (Leviticus 20:10, see your Bible), but in John 8:1-11 (during the dispensation of Grace of which we are now in) we see the account of when Jesus spared a woman caught in the act of adultery from being executed (see your Bible). She was given grace, as those of us are given grace now, who have confessed Jesus Christ as Lord and have confessed the sins that we have committed. Although the principles of the Law still apply, Jesus fulfilled the Law. Therefore, although during the dispensation of the Law, God commanded the nation of Israel to put men and women to death who had sex with

that those who had sexual relations with beasts be put to death, then Identity concludes that during the Dispensation of the Law, white people who had sexual relations with people of color were put to death by the flood because by having sexual relations with people of color they were really having sexual relations with beasts and therefore deserved to have been put to death.

They continue with this disturbing line of reasoning by adding that Seth[5] took the place of Abel (who was murdered by Cain[6]) as the original seed of the white race. They go on to identify Cain as the first Jew, as a man who had sexual relations with those whom they say came from the pre-Adamic people, and as a child of Satan. They believe that people of color and Jews are descendants of Cain. Because of this, they teach that the Jews are literal demons, which is why they believe that the Jews cannot be saved (go to heaven when they die). They also conclude that the serpent was the most highly intelligent beast of the field and that this particular beast was really a "Negro." So, their bottom line is that Eve had sex with the serpent, who was really Satan, who they say was black. Identity theology concludes that the white race must therefore continue to fight an ongoing battle, spiritual and otherwise with what they call the "bastard race-mixed" offspring of Satan and Eve.

Those in the Identity movement believe that the promise[7] that God made to Abraham is a promise that belongs to the white race and no one else.

Although Identity members fancy themselves as the "real" Jews, they will not use the word "Jew," in the sense that the rest of the world uses it and in the sense that the Bible uses it. Instead they prefer to say that they are the actual descendants of the original twelve tribes of Israel spoken of throughout the Old Testament.

---

animals, the part of the command that mandates execution no longer applies since Jesus died for our sins and since those who believe on him are atoned for. However, the immorality of having sex with an animal still applies. It is still wrong to have sex with an animal, but the act, along with all other immoral acts, is no longer subject to capital punishment because Jesus atoned for our sins on the cross through his own death. By saving the woman caught in adultery, Jesus not only saved her from execution, but his action also did away with capital punishment altogether.

[5] Genesis 4:25: "Adam lay with his wife again, and she gave birth to a son and named him Seth, saying, 'God has granted me another child in place of Abel, since Cain killed him.'"

[6] See the historical account of Cain under the heading "The Mormons and their contribution to racism."

[7] See Chapter 7

As stated earlier, the Identity movement also contends that Jesus was not Jewish, despite the many references in the Bible to the contrary. They further teach that Judaism and being Jewish evolved from a satanic pagan religion and that during Jesus' earthly ministry, he preached to the white race only. With this line of reasoning Identity movement members must explain away the word "Gentile" since the Bible tells us repeatedly in the New Testament that the gospel is for the Gentiles (non-Jews) as well as the Jews. They therefore apply a false meaning to the word "Gentile" just as they do to the word "Jew." They erroneously conclude that the word "Gentile" applies to white people who assimilated with other nations during the time of the apostles. However, "ethnos" is the Greek word for Gentile and its meaning refers to nations of people, not a specific "race" of people.

Those who embrace Identity theology also assert that salvation is for white people only. They believe that all other people are satanic in actual nature and can therefore not be saved. This makes for a very dangerous theology because this type of theology says that there are those who were born into damnation and those who were born into salvation. But according to the Bible, God has given everyone an opportunity to accept or reject Christ. According to the Bible, God's free gift of salvation has nothing to do with the color of one's skin but instead with whether or not one has confessed Jesus Christ as Lord and Savior and believes in his/her heart that Jesus was raised from the dead.

Those involved in Identity believe that Jesus Christ was the ultimate racial separatist. Not only do they teach a "racial purity" doctrine which says that whites cannot marry outside of their race and that to do so would be what they call "race-mixing" but they also add that whites should not live with non-whites. Moreover, they declare that all non-Israeli nations that were spoken of in the Bible (especially in the Old Testament), were composed of people who were from the "seed of the serpent," in other words, these they say, are children of the devil.

Those who adhere to Identity theology even go so far as to say that the Holocaust that was perpetrated against the Jews under Hitler's[8] reign, never actually happened and that the historical event itself is nothing but a hoax aimed at eliciting sympathy for the Jewish population.

---

[8] Adolph Hitler ruled Germany from 1933 to 1945. He was also the leader of Germany's Nazi Party (National Socialist German's Worker's Party) at the time. He became the leader of the Nazi's in 1921. He gained great power during his reign. In his quest for "race cleansing" Hitler was the force behind the extermination of 6 million Jews and 5 million others including Soviet POWs, ethnic Polish people, and the disabled. The killing began in 1933 and didn't stop until 1945.

When it comes to their relationship to the United States Government, Identity theorists believe that white people should not be taxed because they say that the land of America really belongs to white people. They feel that non-whites should be taxed.

Identity adherents believe that they are at war against the children of Satan whom they define as anyone who is non-white and they see this war as a religious battle in which the "Children of Light" (whom they identify as themselves) are pitted against the "Children of Darkness" whom they also identify as the "Serpent seed." Because of their belief that they are at war, many of those involved in the Identity movement stockpile weapons and participate in militias in preparation for their perceived inevitability of what they term as a racial holy war. They believe that the "Children of Darkness" sit high in Government seats and that therefore the Government is the main institution conspiring against them. Because of this, they see the Government as an enemy and as an institution to be defeated.

Timothy McVeigh,[9] the man convicted for the 1995 Oklahoma City bombing had similar views as those expressed by Identity advocates. McVeigh belonged to an anti-government white supremacist militia organization and was eventually convicted of eleven charges related to the bombing of the 1995 Alfred P. Murrah Federal Building in Oklahoma city. The blast from that bombing killed 168 people including 19 children. This event gives credibility to the stance that, for the most part, militia organizations in the United States are American homeland terrorist groups and are just as dangerous, as any other terrorist group.

Despite their criticisms of the government and their beliefs in government conspiracy theories against them, Identity advocates are very patriotic. Unfortunately, along with their patriotism comes the belief that all non-whites that are citizens of the United States really have no right to be citizens and that white people should not live in any area which is not white-majority populated. They also believe that the laws of the land do not apply to them and that no woman or person of color should be able to rule over them.

THE MORMONS

Joseph Smith is the founder of the Mormon religion (also referred to as the Church of Jesus Christ of Latter Day Saints) and is an example of a man who twisted the meanings of biblical Scripture in an effort to prove the erroneous belief that the white race is superior. He created his own racist theology by misinterpreting Scripture and unfortunately continued to

---

[9] Discussed in Chapter 5

identify himself as a Christian when in actuality what he had created was and still is a *cult* of Christianity. Mormonism is still practiced world-wide as a religion today.

Joseph Smith was born on December 23, 1805 in Sharon Vermont. He was raised as a Christian. However, when Smith was only 14 years of age, he alleged that he saw a vision of two persons who instructed him not to join any of the Christian denominations existing at the time. He also alleged that one of these "persons" was identified as God's beloved son (only Jesus is identified in this manner in the Bible[10]) who told him that all the sects of Christianity were theologically in error and not to join any of them. Smith further claimed that one of these persons identified himself as Moroni and appeared glorious beyond description. Moroni had supposedly told Smith that there was another book besides the gospel of Jesus Christ which contained "the fullness of the everlasting Gospel." As Smith put it, this book was written on gold tablets which he said he found on a Hill called Cumorah. However, he claimed that characters, not words, were inscribed on the plates. Smith, along with a former schoolteacher of his, claimed to have translated the message on the plates into what Smith called, "The Book of Mormon."

It was not long after, that Smith began to claim he was receiving new divine revelations. Eventually, he authored a second book entitled, "Doctrine and Covenants," in which he wrote about these revelations. Smith basically rewrote certain biblical Scriptures in an effort to support his new "revelations".

Among the many twisted versions of Scripture Smith offered to the public was one that affected how Mormons (and other whites who supported the Latter-Day Saints) thought of blacks. Smith's revision of the Bible introduced a doctrine that taught that the Canaanites were cursed with black skin as punishment for their sins. This *cursed-black* theory added to the already existing theory accepted among many white people at the time (especially those who owned slaves) that blacks were cursed by God to be slaves;[11] hence, it was all right to mistreat them. This misinformation had been passed down through the ages beginning from the sixth century and progressed throughout the years. Unfortunately, without reading or studying for themselves, many blacks began to think that the Bible actually said these things thereby eventually triggering an eventual resistance towards the Bible and Christianity by a significant number of blacks.

---

[10] Matthew 3:16-17 KJV. See your Bible.

[11] This teaching is discussed later in this chapter under the subheading "The False Doctrine of the Black curse."

Joseph Smith was killed in 1844 by an angry mob after having been charged with treason and jailed. However, his altering of Scripture lived on.

The Mormons have taught that everyone pre-existed in heaven before birth and that Lucifer[12] organized a great rebellion in heaven during this pre-existence. Their teaching goes on to say that Lucifer organized this rebellion when he discovered that Christ was chosen to redeem the world and that there were those in heaven that took sides with Christ and those that took sides with Lucifer. The Mormons concluded that those who sided with Satan were born on earth as "Negroes" and that all black people have genealogies that begin with Cain (the man who killed Abel). They further taught that the mark that God gave Cain, to punish him for killing his brother, was a mark of "a flat nose and black skin."[13] Joseph Smith is quoted as saying that Cain became the "father of an inferior race."

The Mormons' account of Lucifer deviates significantly from what the Bible says about him. The Scriptures teach that Lucifer rebelled against God but not because Christ was to redeem the world, as the Mormons teach, but because he became prideful due to his beauty and that he wanted to be like God. Ezekiel 28:12b-17 attests to this. It says:

> [12b]This is what the Sovereign Lord says "You were the model of perfection, Full of wisdom and perfect in beauty.
>
> [13]You were in Eden, the garden of God; every precious stone adorned you: ruby, topaz and emerald, chrysolite, onyx and jasper, sapphire, turquoise and beryl. Your settings and mountings were made of gold. On the day you were created they were prepared.
>
> [14]You were anointed as a guardian cherub, for so I ordained you. You were on the holy mount of God; You walked among the fiery stones.
>
> [15]You were blameless in your ways from the day you were created till wickedness was found in you.
>
> [16]Through your widespread trade you were filled with violence, and you sinned. So I drove you in disgrace from the mount of God, And I expelled you, O guardian cherub, From among the fiery stones.

---

[12] Satan; the devil

[13] The historical account of Cain and Abel is found in Genesis 4:1-16. See your Bible.

¹⁷Your heart became proud on account of your beauty,
and you corrupted your wisdom because of your
splendor. So I threw you to the earth; I made a spectacle
of you before kings (NIV)

The guardian cherub referred to in the passage is Lucifer. Lucifer's heart became proud, so God expelled him from heaven. Lucifer had exalted himself above measure which is even more evident in the following passage:

¹²How are thou fallen from heaven, O Lucifer, son of
the morning! how art thou cut down to the ground,
which didst weaken the nations!
¹³For thou hast said in thine heart, I will ascend into
heaven, I will exalt my throne above the stars of God:
I will sit also upon the mount of the congregation, in
the sides of the North:
¹⁴I will ascend above the heights of the clouds: I will
be like the most High.
¹⁵Yet thou shalt be brought down to hell, to the sides
of the pit. (Isaiah 14:12-15 KJV)

According to the Bible, Lucifer wanted to exalt himself to the position of God. Lucifer became puffed up because of his beauty and position. According to the Bible, because of Lucifer's rebellion, there was a war in heaven between himself and Michael, the archangel. Lucifer lost the war and he and the angels that fought with him were cast from heaven to the earth, as we see below:

⁷And there was war in heaven: Michael and his angels
fought against the dragon; and the dragon fought and his
angels,
⁸And prevailed not; neither was their place found any
more in heaven.
⁹And the great dragon was cast out, that old serpent,
called the Devil, and Satan, which deceiveth the whole
world: he was cast out into the earth, and his angels were
cast out with him. (Revelation 12:7-9 KJV)

Although the Mormons have taught that everyone pre-existed in heaven and that those who were kicked out of heaven with Satan were cursed to be "Negroes" on earth, the verses of Scripture cited above say nothing of the sort. The Scriptures instead indicate that those who were cast out with Satan were angels who rebelled with him (verse 9), not pre-existent human beings. In the verses, the dragon is identified as the devil and the devil is identified as Satan. The name *Satan* means *adversary*. After Lucifer rebelled against God, he became God's adversary, as well as the adversary of mankind. The Bible refers to the angels that were cast out with Satan as demons. The subject of the devil is discussed further in the following chapter.

The Mormon's teaching that black people are cursed with black skin because of a pre-existent alliance with the devil is clearly something that was taught that has no merit. Because of social pressures, the Mormons denounced this belief in 1978, but the damage had already been done. Not only had they taught racist doctrine pertaining to the events that took place in heaven at the time of Lucifer's fall, but they also took it further with their teachings on the mark of Cain. As stated before, the Mormons have taught that the mark that Cain was cursed with, after slaying his brother, was black skin. But let's take a look at what the Bible has to say about the matter. The following is the entire account:

> [1]Now Adam knew Eve his wife, and she conceived and bore Cain, and said, "I have acquired a man from the LORD" [2]Then she bore again, this time his brother Abel. Now Abel was a keeper of sheep, but Cain was a tiller of the ground. [3]And in the process of time it came to pass that Cain brought an offering of the fruit of the ground to the LORD. [4]Abel also brought of the first-born of his flock and of their fat. And the LORD respected Abel and his offering, [5]but He did not respect Cain and his offering, And Cain was very angry, and his countenance fell.
> [6]So the LORD said to Cain, "Why are you angry? And why has your countenance fallen? [7]If you do well, will you not be accepted? And if you do not do well, sin lies at the door. And its desire is for you, but you should rule over it."
> [8]Now Cain talked with Abel his brother; and it came to pass when they were in the field, that Cain rose up against Abel his brother and killed him.
> [9]Then the LORD said to Cain, "Where is Abel your brother?" He said, "I do no know. Am I my brother's keeper?"

[10]And He said, "What have you done? The voice of your brother's blood cries out to Me from the ground. [11]"So now you are cursed from the earth, which has opened its mouth to receive your brother's blood from your hand. [12]"When you till the ground, it shall no longer yield its strength to you. A fugitive and a vagabond you shall be on the earth." [13]And Cain said to the LORD, "My punishment is greater than I can bear! [14]"Surely You have driven me out this day from the face of the ground; I shall be hidden from Your face; I shall be a fugitive and a vagabond on the earth, and it will happen that anyone who finds me will kill me." [15]And the LORD said to him, "Therefore, whoever kills Cain, vengeance shall be taken on him sevenfold." And the LORD set a mark on Cain, lest anyone finding him should kill him. [16]Then Cain went out from the presence of the LORD and dwelt in the land of Nod on the east of Eden. (Genesis 4:1-16 NKJV)

Cain's offering to the Lord was not acceptable. The Scriptures do not really tell us why Cain's offering was not acceptable but just that it wasn't. Cain became angry because his offering wasn't accepted. However, God assured Cain (verse 6 and 7) that there was no reason to be angry because if he did well then his offering would be accepted. With this, God was telling Cain that Cain still had the opportunity to offer something that would be pleasing to the Lord. But Cain did not heed God's words and instead took his anger out on his brother, Abel, by murdering him. As punishment for this murder God cursed Cain to be a fugitive and vagabond (verse 12) and to toil the ground in futility. Cain responded by pleading with the Lord, saying that his punishment was too much for him to bear and that people would set out to kill him because he was now a fugitive guilty of murder. Because of Cain's appeal, God had mercy on Cain declaring that anyone who set out to kill Cain would incur the wrath of God. God therefore put a mark on Cain.

It is important to note that the mark was not an initial part of the curse. God put a mark on Cain after Cain's appeal for mercy. The mark was used as a way of protecting Cain from the vengeance of other people who might set out to kill him. It was a way of giving notice to others not to do Cain any harm. This mark actually protected Cain from his adversaries.

The Scriptures do not tell us what kind of mark this was that God placed on Cain. There is absolutely no indication that the mark was black skin color or a "flat nose." Furthermore, this mark was given as a warning to other people *not to harm* or kill Cain. Being black in America has historically brought the opposite. From the time of slavery up into the 1960s (and even today when it comes to institutional racism) having black skin did more to *insure* mistreatment from others than to prevent it. Therefore, the mark of Cain certainly could not have been black skin, because God gave Cain a mark that would *discourage* harm to the bearer of it.

Before continuing, it should be emphasized that there are clear passages in the Bible that speak against adding to or taking away from the Scriptures, of which Joseph Smith was obviously guilty. Let's look at some of these passages:

> [18]For I testify unto every man that heareth the words of the prophecy of this book, If any man shall add unto these things, God shall add unto him the plagues that are written in this book:
> [19]And if any man shall take away from the words of the book of this prophecy, God shall take away his part out of the book of life, and out of the holy city, and from the things which are written in this book. (Revelation 22:18-19 KJV)

In verse 18 above, "this book" is referencing the book of Revelation. Although the passage specifically references the book of Revelation when speaking of the plagues that will be added to those who add to Revelation and when speaking of the exclusion from the book of life of those who subtract from Revelation, the passage is also indicative of how God feels about all inspired Scripture contained within the texts of the Bible. Without question, no one should add to or take away from the Scriptures of the Bible (the word of God). Galatians 1:8-9 brings the point home even further with the following quote:

> [8]But even if we or an angel from heaven should preach a gospel other than the one we preached to you, let him be eternally condemned! [9]As we have already said, so now I say again: If anybody is preaching to you a gospel other than what you accepted, let him be eternally condemned! (NIV)

192

Paul, the apostle, is the one speaking in the above scriptural quote. He emphasized the disdain of altering the gospel or preaching a totally different gospel other than that of Christ by repeating himself when speaking of one's punishment for doing so. That person will be eternally condemned. Some biblical translations say that the person will be cursed.

Joseph Smith allegedly saw a vision of two men who told him to oppose Christian denominations. He also claimed that one of these men (whose name he says was Moroni) gave him another gospel to preach other than the gospel of Christ. But the Bible warns us about men and women who preach another gospel and God is very clear about how he feels concerning fake prophecies. The following passage of Scripture from the book of Jeremiah makes clear God's stance when it comes to altering his message:

> [23]Am I a God who is only close at hand?" says the LORD. No, I am far away at the same time.
> [24]Can anyone hide from me in a secret place?
> Am I not everywhere in all the heavens and earth?" says the LORD.
> [25]"I have heard these prophets say, 'Listen to the dream I had from God last night.' And then they proceed to tell lies in my name. [26]How long with this go on? If they are prophets, they are prophets of deceit, inventing everything they say. [27]By telling these false dreams, they are trying to get my people to forget me, just as their ancestors did by worshiping the idols of Baal.
> [28]"Let these false prophets tell their dreams, but let my true messengers faithfully proclaim my every word. There is a difference between straw and grain!
> [29]Does not my word burn like fire?" says the LORD.
> "Is it not like a mighty hammer that smashes a rock to pieces?
> [30]"Therefore," says the LORD, "I am against these prophets who steal messages from each other and claim they are from me. [31]I am against these smooth-tongued prophets who say, 'This prophecy is from the LORD!' [32]I am against these false prophets. Their imaginary dreams are flagrant lies that lead my people into sin. I did not send or appoint them, and they have no message at all for my people. I, the LORD have spoken. (Jeremiah 23:23-32 NLT)

God himself has told us that there are those who prophesy, teach, and preach in his name that spread lies in his name. God identifies them as false prophets. Joseph Smith was one of these false prophets. The Bible does not say that black people were cursed. The Bible does not say that black people were pre-existent beings that sided with Satan and were therefore cursed with blackness. The Bible does not say that the mark of Cain was black skin. However, Joseph Smith taught and perpetuated these lies and did so in the name of Christianity. By doing so Joseph Smith fits the description of a false prophet and as one whom God defines in verse 26 as a prophet who lies from the deceit of his own heart. Joseph Smith also fits the description of a false prophet that causes his people to err by his lies, found in verse 32. Many white Americans erred by believing Joseph Smith's racist doctrines. These racist doctrines have been added to the Bible by men who try to prove the false belief that one race of people is superior to another.

THE FALSE DOCTRINE OF THE "BIBLICAL BLACK CURSE"[14]

For many years a substantial number of whites in America justified the enslavement of blacks by saying that blacks were cursed to be slaves by God. There are people who still believe this today and many, including black Americans, feel that the Bible supports this belief.

The false doctrine of cursed blacks stems from the misinterpretation of a particular biblical account of Noah and his three sons. But before moving forward in examining the account, we need to take a look at a certain theological belief that fuels this false doctrine; and that is the belief that Ham was black.

The sons of Noah were Ham, Shem, and Japheth. There is some discrepancy, when looking at different commentaries, as to the Hebrew meanings of their names. In his book, *Beyond Roots*, William Dwight McKissic defines the names as such:

> The name Ham means 'dark or black,' Shem means 'dusky or olive colored,' and Japheth means 'bright or fair.'[15]

---

[14] Dodds, Elreta, *What the Bible Really says about Slavery: This and other Information on the issue of Slavery as it applies to History and Religion,* Press Toward The Mark Publications, Detroit Michigan, Revised Edition, Third Printing, copyright © 2000.The majority of the text under this subheading is taken directly from chapter six of What the Bible Really says about Slavery. All rights reserved. Used by Permission of the publisher.

[15] McKissic, William Dwight Sr., *Beyond Roots: In Search of Blacks in the Bible* (Woodbury, NJ: Renaissance Productions, Inc. 1990) p. 51, Fair use.

Other scholars come to a different conclusion. Strong's Greek and Hebrew Lexicon gives the Hebrew meaning of the name *Ham* as "hot or warm," the Hebrew meaning of the name *Shem* as "reputation or fame," and the meaning of the name *Japheth* as "opened." The Holman Bible Dictionary agrees with Strong and defines Ham's name as meaning "hot" in the Hebrew, Shem's name as meaning "fame" (which correlates with reputation) in the Hebrew, and Japheth's name as meaning "may he have space" (which correlates with "opened") in the Hebrew.

Holman and Strong's Hebrew translation of the three names (Ham, Shem, and Japheth) do not translate the names into *black, olive colored,* and *fair.* Despite this, the meaning of the three names as applying to the races have proliferated much of the literature that has been written about what many refer to as the "curse of Ham."[16] Consequently, the result of this has been a misunderstanding and misconstruing of the scriptural passages that give account to the curse, stemming from the belief that Ham was black, Japheth was white, and Shem was somewhere in between.

However, the belief that Ham was black is not without some reasoning. The Egyptians are descendants of Ham and come from his lineage. Egypt is an African country and historians agree that a substantial portion of ancient Egyptians were people of color. Japheth's sons, according to Genesis 10:2 were Gomer, Magog, Madai, Javan, Tubal, Meshech, and Tiras all of whom, according to Holman, fathered nations associated with Indo-European peoples. Abraham was born through the line of Shem. The Israelites (the Jewish people) came from the Abrahamic line and therefore Shem is considered a patriarch of Semitic peoples. Because of the nations of people that descended from each son, many theologians consider Noah to be the father of all the human races. But this identification comes into question when considering that all human beings come from one bloodline; Adam[17] (discussed in detail in the following chapter).

For the purposes of our discussion, we are most concerned with the meaning of the name *Ham.* Most theologians would agree that if the definition of "hot" were used then the word "hot" itself is referring to the climate in which Ham lived. Strong's Lexicon also informs us that the word *Ham* was later used as a collective name for the Egyptians. Again, historians agree that the majority of ancient Egyptians were people of color. So, for many people this means that Ham was black. Therefore, Mckissic's translation of the name *Ham* is not without some merit. And

---

[16] This author has fallen prey to this in earlier of her writings.

[17] From one man he created all the nations throughout the whole earth. He decided beforehand when they should rise and fall, and he determined their boundaries. (Acts 17:26, NLT)

despite the discrepancy in the definition of the name when exploring commentaries, it appears that the majority of theologians believe that Ham was black and therefore so were the Canaanites (since Canaan was the son of Ham). However, the writers of the New International Version Study Bible contend that the Canaanites were Caucasian.[18] If this is indeed so then the entire *blacks are cursed* doctrine is even more conspiratorial than suspected.

When it comes to the actual curse cited in the Scriptures as related to Ham, the Bible tells us that Canaan (Ham's son) was cursed to be the slave of Shem and Japheth (and his descendants slaves to their descendants). Some have erroneously interpreted this to mean that the black race is altogether cursed to be slaves of the white race and other races since it is believed by many theologians that Ham was black and therefore that his son Canaan was also black (and that descendants of Japheth were white). Genesis 9:18-27 contain the verses of Scripture that have been misinterpreted throughout the centuries by some to mean that blacks are cursed to be slaves, thus the enslavement of blacks and discrimination against them justified. Let's take a look at what Genesis 9:18-27 says:

[18]The sons of Noah who came out of the ark were Shem, Ham and Japheth. (Ham was the father of Canaan.) [19]These were the three sons of Noah, and from them came the people who were scattered over the earth.
[20]Noah, a man of the soil, proceeded to plant a vineyard. [21]When he drank some of its wine, he became drunk and lay uncovered inside his tent. [22]Ham, the father of Canaan, saw his father's nakedness and told his two brothers outside. [23]But Shem and Japheth took a garment and laid it across their shoulders; then they walked in backward and covered their father's nakedness. Their faces were turned the other way so that they would not see their father's nakedness.
[24]When Noah awoke from his wine and found out what his youngest son had done to him, [25]he said, "Cursed be Canaan! The lowest of slaves will he be to his brothers."
[26]He also said, "Blessed be the LORD, the God of Shem! May Canaan be the slave of Shem.
[27]May God extend the territory of Japheth; may Japheth live in the tents of Shem, and may Canaan be his slave." (NIV)

---

[18] Barker, L. Kenneth; NIV Study Bible, 10th Anniversary Edition, Zondervan Publishing Company; Grand Rapids Michigan copyright© 1995, p. 20 (Commentary)

First, it is interesting to note that although many theologians identify this event as the curse of Ham, Canaan (one of Ham's sons), as mentioned earlier, was the one who was actually directly cursed. Canaan's descendants would be slaves of Shem and Japheth's descendants. Most theologians interpret that the brothers that Canaan's descendants will become slaves of to be referring to the descendants of Shem and Japheth. However, Shem and Japheth were technically Canaan's uncles. There are two possible explanations for the identification of Shem and Japheth as Canaan's brothers instead of Canaan's uncles; the first being that the term "brother" is used loosely since Ham who was their actual brother was indirectly cursed through the cursing of Canaan, or the second being that the account is referring to Canaan's literal brothers in addition to Shem and Japheth. Either way, there is no doubt that Canaan's descendants were to be the slaves of the descendants of his close relatives, Shem and Japheth.

Although McKissic's stance that Ham was black and therefore Canaan was black can be questioned, McKissic refutes, with the following words, the false doctrine of blacks being cursed:

> Canaan, Ham's youngest son, is perhaps associated with Ham in most Bible students' minds (more so than his older brothers) because of the curse of Canaan recorded in Genesis 9:20-26. There is no doubt about it; the Canaanites were Black.

> The descendants of Ham led very advanced civilizations that predate Semitic and Japhethic civilizations by at least two thousand years, which may explain the reluctance of some scholars to identify the ancient Egyptians, Canaanites, Libyans and sometimes even the Ethiopians with the modern day Negro. Some scholars label these groups as white with dark skin.

Mckissic goes on to say:

> Biblically speaking, a curse lasted three or four generations (Exodus 20:5). What was the curse? Canaan was assigned servitude to Ham's brothers, Japheth and Shem. Why was Ham not cursed? According to Dr. Custance, in Hebrew thought, Noah could not have cursed Ham without cursing himself. When and how was the curse fulfilled? Most scholars believe that the curse was fulfilled when the Canaanites were conquered by Israel and became subservient to the Israelites. It is interesting to note that

of Ham's four sons (Ethiopia, Egypt, Libya and Canaan), Canaan
is the only one that does not exist today as a nation.[19]

Ham had four sons. They were: Cush, the father of the nation of
Ethiopia, Mizraim, the father of the nation of Egypt, Phut, the father of the
nation of Libya, and Canaan. At one time the Canaanites inhabited what is
now called Palestine. Ethiopia, Egypt, and Libya are African countries.
Native Africans who have African ancestry are usually considered to be
black or to be people of color. Therefore, it stands to reason that if all
blacks had been cursed then Cush, Mizraim and Phut would have had to be
cursed also. However, they were not.

It cannot be denied that theoretically Ham is the original ancestor of
Ethiopia, Egypt, and Libya which are all African countries comprised of
black people. This fact in and of itself gives credence to the viewpoint that
Ham was a person of color in some way.

During the Jim Crow era in America, a person was considered to be
black if he or she had as little as one-eighth ancestral "black blood."
Respectively, if Ham was black then Noah and/or his wife must have also
been black in some way, at least according to early American standards of
racial identification. As previously stated in chapter 3, whites labeled
blacks according to the degree of black ancestry they had in their
genealogical history. American racial identification laws basically
categorized anyone as "Negro" who had as little as one sixteenth "black
blood"[20] or anyone who had discernable black facial characteristics.
Therefore, according to those standards, if we are to say that Ham was
black then Shem and Japheth would have to be defined as having been
black as well no matter how fair-skinned they actually appeared since by
biologically parenting Ham, Noah and/or or his wife would have had to be
black in some way (at least according to early American definitions of
blackness) and since Shem and Japheth were biologically parented by
Noah and his wife also; then they too would have had to have been black
in some way.

To further the argument, we need to bring focus to the fact that the
Scripture passage tells us that Canaan was cursed to serve Shem and
Japheth. Therefore, when taking into account these early American
standards of defining racial identity, we have no other choice but to

---

[19] McKissic, William Dwight, *Beyond Roots: In Search of Blacks in the Bible,*
Renaissance Productions Inc., Woodbury, New Jersey, p.64. Fair use.
[20] There is no such thing as black blood or white blood. Blood is blood. But for the
purposes of explaining the mindset of the time, the terminology "black blood" is
being used.

conclude that one black brother (Canaan) was cursed to serve two other black brothers (Shem and Japheth). If one contends that a person who possesses only a sixteenth of black blood should be defined as black or at least as a person of color subject to denial of certain privileges enjoyed by whites, then that same person must contend that Shem and Japheth were black. Consequently if, according to early American standards of racial identification, Shem and Japheth were black, then the whole theory of the black race being cursed is blown apart by the mere fact that one brother could not serve the other if all were cursed to serve. How can the entire black race be cursed to be slaves of whites if the slave as well as the one to be served were both black?

In taking the argument a step further, a curse lasted three or four generations. In the following quote, the Holman Bible Dictionary gives us a good understanding of what the Bible says the length of a generation is:

> A generation did not necessarily have a specific number of years. Genesis 15:13-16 apparently equates 400 years with four generations, thus 100 years per generation. Numbers 32:11-13 may reckon a generation as 60 years, it including people twenty and above and giving them forty more years to die. Or one may interpret this to mean a generation is the forty years of adulthood between ages 20 and 60. God promised Jehu his sons would rule to the fourth generation, apparently meaning four sons (2 Kings 10:30; 15:12). Jehu began ruling about 841 B.C., his first son Jehoahaz about 814 B.C. and the fourth generation Zechariah died about 752 B.C. The five generations ruled less than 90 years, while the four sons' generations ruled about 60 years. This is reducing a generation to quite a small number. After his tragedies Job lived 140 years and saw four generations (Job 42:16). This would make a generation about 35 years. Basically, generation is not a specific number of years but a more or less specific period of time. (Compare Job 8:8; Isa. 51:9.) The literal Hebrew expression "generation and generation" thus means through all generations or forever (Ps. 49:11). Similarly, 'to you (his, their) generations' means forever (Num. 10:8).[21]

The curse of Canaan was never described in Scripture to have been implemented to last through unlimited generations. This curse was not to last forever. The Canaanites no longer exist as a nation today. The

---

[21] Excerpt taken from Holman Bible Dictionary, Editor, Trent C. Butler, c 1991 Holman Bible Publishers, pgs. 539-540. Used by permission of the Publisher.

Canaanites were among a nation of five other nations that were overthrown by Israel during antiquity. We see this in the following passage of Scripture in which God is speaking to the Israelites:

> [20]Behold, I send an Angel before thee, to keep thee in the way, and to bring thee into the place which I have prepared.
> [21]Beware of him, and obey his voice, provoke him not; for he will not pardon your transgressions: for my name is in him.
> [22]But if thou shalt indeed obey his voice, and do all that I speak; then I will be an enemy unto thine enemies, and an adversary unto thine adversaries.
> [23]For mine Angel shall go before thee, and bring thee in unto the Amorites, and the Hittites, and the Perizzites, and the Canaanites, the Hivites, and the Jebusites: and I will cut them off. (Exodus 23:20-23 KJV)

If the Canaanites, along with the other aforementioned nations, do not exist today, then it would stand to reason that Noah's curse upon Canaan ceased when the nation itself ceased to exist. In the preceding passage of Scripture we see that the Canaanites were grouped with nations that were to be cut off, which means that the generations of Canaanites ceased to be. Even if Ham's sin did result in a curse that was to affect the generations of his descendants; because of God's mercy, the curse would have had no effect after about the third or fourth generation. It could certainly have had no effect if the generation was non-existent.

Although the Canaanites no longer exist, blacks do. Therefore the question becomes: how can a race of people, said to be the generation of a cursed people, live under a curse whereby the original nation of people that were cursed are non-existent and have been for some time? The Canaanites were cut off. There are no more generations of Canaanites. Furthermore, Canaan's descendants were cursed to be slaves because they were *his* descendants, not because they were black. The curse was upon the nation of Canaan, and had nothing to do with the skin color of those who comprised the nation. Skin color is incidental to the matter. To say that all blacks are cursed since Canaan was cursed and he was black is like saying all people who are six feet tall are cursed since Canaan was cursed and he was six feet tall (or whatever height he may have been). We would see the latter conclusion as preposterous. Well, the former conclusion is just as preposterous. Height or any other physical attribute would be incidental to the matter. The curse applied to a nation of people, not a race of people.

When we examine the passage of Scriptures closely that document the lives of Noah and his sons, we can clearly see that blacks are not living under an enslavement curse, or under any other curse for that matter that goes beyond the curses that all human beings are living under resulting from the disobedience of Adam and Eve while they were in the Garden of Eden.

"WHITE CHURCH" / "BLACK CHURCH"

One of the most somber results that have come about from the continued racial divide in America is the racial separation of the church. Just as America is often referred to as two Americas: "white America" and "black America," the church in America is often referred to as two churches: the "white church" and the "black church." Simply put: white Christians and black Christians basically worship God on Sunday mornings, separately. Truly integrated churches do exist in America, but are rare. Most white people attend churches in which over ninety percent of the parishioners are white and most black people attend churches in which over ninety percent of the parishioners are black. This is so much so that the church is seen as divided between racial lines and the terms "black church" and "white church" have as a result, been coined.

There are many reasons why racial groups have a tendency to worship separately from other racial groups as opposed to interactively. Reasons range from different cultural practices of worship, different tastes in musical styles, language barriers, denominational preferences, church locations, and so on. These reasons are not necessarily seen as objectionable reasons. However, the separation of the black and white church began with the white church, specifically during the days of Jim Crow, refusing to worship with blacks. The refusal had only to do with race. Because of the color of their skin, blacks were not allowed in white churches on Sunday mornings. Blacks therefore began forming their own churches and the black pastor ultimately became the most powerful figure in the American black community. Although blacks have, historically, been denied entry into white churches; in general, whites have never been denied entry into black churches.

Not only were blacks denied entry into white churches during the Jim Crow era and/or given the unspoken understanding that they were not welcome during the Civil Rights Movement, but the white Protestant church was, overall, as mentioned before, a strong supporter of the Ku Klux Klan in its hey-day. The white Protestant church would often times allow members of the KKK to speak at their churches on Sunday morning[22] and oftentimes the Klan would visit in full regalia. Many white Protestant pastors were part of the Klan themselves. This made way for even greater racial separation of the church between blacks and whites. The white Protestant church, for the most part, was not only a partaker in the racism that was hurled against blacks during the nineteenth and early twentieth centuries but the white church as a whole, during that time, basically remained silent while blacks struggled for the same freedoms that whites had. And although there are surely white churches today that speak out against racism and there have surely been white churches that have done so in the past, the white church in America, as a whole, for the most part, is still relatively silent today when it comes to taking a stand against institutional racism.

The Bible is clear, however, that there is just one church, overall. Although Scripture speaks of different churches in different cities (e.g. the church of the city of Corinth, the church of the city of Galatia, the church in each of the seven cities spoken of in Revelation, and etc) and even multiple churches were spoken of in certain areas; it is understood that although each church had different concerns that had to be addressed and different problems that had to be sorted out there was still, spiritually speaking, only one church. Scripture refers to the church as a whole as the "body of Christ" as evidenced in Paul's message to the Corinthian church in which he said the following:

> [4]There are different kinds of gifts, but the same Spirit.
> [5]There are different kinds of service, but the same Lord.
> [6]There are different kinds of working, but the same God works all of them in all men.
>
> [7]Now to each one the manifestation of the Spirit is given for the common good. [8]To one there is given through the Spirit the message of wisdom, to another the message of knowledge by means of the same Spirit, [9]to another faith by the same Spirit, to another gifts of healing by that one Spirit, [10]to another miraculous powers, to another prophecy, to another distinguishing between spirits, to another speaking in different kinds of tongues, and to still another the interpretation of tongues. [11]All these are

---

[22] This is not to say that the black church has not been guilty of the same thing in times past, as well, wherein the black church, as a whole, has also invited black leaders into the pulpit that were known to express black supremacist views.

the work of the one and the same Spirit, and he gives them to each one, just as he determines.

[12]The body is a unit, though it is made up of many parts; and though all its parts are many, they form one body. So it is with Christ. [13]For we were all baptized by one Spirit into one body—whether Jews or Greeks, slave or free—and we were all given the one Spirit to drink.

[14]Now the body is not made up of one part but of many. [15]If the foot should say, "Because I am not a hand, I do not belong to the body," it would not for that reason cease to be part of the body. [16]And if the ear should say, "Because I am not an eye, I do not belong to the body," it would not for that reason cease to be part of the body. [17]If the whole body were an eye, where would the sense of hearing be? [18]But in fact God has arranged the parts in the body, every one of them, just as he wanted them to be. [19]If they were all one part, where would the body be? [20]As it is, there are many parts, but one body.

[21]The eye cannot say to the hand, "I don't need you!" And the head cannot say to the feet, "I don't need you!" [22]On the contrary, those parts of the body that seem to be weaker are indispensable, [23]and the parts that are unpresentable are treated with special modesty, [24]while our presentable parts need no special treatment. But God has combined the members of the body and has given greater honor to the parts that lacked it, [25]so that there should be no division in the body, but that its parts should have equal concern for each other. [26]If one part suffers, every part suffers with it; if one part is honored, every part rejoices with it.

[27]Now you are the body of Christ, and each one of you is a part of it. [28]And in the church God has appointed first of all apostles, second prophets, third teachers, then workers of miracles, also those having gifts of healing, those able to help others, those with gifts of administration, and those speaking in different kings of tongues. [29]Are all apostles? Are all prophets? Are all teachers? Do all work miracles? [30]Do all have gifts of

> healing? Do all speak in tongues? Do all interpret? [31]But
> eagerly desire the greater gifts. And now I will show you
> the most excellent way. (1 Corinthians 12:4-31 NIV)

God gives spiritual gifts to the members of the church as he pleases. Paul specifically taught that not every Christian has every gift and that the gifts are divided among Christians the way God sees fit. There were some in the church that were putting more significance on certain gifts as opposed to others. But Paul explained that all the gifts are important because they make up a whole, just as all the different parts of the body are important because they make up a whole body and there is no part of the body that we can do without. Paul therefore compares the church, as a whole, to a body, made up of specific bodily parts. Specific attention is brought to verses 12 and 13 in which the Scriptures teach that those in the church are baptized into one body no matter if they are "Jews or Greeks, slaves or free" and that though there are many parts, there is still only one body of believers; one church altogether.

So, though there are many churches in America, and many church buildings, and many church affiliations and denominations, and though there is what Americans call "the black church" and "the white church," the Scripture teaches that all those who are in the church [and are truly saved] are baptized into *one body* no matter what color they are, no matter what race they are, and no matter what their ethnic background is; there is really only one church. So, just as members of the church are not to put more significance on certain gifts as opposed to other gifts; it would certainly then stand to reason that members of the church should not put more significance on one race of people as opposed to other races of people, particularly since, for those who are in Christ, there is no Jew or Greek which translates into there is no black or white, or Hispanic, or Asian, or Arab or Native American, but we are all one in the Lord. If therefore there is a "black church" and a "white church" due to preferences in worship styles or the like, then that's one thing; but if there is a "black church" and a "white church" due to underlying racism on the part of either of these churches, then that's another thing; a thing that is not acceptable with God.

CHAPTER SUMMATION

There is no doubt that there are people who continue to follow the precepts of certain theological doctrines that teach racism against people of color. Those who are a part of the Aryan Nation, the Ku Klux Klan, and white militia groups embrace the misinterpretations of the Bible that misguidedly justify racism against people of color. It is also questionable whether or not all of Mormonism has truly totally denounced its racist doctrines against blacks that its founder promoted and taught.

It is clear, however, when looking at what has been discussed so far, that the Bible has been unjustly vilified as one of the main religious sources that supports racial discrimination and has been falsely used to justify racial prejudice of one group against another. The Christian Identity movement misrepresents Scripture and adds racist overtures to the Scripture that simply aren't there as had Joseph Smith done when it came to certain doctrines of Mormonism. And when it comes to the account of the curse of Ham, it has been clearly shown that the belief of some that take the curse to mean that all black people are forever cursed to be subservient to white people is indeed a misunderstanding and a misinterpretation of the passage of Scripture that describes the account.

Racism has been so indoctrinated into the society of America that we have seen the development of what is now called the black church and the white church. The irony of this is that the church as a whole appears to be comfortable with these two distinctions when in essence these distinctions speak to the historical infiltration of racism into the church more so than just a cultural phenomenon of worship style preference. In looking further into the question as to whether or not the Bible condones racism and racial discrimination, we will progress into a more detailed discussion, with regard to what the Scriptures teach, in the following chapter.

7.

THE BIBLICAL PERSPECTIVE ON RACE AND RACISM

Before getting into this discussion, it is important to lay a foundation as to some of what the Bible teaches about God. The Bible teaches the following: there is one God who represents himself in three personages: The Father, The Son (Jesus Christ), and The Holy Ghost. The Son (Jesus Christ) was manifest as a man to die on the cross in order that his blood may atone for the sins of the world. Jesus Christ proved that he was God manifested in the flesh by predicting his own death, burial, and resurrection, and then by being raised from the dead, three days after he was crucified, as he predicted.[1] Jesus walked the earth as a testimony to his resurrection for forty days and was seen by over five hundred people during this time. After these forty days Jesus ascended into heaven to be seated (as he initially had been before being manifest as a man and coming to earth) at the right hand side of the Father. In order to go to heaven (to be saved) when one dies, one must have openly confessed (at some point in life) that Jesus is Lord (Savior and God) and that God raised him from the dead (Romans 10:9).

Those who follow the teachings of Jesus Christ and believe in the basic doctrines of the Christian faith are identified as Christians; followers of Christ. Christians believe that the Bible is the infallible unadulterated word of God and that it stands alone as such. A more comprehensive explanation of the tenets of the Christian faith is provided in the Appendix.

Unfortunately, many people believe that the Bible condones racism and because of this belief, they do not embrace the Bible. Grievously, the belief that the Bible condones racism is often fueled by those who are racists themselves and identify themselves as Christians. They misuse the Bible to generate their bigoted views. However, the Bible speaks volumes against racism.

---

[1]Jesus answered them, "Destroy this temple and I will raise it again in three days." The Jews replied, "It has taken forty-six years to build this temple, and you are going to raise it in three days?" But the temple he had spoken of was his body. After he was raised from the dead his disciples recalled what he had said. Then they believed the Scripture and the words that Jesus had spoken. (John 2:19-21). Jesus raised himself from the dead which is proof that he is God, the Son. There is one God who represents himself in three persons: Father, Son, and Holy Ghost.

If God is a racist and if the Bible condones racism, then there should be verses in the Bible that say that one race of people is genetically superior to another race of people. There should also be proof that one race of people has a better chance than another race of people to make it into heaven simply by virtue of their race. If God is a racist then there should be no biblical indication of equality among humans. If God is a racist then we should be able to find Scriptures that speak of skin color and facial structures as characteristics that determine who is superior and who is inferior. But as we will see, there is great biblical evidence of equality among humans, there is no biblical evidence that one race of people is genetically superior to another, and there is no Scripture that focuses on skin color and facial structure as determinants for human superiority or inferiority, nor as determinants for divine favor. This chapter is dedicated to centering upon certain Scriptures that prove that God is not a racist and that the Bible does not teach or condone racism in any way.

THE BIBLE WHEN IT COMES TO RACIAL CATEGORIES

Contrary to what many might believe, the Bible does not place people into racial categories. The Bible places people into two basic categories: children of God and children of the devil. Jesus himself said so as evidenced by the following passage of Scripture:

> [42]Jesus said to them, "If God were your Father, you would love me, for I came from God and now am here. I have not come on my own; but he sent me. [43]Why is my language not clear to you? Because you are unable to hear what I say. [44]You belong to your father, the devil, and you want to carry out your father's desire. He was a murderer from the beginning, not holding to the truth, for there is no truth in him. When he lies, he speaks his native language, for he is a liar and the father of lies. [45]Yet because I tell the truth, you do not believe me! [46]Can any of you prove me guilty of sin? If I am telling the truth, why don't you believe me? [47]He who belongs to God hears what God says. The reason you do not hear is that you do not belong to God. (John 8:42-47 NIV)

The apostle John goes on to elaborate in the first letter that he wrote to the church...

[8]He who does what is sinful is of the devil, because the devil has been sinning from the beginning. The reason the Son of God appeared was to destroy the devil's work. [9]No one who is born of God will continue to sin, because God's seed remains in him; he cannot go on sinning, because he has been born of God. [10]This is how we know who the children of God are and who the children of the devil are: Anyone who does not do what is right is not a child of God; nor is anyone who does not love his brother. (1 John 3:8-10 NIV)

Those who are of God accept Jesus Christ and do not practice sin and those who are of the devil reject the name of Jesus and keep on sinning. In other words, they practice sin without remorse. This is the extent of it. Race is not cited as a factor as to whether or not one is of God or of the devil. Race is not an indicator as to whether or not one can be saved. Instead, the Scriptures teach that in order to be saved one must confess Jesus as Lord (God who was manifested in the flesh) and believe that God raised him from the dead. The following passage of Scripture attests to this:

[9]If you declare with your mouth, "Jesus is Lord," and believe in your heart that God raised him from the dead, you will be saved. [10]For it is with your heart that you believe and are justified, and it is with your mouth that you profess your faith and are saved. [11]As Scripture says, "Anyone who believes in him will never be put to shame. [12]For there is no difference between Jew and Gentile—the same Lord is Lord of all and richly blesses all who call on him, [13]for, "Everyone who calls on the name of the Lord will be saved." (Romans 10:9-13 TNIV)

In the passage of Scripture just quoted, there is no mention of race as being a determinant of who will be saved and who won't be. To be saved means to be saved from eternal hell. Instead of going to hell, those of us who accept the Lordship of Jesus Christ will instead go to heaven to be with him when we die. The Scripture plainly tells us that in order to gain salvation one must believe in the Deity of Christ (that he is Lord) and that he was raised from the dead. The Scripture goes on to say that there is no difference between Jew and Gentile and that everyone who calls on the name of the Lord will be saved. In other words, God does not favor a people over another when it comes to the gift of salvation. Although salvation is open to everyone, no matter what race a person is categorized in, there is only one way, according to the Scriptures, that one can acquire salvation. The apostle Luke puts it plainly in the following account located in the book of Acts:

> [8]Then Peter, filled with the Holy Spirit, said to them: "Rulers and elders of the people! [9]If we are being called to account today for an act of kindness shown to a man who was lame and are being asked how he was healed, [10]then know this, you and all the people of Israel: It is by the name of Jesus Christ of Nazareth, whom you crucified but whom God raised from the dead, that this man stands before you healed.
> [11]Jesus is "the stone you builders rejected, which has become the cornerstone."
> [12]Salvation is found in no one else, for there is no other name given under heaven by which we must be saved. (Acts 4:8-12 TNIV)

Only Jesus saves; no one else does. The Bible is explicit in this teaching. And when it comes to salvation, the Bible is just as explicit in teaching that God does not categorize nor judge people according to race, but instead according to whether or not they have confessed Jesus Christ as Lord and Savior and have lived their lives according to his teachings. But a racist would have one to believe otherwise. Racists would have us to believe that one's eternal destiny depends heavily upon the color of a person's skin. They would have us to believe that certain races of people are cursed and that as a result, God sees those certain races of people as subhuman deserving of discrimination. Racists are blind to the fact that racism is one of the devil's biggest ploys.

God has not created race, man has. Man has created the concept of race. God has simply created human beings with different skin color, hair color, hair texture, facial features and so forth. It is no more than that. However, man has made it into much more because the very core of racism exploits the fact that people look different from one another.

But the Bible never speaks of the racial identity of people. It does not categorize people as white, black, Hispanic, Asian, Indian, etc. In some places the Bible may describe the skin color of a person, but it does not regulate that person into a specific racial category. However, aside from the basic categorization of people as being children of God or children of the devil, God also subcategorizes people by nations. But one's nationality is different from one's race. There can be many different races that make up one nationality. God judges nations of people, not races of people. And God judges nations by whether or not the people of those nations accept and worship him as the only true God. God does not look at the color of a person's skin. To bring the point home further, we need to consider the following Scripture:

> All flesh is not the same flesh: but there is one kind of
> flesh of men, another flesh of beasts, another of fishes,
> and another of birds (1 Corinthians 15:39 KJV)

The verse of Scripture above teaches us that God makes a distinction between the flesh of men (mankind) and the flesh of animals, fish, and birds. The flesh of men is different from the flesh of animals which is different from the flesh of fish which is different from the flesh of birds.

Humans, animals, fish, and birds have different flesh because they are different species of beings, meaning simplistically, that they cannot interbreed with one another. Humans cannot interbreed with fish, fish cannot interbreed birds, birds cannot interbreed with animals, and so forth. But humans can interbreed with all other humans. This therefore means that there is only one species of human being which coincides with the verse just previously quoted which says, "there is one *kind* of flesh of men." In other words, all of mankind has the same *kind* of flesh.

In America, different races are often spoken of as being of different "kinds." We have heard statements such as, "Stick to your own kind" which is a demand for people not to marry outside of their race. But as we see in the Scripture above, the Bible specifically teaches that there is only *one kind* of human flesh. There are no different kinds. There are different colors but no different kinds. The skin of a black person basically functions in the same way as the skin of a white person. Even though it is of a different color, it is of the same kind.

Man's flesh is of the human kind as opposed to the kind of animals, fish, or birds. Human beings are therefore of one species. There are no different kinds of human flesh and therefore there are no different species of human beings. The only difference in the flesh of humans is skin color which is no more significant a difference than the different colors of hair or eyes that humans have. The Bible emphasizes the insignificance of physical flesh in the following passage:

> [24]For all flesh is as grass, and all the glory of man as the
> flower of grass. The grass withereth, and the flower
> thereof falleth away:

²⁵But the word of the Lord endureth for ever. And this is the word which by the gospel is preached unto you. (1 Peter 1:24-25 KJV)

It is not our flesh (our physicality) that we should primarily focus on because what is really important is what lives forever, and that is the Holy Scripture, that has been preached to us; the word of God. Our flesh is just as vulnerable as grass because our flesh, just like grass, eventually withers away and dies. So, we should be careful not to place undue importance on it. This is what Peter was telling us in the passage of Scripture quoted above.

THE BIBLE WHEN IT COMES TO FAVORITISM

There are many biblical passages that teach that it is wrong to show favoritism. We first see God's admonishment against favoritism in the Old Testament Law that he gave to the Israelites, documented in the verses of Scripture below:

²"Do not follow the crowd in doing wrong. When you give testimony in a lawsuit, do not pervert justice by siding with the crowd, ³and do not show favoritism to a poor man in his lawsuit." (Exodus 23:2-3 NIV)

¹⁵ "Do not pervert justice; do not show partiality to the poor or favoritism to the great, but judge your neighbor fairly." (Leviticus 19:15 NIV)

Favoritism should be given to no one when it comes to settling issues regarding human rights abuses. People who are poor and are seeing hard times should be judged no differently than those who are rich or who are great in status. The Scripture passages quoted above teach that everyone should be judged by the same standards. No one should be above the law. No one should be able to get away with doing something wrong simply because of who they are. Everyone should be judged fairly. Proverbs 20:10 teaches that the Lord detests double standards. It reads,

False weights and unequal measures—the LORD detests double standards of every kind. (NLT)

And Proverbs 20:23 reads,

> The LORD detests double standards. He is not pleased by
> dishonest scales. (NLT)

If status and riches should not be factors triggering favoritism and
double standards (of which there should be no practice to begin with), then
skin color is unquestionably a factor that should not trigger favoritism and
double standards. It is so very important that we not show favoritism that
Paul charged Timothy in this matter as he was instructing him as to how to
oversee the churches. The charge reads as such,

> [17]The elders who direct the affairs of the church are well
> worthy of double honor, especially those whose work is
> preaching and teaching. [18]For the Scripture says, "Do not
> muzzle the ox while it is treading out the grain," and
> "The worker deserves his wages." [19]Do not entertain an
> accusation against an elder unless it is brought by two or
> three witness. [20]Those who sin are to be rebuked
> publicly, so that the others may take warning.
> [21]I charge you, in the sight of God and Christ Jesus and
> the elect angels, to keep these instructions without
> partiality, and to do nothing out of favoritism.
> (1 Timothy 5:17-21 NIV)

Verse 21 particularly teaches that to act out of partiality and/or
favoritism is wrong. Therefore, discrimination is wrong because to show
favoritism to one automatically discriminates against another.

The Bible clearly emphasizes that God does not show favoritism and
accepts all men and women who accept him. The following verse of
Scripture attests to this.

> [34]Then Peter began to speak: "I now realize how true
> it is that God does not show favoritism [35]but accepts
> men from every nation who fear him and do what is
> right....." (Acts 10:34-35 NIV)

Favoritism breeds prejudice and discrimination. Therefore, if God does
not show favoritism among those who accept him, then neither does God
discriminate among those who accept him. Everyone who accepts God has
an equal chance with God. Even those who do not accept God initially
have the same opportunities from God as those who do accept him.

When Peter explained that God does not show favoritism he meant it in the sense that everyone has an equal opportunity to be accepted by God as long as they accept him. And to be accepted by God in biblical terms means to be accepted as one of his spiritual children while here on earth and also to be accepted into his kingdom at the point of physical death, in other words, to be guaranteed a place in heaven when one dies.

In examining the totality of the matter, we must take a look at the fact that although God does not show favoritism, he does, at times, show favor. With God, there is a difference between favoritism and favor. When God shows favor he does so in a way in which he selects someone who he has deemed to fulfill his purpose. God's favor is therefore justified. Favoritism, however, is never justified. God gives favor to fulfill a purpose and oftentimes the job that goes along with that purpose is not an easy one. On the other hand, favoritism is given due to no particular qualification or characteristic, but only due to the biased admiration that the giver has towards the receiver. One example of God's favor can be seen when we look at the account of the Virgin Mary, cited below.

[26]In the sixth month of Elizabeth's pregnancy, God sent the angel Gabriel to Nazareth, a town in Galilee, [27]to a virgin pledged to be married to a man named Joseph, a descendant of David. The virgin's name was Mary. [28]The angel went to her and said, "Greetings, you who are highly favored! The Lord is with you."

[29]Mary was greatly troubled at his words and wondered what kind of greeting this might be. [30]But the angel said to her, "Do not be afraid, Mary; you have found favor with God. [31]You will conceive and give birth to a son, and you are to call him Jesus. [32]He will be great and will be called the Son of the Most High. The Lord God will give him the throne of his father David, [33]and he will reign over the house of Jacob forever, his kingdom will never end."

[34]"How will this be," Mary asked the angel, "since I am a virgin?"

[35]The angel answered, "The Holy Spirit will come on you, and the power of the Most High will overshadow you. So the holy one to be born will be called the Son of God. [36]Even Elizabeth your relative is going to have a child in her old age, and she who was said to be unable to conceive is in her sixth month. [37]For no word from God will ever fail."

213

[38]"I am the Lord's servant," Mary answered. "May it be to me according to your word." Then the angel left her. (Luke 1:26-38 TNIV)

God found favor with Mary in that he called her to do a mighty work. He favored her in the sense that he knew that she would carry his work through and she possessed the qualities that he was looking for. The same can be said of many others that the Bible gives account of whom God called to do a great work. The favor of God is therefore different than favoritism. With the favor of God also comes hard work and possible persecution. We see this when we look at Moses (who had favor with God) and how difficult it was for him to lead the Israelites to the Promised Land because they kept turning against him. Even the Virgin Mary was initially persecuted by her husband, Joseph, who was at first considering divorcing her when he learned she was pregnant but stopped his plans to do so after an angel of the Lord appeared to him in a dream and told him that what was conceived in her was from the Holy Spirit, that she would give birth to a son, and that they were to give him the name Jesus because he would save his people from their sins (Matthew 1:18-21)[2].

So, whereas favoritism gives privilege and reward simply based on incidental things such as outward appearance, God's favor is given to those who he knows can carry out his will even in the face of much adversity.

Racism is a dysfunctional extreme of favoritism. Racism gives privilege and esteem to one set of people based solely on skin color or other physical features while denying those same privileges and esteem to another set of people based on the same factors. The following passage of Scripture further confirms that the Bible does not condone favoritism and specifically speaks against class favoritism:

[1]My brothers and sisters, believers in our glorious Lord Jesus Christ must not show favoritism. [2]Suppose someone comes into your meeting wearing a gold ring and fine clothes, and a poor person in filthy old clothes also comes in. [3]If you show special attention to the one wearing fine clothes and say, "Here's a good seat for you," but say to the one who is poor, "You stand there" or "Sit on the floor by my feet," [4]have you not discriminated among yourselves and become judges with evil thoughts?

---

[2] See your Bible.

214

[5]Listen, my dear brothers and sisters: Has not God chosen those who are poor in the eyes of the world to be rich in faith and to inherit the kingdom he promised those who love him? [6]But you have dishonored the poor. Is it not the rich who are exploiting you? [7]Are they not the ones who are dragging you into court? Are they not the ones who are blaspheming the noble name of him to whom you belong?
[8]If you really keep the royal law found in Scripture, "Love your neighbor as yourself," you are doing right. [9]But if you show favoritism, you sin and are convicted by the law as lawbreakers. [10]For whoever keeps the whole law and yet stumbles at just one point is guilty of breaking all of it. [11]For he who said, "you shall not commit adultery," also said, "You shall not murder." If you do not commit adultery but do commit murder, you have become a lawbreaker. (James 2:1-11 TNIV)

The Bible teaches against giving privileges to those who are in the financial upper class while not allowing those same privileges to those who are in the lower class. God is not a respecter of persons as attested to in the following passage of Scripture:

[13]Wherefore gird up the loins of your mind, be sober, and hope to the end for the grace that is to be brought unto you at the revelation of Jesus Christ;
[14]As obedient children, not fashioning yourselves according to the former lusts in your ignorance:
[15]But as he which hath called you is holy, so be ye holy in all manner of conversation;
[16]Because it is written, be ye holy; for I am holy.
[17]And if ye call on the Father, who without respect of persons judgeth according to every man's work, pass the time of your sojourning here in fear:
[18]Forasmuch as ye know that ye were not redeemed with corruptible things, as silver and gold, from your vain conversation received by tradition from your fathers.
[19]But with the precious blood of Christ, as of a lamb without blemish and without spot:
(1 Peter 1:13-19 KJV)

Verse 17 above teaches that God judges people according to what they have done not according to who they are or what position they have in life. Caleb Colley is quoted as saying the following in his on-line article entitled "God is no Respecter of Persons":

> God offers salvation to every man, no matter what external circumstances, such as socioeconomic status or nationality, might apply to him. God does not offer salvation only to the Jew, just because he is a Jew, or only to the Gentile because he is a Gentile. The Greek word translated 'respecter of persons" in the King James Version of Acts 10:34 ("God is no respecter of persons") is *prosopolemptes*, a word that refers to a judge who looks at a man's face instead of at the facts of the case, and makes a decision based on whether or not he likes the man (Lenski, 1961, p. 418).[3]

If then God does not judge a person based on his or her outer appearance and whether or not he likes that person, the color of one's skin certainly has no place in God's judgment either. Skin color quickly then, becomes a non-issue. Then, we too, should not judge a person by how they look either. 1 Peter 2:17[4] goes on to admonish us to honor all men while Jesus is quoted in Matthew 7:12 as saying that we should do unto others as we would want others to do unto us (the actual verse reads as follows in the King James Version, "Therefore all things whatsoever ye would that men should do to you, do ye even so to them: for this is the law and the prophets."). It is safe to say that people do not want to be discriminated against or treated unequally. Most of us want others to treat us fairly and not to discriminate against us. In accordance then to what Jesus has taught about treating people the way we want to be treated (doing unto others) we must conclude that discriminating against someone is not something that we should be doing to others. We can even go further to say that if we treat a person in a way that we would not want to be treated then we have sinned, not only against that person, but against God.

---

[3] Colley, Caleb, Apologetics Press, article, *God is no Respecter of Persons,* copyright 2004, www.apologeticspress.org, reference quoted taken from R.C.H Lenski's book The Interpretation of the Acts of the Apostles (Minneapolis MN: Augsburg) 1961 Reprint, p. 418. Apologetics Press article: used by permission, otherwise; Fair use.

[4] "Honour all men. Love the brotherhood. Fear God. Honour the king." KJV

If then the Scriptures teach against discrimination when it comes to societal status and money, there is no question, that the color of one's skin is certainly not enough to warrant any type of favoritism. As we saw earlier, James 2:8 tells us to love our neighbors as we love ourselves. The book of Luke also records Jesus giving this same command. Jesus explains the command through a parable, most commonly known as "The Good Samaritan." The parable teaches us that our neighbors could very well be someone that we think little of or that we consider an enemy. But no matter what we think of them, we are still supposed to love them and treat them as we would want to be treated. Jesus' parable of the good Samaritan cited below, teaches us this:

> [25]On one occasion an expert in the law stood up to test Jesus. "Teacher," he asked, "what must I do to inherit eternal life?"
>
> [26]What is written in the Law?" he replied. "How do you read it?"
>
> [27]He answered: "'Love the Lord your God with all your heart and with all your soul and with all your strength and with all your mind; and 'Love your neighbor as yourself.'"
>
> [28]"You have answered correctly," Jesus replied. "Do this and you will live."
>
> [29]But he wanted to justify himself, so he asked Jesus, "And who is my neighbor?"
>
> [30]In reply Jesus said: "A man was going down from Jerusalem to Jericho, when he fell into the hands of robbers. They stripped him of his clothes, beat him and went away, leaving him half dead. [31]A priest happened to be going down the same road, and when he saw the man, he passed by on the other side. [32]So too, a Levite, when he came to the place and saw him, passed by on the other side. [33]But a Samaritan, as he traveled, came where the man was; and when he saw him, he took pity on him. [34]He went to him and bandaged his wounds, pouring on oil and wine. Then he put the man on his own donkey, took him to an inn and took care of him. [35]The next day he took out two silver coins and gave them to the innkeeper. 'Look after him,' he said, 'and when I return, I will reimburse you for any extra expense you may have.'

[36]"Which of these three do you think was a neighbor to the man who fell into the hands of robbers?"
[37]The expert in the law replied, "The one who had mercy on him." Jesus told him, "Go and do likewise." (Luke 10:25-37 NIV)

The New Testament Samaritans were identified as a people who came about from the intermarriage of Jews and Gentiles who lived in the city of Samaria. The intermarriages came about when a small number of Jews were left in Samaria after the Assyrians had conquered Israel and exiled the majority of the Jews away from the city. The remaining Jews intermarried with the Gentiles that had settled in the land after the exile. During the time of this parable, the Samaritans and the Jews were enemies. They did not think well of one another. At the time, the Israelite Jews looked upon the Samaritans as inferior. More will be said about the Samaritans later on in the chapter, but for now the emphasis is on the fact that although these two groups of people didn't get along, God still considered them to be neighbors of one another. Neither was justified in mistreating the other despite any differences they may have had. Neither group of people was humanly superior to the other. Jesus taught that we are to treat one another with mercy whether or not they are a part of "our group" or not. In his parable, Jesus depicted a man who helped another man that belonged to a group that despised him; but he helped him regardless. We are all to treat one another in a neighborly way despite our differences. This type of teaching certainly flies in the face of any attempt to justify undue privilege, racial discrimination, nepotism, cronyism, and a host of racial injustices which are all types of favoritism.

If we are to have mercy on our neighbors (which means symbolically that we should have mercy on everyone) and love them as we love ourselves (meaning we are to love everyone as we love ourselves) then we must treat everyone the way we would want to be treated (as long as in doing so we do not condone sin). This is what the Bible teaches. The word of God doesn't allow favoritism. If we show favoritism, then we are not acting in love and mercy. Loving our neighbors and having mercy on them even applies when it comes to how foreigners and immigrants should be treated, as attested to in the following Scripture verses:

[12]And now, O Israel, what does the Lord your God ask of you but to fear the Lord your God, to walk in all his ways, to love him, to serve the Lord your God with all your heart and with all your soul, [13]and to observe the

Lord's commands and decrees that I am giving you today for your own good? [14]To the LORD your God belong the heavens, even the highest heavens, the earth and everything in it. [15]Yet the LORD set his affection on your forefathers and loved them, and he chose you, their descendants, above all the nations, as it is today. [16]Circumcise your hearts, therefore, and do not be stiff-necked any longer. [17]For the LORD your God is God of gods and LORD of lords, the great God, mighty and awesome, who shows no partiality and accepts no bribes. [18]He defends the cause of the fatherless and the widow, and loves the alien, giving him food and clothing. [19]And you are to love those who are aliens, for you yourselves were aliens in Egypt. (Deuteronomy 10:12-19 NIV)

God admonished the Israelites to treat well those persons from other countries that were living in the land; the aliens. The Israelites were not to mistreat them. They were to treat them with love. The aliens were not to be discriminated against. Although God was speaking to the Israelites at the time; we can certainly apply this principle to today's time. Apparently, God considers an alien to be no less a neighbor to a countryman than another citizen of that country. So, Jesus' command to love one's neighbor as one would love one's self includes *anyone* who is a neighbor, regardless of skin color and even regardless of nationality or citizenship. The Scripture passage above shows us that God reminded Israel how badly they were treated when they were aliens in Egypt and alludes to the fact that the Israelites were not loved by the Egyptians during the time the Egyptians had the Israelites under their authority. The Israelites were instead enslaved and treated so harshly by the Egyptians that God intervened by calling upon Moses to lead the way to their deliverance resulting in ten plagues that Egypt first suffered through as God's chastisement for Pharaoh's initial refusal to free the Israelite slaves.[5]

Not only does the Bible teach that favoritism (and therefore discrimination) is wrong and is a sin, but the Scripture passage below goes further to teach that we are to regard others as more important than ourselves. This is a far cry from what defines prejudice and discrimination.

[1]Therefore if there is any encouragement in Christ, if there is any consolation of love, if there is any

---

[5] Exodus, Chapters 7-12. See your Bible.

219

fellowship of the Spirit, if any affection and
compassion,
²make my joy complete by being of the same mind,
maintaining the same love united in spirit, intent on
one purpose.
³Do nothing from selfishness or empty conceit, but
with humility of mind let each of you regard one
another as more important than himself;
⁴Do not merely look out for your own personal
interests, but also for the interests of others.
(Philippians 2:1-4 NASB)

The above verses of Scripture are taken from the Apostle Paul's letter to the people of Philippi. Most of the inhabitants there were Christians and much of Paul's letter admonishes the Philippians in the correct ways of Christian living. In verses 1 and 2 Paul begins by speaking of the consolation of love, affection, and compassion and relating those attributes to Christ. Then he goes on by indicating that one of the ways of showing the love of Christ is to abstain from conceit and to regard others as more important than oneself. This type of thinking is certainly not compatible with the type of thinking that allows a person to believe he or she is superior to, or better than, another person.

THE BIBLE WHEN IT COMES TO HUMAN EQUALITY

Although the Bible does teach that mankind was given dominion over "the fish of the sea, and over the fowl of the air, and over the cattle, and over all the earth, and over every creeping thing that creepeth upon the earth (Genesis 1:26)," there is no Scripture that says that one man was created to have dominion over another man. This is because, as human beings, none of us are superior to any other human being. We are all equally created in the image of God as found in Genesis 1:27 which says,

So God created human beings in his own image, in the
image of God he created them; male and female he
created them. (NLT)

This means that God created every man and every woman in his image. There is no indication in the Bible whatsoever that one race of people was not created in God's image. All human beings were created in the image of God regardless of skin color. There are no separate species of human

220

beings. In their book entitled, "One Blood," Ken Ham, Carl Wieland, and Don Batten put it the following way:

> As a result of Darwinian evolution, many people started thinking in terms of the different people groups around the world representing different "races," but within the context of evolutionary philosophy. This has resulted in many people today consciously or unconsciously, having ingrained prejudices against certain other groups of people.
>
> All human beings in the world today, however, are classified as *Homo sapiens*. Scientists today admit that, biologically, there really is only one race of humans. For instance, a scientist at the Advancement of Science Convention in Atlanta in 1997 stated, "Race is a social construct derived mainly from perceptions conditioned by events of recorded history, and it has no basic biological reality." This person went on to say, "Curiously enough, the idea comes very close to being of American manufacture."
>
> Reporting on research conducted on the concept of race, the American ABC News science page stated, "More and more scientists find that the differences that set us apart are cultural, not racial. Some even say that the word 'race' should be abandoned because it's meaningless." The article went on to say that "we accept the idea of race because it's a convenient way of putting people into broad categories, frequently to suppress them...The most hideous example was provided by Hitler's Germany. And racial prejudice remains common throughout the world.[6]

The Bible supports the position that race is a social construct and that it has been manufactured by societies. It is interesting to note that the quote specifies America as the main manufacturer. Biblically speaking, there really is no such thing as race because when we get right down to it, every human being who lives or who has ever lived has the same ancestry since

---

[6] From *One Blood: The Biblical Answer to Racism,* by Ken Ham; Carl Wieland; and Don Batten. First printing 1999, sixth printing 2002, copyright 1999, pgs. 52-53. Used with permission from the publisher, Master Books Inc., (a division of New Leaf Press) Green Forest Arizona, copyright 1999.

we all came from one man...Adam. The following passage of Scripture attests to this:

> [24]The God who made the world and everything in it is the Lord of heaven and earth and does not live in temples built by hands. [25]And he is not served by human hands, as if he needed anything, because he himself gives all men life and breath and everything else. [26]From one man he made every nation of men, that they should inhabit the whole earth; and he determined the times set for them and the exact places where they should live." (Acts 17:24-26 NIV)

Verse 26 tells us that God made all nations of men from one man (some translations read, "from one blood"). This is a striking blow to any devout racist. If we are all made from one blood how then are any of us superior to the other? With just this one Scripture alone, the Bible backs up scientific evidence that says that there is really no such thing as race aside from the human race. We are all cut from the same cloth.

Since God made every nation of men from one man, this means that if everyone in the entire world could construct an individual family tree that could go all the way back to the very beginning of each one's genealogy, we'd all have Adam at the beginning of that tree. Adam (along with Eve) would be at the top of everyone's genealogical chart. This means that Adam is everyone's initial ancestral patriarch which in turn means that we're all really related to one another despite our physical differences. We are all cousins, very distant cousins, but cousins all the same. We all share the same bloodline.

Once again we see that there are therefore no different species of human beings. In other words, men and women from any race can breed together and produce other humans. But it is not the same for all creatures. For example, all birds cannot breed with one another because there are many birds that are not physically able to interbreed with other birds and produce offspring. It is not possible for an ostrich and an eagle to interbreed and produce offspring even though the ostrich and the eagle are both birds. The ostrich and the eagle are two different species of birds; two different kinds. However, despite the differences between skin color, facial features, and hair texture, there is no particular group of people that cannot "breed" with another group of people. Our physical differences do not separate us into different species because if they did then one group of people could not successfully procreate with another group of people. But this is not the case. People fall in love, get married, and have children

222

across "racial" lines all the time. The children who are a product of these "interracial" marriages are just as normal as anybody else is.

As human beings, we are all one species joined together by one common ancestor...well, actually two, since Eve is identified as the "mother of all living" in Genesis 3:20 which reads "And Adam called his wife's name Eve; because she was the mother of all living (KJV)."

The fact that Eve is the mother of all human beings goes hand in hand with the fact that all nations of men are made from one blood. If God were going to make distinctions in superiority between races it does not compute that he'd give us all the same initial ancestry because to do so would make the argument of superiority a difficult one indeed. How can a person say that he is superior to another person if both people have the same beginnings? Whether we like it or not, we're all related to one another according to the Bible. Furthermore, none of us are better than any of the rest of us because all of us were created by the same God, of which there is only one.[7] Therefore, when looking at things from a biblical perspective, we should never look down on anyone and we should not think of anyone as beneath us or treat anyone as if they were beneath us. No one is beneath anyone as attested to in the following passage of Scripture:

> [13]If I have denied justice to any of my servants, whether
> male or female, when they had a grievance against me,
> [14]what will I do when God confronts me?
> What will I answer when called to account?
> [15]Did not he who made me in the womb make them?
> Did not the same one form us both within our mothers?
> (Job 31:13-14 TNIV)

The preceding passage of Scripture comes from the book of Job. Job himself is speaking. In the first chapter of the book of Job, Job is described by God himself as a man who was "blameless, upright, feared God, and shunned evil." Job was a very righteous man and his righteousness was recognized by God.

In the Scripture passage above, Job espouses the cause of his servants by explaining that he would be wrong were he to deny them a voice to grieve any complaint that they might have against him. He then took it further by indicating that he had no right to deny his servants justice for

---

[7] See now that I myself am He! There is no God besides me. I put to death and I bring to life, I have wounded and I will heal, and no one can deliver out of my hand. (Deuteronomy 32:39 NIV)

any complaint or grievance that they brought to him concerning his treatment of them because he was no better than they were although he was in authority over them. The authority that Job had over his servants did not give him the right to mistreat them because, when it came right down to it, his servants were created by God just as he was and were therefore no different than he was. His servants were humanly equal to him even though they were under his authority. And Job knew that if he began thinking that he was better than his servants and consequently began to mistreat them, then he would have to account to God for it. What is being taught here speaks volumes, and that is that all humans are equal no matter their position in life. If skin color and facial features are to be a determinant as to one's superiority over another, then it would seem that Job would have certainly said something about it. Moreover, there are some translations that actually translate the word *servant* as *slave*.

Along with Job, Paul also makes it clear, by what he wrote to the Colossians below, that slaves are not inferior to those who are free:

> [8]But now you also, put them all aside; anger, wrath, malice, slander, and abusive speech from your mouth.
> [9]Do not lie to one another, since you laid aside the old self with its evil practices,
> [10]and have put on the new self who is being renewed to a true knowledge according to the image of the One who created him
> [11]—a renewal in which there is no distinction between Greek and Jew, circumcised and uncircumcised, barbarian, Scythian, slave and freeman, but Christ is all, and in all. (Colossians 3:8-11 NASB)

Verse 11 in the above Scripture tells us that God makes no distinction between a Jew and a non-Jew (Gentile) and a slave and a freeman as long as they are in Christ. The Scripture is clear; for those who are renewed in Christ, God does not make a difference between people no matter their race, no matter their ethnicity (Greek or Jew), and no matter their status (slave or free). Even slaves are humanly equal to those who are free. The master is not superior to the slave, and the slave is not inferior to the master, which brings us to our next topic of discussion.

THE BIBLE WHEN IT COMES TO SLAVERY[8]

Since the Bible has been used by many in times past, and even today, to justify the past enslavement of blacks in America, it is important to take a look at what the Bible actually teaches regarding the practice of slavery. During the years in America in which blacks were enslaved, it was illegal to teach black people to read and write. This was partly due to the attempt to withhold certain biblical truths from blacks such as the fact that salvation is a gift given to all men and that Jesus shed his blood for the spiritual redemption of everyone, including black people and other minorities. We will take a look at scriptural passages that give evidence that the type of slavery that was forced upon African men and women during the slave trade was clearly against the word of God.

To begin with, African men and women were kidnapped from their native land, forced into slave ships and transported against their will across the Atlantic Ocean to America. However, if we turn to the Mosaic Law of the Old Testament, we find the following:

> And he who kidnaps a man, whether he sells him or he is found in his possession, shall surely be put to death. (Exodus 21:16 NIV)

> If a man be found stealing any of his brethren of the children of Israel, and maketh merchandise of him, or selleth him; then that thief shall die, and thou shalt put evil away from among you." (Deuteronomy 24:7 KJV)

Although God was speaking to the nation of Israel when he made the decrees cited above, the basic premise still stands; kidnapping and selling a person, for whatever reason, is a sin against God. We can therefore safely surmise that slavery in early America was a sin since Africans were kidnapped and forced across the Atlantic to be sold.

New Testament Scripture also coincides with Old Testament Scripture when it comes to the issue of slavery. Let's take a look:

> [9]We also know that law is made not for the righteous but for lawbreakers and rebels, the ungodly and sinful, the

---

[8] Dodds, Elreta; *What the Bible Really says about Slavery*, copyright ©2000, Revised Edition, Press Toward The Mark Publications, Detroit Michigan. Most of the material under this subheading is quoted directly from this book. Used by Permission.

unholy and irreligious; for those who kill their fathers or mothers, for murderers, [10]for adulterers and perverts, for slave traders and liars and perjurers and for whatever else is contrary to the sound doctrine [11]that conforms to the glorious gospel of the blessed God which he entrusted to me. (1 Timothy 1:9-11 NIV)

The focus here is on the phrase "slave traders" which the King James Version of the Bible translates as "menstealers." Slave traders and menstealers are made synonymous when taking into consideration the fact that slave traders are those who kidnap people and sell them into slavery; hence, they steal men (as well as women and children). The Scripture puts slave traders in the same category as lawbreakers, rebels, the ungodly, the sinful, the unholy, the irreligious, those who kill their fathers or mothers, murderers, adulterers, perverts, liars, and perjurers.

Despite the fact that slavery that involves kidnapping is a sin, there were instances in the Bible in which slavery was acceptable as long as the practice met certain regulations set by God. For instance, it was commonplace for the Israelites to sell themselves into slavery to pay a debt. Selling oneself into slavery was acceptable. However, there were certain rules that the slave masters had to follow, as attested to in the following passage of Scripture:

[12]If a fellow Hebrew, a man, or a woman, sells himself to you and serves you six years, in the seventh year you must let him go free. [13]And when you release him, do not send him away empty-handed. [14]Supply him liberally from your flock, your threshing floor and your winepress. Give to him as the LORD your God redeemed you. [15]Remember that you were slaves in Egypt and the LORD your God redeemed you. That is why I give you this command today. (Deuteronomy 15:12-15 NIV)

In the scenario above, God commanded a slave to be set free after six years of servitude (in the seventh year). Not only did God command that the slave go free in the seventh year but when the slave was set free he was not to go free empty-handed. Upon setting his slave free, the slave master was to supply his slave liberally from his flock, threshing floor and winepress. In today's time this would mean that the slave master would be mandated to supply the slave with enough money and resources for the slave to get off to a very good start.

226

Additionally, any runaway slave was not to be oppressed by those who found him and was not to be handed back over to the master from whom he had fled. This is seen in the following passages of Scripture:

> [15]If a slave has taken refuge with you, do not hand him over to his master. [16]Let him live among you wherever he likes and in whatever town he chooses. Do not oppress him. (Deuteronomy 23:15-16 NIV)

> Thou shalt neither vex a stranger, nor oppress him: for ye were strangers in the land of Egypt. (Exodus 22:21 KJV)

God mandated that any slave who ran away from his master was not to be hunted down and sent back to his master against his will but was instead to be a welcome refugee in whatever town he was pleased to live in. Moreover, he was not to be oppressed. This is a far cry from how runaway slaves were treated during America's slavery era.

When reading the account in the Bible of how God used Moses to free the Jews from the slavery imposed on them by the Egyptians,[9] God's initial conversation with Moses regarding his assignment to deliver the Jews is very telling. The account reads as follows:

> [7]The LORD said, "I have indeed seen the misery of my people in Egypt. I have heard them crying out because of their slave drivers, and I am concerned about their suffering. [8]So I have come down to rescue them from the hand of the Egyptians and to bring them up out of that land into a good and spacious land, a land flowing with milk and honey—the home of the Canaanites, Hittites, Amorites, Perizzites, Hivites and Jebusites. [9]And now the cry of the Israelites has reached me, and I have seen the way the Egyptians are oppressing them. [10]So now, go. I am sending you to Pharaoh to bring my people the Israelites out of Egypt. (Exodus 3:7-10 NIV)

As we can see, God stepped in to deliver the Israelites from slavery because those who were enslaving them were also oppressing them. The fact that the Jews were slaves of the Egyptians did not give the Egyptians the right to mistreat the Jews. The Egyptians were wrong to mistreat them.

---

[9] Exodus chapters 1 through 14. See your Bible.

Mistreatment of slaves is therefore an action that goes against morality and the teachings of the Bible. The Bible teaches us that slavery in and of itself is not a sin but that the mistreatment of slaves is. We see this in the following passage of Scripture:

> [5]Slaves obey your earthly masters with respect and fear, and with sincerity of heart, just as you would obey Christ. [6]Obey them not only to win their favor when their eye is on you, but like slaves of Christ doing the will of God from your heart. [7]Serve wholeheartedly, as if you were serving the Lord, not men, [8]because you know that the Lord will reward everyone for whatever good he does, whether he is slave or free.
>
> [9]And masters, treat your slaves in the same way. Do not threaten them, since you know that he who is both their Master and yours is in heaven, and there is no favoritism with him. (Ephesians 6:5-9 NIV)

There is also a similar passage in Colossians 3:22-25 which reads:

> [22]Slaves, obey your earthly masters in everything; and do it, not only when their eye is on you and to win their favor, but with sincerity of heart and reverence for the Lord. [23]Whatever you do, work at it with all your heart, as working for the Lord, not for men, [24]since you know that you will receive an inheritance from the Lord as a reward. It is the Lord Christ you are serving. [25]Anyone who does wrong will be repaid for his wrong, and there is no favoritism. (NIV)

Many theologians interpret these passages of Scripture as meaning that employees are to be obedient to their bosses. But the passages are referencing literal slavery; not workplace relations (although the passages can be applied to workplace relations). The Greek word for slave used in the text is "doulos" which means a literal *slave* as we understand the term. There is no way around this. Slaves are commanded to obey their masters and serve them to the best of their ability just as they would serve Christ to the best of their ability. This does not mean that the slave master is on the same level as or equal to Christ and this does not mean that a slave master is at liberty to make demands of his slave that are unreasonable or sinful. The Scripture commands the slave to respect the authority of the slave master no differently than he (or she) respects the authority of Jesus Christ.

228

The issue here is respect for authority figures. The slave master is an authority figure over the slave and therefore the Bible says that that authority should be respected.

God is the one who places people in authority according to his purpose (Psalms 75:6-7)[10]. So it is in this sense that when we serve those in authority, we are serving the Lord. Therefore, those of us who are under any kind of authority should have the same respect for that authority as we do for the authority of Christ. This does not mean that the one in authority is Christ or that we are to worship that person; nor does it mean that the person in authority is infallible and that there are not times when we must resist their authority; particularly if they have asked us to do something ungodly or that we believe is ungodly. However, the Bible often times points out the importance of Christians abiding by authority. This becomes evident when considering the authority of the Government (Romans 13:1-7)[11], when it comes to people who are in authoritative positions (1 Peter 2:13-17)[12], and when it comes to a husband's position in the home (Ephesians 5:22-24).[13]

Despite the fact that people are supposed to submit to those who are in authority over them; the Bible specifies that there are certain situations in

---

[10] See your Bible

[11] See your Bible

[12] [13]Submit yourselves for the Lord's sake to every authority instituted among men: whether to the king, as the supreme authority, [14]or to governors, who are sent by him to punish those who do wrong and to commend those who do right. [15]For it is God's will that by doing good you should silence the ignorant talk of foolish men. [16]Live as free men, but do not use your freedom as a cover-up for evil; live as servants of God. [17]Show proper respect to everyone: Love the brotherhood of believers, fear God, honor the king. (NIV)

[13] [22]Wives, submit to your husbands as to the Lord. [23]For the husband is the head of the wife as Christ is the head of the church, his body, of which he is the Savior. [24]Now as the church submits to Christ, so also wives should submit to their husbands in everything." [The word for *submit* in the original Greek language means to "tend to the needs of" or "be supportive of", it does not mean to be a slave. The Greek word for *head* is "Kephale" and it means to be on the front line as a soldier is on the front line. It does not mean dictatorship. Wives submitting to their husbands in everything is a figure of speech. She cannot submit to sin, what she thinks is a sin, or anything that would have her go against God's purpose for her life. Men are mandated to love their wives as Christ loved the church (Ephesians 5:25). They are also commanded not to be bitter towards their wives (Colossians 3:19). Jesus taught that the greatest commandment is to love God with all heart, mind, and soul and then the second greatest commandment is to love your neighbor (Matthew 22:36-40). Therefore, the command to love is greater than the command to submit.

which those under authority can indeed refuse to submit to those who are in authority over them (the mandate in Ephesians 5:24 for wives to submit to their husbands in "everything" is not literal but is a figure of speech). These situations include any mandate from authoritative figures that instructs people to do things that are immoral, to do things that they *believe* are immoral (Romans 14)[14] or to do things that go against the assignment that God has given them. The account of Shadrach, Meshach, and Abednego serves as an example when they refused to submit to King Nebuchadnezzar's mandate to worship an idol (Daniel 3).[15] In addition, Paul's refusal to abide by the authority of the Sadducees recorded in Acts 5:17-40[16] where Paul and the other apostles were mandated to stop teaching in the name of Jesus, is another example of a circumstance that would necessitate resistance against an authority figure. They did not stop teaching and instead told the Sadducees that they "must obey God rather than man (specifically, Acts 5:29).

The mandate for slaves to obey their masters also in no way gives license for those in authority to mistreat those who are under their rule as attested to in verse 25 of the preceding Scripture text quoted from Colossians which reads, "anyone who does wrong will be repaid for his wrong, and there is no favoritism." If a slave does wrong then he is to be repaid for his wrong and if a master or one in authority does wrong then he is to be repaid for his wrong. Ephesians 6:9 corroborates this. As quoted earlier, it reads,

> And masters, treat your slaves in the same way. Do not
> threaten them, since you know that he who is both their
> Master and yours is in heaven, and there is no favoritism
> with him. (NIV)

Slave masters are not to be threatening towards their slaves. They are supposed to treat slaves in the same manner that slaves are supposed to treat them. Slaves are commanded to obey their masters with sincerity and respect as they would obey Christ. If masters are to treat their slaves in the same manner, then they are to treat slaves with sincerity and respect and they are to treat slaves with the same love for them that Christ has for us. God does not esteem the master better than the slave. In God's eyes, there is no difference between the two that would justify favoritism of one over the other. We've seen earlier that God opposes favoritism. Moreover, if masters are to treat their slaves in the same manner as slaves are to treat

---

[14] See your Bible

[15] See your Bible

[16] See your Bible

their masters, and if masters are to be non-threatening towards their slaves, then we can conclude, with certainty, that any kind of abuse of a slave is a sin.

However, somewhere along the line in Antebellum America; Ephesians 6:9 got buried, so to speak. Slave masters instead focused on Ephesians 6:5 which reads, "Slaves obey your earthly masters with respect and fear, and with sincerity of heart, just as you would obey Christ" and ignored 6:9 which commands masters to treat their slaves "in the same way" (with respect) and not to threaten them. The Scriptures that regulate a humane and non-oppressive system of slavery were kept away from black slaves of times past. And even now, many black people are not aware that there are Scriptures in the Bible that speak against the mistreatment of a slave.

Moreover, Ephesians 6:9 essentially tells us that the master was no better than the slave; that God does not esteem one over the other and that God is Master over them both. The slave master is not superior. The slave is not inferior. Both have the same Master in heaven and neither is more worthy or greater than the other. When it's all said and done, both the master and the slave will have to answer to the same God.

In general, this doctrine of equals between slave and master was something that the white slave masters did not want their black slaves to know. They did not want blacks on any equal footing with themselves, neither humanly nor spiritually. But as we have seen earlier when looking at Job 31:13-15, black slaves of antebellum America and their slave masters were on equal footing in the eyes of God. When revisiting the passage in the New American Standard Bible, the Scripture reads:

> [13]If I have despised the claim of my male or female slaves when they filed a complaint against me,
> [14]What then could I do when God arises, and when he calls me to account, what will I answer him?
> [15]Did not He who made me in the womb make him, and the same one fashion us in the womb? (Job 31:13-15 NASB)

As we saw earlier, Job is identified in the Bible as a man who was blameless, upright, and shunned evil. Since this was so, then we can conclude that the way Job treated his slaves was the right way. As discussed earlier, Job felt it would be wrong of him to despise any of his slaves' complaints against him. His slaves were free to complain and if they did; he was obligated not to hold their complaints against them but to address the complaint and offer resolution without malice. But this is not how America's slave masters treated black slaves. For the most part, black slaves were not at liberty to complain; and if they did, they risked retaliation from their slave masters in the form of floggings, whippings, beatings, rape and other forms of mistreatment. This was certainly not the Christian way that masters were to treat their slaves. As we can see, masters were supposed to hear out any complaints and work to make their slaves as comfortable as possible.

Not only did Job, one of the most righteous men whoever lived, indicate that masters are to embrace the complaints of their slaves in a respectful and loving way, but Job also argued that he had no right to despise the complaints of his slaves because he was no better than them and that both he and his slaves were made equally in the womb by God. Passages of Scripture (like the passage cited in Job) that condemns the mistreatment of slaves and puts slaves on the same human level as the slave master were kept from black slaves by white slave masters. The Scriptures that emphasized slaves obeying their masters were instead focused upon by slave masters as if no other biblical regulation of slavery existed. Consequently, there has been a grave misunderstanding throughout the centuries as to what the Bible really teaches when it comes to the issue of slavery.

Job's understanding of how wrong it is for a slave master to mistreat his slave is backed up in New Testament writings as well. In the book of Colossians, Paul the Apostle gives the following command:

> [1]Masters provide your slaves with what is right and fair, because you know that you also have a Master in heaven. (Colossians 4:1 NIV)

The theme of how masters are to treat their slaves is consistent throughout the Scriptures. Masters are to give to slaves what is right and fair. Masters are to be non-threatening towards their slaves. Masters are to be willing to listen to their slaves if they complain and to address the complaints in a loving and respectful manner. Masters are not to abuse their slaves and are to give to them liberally. It's no wonder that these mandates of how slave masters were to treat slaves were kept from black slaves and the Scriptures that command the obedience of slaves to their masters were instead emphasized. This way the master could exploit the slave without the slave being able to point to the Scriptures that speak against such exploitation. But although these Scriptures were hidden from black slaves, the Scriptures were not deleted from the Bible. To do so

232

would have been an abomination. Slave masters knew better than to tamper with the word of God.[17]

THE BIBLE WHEN IT COMES TO "INTERRACIAL" MARRIAGE

We saw in chapter 6 that the Christian Identity movement teaches that God flooded the earth in Noah's day because of pre-Adamic "race mixing" between whites and persons of color. But the Bible says differently as attested to in the Scripture passage below.

> [1]When men began to increase in number on the earth and daughters were born to them, [2]the sons of God saw that the daughters of men were beautiful, and they married any of them they chose. [3]Then the LORD said, "My Spirit will not contend with man forever, for he is mortal; his days will be a hundred and twenty years."
> [4]The Nephilim were on the earth in those days—and also afterward—when the sons of God went to the daughters of men and had children by them. They were the heroes of old, men of renown.
> [5]The LORD saw how great man's wickedness on the earth had become, and that every inclination of the thoughts of his heart was only evil all the time. [6]The LORD was grieved that he had made man on the earth, and his heart was filled with pain. [7]So the LORD said, "I will wipe mankind, whom I have created, from the face of the earth—men and animals, and creatures that move along the ground, and birds of the air—for I am grieved that I have made them." [8]But Noah found favor in the eyes of the LORD. (Genesis 6:1-8 NIV)

The passage of Scripture quoted above informs us that in those days the sons of God were having sex and marrying the daughters of men. Apparently this was some kind of unholy alliance that had spread throughout the human race. There is great debate theologically as to the identity of the sons of God. Some theologians believe that the phrase refers

---

[17]The fact that scriptural mandates for slave masters to treat their slaves humanely have not been deleted from the Bible, and that there is scripture that defines slave trading as a sin, is strong evidence (among many other evidences) that the doctrinal teachings of the Bible have not been tampered with.

to angels, partly due to the fact that when used in Job 1:6 and Job 2:1[18] the phrase does indeed refer to angels and partly due to the fact that the word *Nephilim* is translated into Hebrew as "fallen ones." Many theologians therefore believe that the sons of men are the fallen angels (demonic angels, spirits) that were thrown out of heaven along with Lucifer before the creation of man.[19]

However, others believe that the sons of God could not be referring to angels because Jesus taught that angels in heaven neither marry nor are given in marriage.[20]

Still, there are those theologians that point out that there are places in Scripture in which human beings are referred to as being the sons and daughters of God and that therefore the phrase "sons of God" could refer to godly men. And then there are those who believe that the phrase "sons of God" might refer to ungodly earthly kings that had harems.

There are three possible reasons why the alliance was unholy: because one of the groups was pagan, or because the men and women of these groups were not married to one another (v.4)[21], or because the sons of God were not human beings. If the sons of God were not human then the unholy sexual alliance would have to be due to the fact that the alliance was physically unnatural.

Aside from these possible explanations, there is absolutely no biblical indication that the unholy sexual alliance between the sons of God and the daughters of men was unholy because one group of participants was white and the other group was non-white. Race is never mentioned in the text. As a matter of fact, what's cited as God's reason for destroying the inhabitants of the earth with a flood is not "race-mixing," but instead the extent of people's wickedness at the time (which apparently had a lot to do with the sexual interaction that was taking place between the sons of God and the daughters of men) and evil thoughts. Clearly, the sexual intercourse that was taking place between the sons of God and the daughters of men was immoral. Why it was viewed that way by God we may never clearly understand, as stated before, maybe the sons of God were beings that were not human; but what we do understand is that the sons of God and the daughters of men were not supposed to be marrying one another and having sex. Theirs was an unholy sexual alliance in some way. However, we know that skin color could not be the reason that the

---

[18] See your Bible.

[19] Ezekiel 28:13-19 and Revelation 12:7-9, see your Bible.

[20] Matthew 22:28-30, see your Bible.

[21] The Bible teaches that it is a sin to have sexual intercourse prior to marriage (1 Corinthians chapter 7, see your Bible).

union was deemed unholy because nowhere in the Bible is it indicated that it is unholy or unnatural for two people of different races to marry one another.

Moses and his Ethiopian wife

One argument that helps to give credibility to the position that the Bible is not against interracial marriages has to do with the reaction of Moses' family to his marriage of an Ethiopian woman. The account is given below.

> [1]Miriam and Aaron began to talk against Moses because of his Cushite wife, for he had married a Cushite. [2]"Has the Lord spoken only through Moses?" they asked. "Hasn't he also spoken through us? And the Lord heard this.
> [3](Now Moses was a very humble man, more humble than anyone else on the face of the earth).
> [4]At once the Lord said to Moses, Aaron, and Miriam, "Come out to the tent of meeting all three of you." So the three of them went out. [5]Then the Lord came down in a pillar of cloud; he stood at the entrance to the tent and summoned Aaron and Miriam. When the two of them stepped forward, [6]he said, "Listen to my words: "When there are prophets of the Lord among you, I reveal myself to them in visions, I speak to them in dreams.
> [7]But this is not true of my servant Moses; he is faithful in all my house.
> [8]With him I speak face to face, clearly and not in riddles; he sees the form of the Lord. Why then were you not afraid to speak against my servant Moses?
> [9]The anger of the Lord burned against them, and he left them. (Numbers 12:1-9 NIV).

One of Ham's sons was Cush. As discussed in the previous chapter, Cush was the father of the Ethiopian nation. Many translations therefore opt to translate the identification of Moses's wife in the above passage as Ethiopian. Israel is a nation composed of twelve original tribes. The Cushites were not Israelites. They were of a different nationality than the Israelites. However, it should be noted that Abraham (whose name was at

235

first Abram until God changed it to Abraham[22]), the father of the Israelites, was a descendant of Shem who was the brother of Ham and therefore the uncle to Cush. It is believed, however, that Miriam and Aaron spoke against the marriage of Moses and his Cushite (Ethiopian) wife because she was not an Israelite. However, there are some who believe that they spoke against the marriage because she was an African woman and therefore, more likely than not, a black woman. Whatever the reason, the Scriptures quite clearly indicate that God was not pleased with the attitude of Miriam and Aaron. His anger burned against them both. The account goes on as follows:

> [10]As the cloud moved from above the Tabernacle, there stood Miriam, her skin as white as snow from leprosy. When Aaron saw what had happened to her, [11]he cried out to Moses, "Oh, my master! Please don't punish us for this sin we have so foolishly committed. [12]Don't let her be like a stillborn baby, already decayed at birth. [13]So Moses cried out to the LORD, "Oh God I beg you, please heal her!"
> [14]But the LORD said to Moses, "If her father had done nothing more than spit in her face, wouldn't she be defiled for seven days? So keep her outside the camp for seven days, and after that she may be accepted back."
> [15]So Miriam was kept outside the camp for seven days, and the people waited until she was brought back before they traveled again." (Numbers 12:10-15 NLT).

God began to punish both Aaron and Miriam for speaking against Moses. God punished Miriam first by cursing her with leprosy. Although most translations define the disease as leprosy, theologians agree that the word in the Hebrew that is used for leprosy in the text was also used for many other various diseases of the skin. Therefore, the disease might not have been leprosy, but clearly God vexed her with some sort of disease. The passage of Scripture implies that God was about to chastise Aaron with a similar punishment, but Aaron pleaded with Moses for himself and for Miriam. Then Moses pleaded that Miriam be healed. God had mercy and did not vex Aaron. But Miriam was already deemed unclean according to the Laws that God had handed down to the people through Moses. Therefore, God ordered that Miriam be separated from the camp until

---

[22] Genesis 17:1-8 is discussed later on in this chapter.

seven days had passed. Seven days was the usual time it took to be ceremonially cleansed.

If it had been wrong for Moses to marry this Ethiopian woman because she was a black woman and he was an Israelite (a Jew), then God would not have responded the way he did towards Miriam and Aaron but would have instead chastised Moses and his wife. But he did not punish Moses and his wife. He instead chastised Miriam and Aaron for speaking against, what we would refer to today as an interracial marriage.

Marriages that the Bible speaks against

When looking at the marriages that God authorized in the Bible, we see time and time again that God forbade the Israelites to marry people from other nations that worshipped pagan Gods. They were to only marry people who worshipped the one true God; whether that person was an Israelite or not didn't matter, as long as they worshipped the one true God. We can therefore safely assume that Moses' Ethiopian wife, although African and not necessarily ethnically Jewish (although she may have been), accepted the God of the Hebrews (the Jews) and worshipped the same God as Moses did. Otherwise, God would have not accepted the marriage and he would not have chastised Aaron and Miriam for speaking against it.

This becomes clearer when looking at the New Testament Scriptures on marriage. Although there is no biblical command that forbids interracial marriage; there are Old Testament commands that forbade marriages between Jewish believers and pagans and New Testament commands that forbid marriage between Christians and non-Christians. This has nothing to do with race, but instead with belief, as attested to in the following passage of Scripture:

> [14]Do not be yoked together with unbelievers. For what do righteousness and wickedness have in common? Or what fellowship can light have with darkness? [15]What harmony is there between Christ and Belial? Or what does a believer have in common with an unbeliever? [16]What agreement is there between the temple of God and idols? For we are the temple of the living God. As God has said "I will live with them and walk among them, and I will be their God, and they will be my people."
> [17]"Therefore come out from them and be separate, says the Lord.

Touch no unclean thing and I will receive you,
¹⁸"I will be a Father to you,
and you will be my sons and daughters, says the Lord
Almighty." (2 Corinthians 6:14-18 NIV)

The above Scripture passage was written by the Apostle Paul who wrote
two-thirds of the New Testament and was, at one point, the most feared
persecutor of Christians until the risen Lord, Jesus Christ, confronted him
on the road to Damascus;[23] after which he became one of the most
dedicated followers of Christ that ever lived. The passage was written to
the Corinthian church and under inspiration of God. Paul specifically
taught that believers in Christ are not to team up with unbelievers for
"what fellowship can light have with darkness?" and "what does a believer
have in common with an unbeliever?" There's no doubt that this
admonishment for believers not to join together with unbelievers would
especially apply to marriage since marriage is the most serious of
partnerships men and women enter into; second only to getting saved and
walking with Christ. With this said, as we can see; Paul makes no mention
of race when it comes to who believers can marry and not marry; so,
therefore, it is not an issue. However, the following passage of Scripture is
one that some opponents of this view might try to use to argue against this
point. It reads,

¹After these things had been done, the leaders came to
me and said, "The people of Israel, including the priests
and the Levites, have not kept themselves separate from
the neighboring peoples with their detestable practices,
like those of the Canaanites, Hittites, Perizzites,
Jebusites, Ammonites, Moabites, Egyptians, and
Amorites. ²They have taken some of their daughters as
wives for themselves and their sons and have mingled
the holy race with the peoples around them. And the
leaders and officials have led the way in this
unfaithfulness.
³When I heard this, I tore my tunic and cloak, pulled hair
from my head and beard and sat down appalled. ⁴Then
everyone who trembled at the words of the God of Israel
gathered around me because of this unfaithfulness of the
exiles. And I sat there appalled until the evening
sacrifice.

---

[23] Acts 22:6-10, see your Bible.

[5]Then, at the evening sacrifice, I rose from my self-abasement, with my tunic and cloak torn, and fell on my knees with my hands spread out to the LORD my God [6]and prayed: "O my God, I am too ashamed and disgraced to lift up my face to you, my God, because our sins are higher than our heads and our guilt has reached to the heavens. [7]From the days of our forefathers until now, our guilt has been great. Because of our sins, we and our kings and our priests have been subjected to the sword and captivity, to pillage and humiliation at the hand of foreign kings, as it is today.

[8]"But now, for a brief moment, the LORD our God has been gracious in leaving us a remnant and giving us a firm place in his sanctuary, and so our God gives light to our eyes and a little relief in our bondage. [9]Though we are slaves, our God has not deserted us in our bondage. He has shown us kindness in the sight of the kings of Persia: He has granted us new life to rebuild the house of our God and repair its ruins, and he has given us a wall of protection in Judah and Jerusalem.

[10]"But now, O our God, what can we say after this? For we have disregarded the commands [11]you gave through your servants the prophets when you said: 'The land you are entering to possess is a land polluted by the corruption of its peoples. By their detestable practices they have filled it with their impurity from one end to the other. [12]Therefore, do not give your daughters in marriage to their sons or take their daughters for your sons. Do not seek a treaty of friendship with them at any time, that you may be strong and eat the good things of the land and leave it to your children as an everlasting inheritance.'

[13]"What has happened to us is a result of our evil deeds and our great guilt, and yet, our God, you have punished us less than our sins have deserved and have given us a remnant like this. [14]Shall we again break your commands and intermarry with the peoples who commit such detestable practices? Would you not be angry enough with us to destroy us, leaving us no remnant or survivor? [15] O LORD, God of Israel, you are righteous! We are left this day as a remnant. Here we are before you in our

guilt, though because of it not one of us can stand in
your presence." (Ezra, chapter 9 NIV)

Special attention needs to be called to verse 2 which says, "they have
taken some of their daughters as wives for themselves and their sons and
have mingled the holy race with the peoples around them." The leaders of
Israel came to the prophet Ezra and made this accusation, among other
accusations, against the Hebrews (Jews) to Ezra. The accusation was that
the Jews had allowed other people to mix with them; "the holy race."
Some would say that the use of the word *race* in the passage proves God
made different races of human beings. They would probably go on to say
that the fact that one group of people has been identified in the Bible as
"the holy race" adds even more to their argument that one race of people
can be superior to another. The rebuttal to such an argument would be
threefold.

First, the original language of the Old Testament was Hebrew and the
actual Hebrew word for the word *race* that is used in the English
translation of the text is *zera* which more accurately translates as
descendants or *offspring* which is quite different from the way the word
race is used in American society. Secondly, some Bible translations use
the word *race* when translating the passage while other translations use
the word *seed* or *offspring* (a more exact translation) depicting more
clearly a blessed people through ancestral roots and not through physical
characteristics. Thirdly, those who insist that the Bible teaches that one
group of people are superior to another, who espouse racism, and who
misuse the Bible to support their beliefs often target the Jews as one of the
"races" of people that they say is inferior. However, Ezra 9:2 is
undoubtedly referring to the Jews as "the holy race." Certainly then, the
Jews are by no means inferior. But Jews are called holy, not because they
are automatically righteous because they are Jews, but because they are
set apart due to a promise God made to their forefather, Abraham. To be
holy means to be set apart. A more precise translation would be "set apart
offspring" instead of "holy race." This does not make the Jews superior,
but it does make them special.

The passage tells us that the Israelites were wrong for marrying the
neighboring people, not because of the color of their skin, but because of
their detestable practices that were similar to the detestable practices of
other pagan nations like the Canaanites and Hittites. The detestable
practices not only included the worshipping of false gods but deviant
sexual practices as well.[24]

---

[24] Exodus 34:1-15, see your Bible

THE BIBLE WHEN IT COMES TO THE COLOR OF GOD

The answer to the question as to what color God is, particularly among those who embrace racist ideologies, has long been the focus of great debate; the idea being that if God can be categorized as belonging to a particular race, then it would stand that whatever race God belongs to is superior to every other race.

Over the centuries, white America has depicted all biblical characters as white. Hollywood has been the main culprit of this. But the visual racial identification of biblical characters, particularly Jesus (God manifested in the flesh), as white that has permeated America is not only seen in movies but also in church stain glass windows, Bible graphics, art, books, and the like. These depictions of Jesus as white eventually helped to turn many blacks against Christianity because they saw whites as oppressive and therefore saw Jesus as oppressive since he too was portrayed as white. Many blacks began to believe the lie that Christianity was the "white man's religion."[25]

During the mid to late sixties amid the struggle for racial equality, many Christian blacks began portraying Jesus as black in order to counteract the American depiction of him as white. Jesus' race, for some, became more of a focus than his message. The irony of this is that, there is no doubt that Jesus was a Jew; and in today's American society, as in most societies of the world, that would mean that technically, he was neither black nor white. Moreover, and ironically, while white America claims him as white and black America claims him as black, Orthodox Jews reject him as the Messiah (Lord God and Savior), even though Jesus came in the flesh as a Jew.

There is no Scripture that describes what color Jesus was. We don't know if he looked white or if he looked black. We don't know if he was of a fair complexion or dark-skinned. The Bible never says. Some, would however disagree. Blacks that attempt to prove that Jesus was black, usually use the following passage of Scripture as their argument :

> [12]I turned around to see the voice that was speaking to me. And when I turned I saw seven golden lampstands, [13]and among the lampstands was someone "like a son of man," dressed in a robe reaching down to his feet and with a golden sash around his chest. [14]His head and hair was white like wool, as white as snow, and his eyes were

---

[25] A teaching of Elijah Muhammad, successor to the founder of the Nation of Islam.

> like blazing fire. [15]His feet were like bronze glowing in a furnace, and his voice was like the sound of rushing waters. [16]In his right hand he held seven stars, and coming out of his mouth was a sharp, double-edged sword. His face was like the sun shining in all his brilliance. (Revelation 1:12-16 NIV)

This passage comes from the biblical book of Revelation and depicts the Apostle John receiving revelation from Jesus Christ. Jesus Christ is identified in the first chapter of Revelation as the person from which the revelation comes. The main focus in the above passage has to do with the description of Jesus' hair being "white like wool." Most black Americans who use this Scripture to defend their position that Jesus was black, argue that the Bible says that his hair was like wool, meaning that his hair was the same texture as is the hair of African peoples (wooly) and therefore Jesus had to be black. The problem with this line of reasoning is that the biblical description references the *color* of Jesus' hair, not the texture. "White like wool" indicates that his hair was the same color as wool: white. Moreover, if we are to say that Jesus was black because the Scripture depicts his hair as white like wool and his feet the color of bronze, then the same argument could be used to say that Jesus is white because the passage of Scripture also describes his head as white. But when looking at the passage it is obvious that there is a great deal of symbolism in the vision of Jesus that John saw and that the Jesus he saw was not Jesus in human form that he had once seen when Jesus walked the earth, but Jesus in a glorified heavenly appearance.

When looking for a description of Jesus during the time he walked the earth in human flesh, the Scripture passage below is the only passage that describes how Jesus looked; it reads…

> He had no beauty or majesty to attract us to him, nothing in his appearance that we should desire him. (Isaiah 53:2b NIV)[26]

The prophet Isaiah described Jesus as very average looking. He was not beautiful. There was nothing about his appearance that would have made a person want to be around him. It would appear that God set it up this way so that people who came to follow Jesus would do so out of a sincere heart. There is no mention of skin color or facial features. There

---

[26] See your Bible for the entire examination of the chapter so that there is no doubt that the person being spoken of is Jesus.

were no cameras during those times so there is no picture of him.[27] Isaiah, however, does predict how Jesus would look after suffering the cruelties of the cross. The description is as follows:

> [13]See, my servant will act wisely, he will be raised and
> lifted up and highly exalted.
> [14]Just as there were many who were appalled at him—
> his appearance was so disfigured beyond that of any man
> and his form marred beyond human likeness—
> [15]so will he sprinkle many nations, and kings will shut
> their mouths because of him. (Isaiah 52:13-15a NIV)

Although the apostles and many disciples walked with Jesus during his earthly ministry, none of them ever wrote down a description of him as far as skin color, facial features, height, weight, hair color/texture, and so forth. This in itself speaks volumes as to whether or not his looks were important. Apparently, the color of Jesus' skin wasn't important enough for those who walked with him in his ministry to record it in the Bible. Therefore, it is apparently not important at all and had absolutely no bearing upon what he was called to this earth to do. Aside from the second personage of God (Jesus Christ) having had been manifested in the flesh in order to make an ultimate blood sacrifice for the atonement of sins; God is a Spirit, as attested to in John 4:24 (KJV) which says, "God is a Spirit, and they that worship him must worship him in spirit and in truth." Ultimately, there is no racial category that we can fit God into because God is a Spirit, which is a different order of being altogether from a human being.

THE BIBLE WHEN IT COMES TO VERY DARK SKIN

As discussed in Chapter 5, in America, as well as in many other parts of the world, the darker one's skin tone, the more likely one is to be discriminated against in some way even if it is only to experience the scorn and disapproval of the close friends and relatives of a dating partner. Darker-skinned people (especially those who are very dark) are often times considered as less attractive than lighter-skinned people, simply by virtue of their skin color and nothing else. This type of discrimination not only plays into the mate selection process but might also be present inconspicuously and even unconsciously during employee interview processes and the like. Black America has been just as guilty of light-

---

[27] However, some believe that the Shroud of Turin depicts the face of Jesus.

skinned/dark-skinned lookism[28] as has white America. And when looking at things biblically, we see that there is also some indication that persons living in ancient times may have similarly had a tendency to label darker-skinned peoples as less attractive. We see this possibility when examining the biblical book of the Song of Solomon.

Song of Solomon

The Song of Solomon is a book of the Bible that portrays the depth of love between two young newlyweds. The passage of Scripture that alludes to the possibility of a society in which dark-skinned peoples were thought of as less attractive is documented below:

[1]This is Solomon's Song of Songs, more wonderful than any other.
Young woman:
[2]Kiss me and kiss me again, for your love is sweeter than wine.
[3]How fragrant your cologne; your name is like its spreading fragrance. No wonder all the young women love you!
[4]Take me with you; come, let's run! The king has brought me into his bedroom.
Young women of Jerusalem
How happy we are for you, O king. We praise your love even more than wine
Young woman
How right they are to adore you.
[5]I am dark but beautiful, O women of Jerusalem—dark as the tents of Kedar, dark as the curtains of Solomon's tents.
[6]Don't stare at me because I am dark—the sun has darkened my skin. My brothers were angry with me; they forced me to care for their vineyards, so I couldn't care for myself—my own vineyard.
[7]Tell me, my love, where are you leading your flock today? Where will you rest your sheep at noon? For why should I wander like a prostitute among your friends and their flocks?

---

[28] See chapter 5

Young Man
[8]If you don't know, O most beautiful woman, follow the trail of my flock, and graze your young goats by the shepherd's tents.
[9]You are as exciting, my darling, as a mare among Pharaoh's stallions.
[10]How lovely are your cheeks; your earrings set them afire! How lovely is your neck, enhanced by a string of jewels.
[11]We will make for you earrings of gold and beads of silver.

Young Woman
[12]The king is lying on his couch, enchanted by the fragrance of my perfume.
[13]My lover is like a sachet of myrrh lying between my breasts.
[14]He is like a bouquet of sweet henna blossoms from the vineyards of En-gedi.

Young Man
[15]How beautiful you are, my darling, how beautiful! Your eyes are like doves.

Young Woman
[16]You are so handsome, my love, pleasing beyond words! The soft grass is our bed;
[17]fragrant cedar branches are the beams of our house, and pleasant smelling firs are the rafters.
(Song of Solomon 1:1-17 NLT)

Solomon was Israel's third king. He reigned as king over Israel for roughly forty years. God blessed Solomon with unprecedented wisdom. He wrote the book of proverbs and was known during his lifetime as being full of wisdom. The book of the Song of Solomon is a song that King Solomon wrote depicting a newly married man and woman serenading one another poetically.

In Verse 5 above, the young woman identifies herself as "dark but beautiful." The description is translated as "black but comely" in the King James Version, the American Standard Version, the Webster's Bible Translation, the English Revised Version, the Darby Bible Translation, and the Young's literal Translation. The description is translated as "black but lovely" in the New American Standard Bible and in the Word English Bible. The description is translated as "black but beautiful" in the New Living Translation and the New International Version translates the description as "dark yet lovely." History tells us that the tents of Kedar refer to the tents of an ancient Northern Arabic tribe who made their tents from the wool of black goats. There is therefore little argument against the conclusion that the woman depicted in Solomon's song is what Americans would refer to as a very dark-skinned black woman and not a white woman with a tan nor a light-skinned black woman.

The woman goes on to admonish the women of Jerusalem not to stare at her because she is dark and then she excuses her blackness by explaining that she was made to work in the sun for hours every day. The fact that Solomon depicts the woman as excusing her blackness indicates that there was prejudice against very dark-skinned black people at that time. It is interesting to note that out of all the women Solomon could have chosen to depict to sing about; he chose to depict a very dark-skinned black woman. As the song continues, we see that the husband (the young lover) never addresses the fact that her skin is black. For him, it is a non-issue. Instead he calls her beautiful throughout the song and not only refers to her as beautiful but is absolutely enamored by her beauty. The woman says that she is beautiful despite her blackness, but the response that Solomon applies to the lover implies that her lover sees her blackness as part of her beauty. Her lover continuously tells her throughout the song that she is the "most beautiful of women." Her friends also refer to her as "most beautiful of women" which is seen in Song of Solomon 5:9 and 6:1.[29]

The Song of Solomon celebrates the love between two newlyweds[30] and depicts a black woman (a very dark-skinned black woman at that) being praised for her beauty. If the Bible were truly a book that, in particular, elevates whites over blacks (as some believe that it does) it stands to reason that we would not expect a book in the Bible to in any way celebrate the beauty of a black woman. But the biblical book of the Song of Solomon does just that. This kind of thing is simply hard to overlook.

But it doesn't stop there. In Song of Solomon 5:10 most Bible translations translate the description of the young man (as described by the young woman) as being "white and ruddy." In the King James Version the verse reads, "My beloved is white and ruddy, the chieftest among ten thousand (KJV)." The specific descriptive phrase "white and ruddy" also reads the same in the following Bible translations: the New King James Version, the 21st Century King James Version, the American Standard

---

[29] See your Bible.

[30] In Song of Solomon 5:1 the young man refers to the young woman as his bride. See your Bible.

Version, the Darby Bible, the English Bible, and the Webster's Bible Translation. The New International Version translates the description as "radiant and ruddy." The actual ancient Hebrew words for the description are "sah" and "adom" respectively. However, according to the NIV Exhaustive Concordance, the Hebrew word "sah" translates literally into English as *clear, radiant, scorching, or shimmering*. But when looking further into the Concordance listings we find that *sahah*, (apparently a derivative of the word "sah") translates into the English word "whiter." It follows then that if *sahah* means *whiter* then *sah* could mean *white* and that the terms *radiant* and *shimmering* could possibly refer to a white hue.

A further description of the young man is seen in verse 14 of that same chapter in which his body is described as "polished ivory." Ivory is indeed white, which is probably the reason that many biblical translators chose to assume that the radiance of the young man had to do with a lighter color of skin. However, the Hebrew word "adom" translates literally into English as *red*, which brings question to the translation of "sah" as white. Some might say that a facial blush of his skin may contribute to the redness. Overall, we must keep in mind that the Song of Solomon is indeed that; a song, which means that the verses of Scripture contained in it are lyrics giving rise to the position that the two newlywed lovers depicted in the song are fictional. Some would however say that they are not fictional but instead represent two actual people, the young man being Solomon himself. Let's take a look at the particular verses that we've been referring to in context:

Friends
[9]How is your beloved better than others,
Most beautiful of women?
How is your beloved better than others,
That you charge us so?

Beloved
[10]My lover is radiant and ruddy,
Outstanding among ten thousand.
[11]His head is purest gold;
His hair is wavy
And black as a raven.

[12]His eyes are like doves
by the water streams,
washed in milk,
mounted like jewels.

247

¹³His cheeks are like beds of spice
yielding perfume.
his lips are like lilies
dripping with myrrh.

¹⁴His arms are rods of gold
set with chrysolite.
His body is like polished ivory
decorated with sapphires.
(Song of Solomon 5:9-14 NIV)

The "Beloved" in the above translation is the same as "the Young Woman" in the New Living Translation previously used. As indicated earlier, verse 10 is the verse in question. Some translations render the word "radiant" as having a definite correlation with the word "white."[31] We see this correlation between radiance (brightness) and whiteness when looking at how princes are described in the following passage of Scripture from the book of Lamentations:

> Their princes were brighter than snow and whiter than milk, their bodies more ruddy than rubies, their appearance like sapphires. (Lamentations 4:7 KJV)

Despite this correlation, verse 11 describes the young man's head as purest gold. If we look to this as describing skin color then we have a contradiction. How can he be white (radiant) if his head is purest gold? Pure gold is light brownish tan in color. It is not the color of white. Is the description of the young man's gold head referring to color or is the description simply an exuberant metaphor expressed from the young woman relating to his overall beauty? It's hard to say. But if we take the premise that his head is brown then we must do away with the depiction of him as white and instead use the word "radiant" to denote him as does the NIV translation and conclude that his ivory polished body is not speaking of color but of the smoothness of skin texture.

All this said, even though there is no question that the young woman is black; there is some question as to the skin color of the young man; is he

---

[31] The New Living Translation renders the description "dark and dazzling and is the only translation to use the word "dark." This might have to do with the fact that the word *sah* used there in the Greek translates into English as all of the following: *clear, radiant, scorching,* or *shimmering.* Some would therefore look at the description of "scorching" as indicative of a dark color.

white, tan, or red? Some would say the question is very important because of verse 9 in which the friends of the young woman are depicted as asking the following question: "How is your beloved better than others, most beautiful of women?" Those who look to the Bible to find some proof that the Bible supports racism would be prone to render the phrase "better than others" as "superior to others" making it understandable why, in such cases, the translation of her response is so important, for the young woman replies by saying that her beloved is "radiant and ruddy." If then the translation of "radiant" is white, then the answer to the question, "why is your beloved better than others?" becomes, "because he is white" when actually it is because he is radiant and glowing which can be attributed to any skin color; literally, he is "clear" (the literal meaning) which could also mean that his skin is flawless and glowing. Furthermore, the phrase "better than others" literally translates into "above any other," which then basically points towards the depiction of a woman holding her husband in high esteem above any other man, which as his wife, she is expected to do. The descriptions therefore of the physicality of the young woman and the young man are not a testament to the superiority of one skin color over another but instead is a testament to the physical beauty each of them see in one another because of the profound love that they have for one another.

The main point in examining the text is to emphasize the fact that Solomon, the wisest man who was living at the time and probably who ever lived,[32] chose to depict a black woman (literally black, very dark-skinned) as a woman with great beauty. It looks like he also may have chosen to depict a white man as a man with equally great beauty (although some could justifiably argue that the man was brown-skinned or red-skinned). If we go with the majority of translations that depict Solomon's newlywed couple in his song as the woman having black skin and the man having white skin then not only is it safe to say that the Bible emphasizes the beauty of both skin colors but it is also safe to say that the Bible devotes an entire book towards celebrating a marriage that we would define as interracial. It is therefore not surprising that those who misuse and misinterpret the Bible in attempts to justify racist and discriminatory views rarely venture into the pages of the Song of Solomon; for if they did they would have a lot of explaining to do.

Skin colors of disease

In the Bible, skin color is often spoken of as a result of certain skin diseases. Those who try to find something in the Bible to support racial

---

[32] 1 Kings 4:29-34, see your Bible

bigotry might turn to those Scriptures. We will take a look at some of those Scriptures. We will first look at Scriptures that white supremacists might use in order to try to prove that black skin is inferior and then we will take a look at the Scriptures that black supremacists might use in order to try to prove that white skin is inferior.

> [7]So Satan went out from the presence of the LORD and afflicted Job with painful sores from the soles of his feet to the top of his head. (Job 2:7 NIV)

> [28]I go about blackened, but not by the sun; I stand up in the assembly and cry for help.
> [29]I have become a brother of jackals, a companion of owls.
> [30]My skin grows black and peels; my body burns with fever.
> [31]My harp is tuned to mourning, and my flute to the sound of wailing. (Job 30:28-31 NIV)

The book of Job[33] is an historical account of an upright and blameless man named Job who Satan attacked in an effort to prove to God that Job would curse God if he lost his health and wealth. Although Job became distressed during the ordeal, he never cursed God. In Satan's quest to discredit Job, Satan attacked Job's health and made him very ill. At one point Job's whole body became infected with boils which eventually turned his skin black. We cannot say that since Job was afflicted and his skin became black (as a result of his affliction) that black skin is inferior. If we were to say this then we'd have to say the same thing about white skin when taking the following account into consideration that we looked at previously:

> [9]And the anger of the LORD was kindled against them; and he departed.
> [10]And the cloud departed from off the tabernacle; and, behold, Miriam became leprous, white as snow: and Aaron looked upon Miriam, and, behold, she was leprous. (Numbers 12:9-10 KJV)

Miriam's skin became as white as snow as a consequence of a disease. However, the white skin was a result of a disease but not the disease itself.

---

[33] See your Bible for the book of Job.

White skin is not a disease just as black skin is not a disease. Even when taking into consideration the condition of vitiligo in which the skin begins to lose its pigmentation and turns white, the loss of pigmentation is the actual ailment and the white skin is the result of that loss of pigmentation but is not the ailment itself. We see the same kind of occurrence in Job 2:7 when Job describes his misery that results from being afflicted by Satan with painful sores.[34] Later on, he describes his skin as being blackened from the disease (Job 30:28-31).[35] The blackened skin is a result of the sores but is not the disease itself. The natural color of one's skin and the unnatural coloring of it resulting from disease are two different issues. One has no bearing on the other. Therefore, the discoloration of Miriam's skin and the discoloration of Job's skin due to disease cannot be used to justify the notion that one skin color is superior to another.

Still there are some that might persist in their erroneous argument as to the superiority of one skin color over another and they might use the following passage of Scripture in their attempt at justification:

[2]How the precious sons of Zion,
once worth their weight in gold,
are now considered as pots of clay,
the work of a potter's hands!

[3]Even jackals offer their breasts
to nurse their young,
but my people have become heartless
like ostriches in the desert.

[4]Because of thirst the infant's tongue
sticks to the roof of its mouth;
the children beg for bread,
but no one gives it to them.

[5]Those who once ate delicacies
are destitute in the streets.
Those nurtured in purple
now lie on ash heaps.

[6]The punishment of my people
is greater than that of Sodom,

---

[34] See your Bible
[35] Previously quoted.

which was overthrown in a moment
without a hand turned to help her.

[7]Their princes were brighter than snow
and whiter than milk,
their bodies more ruddy than rubies,
their appearance like sapphires.

[8]But now they are blacker than soot;
they are not recognized in the streets.
Their skin has shriveled on their bones;
it has become as dry as a stick.

[9]Those killed by the sword are better off
than those who die of famine;
racked with hunger, they waste away
for lack of food from the field.
(Lamentations 4:2-9 NIV)

There are some white supremacists who might look at verse 8 of the Scripture passage just quoted and say that since the skin blackening of the white royal princes was a bad thing then black skin overall is therefore bad. What is quite evident in the passage is that the blackening of the skin was due to some human ailment; this time it wasn't directly caused by disease but by starvation which no doubt weakened the immune system giving way to disease. Verse 9 clearly indicates that the reason for the skin turning from white to black had to do with famine and hunger. One would therefore be hard pressed to make an argument that black skin is inferior by using this Scripture.

White supremacists may also attempt to use the following Scripture to justify their racism:

[7]Cleanse me with hyssop, and I will be clean; wash me,
and I will be whiter than snow. (Psalms 51:7 NIV)

Some would be quick to say that the above verse of Scripture indicates that white skin represents cleanliness and purity. It is not the color of skin but the color *itself* that often times represents purity in the Bible. The biblical symbolisms attached to colors have nothing to do with skin. An easy rebuttal for those who would want to misuse the above verse to attempt to justify racism is presented in the Scripture below:

252

[18]"Come now, let us reason together,"
says the LORD.
"Though your sins are like scarlet,
they shall be as white as snow;
though they are red as crimson,
they shall be like wool.
(Isaiah 1:18 NIV)

Sins are compared to the color scarlet and crimson (red) but once we reason together with the Lord and turn from our sins they will be as white as snow. Sins are actions and therefore intangible. The colors associated with them are used symbolically, not literally. The color of crimson is used to symbolize sin, but the color itself is not sinful. It is not a sin to wear apparel that is crimson colored and wearing white does not make one pure or clean. The colors are used symbolically.

THE BIBLE WHEN IT COMES TO THE JEWS AS THE CHOSEN PEOPLE

Because the Bible gives account of God as having made certain promises to the nation of Israel (the Jews) that he has not made to any other nation, many believe that the Bible is discriminatory in favor of the Jews. There are those who argue that in having made the Jews certain promises, God has placed the Jews over everyone else. Bible opponents will argue that God has given the Jews special treatment, and they will say that this is not fair to the rest of us. Because of the complexity of this topic, we will need to explore the matter from its roots and build upon that. The root begins with Abraham.

Abraham: the father of the Jews; a Great Nation

According to the Bible, Abraham is the ancestral father of the nation of Israel, the Jews. Abraham and Sarah had a son that they named Isaac and Isaac had a son named Jacob whom God eventually renamed Israel. Israel had twelve sons which developed into what is now known as the twelve tribes of Israel. Judah was one of these twelve tribes named after the son that fathered the tribe. It is believed that most of Abraham's descendants who are now living are descendants of the tribe of Judah. Therefore the Israelites are most commonly associated with Judah which is the tribal name that the ethnic term *Jew* originates from. Moreover, Jesus Christ is a descendent of the tribe of Judah. Once God changed Jacob's name to

253

Israel, the Jews were also referred to and became known as the Israelites. Prior to this, Abraham's offspring were referred to as Hebrews.

Abraham is introduced in the Bible in the 11th Chapter of Genesis as Abram.[36] He is from the family line of Shem, one of Noah's three sons. Abraham's name was at first *Abram* before God changed it to Abraham. The following Scripture text is the account of God's first promise to Abraham:

> [1]The LORD had said to Abram, "Leave your country, your people and our father's household and go to the land I will show you.
> [2]I will make you into a great nation and I will bless you: I will make your name great, and you will be a blessing.
> [3]I will bless those who bless you, and whoever curses you I will curse; and all peoples on earth will be blessed through you." (Genesis 12:1-3 NIV)

Some would argue that God promised to bless Abraham by making him into a great nation without Abraham having had done anything to deserve it. But God is all knowing. The Bible describes God as the Alpha and Omega; the Beginning and the End.[37] This tells us therefore that God is not only knowledgeable about the past and present but also has knowledge of future things. God knew that Abraham would do anything that God required of him; even if it meant giving up his son to be sacrificed, which eventually is how God tested him. God came to Abraham a second time and promised him that his offspring for generations to come would be as numerous as the stars in the sky. The passage of Scripture below gives the account:

> [1]After this, the word of the LORD came to Abram in a vision: "Do not be afraid, Abram. I am your shield, your very great reward.
> [2]But Abram said, "Sovereign LORD, what can you give me since I remain childless and the one who will inherit my estate is Eliezer of Damascus? [3]And Abram said, "You have given me no children; so a servant in my household will be my heir."

---

[36] See your Bible.

[37] "I am the Alpha and the Omega," says the Lord God, "who is, and who was, and who is to come, the Almighty." (Revelation 1:8 NIV)

> [4]Then the word of the LORD came to him: "This man will not be your heir, but a son coming from your own body will be your heir. [5]He took him outside and said, "Look up at the heavens and count the stars—if indeed you can count them." Then he said to him, "So shall your offspring be."
> [6]Abram believed the LORD and he credited it to him as righteousness. (Genesis 15:1-6 TNIV)

Abraham asked God to bless him and God honored his request by reiterating, in a manner of speaking, that he would make Abraham into a great nation (meaning numerous generations of offspring would come from him). The account continues:

> [15]God also said to Abraham, "As for Sarai your wife, you are no longer to call her Sarai; her name will be Sarah. I will bless her and will surely give you a son by her. [16]I will bless her so that she will be the mother of nations; kings of peoples will come from her.
> [17]Abraham fell facedown, he laughed and said to himself, "Will a son be born to a man a hundred years old? Will Sarah bear a child at the age of ninety?? [18]And Abraham said to God, "If only Ishmael might live under your blessing!" (Genesis 17:15-18 TNIV)

Abraham laughed at the thought that he and his wife (since they were both old and Sarah was beyond the years of childbearing) would have a child. Abraham also suggested indirectly that his son Ishmael[38] reap these blessings since he felt, despite what God had told him, that he and Sarah were not able to produce children together. God responds:

> [19]"Then God said, "Yes, but your wife Sarah will bear you a son, and you will call him Isaac. I will establish my covenant with him as an everlasting covenant for his descendants after him. [20]And as for Ishmael, I have heard you: I will surely bless him; I will make him

---

[38] Ishmael was the son that Abraham fathered through his Egyptian servant Hagar under the prompting of his wife Sarah who, in the quest to orchestrate a surrogate pregnancy, asked Abraham to sleep with Hagar, since she herself was unable, at the time to bear him children and had become impatient. Genesis chapter 16, see your Bible.

> fruitful and will greatly increase his numbers. He will be
> the father of twelve rulers, and I will make him into a
> great nation. [21]But my covenant I will establish with
> Isaac, whom Sarah will bear to you by this time next
> year." (Genesis 17:19-21 TNIV)

Despite Abraham's laughter and unbelief, God reiterated what he had told Abraham confirming that Abraham and his wife would indeed have a son around that same time the following year. God commanded that the child be given the name Isaac. In the Hebrew language, Isaac means "he laughs." This seemed to be God's way of reminding Abraham of his initial unbelief and laughter at the promise of a son coming from the womb of his wife.

With regard to Abraham's mention of Ishmael, God assured Abraham that he heard him (in other words, he accepted Abraham's appeal regarding Ishmael) and promised to bless Ishmael, as well, by making him fruitful and by making his offspring into a numerous great nation also. Here is the first event in the historical account of Abraham that gives support to the argument that God did not "racially" discriminate between Isaac and Ishmael. Both sons were to become great nations.

Favor, in that God would establish a covenant (promise), did however, rest with Isaac; but not because Isaac was a full-blooded Hebrew and Ishmael was of mixed heritage (Hagar, Ishmael's mother, was an Egyptian), but speculatively because Isaac was born from the marital union and Ishmael was not. Ishmael was born by another woman other than Abraham's wife out of the impatience and disappointment experienced by that wife; Sarah. Despite this, God had always been very merciful to Hagar and her son, Ishmael.[39] God never blamed Hagar or Ishmael for events that eventually led to the surrogate parentage. If God would have viewed Ishmael, based on his heritage, as somehow inferior to Isaac, then it stands to reason that God would not have blessed Ishmael in any way. But this is not the case. God blessed Ishmael similar to how he blessed Isaac in that both Ishmael and Isaac would father great nations.

Later on when Isaac had become a boy, the Lord tested Abraham. Abraham's response to this test is the reason behind the promises that God had initially made to him. The account of this test is given below:

> [1]Some time later God tested Abraham. He said to him,
> "Abraham!" "Here I am," he replied.

---

[39] Genesis chapter 16 gives the full account. See your Bible

256

²Then God said, "Take your son, your only son, Isaac, whom you love, and go to the region of Moriah. Sacrifice him there as a burnt offering on one of the mountains I will tell you about."

³Early the next morning Abraham got up and saddled his donkey. He took with him two of his servants and his son Isaac. When he had cut enough wood for the burnt offering, he set out for the place God had told him about. ⁴On the third day Abraham looked up and saw the place in the distance. ⁵He said to his servants, "Stay here with the donkey while I and the boy go over there. We will worship and then we will come back to you."

⁶Abraham took the wood for the burnt offering and placed it on his son Isaac, and he himself carried the fire and the knife. As the two of them went on together, ⁷Isaac spoke up and said to his father Abraham, "Father?" "Yes, my son?" Abraham replied. "The fire and wood are here," Isaac said, "but where is the lamb for the burnt offering?"

⁸Abraham answered, "God himself will provide the lamb for the burnt offering, my son." And the two of them went on together.

⁹When they reached the place God had told him about, Abraham built an altar there and arranged the wood on it. He bound his son Isaac and laid him on the altar, on top of the wood. ¹⁰Then he reached out his hand and took the knife to slay his son. ¹¹But the angel of the LORD called out to him from heaven, "Abraham! Abraham!" "Here I am," he replied.

¹²"Do not lay a hand on the boy," he said. "Do not do anything to him. Now I know that you fear God, because you have not withheld from me your son, your only son."

¹³Abraham looked up and there in a thicket he saw a ram caught by its horns. He went over and took the ram and sacrificed it as a burnt offering instead of his son. ¹⁴So Abraham called that place The LORD Will Provide. And to this day it is said, "On the mountain of the LORD it will be provided."

¹⁵The angel of the LORD called to Abraham from heaven a second time ¹⁶and said, "I swear by myself, declares the LORD, that because you have done this and

have not withheld your son, your only son, [17]I will surely bless you and make your descendants as numerous as the stars in the sky and as the sand on the seashore. Your descendants will take possession of the cities of their enemies, [18]and through your offspring all nations on earth will be blessed, because you have obeyed me." (Genesis 22:1-18 NIV)

Verses 16-17 bring us to the main reason all along why God blessed Abraham. He did so because Abraham was willing to do anything God asked even if it meant giving up his only son for him. God knew that Abraham would pass this test and that his faith would prove solid. It must also be noted that Abraham's willingness to sacrifice his only son is akin and is symbolic to God being willing to sacrifice his only Son: Jesus Christ. This sacrifice is evident in John 3:16-18 which reads,

[16]For God so loved the world, that he gave his only begotten Son, that whosoever believeth in him should not perish, but have everlasting life.
[17]For God sent not his Son into the world to condemn the world; but that the world through him might be saved.
[18]He that believeth on him is not condemned: but he that believeth not is condemned already, because he hath not believed in the name of the only begotten Son of God. (KJV)

We see here that God the Father, gave up his only Son, Jesus Christ just as Abraham was willing to give up his only 'legitimate" son, Isaac. As discussed earlier, Abraham had two sons; Isaac and Ishmael. Isaac's birth was lawful whereas Ishmael's birth was not, which is why God identified Isaac as Abraham's "only son." Isaac was Abraham's only legal son. We see this even today. In America, there is a difference between a legal father and a biological father. Every legal father is not always the biological father and every biological father is not always the legal father.[40] A man automatically has legal claim to a child if that child was born to him inside of a marriage. However, in America, if a child is born to a man outside of marriage then he is not legally the father of that child unless his paternity has been established. Although, biologically the child is his; if paternity

---

[40] In most states, when a child is born inside of a marriage in which that child was conceived by a man other than the wife's husband, the husband is the legal father while the biological father is not.

has not been established, then legally the child is not his, and consequently the child has no right to any inheritance from the father. A similar consequence applied to Ishmael. He had no right to the inheritance of the covenant that God would pass down from Abraham to his son. When God referred to Isaac as Abraham's "only son" the meaning is that Isaac was Abraham's only legal son, so to speak. He had another son, Ishmael, but that son was not born through the proper channels. Despite this, God also promised to make Ishmael into a great nation as well. God kept his promise (Genesis 17:20) and Ishmael also had twelve sons whose descendants developed into great nations. The sons of Ishmael are recorded in the following passage of Scripture:

> [13] These are the names of the sons of Ishmael, listed in the order of their birth: Nebaioth the firstborn of Ishmael, Kedar, Adbeel, Mibsam, [14] Mishma, Dumah, Massa, [15] Hadad, Tema, Jetur, Naphish and Kedemah. [16]These were the sons of Ishmael, and these are the names of the twelve tribal rulers according to their settlements and camps. (Genesis 25:13-16 NIV)

Many of these names cited above are Arabic names giving way to the belief of many theologians that Ishmael was the father of the Arabic nations. Although Isaac was heir to the promise; he was heir not because of his race, but because he was a son of Abraham that was born of the marital union between Abraham and his wife Sarah while Ishmael was born of the union between Abraham and his servant Hagar as a result of Sarah's impatience. Both Isaac and Ishmael had the same father. Race was never an issue.

Isaac would eventually father Jacob and Jacob (Israel) would go on to father twelve sons that would produce twelve nations as well.[41] Jacob's sons were Reuben, Simeon, Levi, Judah, Issachar, Zebulun, Joseph, Benjamin, Dan, Naphtali, Gad, and Asher. These are the names of the nations that compose the twelve nations of Israel.

The Promised Land

Not only did God promise Abraham that he would be the father of a great nation, but he also promised to give a certain area of land to this great nation. We have seen this in Genesis 15:1-6 quoted previously and we

---

[41] Genesis 35:21-26 and Genesis chapter 49, see your Bible.

learn more about this land when examining the following passage of Scripture:

> [13]Then the Lord said to him, "Know for certain that for four hundred years your descendants will be strangers in a country not their own and that they will be enslaved and mistreated there. [14]But I will punish the nation they serve as slaves, and afterward they will come out with great possessions. [15]You, however, will go to your ancestors in peace and be buried at a good old age. [16]In the fourth generation your descendants will come back here, for the sin of the Amorites has not yet reached its full measure."
>
> [17]When the sun had set and darkness had fallen, a smoking firepot with a blazing torch appeared and passed between the pieces. [18]On that day the LORD made a covenant with Abram and said, "To your descendants I give this land, from the Wadi of Egypt to the great river, the Euphrates—[19]the land of the Kenites, Kenizzites, Kadmonites, [20]Hittites, Perizzites, Rephaites, [21]Amorites, Canaanites, Girgashites, and Jebusites." (Genesis 15:13-21 TNIV)

There is some debate among theologians as to how much land the promise actually entails and whether or not portions of Egypt, Iraq, Palestine, Lebanon, Jordan, and Kuwait are included; but in general, all theologians agree that the land of Israel is the centerpiece of the promise. God promised this particular piece of land to the descendants of Abraham; the Jews. God continues blessing Abraham in the account cited below:

> [1]When Abram was ninety-nine years old, the Lord appeared to him and said, "I am God Almighty, walk before me faithfully and be blameless. [2]Then I will make my covenant between me and you and will greatly increase your numbers.
>
> [3]Abram fell facedown, and God said to him, [4]"As for me, this is my covenant with you: You will be the father of many nations. [5]No longer will you be called Abram; your name will be Abraham, for I have made you a father of many nations. [6]I will make you very fruitful; I will make nations of you, and kings will come from you. [7]I will establish my covenant as an everlasting covenant

between me and you and your descendants after you.
⁸The whole land of Canaan, where you now reside as a
foreigner, I will give as an everlasting possession to you
and your descendants after you; and I will be their God."
(Genesis 17:1-8 TNIV)

As we see, this is the point where God changed Abram's name to
Abraham. God already knew that Abraham would walk with him faithfully
and blamelessly, which is why he began to bless him so abundantly. His
offspring was blessed, not on their own merit, but on the merit of their
ancestral father, Abraham. The account below documents the blessing that
Isaac passes from himself to Jacob (Israel) with regard to possession of the
land that was promised. It reads,

¹So Isaac called for Jacob and blessed him. Then he
commanded him: 'Do not marry a Canaanite woman.
²Go at once to Paddan Aram, to the house of your
mother's father Bethuel. Take a wife for yourself there,
from among the daughters of Laban, your mothers'
brother. ³May God Almighty bless you and make you
fruitful and increase your numbers until you become a
community of peoples. ⁴May he give you and your
descendants the blessing given to Abraham, so that you
may take possession of the land where you now reside as
a foreigner, the land God gave to Abraham." (Genesis
28:1-4 TNIV)

In the Scripture passage above, the blessing of the Promised Land is
passed from Isaac to Jacob. Isaac's admonishment of Jacob not to marry a
Canaanite woman had nothing to do with race but instead had to do with
the Canaanites' propensity towards the worshipping of false gods. Because
of their worshipping of false gods, the Canaanites are included among the
nations that God commanded the Israelites to completely destroy during
the time of Moses, as attested to below in the command given by God to
the Israelites:

¹⁶However, in the cities of the nations the LORD your
God is giving you as an inheritance, do not leave alive
anything that breathes. ¹⁷Completely destroy them—the
Hittites, Amorites, Canaanites, Perizzites, Hivites and
Jebusites—as the LORD your God has commanded you.
¹⁸Otherwise, they will teach you to follow all the

261

detestable things they do in worshipping their gods, and you will sin against the LORD your God. (Deuteronomy 20:16-18 TNIV)

The land that is spoken of is the same land that was promised to Abraham by way of his descendants; Isaac and Jacob.[42] God eventually changes Jacob's name to Israel. This account is seen in Genesis 35:9-12, which reads:

[9]After Jacob returned from Paddan Aram, God appeared to him again and blessed him. [10]God said to him, 'Your name is Jacob, but you will no longer be called Jacob; your name will be Israel. So he named him Israel.
[11]And God said to him, "I am God Almighty; be fruitful and increase in number. A nation and a community of nations will come from you, and kings will come from your body. [12]The land I gave to Abraham and Isaac I also give to you, and I will give this land to your descendants after you." (NIV)

As stated earlier, Israel (Jacob) had twelve sons and each son eventually produced a tribe, which makes up the twelve tribes of Israel, and is more commonly known as the Jewish nation. As indicated earlier, the land of Israel today, according to most theologians, is the Promised Land that God promised to the Jews. Israel was referred to as Palestine and was home to Arab Palestinians before it was established as the Jewish state of Israel in May of 1948.

Chosen Israel

The Jews are referred to as the chosen people partly due to the fact that they have been promised a certain area of land and partly due to the fact that God promised to make them a great nation; great in numbers. But in addition to those things, what makes the Jews the chosen people of God is the fact that God himself called them chosen through the writings of the Old Testament prophet Isaiah. The following passage of Scripture attests to this.

---

[42] More details. regarding the perimeters of the land are given in Exodus 23:31 which describes it as land that borders "the Red Sea to the Mediterranean Sea, and from the desert to the Euphrates River." (TNIV)

⁸But you O Israel, my servant
Jacob, whom I have chosen,
you descendants of Abraham my friend,

⁹I took you from the ends of the earth,
from its farthest corners I called you.
I said, 'You are my servant',
I have chosen you and have not rejected you.

¹⁰So do not fear, for I am with you;
do not be dismayed, for I am your God.
I will strengthen you and help you;
I will uphold you with my righteous right hand.

¹¹All who rage against you
will surely be ashamed and disgraced;
those who oppose you
will be as nothing and perish. (Isaiah 41:8-11 NIV)

God chose to bless Jacob (Israel) and his descendants (the Jews) not only with the promise of land and with the promise of becoming a great nation, but also with protection from total annihilation. This becomes clearer in the next two passages of Scripture.

¹But now, this is what the LORD says—
he who created you, Jacob,
he who formed you, Israel:
"Do not fear, for I have redeemed you;
I have summoned you by name; you are mine.

²When you pass through the waters,
I will be with you;
and when you pass through the rivers,
they will not sweep over you.
When you walk through the fire,
you will not be burned;
the flames will not set you ablaze.

³For I am the LORD your God,
The Holy One of Israel, your Savior,
I give Egypt for your ransom,
Cush and Seba in your stead.

> ⁴Since you are precious and honored in my sight,
> and because I love you,
> I will give nations in exchange for you,
> and people in exchange for your life.
>
> ⁵Do not be afraid, for I am with you;
> I will bring your children from the east
> and gather you from the west.
>
> ⁶I will say to the north, 'Give them up!'
> and to the south, 'Do not hold them back.'
> bring my sons from afar
> and my daughters from the ends of the earth—
>
> ⁷everyone who is called by my name,
> whom I created for my glory,
> whom I formed and made (Isaiah 43:1-7 NIV)

Verse 4 gives account of God saying to Israel, "I give Egypt for your ransom, Cush and Seba in your stead." It must be emphasized that the text is speaking of nations of people, not races of people and that all three of these nations were heathen nations at the time. The text is referring to a historical event. The commentary of Adam Clarke (early 19th century theologian) gives the following understanding to the text:

> *I gave Egypt for thy ransom.*[43] This is commonly supposed to refer to the time of Sennacherib's invasion; who, when he was just ready to fall upon Jerusalem, soon after his entering Judea, was providentially diverted from that design, and turned his arms against the Egyptians, and their allies the Cushean Arabians, with their neighbors the Sabeans, probably joined with them under Tirhakah. See chap. XX and chap. XXXVii. Or as there are some reasonable objections to this opinion, perhaps it may mean more generally that God has often saved His people at the expense of other nations whom He had, as it were in their stead, given up to destruction.

---

[43] "Gave" is the translation of the KJV as opposed to "give." The Assyrian invasion of Senncherib (the Assyrian king at the time) took place701 B.C. Tirhakah was a Cushite king of Egypt at the time. The account is documented in Isaiah 37. See your Bible.

264

Kimchi refers all this to the deliverance of Jerusalem from the invasion of Sennacherib, Tirhakah, king of Ethiopia, had come out to war against the king of Assyria, who was thereupon obliged to raise the siege of Jerusalem. Thus the Ethiopians, Egyptians, and Sabeans were delivered into the hands of the Assyrians as a ransom for Israel. I cannot help thinking this to be a very rational solution of the text.[44]

The text also tells us that God promised the Nation of Israel a special protection from those who might want to harm them. This does not mean that the Jewish people will never suffer persecution from other nations for history tells us that they did suffer Babylonian captivity in 70 A.D. and that they also suffered through attempted genocide during Hitler's German Nazi reign. The biblical book of Esther also recounts the attempt of Haman (a noble of the king at the time) to totally annihilate all of Israel during the reign of Xerxes (Persian king) who ruled from 486 to 465 B.C. This first attempt at Jewish genocide was thwarted by Xerxes' wife, a Jewish woman named Esther.[45] Although there have been two attempts in history to completely obliterate the nation of Israel (Haman's and Hitler's), God has sustained Israel because of his promises to Abraham, Isaac, and Jacob. Israel, the Jewish nation, has the favor of God. God specifically claims Israel as his chosen people. This is further illustrated in the following passage of Scripture:

> [1]"But now listen, Jacob, my servant,
> Israel, whom I have chosen.
> [2]This is what the Lord says—
> he who made you, who formed you in the womb,
> and who will help you:
> Do not be afraid, Jacob, my servant,
> Jeshurun, whom I have chosen.
> [3]For I will pour water on the thirsty land,
> and streams on the dry ground;
> I will pour out my Spirit on your offspring,
> and my blessing on your descendants.
> [4]They will spring up like grass in a meadow,
> like poplar trees by flowing streams.

---

[44] Adam Clarke Commentary. 1830. Public Domain.
[45] Esther, the entire book. See your Bible.

> ⁵One will say, 'I belong to the Lord;'
> another will call himself by the name of Jacob;
> still another will write on his hand, 'The
> LORD'S' and will take the name Israel.
> (Isaiah 44:1-5 NIV)

In verse 2 the name *Jeshurun* is used interchangeably with the name *Jacob* (which is used interchangeably with the name *Israel*). Jeshurun is another name for Israel and specifically means "the upright one." God says that he has "chosen" Israel by blessing his descendants and that his descendants will take the name of Israel. The Jews are the descendants of Abraham, Isaac, and Jacob. They are the descendants of Israel. The land that belongs to them is the land of Israel which was named after the man himself. This is attested to in the following passage of Scripture in which we see the word of God coming to the prophet Ezekiel:

> ¹⁴The word of the Lord came to me: ¹⁵"Son of man, the people of Jerusalem have said of fellow exiles and the whole house of Israel, 'They are far away from the Lord; this land was given to us as our possession.'
> ¹⁶Therefore say: 'This is what the Sovereign Lord says: Although I sent them far away among the nations and scattered them among the countries, yet for a little while I have been a sanctuary for them in the countries where they have gone."
> ¹⁷Therefore say: 'This is what the Sovereign Lord says: I will gather you from the nations and bring you back from the countries where you have been scattered, and I will give you back the land of Israel again.' (Ezekiel 11:14-17 TNIV)

Many theologians believe that the gathering of the Jews from many nations to bring them from the countries from which they were scattered back into the land of Israel took place when Israel became a nation again in 1948. Since then, Jews from all over the world have gathered back to the Promised Land of Israel just as Ezekiel predicted.[46] Unfortunately, there has been much bloodshed between the Palestinians and the Israeli citizens over the rights to the land.

---

[46] One of the reasons Christians believe that the Bible is the unadulterated word of God has to do with the many biblical prophecies that have been fulfilled through over the centuries.

The main point here is that the Jews are indeed chosen of God as his people in order that God may fulfill the promise that he made to Abraham due to Abraham's extraordinary loyalty to God. This does not mean simply by virtue of being Jewish that all Jews will automatically go to heaven regardless as to whether or not they confess Christ. They must still confess Christ, along with everyone else, in order to obtain salvation.[47] What this does mean however is that, even if a nation, people, or person tries to completely do away with them, the Jews will never be totally annihilated. The Jewish nation is protected by God and because of this protection; there is a remnant of Jews who will always survive even the worse attempts of genocide by others. This is made even clearer below:

> [3]"I myself will gather the remnant of my flock out of all the countries where I have driven them and will bring them back to their pasture, where they will be fruitful and increase in number. [4]I will place shepherds over them who will tend them, and they will no longer be afraid or terrified, nor will any be missing, declares the LORD. (Jeremiah 23:3-4 NIV)

A remnant is a small part of a whole. Some theologians would say that the remnant that God is speaking of refers to modern times and is the Jewish nation that is now in Israel; that despite the atrocities the Jews suffered at the hands of the Hitler Nazi regime, a remnant of the Jews reestablished themselves as a nation in the land of Israel that God promised to them. Yet, other theologians hold the position that the remnant God is speaking of refers to the 144,000 Jews (12,000 from each of the twelve tribes) that will be saved during the seven-year tribulation rule of the antichrist; detailed in the book of Revelation. Still others hold the position that the remnant refers to any Jew who has ever been spared premature death at any time through the annals of time. And then there are those who believe that the remnant is speaking of those Jews who accepted the true God[48] during Old Testament times before the advent of Christ and the Jews who have accepted Jesus Christ as Lord and Savior after his advent. Despite the differing opinions there is no question that, because of God's promise, a remnant of Jews will always be present; which means that the nation of Israel will never be totally destroyed and the Jews will never be totally annihilated.

---

[47] The tenants of the Christian faith are provided in the Appendix.
[48] See the Appendix

Salvation is available to Jews and non-Jews alike

Although the Jews are God's chosen people in that he has promised them the land of Israel, he has promised to make them into a great nation; (meaning a nation of millions), and he has promised never to annihilate them but to spare a remnant even if they turn against him; this does not mean that salvation is automatically guaranteed to descendants of Abraham, Isaac, and Jacob (the Jews). This also does not mean that other people from other non-Jewish nations (referred to as Gentiles in the Bible) cannot be saved. Paul speaks about this in the 9th chapter of the Book of Romans. We will begin by looking at verses 1-13:

> [1]With Christ as my witness, I speak with utter truthfulness. My conscience and the Holy Spirit confirm it. [2]My heart is filled with bitter sorrow and unending grief [3]for my people, my Jewish brothers and sisters. I would be willing to be forever cursed—cut off from Christ!—if that would save them. [4]They are the people of Israel, chosen to be God's adopted children. God revealed his glory to them. He made covenants with them and gave them his law. He gave them the privilege of worshipping him and receiving his wonderful promises. [5]Abraham, Isaac, and Jacob are their ancestors, and Christ himself was an Israelite as far as his human nature is concerned. And he is God, the one who rules over everything and is worthy of eternal praise! Amen.
> [6]Well then, has God failed to fulfill his promise to Israel? No, for not all who are born into the nation of Israel are truly members of God's people! [7]Being descendants of Abraham doesn't make them truly Abraham's children. For the Scriptures say, "Isaac is the son through whom your descendants will be counted," though Abraham had other children, too. [8]This means that Abraham's physical descendants are not necessarily children of God. Only the children of the promise are considered to be Abraham's children. [9]For God had promised, "I will return about this time next year, and Sarah will have a son."
> [10]This son was our ancestor Isaac. When he married Rebekah, she gave birth to twins. [11]But before they were born, before they had done anything good or bad, she

received a message from God. (This message shows that God chooses people according to his own purposes; [12]he calls people, but not according to their good or bad works.) She was told, "Your older son will serve your younger son." [13]In the words of the Scriptures, "I loved Jacob, but I rejected Esau." (Romans 9:1-13 NLT)

The Apostle Paul is the one speaking here. He is filled with bitter sorrow because the Jews had a history of rejecting God. We see one example of this (there are several others documented in the Bible) when looking at the historical account (in the 32nd chapter of Exodus)[49]of the Jews' worship of a golden calf that they had created when they became impatient with Moses because he was taking a longer time, than they had expected, to return from Mount Sinai. Paul has also indicated that the children of the promise are the children of Israel, not the children of Ishmael. Then he asks, as we see below, whether or not God is unfair in making this distinction. Let's continue along in the passage to see what he says about this...

[14]Are we saying, then, that God was unfair? Of course not! [15]For God said to Moses,
"I will show mercy to anyone I choose, and I will show compassion to anyone I choose."
[16]So it is God who decides to show mercy. We can neither choose it nor work for it.
[17]For the Scriptures say that God told Pharaoh, "I have appointed you for the very purpose of displaying my power in you and to spread my fame throughout the earth. [18]So you see, God chooses to show mercy to some, and he chooses to harden the hearts of others so they refuse to listen.
[19]Well then, you might say, "Why does God blame people for not responding? Haven't they simply done what he makes them do?"
[20]No, don't say that. Who are you, a mere human being, to argue with God? Should the thing that was created say to the one who created it, "Why have you made me like this?" [21]When a potter makes jars out of clay, doesn't he have a right to use the same lump of clay to make one jar for decoration and another to throw garbage into? [22]In

---

[49] Exodus chapter 32, see your Bible.

the same way, even though God has the right to show his anger and his power, he is very patient with those on whom his anger falls, who are destined for destruction. [23]He does this to make the riches of his glory shine even brighter on those to whom he shows mercy, who were prepared in advance for glory. [24]And we are among those whom he selected, both from the Jews and from the Gentiles.

[25]Concerning the Gentiles, God says in the prophecy of Hosea, Those who were not my people, I will now call my people. And I will love those whom I did not love before."

[26]And, "Then, at the place where they were told, 'You are not my people,' there they will be called 'children of the living God.'" (Romans 9:14-26 NLT).

In answering the question as to whether or not God is unfair in choosing the descendants of Israel as his children of the promise and not also the descendants of Esau and Ishmael, Paul uses Pharaoh for an example. In verses 17-18 above, Paul talks about Pharaoh's heart being hardened by God so that he refused to listen and that Pharaoh was therefore created for the very purpose of being defeated in order to display God's power. In verses 20-22 Paul goes on to say (in using Pharaoh as an example) that some people are destined for destruction. Some Christians therefore believe that when people like Pharaoh were born that they were on their way to hell in the womb and could have never been saved. But Pharaoh's heart was hardened against God long before God added to that hardening. It is not as if Pharaoh was a nice guy and God turned him into an evil person. Pharaoh was evil to begin with and by hardening Pharaoh's heart, God used Pharaoh's own evil against Pharaoh himself for God's own purpose. We see the account of God hardening Pharaoh's heart when looking at Exodus 4:21 which reads:

[21]The LORD said to Moses, "When you return to Egypt, see that you perform before Pharaoh all the wonders I have given you the power to do. But I will harden this heart so that he will not let the people go."(NIV)

Pharaoh's heart was already hard as attested to when reading the following passage of Scripture:

270

[8]Then a new king, to whom Joseph meant nothing, came to power in Egypt. [9]"Look," he said to his people, "the Israelites have become far too numerous for us. [10]Come, we must deal shrewdly with them or they will become even more numerous and, if war breaks out, will join our enemies, fight against us and leave the country. [11]So they put slave masters over them to oppress them with forced labor, and they built Pithom and Rameses as store cities for Pharaoh. [12]But the more they were oppressed, the more they multiplied and spread: so the Egyptians came to dread the Israelites [13]and worked them ruthlessly. [14]They made their lives bitter with harsh labor in brick and mortar and with all kinds of work in the fields; in all their harsh labor the Egyptians used them ruthlessly. [15]The king of Egypt said to the Hebrew midwives, whose names were Shiphrah and Puah, [16]"When you help the Hebrew women in childbirth and observe them on the delivery stool, if it is a boy, kill him; but if it is a girl, let her live." (Exodus 1:8-16 NIV)

From examining the text above, we see that Pharaoh was an evil man before God hardened his heart. It was Pharaoh's choice to do evil deeds. God did not create Pharaoh as an evil being but God did create him knowing that he would do evil. In order to reveal his own glory, God used Pharaoh's evil against him.

We've taken some time to look at this because there are those who would go so far as to say that certain races of people are destined for destruction just as Pharaoh was destined for destruction. But people are only destined for destruction in the sense that God knows that they will never accept him and yet he created them anyway. There is no one race of people that fits into the category of those destined for destruction and only God knows those whom he has created that will never accept him and those whom he has created that will accept him. Some say, however, that the Jews are automatically saved simply because they are Jews and that this proves that God esteems one race of people over another. The counterargument is three-fold; first that the Jews are not a race of people but instead a nation of people; secondly, if all Jews are to be saved then the Bible would never talk about only a remnant being saved (which we have seen in Romans 9:27), and thirdly, the Bible is clear that even though the Jews were chosen by God as heirs to a promise, as we shall soon see, being Jewish does not automatically get one into heaven. Consider the following:

> [6]God "will give to each person according to what he has done." [7]To those who by persistence in doing good seek glory, honor and immortality, he will give eternal life. [8]But for those who are self-seeking and who reject the truth and follow evil, there will be wrath and anger. [9]There will be trouble and distress for every human being who does evil: first for the Jew, then for the Gentile; [10]but glory, honor, and peace for everyone who does good: first for the Jew, then for the Gentile. [11]For God does not show favoritism. (Romans 2:6-11 NIV)

Since the Jews are God's chosen children, they are first in line, so to speak, when it comes to reaping eternal life. But they are also first in line when it comes to the wrath of God in response to evildoing. God is not unfair. Those who are second in line have the same opportunity for salvation and punishment for evildoing as do the Jews, its just that rewards, as well as judgment, will first come to the Jews. Those who do not accept God, Jews and Gentiles alike, reject him, not because God hardened their hearts necessarily, but because their hearts were always hardened just as Pharaoh's heart was. If God hardens a heart, then what he is doing is furthering the hardening of a heart that was already hard to begin with.

To do good means to live holy and in order to live holy and therefore do good, we must accept the gospel of Christ and thereby accept him as Lord and Savior and then set out to live according to the mandates of the Scriptures. This is made apparent in Romans 6:22 when Paul explains that being set free from sin and becoming slaves to God means being holy (doing good) which results in eternal life. The passage reads,

> [22]But now that you have been set free from sin and have become slaves to God, the benefit you reap leads to holiness, and the result is eternal life. (NIV)

As we saw earlier, Paul explains (in Romans 2:8 quoted above) that those who reject the truth (the truth of the gospel) will encounter the wrath of God. He goes on to further explain that Jews who reject the truth are no more exempt from God's wrath than are Gentiles who reject the truth and that this is so because God does not show favoritism. Paul goes on to say:

> [28]A person is not a Jew who is only one outwardly, nor is circumcision merely outward and physical. [29]No, a person is a Jew who is one inwardly; and circumcision is circumcision of the heart, by the Spirit, not by the

272

written code. Such a person's praise is not from other people, but from God." (Romans 2:28-29 TNIV)

God made a covenant with Abraham by promising him that his numbers would greatly increase (meaning his descendants) and that he would be the father of many nations. God went on to tell Abraham that every Hebrew male who was eight days old or older had to be circumcised and that this circumcision would be a sign of this covenant between God and Abraham. He further declared that an uncircumcised male was to be cut off from the Hebrew nation because in being uncircumcised, the covenant was broken. We see this in the following passage of Scripture:

> [9]Then God said to Abraham, "As for you, you must keep my covenant, you and your descendants after you for the generations to come. [10]This is my covenant with you and your descendants after you, the covenant you are to keep: Every male among you shall be circumcised. [11]You are to undergo circumcision, and it will be the sign of the covenant between me and you. [12]For the generations to come every male among you who is eight days old must be circumcised, including those born in your household or bought with money from a foreigner—those who are not your offspring. [13]Whether born in your household or bought with your money, they must be circumcised. My covenant in your flesh is to be an everlasting covenant. (Genesis 17:9-13 NIV)

With the first coming of Jesus Christ came the gospel and a New Testament. With this gospel came the fulfillment of the Law through Jesus Christ. Therefore, physical circumcision is no longer necessary in order to be a part of God's people, but instead a circumcision of the heart is now what is necessary. This means that those of us who are not physical Jews can still be spiritual Jews if we circumcise our hearts by accepting Jesus Christ as Lord and those Jews who are physical Jews but have not accepted Christ are only Jews outwardly, but not inwardly, the latter being what really brings one to salvation. The following passage of Scripture confirms this; in it, Paul is speaking:

> [1]Brothers and sisters, my heart's desire and prayer to God for the Israelites is that they may be saved. [2]For I can testify about them that they are zealous for God, but their zeal is not based on knowledge. [3]Since they did not

know the righteousness of God and sought to establish their own, they did not submit to God's righteousness. [4]Christ is the culmination of the law so that there may be righteousness for everyone who believes. [5]Moses writes about the righteousness that is by the law: "Whoever does these things will live by them." [6]But the righteousness that is by faith says: "Do not say in your heart, 'Who will ascend into heaven? (that is, to bring Christ down) [7]or 'Who will descend into the deep? (that is, to bring Christ up from the dead). [8]But what does it say? "The word is near you; it is in your mouth and in your heart," that is, the message concerning faith that we proclaim: [9]If you declare with your mouth, "Jesus is Lord," and believe in your heart that God raised him from the dead, you will be saved. [10]For it is with your heart that you believe and are justified, and it is with your mouth that you profess your faith and are saved. (Romans 10:1-10 TNIV)

The road to salvation by confessing the Lordship (Deity) of Jesus Christ and by believing that God raised him from the dead, is not just available to the Jews, but is available to everyone, as attested to in the continuation of the passage below:

[11]As Scripture says, "Anyone who believes in him will never be put to shame. [12]For there is no difference between Jew and Gentile—the same Lord is Lord of all and richly blesses all who call on him, [13]for "Everyone who calls on the name of the Lord will be saved." (Romans 10:11-13 TNIV)."

The Scripture does not exclude anyone. Everyone means everyone. There is no indication that any person has any more access to salvation than any other person. The way to salvation is the same for everyone. When taking the preceding passage of Scripture into account, one would be hard-pressed to say that the Bible teaches racism; for if this were the case, Paul would have said that only Jews who call on the Lord will be saved or only white people who call on the Lord will be saved or only black people who call on the Lord will be saved or only Asians who call on the Lord will be saved, and so forth; but the Scripture doesn't say these things; instead it says that *everyone* who calls on the name of the Lord (Jesus

Christ), confesses him as Lord (God) and Savior, and believes God raised him from the dead, will be saved. Paul goes on to say the following:

> [14]How, then, can they call on the one they have not believed in? And how can they believe in the one of whom they have not heard? And how can they hear without someone preaching to them? [15]And how can anyone preach unless they are sent? As it is written: "How beautiful are the feet of those who bring the good news!" [16]But not all the Israelites accepted the good news. For Isaiah says, "Lord, who has believed our message?" [17]Consequently, faith comes from hearing the message, and the message is heard through the word about Christ." (Romans 10:14-17 TNIV)

Paul tells us that not all of the Israelites (the Jews) will accept the good news of the gospel (v.16); this after he earlier explained that only a remnant of Israel will be saved. To support this, we will look at an additional passage of Scripture that speaks of the remnant:

> [27]And concerning Israel, Isaiah the prophet cried out, "Though the people of Israel are as numerous as the seashore, only a remnant will be saved.
> [28]For the Lord will carry out his sentence upon the earth quickly and with finality.
> [29]And Isaiah said the same thing in another place: "If the Lord of Heaven's Armies had not spared a few of our children, we would have been wiped out like Sodom, destroyed like Gomorrah."
> [30]What does all this mean? Even though the Gentiles were not trying to follow God's standards, they were made right with God. And it was by faith that this took place. [31]But the people of Israel, who tried so hard to get right with God by keeping the law, never succeeded. [32]Why not? Because they were trying to get right with God by keeping the law instead of by trusting in him. They stumbled over the great rock in their path. [33]God warned them of this in the Scriptures when he said,
> "I am placing a stone in Jerusalem that makes people stumble, a rock that makes them fall. But anyone who trusts in him will never be disgraced."
> (Romans 9:27-33 NLT)

Despite the fact that the Jews are the chosen people of a promise they must have faith in the Lord Jesus Christ just like everyone else if they want to get into heaven; in this respect they are no different. However, they are indeed to be respected as children of the promise; as children of God's favor but not of favoritism; for as we have seen earlier, there is no favoritism with God. Those who confess Christ become Jews in a spiritual sense. They are adopted into the family of God and are no less children of God than the Jews are, as attested to in the following passage of Scripture in which Paul is talking to the Galatians. It reads:

> [23]Before this faith came, we were held prisoners by the law, locked up until faith should be revealed. [24]So, the law was put in charge to lead us to Christ that we might be justified by faith. [25]Now that faith has come, we are no longer under the supervision of the law. [26]You are all sons of God through faith in Christ Jesus, [27]for all of you who were baptized into Christ have clothed yourselves with Christ. [28]There is neither Jew nor Greek, slave nor free, male nor female, for you are all one in Christ Jesus. [29]If you belong to Christ, then you are Abraham's seed, and heirs according to the promise.
> (Galatians 3:23-29 NIV)

If we belong to Christ, if we have truly confessed him as Lord God and Savior, and if we have believed in our hearts that he rose from the dead then we are just as much Abraham's seed as the Jews are. This is a profound statement but this is what the Bible says. The Bible also says that those of us who are in Christ (Christians) are equal to everyone else who is in Christ. In other words, no Christian is any better than any other Christian. So, white Christians are no better than black Christians, and vise-versa. Men are no better than women, and vice-versa. Those who are free are no better than slaves; and vice-versa. In Christ, all are equal. This Scripture literally blows any argument out of the water that says God prefers one race of people over another.

The fact that those who belong to Christ are actually Abraham's seed (spiritual Jews and therefore descendants; the same as one who is adopted into a family), brings us into a better understanding of what the following passage of Scripture really means:

> [25]My friends, I don't want you Gentiles to be too proud of yourselves. So I will explain the mystery of what has

happened to the people of Israel. Some of them have become stubborn, and they will stay like that until the complete number of you Gentiles has come in. [26]In this way all of Israel will be saved, as the Scriptures say, "From Zion someone will come to rescue us. Then Jacob's descendants will stop being evil. [27]This is what the Lord has promised to do when he forgives their sins." (Romans 11:25-27 CEV)

The full number of non-Jews (Gentiles) must be saved before the full remnant of Jews are saved; because the inheritance of the gospel first belonged to the Jews but with the onset of Christ's ministry it now belongs to the Gentiles as well who have been adopted into the family of God. In this way, all of Israel is saved, meaning that non-Jews who confess Christ are also a part of Israel because they too are Abraham's seed through spiritual adoption and therefore cannot be left out. They must have a chance to be saved too. They are spiritually a part of "all Israel;" so if the saving of the Gentiles were to be discounted then all of Israel would not be saved. Paul again makes clear that not all of physical Israel will be saved and not all Gentiles will be lost (many Gentiles will be adopted into spiritual Israel through their faith). The following two passages give strength to this position:

[27]Isaiah cries out concerning Israel: "Though the number of Israelites be like the sand by the sea, only the remnant will be saved. [28]For the Lord will carry out his sentence on earth with speed and finality. (Romans 9:27-28 TNIV)

If only a remnant of Jews will be saved then it follows that Jews are not automatically saved simply because they are Jews, otherwise all Jews dating back to Abraham, would be saved regardless of what they believe, and we know this is not the case. However, it should never be overlooked that the Jews were the ones that God entrusted with his Word. They are the ones who wrote the Bible that was inspired from God himself. But despite the great favor they have; Jews are not superior people, as seen below:

[1]Then what's the advantage of being a Jew? Is there any value in the ceremony of circumcision? [2]Yes, there are great benefits! First of all, the Jews were entrusted with the whole revelation of God. [3]True, some of them were unfaithful; but just because they were unfaithful, does

277

that mean God will be unfaithful? [4]Of course not! Even
if everyone else is a liar, God is true. As the Scriptures
say about him, "You will be proved right in what you
say, and you will win your case in court."
[5] "But," some might say, "our sinfulness serves a good
purpose, for it helps people see how righteous God is.
Isn't it unfair, then, for him to punish us?" (This is
merely a human point of view.) [6]Of course not! If God
were not entirely fair, how would he be qualified to
judge the world? [7]"But," someone might still argue,
"how can God condemn me as a sinner if my dishonesty
highlights his truthfulness and brings him more glory?"
[8]And some people even slander us by claiming that we
say, "The more we sin, the better it is!" Those who say
such things deserve to be condemned.
[9]Well then, should we conclude that we Jews are better
than others? No, not at all, for we have already shown
that all people, whether Jews or Gentiles, are under the
power of sin. (Romans 3:1-9 NLT)

Although the Jews are highly favored of God and there are great
advantages to being Jewish because the word of God has been presented to
the entire world through the Jews; Paul emphatically states that the Jews
are no better than anyone else. The Jews are not a superior people and
circumcision of the heart applies to them just as much as it applies to non-
Jewish persons. Jews and Gentiles alike are both prone to sin. Jews are
equal to everyone else and everyone else is equal to the Jews; this is so
even though Jesus came in the flesh as a Jew and is identified in John
1:14[50] as God manifest in the flesh (God incarnate) who walked among us
as God the Son. God incarnate (Jesus Christ) came to us through the Jewish
nation. If then God can come through a nation of people and deem that
particular nation of people to be no better than anyone else; then it is more
than reasonable to conclude that no race of people is better than any other
race of people; because if the Jews aren't better than anyone else (the very
people from which God incarnate [Jesus] came and the very people who
have presented the word of God to the whole world), then nobody is better;
because if anyone were to be better, it would certainly be the Jews.

---

[50] The Word became Flesh and made his dwelling place among us. We have seen
his glory, the glory of the One and Only, who came from the Father, full of grace
and truth. (John 1:14 NIV).

278

Not only are Jews and Gentiles equal in the Lord but those who accept Jesus Christ are also identified as God's chosen people along with the Jews as confirmed below:

> [7]Yes, you who trust him recognize the honor God has given him. But for those who reject him,
> "The stone that the builders rejected has now become the cornerstone."
> [8]And, "He is the stone that makes people stumble, the rock that makes them fall."
> They stumble because they do not obey God's word, and so they meet the fate that was planned for them.
> [9]But you are not like that, for you are a chosen people. You are royal priests, a holy nation, God's very own possession. As a result, you can show others the goodness of God, for he called you out of the darkness into his wonderful light. (1 Peter 2:7-9 NLT)

Those who trust God and do not reject him are identified as a chosen people, royal priests, and a holy nation. They are identified as possessions of God. So, although the Jewish nation, because of Abraham's faithfulness, was chosen for the promise of land and the promise of being made a great nation so much so that God will keep the nation of Israel alive so that at least a remnant will be saved; those who are not Jews but who have accepted Jesus as Lord are also identified as chosen. They too are a chosen people primed to reap the promises of God as well. What Peter is saying here is that all followers of Christ (whether Jew or Gentile, male or female, master or slave), are chosen people and are royal priests. Race and ethnicity have nothing to do with being chosen; nationality does but only to a limited extent. Ultimately, it is one's belief that determines whether or not one is chosen of God. Belief is a choice, not a skin color.

To bring the point home even further, God embraces all nations of people who embrace him. Foreigners (immigrants) are welcome as confirmed in Isaiah 56:1-3 coupled with Isaiah 56:6-8 where we see God speaking to Israel:

> [1]This is what the Lord says: 'Be just and fair to all. Do what is right and good, for I am coming soon to rescue you and to display my righteousness among you.
> [2]Blessed are all those who are careful to do this. Blessed are those who honor my Sabbath days of rest and keep themselves from doing wrong.

> ³Don't let foreigners who commit themselves to the
> LORD say, 'The LORD will never let me be part of his
> people.' (Isaiah 56:1-3 NLT)

> ⁶"I will also bless the foreigners who commit themselves
> to the LORD, who serve him and love his name, who
> worship him and do not desecrate the Sabbath day of
> rest, and who hold fast to my covenant.
> ⁷I will bring them to my holy mountain of Jerusalem and
> will fill them with joy in my house of prayer. I will
> accept their burnt offerings and sacrifices, because my
> Temple will be called a house of prayer for all nations.
> ⁸For the Sovereign LORD, who brings back the outcasts
> of Israel, says: I will bring others, too, besides my
> people Israel." (Isaiah 56:6-8 NLT)

To clarify, as a result of the gospel of Jesus Christ, *everyday*, for those
who have accepted Christ and confessed him as Lord God and Savior, is
now a Sabbath day of rest according to Hebrews 4:6-10.[51] Also, "a house
of prayer for all nations" means that no person from any nation is excluded
from the opportunity to be saved. God says that he will bless the foreigners
who commit themselves to him and that no one should ever think that God
will never let him be a part of his people. God will let anyone become a
part of his people and his kingdom as long as they have faith in him and
worship only him. Israel is no exception as attested to below:

> ³⁰What does all this mean? Even though the Gentiles
> were not trying to follow God's standards, they were
> made right with God. And it was by faith that this took
> place. ³¹But the people of Israel, who tried so hard to get
> right with God by keeping the law, never succeeded.

---

[51] ⁶So God's rest is there for people to enter, but those who first heard this good
news failed to enter because they disobeyed God. ⁷So God set another time for
entering his rest, and that time is today. God announced this through David much
later in the words already quoted: Today when you hear his voice, don't harden
your hearts. ⁸Now if Joshua had succeeded in giving them this rest, God would not
have spoken about another day of rest still to come. ⁹So there is a special rest still
waiting for the people of God. ¹⁰For all who have entered into God's rest have
rested from their labors, just as God did after creating the world. (Hebrews 4:6-10
NLT)

> ³²Why not? Because they were trying to get right with God by keeping the law instead of trusting him. They stumbled over the great rock in their path. (Romans 9:30-32 NLT)

> For it is by grace that you have been saved, through faith—and this not from yourselves, it is the gift of God—not by works, so that no one can boast. For we are God's workmanship, created in Christ Jesus to do good works, which God prepared in advance for us to do. (Ephesians 2:8-10 NIV)

The Scripture teaches us that faith in Jesus Christ is what saves us; not doing good works. But once we are saved we will have the mindset to do good works, which God has planned for us to do in advance for those of us who have accepted him; for he knew who would accept him and who wouldn't. There is no bias here. Everyone gets a fair chance to repent of their sins, confess Jesus Christ as Lord and Savior, and believe in his resurrection; thereby reaping salvation. God has even placed all of us in the exact place in the world that we need to be at the exact time we would have needed to be there (according to his knowledge of us) in order for us to have the greatest opportunity of knowing him. Where we were born, when we were born, and who we were born of; happened by God's design. The passage of Scripture below from the book of Acts supports this. It reads:

> ²⁴The God who made the world and everything in it is the Lord of heaven and earth and does not live in temples built by hands. ²⁵And he is not served by human hands, as if he needed anything, because he himself gives all men life and breath and everything else. ²⁶From one man he made every nation of men, that they should inhabit the whole earth; and he determined the times set for them and the exact places where they should live. ²⁷God did this so that men would seek him and perhaps reach out for him and find him, though he is not far from each one of us. (Acts 17:24-27 NIV)

This means that no matter what country a person is born in and no matter how much a person is influenced religiously by his or her family, each person has as much a chance of reaching out and finding Jesus as anyone else does. God knows who to place when and where. This is certainly not the description of a God who is biased towards one race of

281

people as opposed to another, for if that were the case then he would do the opposite: that is to say hypothetically that if God were biased towards one particular race then he'd have the people of that race born in places where they'd be most *unlikely* to reach out and find God; but this is not the case. God is fair to all races of men. The gospel of Jesus Christ is available to everyone no matter what one's nationality or skin color is. But there is one apostle who had a difficult time understanding this at first. We will take a look at him now.

Peter's prejudice

We learn through the Scriptures that Peter, the Apostle (also referred to as Simon) was at first prejudiced against the Gentiles in that he felt that he should not be sharing the gospel with them because he saw them as unclean. In other words, he felt that the Gentiles, by virtue of their nationality alone, were not deserving of salvation and that the privilege of a heavenly existence after death was only reserved for the Jews. God himself corrected Peter. The account begins in the 10th chapter of Acts:

> [9]About noon the following day as they were on their journey and approaching the city, Peter went up on the roof to pray. [10]He became hungry and wanted something to eat, and while the meal was being prepared, he fell into a trance. [11]He saw heaven opened and something like a large sheet being let down to earth by its four corners. [12]It contained all kinds of four-footed animals, as well as reptiles and birds. [13]Then a voice told him, 'Get up, Peter. Kill and eat.'
> [14]"Surely not, Lord!" Peter replied. 'I have never eaten anything impure or unclean."
> [15]The voice spoke to him a second time, "Do not call anything impure that God has made clean."
> [16]This happened three times, and immediately the sheet was taken back to heaven (Acts 10:9-16 TNIV)

Peter would soon discover that the meaning of the vision had not as much to do with God declaring foods clean that once weren't, but more to do with rebuking the prejudice that many of the Jews, including Peter, had levied against non-Jewish people. We see this when looking further at the passage:

[17]While Peter was wondering about the meaning of the vision, the men sent by Cornelius found out where Simon's house was and stopped at the gate. [18]They called out asking if Simon who was known as Peter was staying there.

[19]While Peter was still thinking about the vision, the Spirit said to him, 'Simon, three men are looking for you. [20]So get up and go downstairs. Do not hesitate to go with them, for I have sent them."

[21]Peter went down and said to the men, 'I'm the one you're looking for. Why have you come?'

[22]The men replied, "We have come from Cornelius the centurion. He is a righteous and God-fearing man, who is respected by all the Jewish people. A holy angel told him to ask you to come to his house so that he could hear what you have to say." [23]Then Peter invited the men into the house to be his guests.

The next day Peter started out with them, and some of the believers from Joppa went along. [24]The following day he arrived in Caesarea. Cornelius was expecting them and had called together his relatives and close friends. [25]As Peter entered the house, Cornelius met him and fell at his feet in reverence. [26]But Peter made him get up. 'Stand up,' he said, 'I am only human myself.'

[27]While talking with him, Peter went inside and found a large gathering of people. [28]He said to them: 'You are well aware that it is against our law for a Jew to associate with Gentiles or visit them. But God has shown me that I should not call anyone impure or unclean. [29]So when I was sent for, I came without raising any objection. May I ask why you sent for me?'
(Acts 10:17-29 TNIV)

Cornelius was a Gentile centurion from Italy.[52] He was not a Jew and was therefore not a descendant of Israel but he was a devout follower of God. However, Peter looked at all people who were not physical Jews as unclean and he abided by the discriminatory law at the time that made it a crime for Jews to associate with Gentiles or even visit them. Apparently Peter upheld this law with no problem and saw the Jews as somehow better than the Gentiles. But God brought Cornelius and Peter together by

---

[52] Acts 10:1-7

283

sending an angel to Cornelius and by giving Peter a vision with similar messages for the two of them (Cornelius and Peter) should come together.

Peter knew that God brought him together with Cornelius so that he could understand the vision. God rebuked Peter because of his racism and let him know that nationality or ethnicity does not make one Christian any better than another. In other words, the Jewish Christians were no better than the Gentile Christians. The account of Peter coming to this realization is captured in the continuation of the account, which is below:

> [30]Cornelius answered: "Three days ago I was in my house praying at this hour, at three in the afternoon. Suddenly a man in shining clothes stood before me [31]and said, 'Cornelius, God has heard your prayer and remembered your gifts to the poor. [32]Send to Joppa for Simon who is called Peter. He is a guest in the home of Simon the tanner, who lives by the sea.' [33]So I sent for you immediately, and it was good of you to come. Now we are all here in the presence of God to listen to everything the Lord has commanded you to tell us."
> [34]Then Peter began to speak: "I now realize how true it is that God does not show favoritism [35]but accepts those from every nation who fear him and do what is right. (Acts 10:30-35 TNIV)

Luke (the author of Acts) goes on to further explain Peter's change of heart in chapter 11, when he says:

> [1]The apostles and the believers throughout Judea heard that the Gentiles also had received the word of God. [2]So when Peter went up to Jerusalem, the circumcised believers criticized him [3]and said, "You went into the house of the uncircumcised and ate with them."
> [4]Starting from the beginning, Peter told them the whole story: [5]"I was in the city of Joppa praying, and in a trance I saw a vision. I saw something like a large sheet being let down from heaven by its four corners, and it came down to where I was. [6]I looked into it and saw four-footed animals of the earth, wild beasts, reptiles and birds. [7]Then I heard a voice telling me, 'Get up, Peter. Kill and eat.'
> [8]"I replied, 'Surely not, Lord! Nothing impure or unclean has ever entered my mouth.'

[9]"The voice spoke from heaven a second time, 'Do not call anything impure that God has made clean.' [10]This happened three times, and then it was all pulled up to heaven again.

[11]"Right then three men who had been sent to me from Caesarea stopped at the house where I was staying. [12]The Spirit told me to have no hesitation about going with them. These six brothers also went with me, and we entered the man's house. [13]He told us how he had seen an angel appear in his house and say, 'Send to Joppa for Simon who is called Peter. [14]He will bring you a message through which you and all your household will be saved.'

[15]As I began to speak, the Holy Spirit came on them as he had come on us at the beginning. [16]Then I remembered what the Lord had said; 'John baptized with water, but you will be baptized with the Holy Spirit.' [17]So if God gave them the same gift he gave us who believed in the Lord Jesus Christ, who was I to think that I could stand in God's way?"

[18]When they heard this, they had no further objections and praised God, saying, "So then, even to Gentiles God has granted repentance that leads to life."
(Acts11:1-18 TNIV)

Peter was biased and prejudiced against non-Jewish people. God stepped in and corrected Peter. Peter realized that, when it comes to obtaining salvation God is not a respecter of persons. And it is wrong to teach otherwise. Although the gospel was preached first to the Jews, the gift of salvation is available to anyone who accepts God; even the Gentiles. We see this in Paul's letter to the Galatians:

[13]For you have heard of my previous way of life in Judaism, how intensely I persecuted the church of God and tried to destroy it. [14]I was advancing in Judaism beyond many of my own age among my people and was extremely zealous for the traditions of my fathers. [15]But when God, who set me apart from birth and called me by his grace, was pleased [16]to reveal his Son in me so that I might preach him among the Gentiles my immediate response was not to consult any human being. (Galatians 1:13-16 TNIV)

285

In the Scripture passage above, Paul is speaking to the Galatians, who were Gentiles. He doesn't hide the fact that, before being called of God to preach the gospel to the Gentiles, he used to persecute Christians by having them put to death. Paul was a Jew but he was also a Roman citizen. Before his calling to preach the gospel, Paul was an avid enemy of the Christians. But through his conversion, Paul became one of the most noted apostles of all ages; and God specifically assigned Paul the task of preaching the gospel to the Gentiles. Although his immediate response, after Jesus appeared to Paul on the Damascus road, was not to consult any human being, he eventually did consult Cephas and James after spending three years in Arabia.[53]

If God was to esteem one race or ethnic group over another then he would have never assigned anyone to preach the gospel to non-Jews and only Jews would be able to be saved. But this is not the case. Paul goes on to confirm once again that there is no favoritism with God when it comes to the gift of salvation. He says:

> [6]As for those who were held in high esteem—whatever they were makes no difference to me; God does not show favoritism—they added nothing to my message. [7]On the contrary, they saw that I had been entrusted with the task of preaching the gospel to the Gentiles, just as Peter had been to the Jews. [8]For God, who was at work in Peter as an apostle to the Jews, was also at work in me as an apostle to the Gentiles. (Galatians 2:6-8 TNIV)

Paul makes it clear that a man or woman's "importance" in society means nothing, and that it means nothing to God when compared to spreading the good news of the gospel of Jesus Christ. Although racial supremacists in today's time believe that salvation is just for the race that they belong to and that their race is more "important" than other races; without question, the Bible does not teach this. Furthermore, although Paul's ministry was to preach the gospel to the Gentiles and Peter's ministry was to preach the gospel to the Jews, Paul had the authority along with the responsibility to preach to the Jews if the situation arose just as Peter had that same responsibility and authority to preach to the Gentiles whenever the occasion arose (as we saw earlier). Moreover, Paul makes it clear in verse 8 above that the God who led Peter to preach to the Jews about the gospel is the same God who led Paul to talk to the Gentiles. Paul

---

[53] Acts 22:1-21 (Paul's experience on the Damascus road). Galatians 1:15-20 (Paul spends three years in Arabia after meeting the Lord), see your Bible.

rebuked Peter for his prejudice against the Gentiles as documented in the following passage of Scripture:

> [9]James, Cephas and John, those esteemed as pillars, gave me and Barnabas the right hand of fellowship when they recognized the grace given to me. They agreed that we should go to the Gentiles, and they to the Jews. [10]All they asked was that we should continue to remember the poor, the very thing that I had been eager to do all along.

> [11]When Cephas came to Antioch, I opposed him to his face, because he stood condemned. [12]For before certain people came from James, he used to eat with the Gentiles. But when they arrived, he began to draw back and separate himself from the Gentiles because he was afraid of those who belonged to the circumcision group. [13]The other Jews joined him in his hypocrisy, so that by their hypocrisy even Barnabas was led astray." (Galatians 2:9-13 TNIV)

Cephas is the Aramaic name for Peter.[54] Paul reveals that Peter would eat with the Gentiles without concern about the law that forbade Jews to eat with Gentiles. But when Peter found himself among Jews, he would not eat with the Gentiles for fear that the Jews might see him doing so and that he'd lose the company or approval of his Jewish friends. Other Jews who had also eaten with the Gentiles followed Peter's hypocrisy and withdrew from the Gentiles when Jews were present in order to hide the fact that they associated with Gentiles. Paul rebuked Peter for his hypocrisy.

Not only was it wrong to think that Gentiles were somehow beneath the Jews and shun them publicly while eating with them privately, but Paul again gives the argument that those who are of the faith are just as much Abraham's seed as the Jews are. He says,

> [5]Does God give you his Spirit and work miracles among you by your observing the law, or by your believing what you heard? [6]So also Abraham believed God, and it was credited to him as righteousness.

---

[54] [41]The first thing Andrew did was to find his brother Simon and tell him, "We have found the Messiah" (that is the Christ). [42]And he brought him to Jesus. Jesus looked at him and said, "You are Simon son of John. You will be called Cephas" (which, when translated, is Peter). (John 1:42-42 NI)

> [7]Understand then, that those who have faith are children of Abraham. [8]Scripture foresaw that God would justify the Gentiles by faith, and announced the gospel in advance to Abraham: "All nations will be blessed through you." [9]So those who rely on faith are blessed along with Abraham, the man of faith. (Galatians 3:5-9 TNIV)

As indicated before, people from all nations, that accept Jesus as Lord and Savior, are part of the nations that are blessed through Abraham, and those who have faith (who believe in the Deity of Christ) are just as much children of Abraham as Abraham's biological children, the Jews, are. Therefore, as discussed earlier, in a spiritual sense, the chosen people of God are not only those who are physical Jews but are also those who are spiritual Jews. There is no racism with God. The color of a man's skin is neither here nor there with God and when taking into consideration the passages of Scripture that we have looked at in this chapter, it cannot be denied that the Bible supports this view.

As discussed earlier, the Bible does not record Jesus as making any racial distinctions but does record distinctions Jesus made between believers and unbelievers; herein is where God makes a difference between people. As discussed earlier, Jesus makes the distinction between children of God and children of the devil, in the following passages:

> [31]To the Jews who had believed him, Jesus said, "If you hold to my teaching, you are really my disciples. [32]Then you will know the truth, and the truth will set you free."
> [33]They answered him "We are Abraham's descendants and have never been slaves of anyone. How can you say that we shall be set free?"
> [34]Jesus replied, "I tell you the truth, everyone who sins is a slave to sin. [35]Now a slave has no permanent place in the family, but a son belongs to it forever. [36]So if the Son sets you free, you will be free indeed. [37]I know you are Abraham's descendants. Yet you are ready to kill me, because you have no room for my word. [38]I am telling you what I have seen in the Father's presence, and you do what you have heard from your father."
> [39]"Abraham is our father," they answered.
> "If you were Abraham's children," said Jesus, "then you would do the things Abraham did. [40]As it is, you are determined to kill me, a man who has told you the truth

that I heard from God. Abraham did not do such things. [41]You are doing the things your own father does."

"We are not illegitimate children," they protested. "The only Father we have is God himself."

[42]Jesus said to them, "If God were your Father, you would love me, for I came from God and now am here. I have not come on my own; but he sent me. [43]Why is my language not clear to you? Because you are unable to hear what I say. [44]You belong to your father, the devil, and you want to carry out your father's desire. He was a murderer from the beginning not holding to the truth, for there is no truth in him. When he lies, he speaks his native language, for he is a liar and the father of lies. [45]Yet because I tell the truth, you do not believe me! [46]Can any of you prove me guilty of sin? If I am telling the truth, why don't you believe me! [47]He who belongs to God hears what God says. The reason you do not hear is that you do not belong to God." (John 8:31-47 NIV)

Jesus described himself as having come directly from God, meaning that he is the second personage of the Godhead; the literal Son of God, the other personages being the Father and the Holy Spirit. Jesus plainly said that those who do not accept his gospel are children of the devil. John supports this teaching with the following words that we will look at again:

[1]How great is the love the Father has lavished on us, that we should be called children of God! And that is what we are! The reason the world does not know us is that it did not know him. [2]Dear friends, now we are children of God, and what we will be has not yet been made known. But we know that when he appears, we shall be like him, for we shall see him as he is. [3]Everyone who has this hope in him purifies himself, just as he is pure.

[4]Everyone who sins breaks the law; in fact, sin is lawlessness. [5]But you know that he appeared so that he might take away our sins. And in him is no sin. [6]No one who lives in him keeps on sinning. No one who continues to sin has either seen him or known him.

[7]Dear children, do not let anyone lead you astray. He who does what is right is righteous, just as he is righteous. [8]He who does what is sinful is of the devil,

because the devil has been sinning from the beginning. The reason the Son of God appeared was to destroy the devil's work. [9]No one who is born of God will continue to sin, because God's seed remains in him; he cannot go on sinning, because he has been born of God. [10]This is how we know who the children of God are and who the children of the devil are: Anyone who does not do what is right is not a child of God; nor is anyone who does not love his brother." (1 John 3:1-10 NIV)

It must be pointed out that although John said that he who does what is sinful is of the devil (v.8) he clarifies this by saying that no one who is born of God will continue to sin. The operative word is *continue* thus clarifying that those who are children of the devil are not those who sin, per se, (for all have sinned, [except Jesus; 2 Corinthians 5:20-21[55]], and come short of the glory of God[56]), but instead those who sin and keep on sinning without care or remorse; in other words, those who practice sin with no thought about it, or those who practice sin and try to justify it. And they do this because they do not walk with God and are therefore not convicted to change.

The point to this is that the distinction that the Bible makes between people has to do with those who accept the gospel and those who don't; not between those of one race or another. Peter therefore had the right to distinguish the believer from the unbeliever but not the Jew from the Greek.

Jesus and the Greek woman

There are some who would argue that the Bible teaches racism based on the following historical account:

[24]Jesus left that place and went to the vicinity of Tyre. He entered a house and did not want anyone to know it; yet he could not keep his presence secret. [25]In fact, as soon as she heard about him, a woman whose little daughter was possessed by an evil spirit came and fell at

---

[55]We are therefore Christ's ambassadors, as though God were making his appeal through us. We implore you on Christ's behalf: Be reconciled to God. [21]God made him who had no sin to be sin for us, so that in him we might become the righteousness of God. (2 Corinthians 5:20-21 NIV)
[56] Romans 3:23 KJV

his feet. [26]The woman was a Greek, born in Syrian Phoenicia. She begged Jesus to drive the demon out of her daughter.

[27]"First let the children eat all they want," he told her, "for it is not right to take the children's bread and toss it to their dogs."

[28]"Yes, Lord," she replied, "but even the dogs under the table eat the children's crumbs."

[29]Then he told her, "For such a reply, you may go; the demon has left your daughter."

[30]She went home and found her child lying on the bed, and the demon gone. (Mark 7:24-30 TNIV)

This woman came to Jesus and begged him to cast the demon out of her daughter. Jesus' initial response to the woman was to tell her that the children first need to eat all that they want and that one shouldn't take the children's bread and toss it to their dogs. In other words; the miraculous healings and casting out of demons that Jesus was performing was first for the Jews; the chosen people of God; Jesus was basically telling the woman that those who are in the family of God should be first served when it comes to reaping the benefits of the miraculous. He then proceeded to compare her to a dog. However, Jesus' comparison of this woman to a dog was not because she was a Greek, but (one of the reasons) was because Jesus was sent from the Father to the lost sheep of Israel, which meant that the message of the gospel was to first be given to the Jews, not because of their "ethnicity" but because "salvation is of the Jews" (John 4:22 KJV). In other words, it is through the Jews that the gospel message was brought to the world since Jesus came from the line of the Jewish tribe of Judah.

Matthew's account of the incident gives additional information regarding Jesus being sent from the Father to the lost sheep of Israel. It reads:

[21]Leaving that place, Jesus withdrew to the region of Tyre and Sidon. [22]A Canaanite woman from that vicinity came to him, crying out, "Lord, Son of David, have mercy on me! My daughter is demon-possessed and suffering terribly?

[23]Jesus did not answer a word. So his disciples came to him and urged him, "Send her away, for she keeps crying out after us."

[24]He answered, "I was sent only to the lost sheep of Israel."

^{25}The woman came and knelt before him. "Lord, help me!" She said.
^{26}He replied, "It is not right to take the children's bread and toss it to the dogs."
^{27}Yes it is, Lord," she said. 'Even the dogs eat the crumbs that fall from their master's table."
^{28}Then Jesus said to her, "Woman, you have great faith! Your request is granted." And her daughter was healed from that very hour. (Matthew 15:21-28 TNIV)

In the book of Mark, the woman is identified as a Greek, whereas in the book of Matthew she is identified as a Canaanite. It is believed that the identification of her as a Canaanite in Matthew is a description of her in colloquial terms since there was no country named Canaan and the actual nation of the Canaanites had been extinguished long beforehand. But the most pressing point is the statement that Jesus makes in verse 24 of Matthew's account when he tells the woman that he was sent only to the lost sheep of Israel. Then he goes on to compare Gentiles (anyone who was not a Jew, including the Greeks) to dogs. The woman responds by referring to Jesus as Lord and places herself into the Jewish nation by symbolically and metaphorically making herself part of the family; if not humanly, at least as a pet scrambling for the crumbs beneath the table.

With such a response; what the woman was really saying was that, by faith, she too had a right to the bread even though she was compared to a dog; even pet dogs are treated like family and are given the rights to the family blessings. With this, Jesus granted her request. He did so because she expressed faith and belief in him. The reference to her as a dog, therefore, did not really have to do with her ethnicity, but actually had to do with whether or not she was a believer. As we have seen earlier, all those who believe are really the true Jews and in Christ there is no Greek or Jew but all those who are in Christ are equal. Therefore, when this woman expressed her belief in Jesus, she immediately became a spiritual Jew with all spiritual rights and privileges attributed to them.

To reiterate, Jesus' reference to the woman as a dog does not have to do with race and/or ethnicity but has instead to do with belief and non-belief. This is supported even further by the following five passages of Scripture:

"Watch out for false prophets. They come to you in sheep's clothing, but inwardly they are ferocious wolves." (Matthew 7:15 NIV)

292

Jesus warned us to watch out for false prophets and then referred to them as wolves. False prophets are those who promote spiritual teachings other than the teachings of the gospel of Jesus Christ and the Bible as a whole, and/or who promote teachings that they identify as Christian teachings but when examined closely, are not. False prophets do not believe in the gospel of Jesus Christ. Jesus called them wolves. A wolf is a type of dog and belongs to the canine family. So, essentially what Jesus has done is compare a false prophet to a dog which is no different from his comparison of the Greek woman to a dog. In general, New Testament writings basically compare non-believers to dogs. The comparison has nothing to do with racial issues but instead has everything to do with belief issues. In looking further, this comparison of non-believers to dogs becomes even more descriptive:

> [1]But there were also false prophets among the people, just as there will be false teachers among you. They will secretly introduce destructive heresies, even denying the sovereign Lord who bought them—bringing swift destruction on themselves. [2]Many will follow their shameful ways and will bring the way of truth into disrepute. [3]In their greed these teachers will exploit you with stories they have made up. Their condemnation has long been hanging over them, and their destruction has not been sleeping. (2 Peter 2:1-3 NIV)

Further along the passage continues...

> [17]These men are springs without water and mists driven by a storm. Blackest darkness is reserved for them. [18]For they mouth empty, boastful words and, by appealing to the lustful desires of sinful human nature, they entice people who are just escaping from those who live in error. [19]They promise them freedom, while they themselves are slaves of depravity—for a man is a slave to whatever has mastered him. [20]If they have escaped the corruption of the world by knowing our Lord and Savior Jesus Christ and are again entangled in it and overcome, they are worse off at the end than they were at the beginning. [21]It would have been better off for them not to have known the way of righteousness, than to have known it and then to turn their backs on the sacred command that was passed on to them. [22]Of them the

proverbs are true: "A dog returns to its vomit," and, "A sow that is washed goes back to her wallowing in the mud." (2 Peter 2:17-22 NIV)

Peter refers to false doctrine and teaching as vomit and mud; both of which are very dirty and unclean. Those who teach false doctrine and ascribe to it are promoting something that is unclean. Those who teach or ascribe to false doctrine are compared to dogs and pigs that return to vomit or mud respectively. Paul takes it even further by calling evil men dogs. He warns the Philippians as such:

Watch out for those dogs, those men who do evil, those mutilators of the flesh (Philippians 3:2 NIV)

Jesus makes it even plainer by comparing those who practice magic, sexual immorality, murder, idolatry, and everyone who loves falsehood, to dogs. This is documented in the book of Revelation. It reads:

[10]Then he told me, "Do not seal up the words of the prophecy of this book, because the time is near. [11]Let him who does wrong continue to do wrong; let him who is vile continue to be vile; let him who does right continue to do right; and let him who is holy continue to be holy."
[12]"Behold, I am coming soon! My reward is with me, and I will give to everyone according to what he has done. [13]I am the Alpha and the Omega, the First and the Last, the Beginning and the End.
[14]"Blessed are those who wash their robes, that they may have the right to the tree of life and may go through the gates into the city. [15]Outside are the dogs, those who practice magic arts, the sexually immoral, the murderers, the idolaters and everyone who loves and practices falsehood.
[16]I, Jesus, have sent my angel to give you this testimony for the churches. I am the Root and the Offspring of David, and the bright and Morning Star."
[17]The Spirit and the bride say, "Come!" And let him who hears say, "Come!" Whoever is thirsty, let him come; and whoever wishes, let him take the free gift of the water of life. (Revelation 22:10-17 NIV)

Jesus, Peter, and Paul compared unbelievers, particularly false prophets, evil men, magicians, fornicators, murderers, idol worshippers, and those who embrace false teachings, to dogs and to pigs (sows). It should be emphasized that the comparison has to do with how unbelievers *behave* when compared to how dogs and pigs behave. Unbelievers, particularly false prophets return to the "vomit" and the "mud" (2 Peter 2:17-22, quoted previously) of the false doctrine that they propagate just as dogs return to vomit to consume it and pigs return to mud to bask in it. This is not to say that unbelievers are dogs and pigs. It is not to say that they are animals and are somehow inferior to believers. That is not what the Scriptures are teaching. Instead, the comparison has to do with the *behavior* of the person in question, not his or her humanity.

When evil men (and/or women), magicians, fornicators, idol worshippers, false prophets, and those who embrace false teachings behave the way they do, then it is the same as a dog lapping up filthy vomit or a pig wallowing in dirty mud. The comparison has nothing to do with race whatsoever.

The Samaritans

Samaria was a city north of Jerusalem and is initially referenced in 1 Kings 13:32[57] in which the city is described as a town wherein the word of the Lord came against the shrines that were there. This means that the people of Samaria (the Samaritans) were worshipping false gods and that, because of this, God was not pleased with them and came against them. There are some who will say that the Bible depicts the Samaritans as inferior to the Jews. But we will see (as we saw with the Greek woman) that the distinction God made between the Samaritans and the Jews had nothing to do with race or ethnicity but rather with belief and unbelief. In order to look into this we must first begin by gaining a proper understanding of how the Samaritans came to be. In doing so, we will need to look at their entire account that is documented in 2 Kings chapter 7 which reads:

> [1-2]In the twelfth year of Ahaz of Juday, Hoshea son of Elah became king of Israel. He ruled in Samaria for nine years. As far as GOD was concerned, he lived a bad life, but not nearly as bad as the kings who had preceded him.

---

[57] For the message he declared by the word of the LORD against the altar in Bethel and against all the shrines on the high places in the towns of Samaria will certainly come true. (1 Kings 13:32 NIV)

295

³⁻⁵Then Shalmaneser king of Assyria attacked. Hoshea was already a puppet of the Assyrian king and regularly sent him tribute, but Shalmaneser discovered that Hoshea had been operating traitorously behind his back—having worked out a deal with King So of Egypt. And, adding insult to injury, Hoshea was way behind on his annual payments of tribute to Assyria. So the king of Assyria arrested him and threw him in prison, then proceeded to invade the entire country. He attacked Samaria and threw up a siege against it. The siege lasted three years.

⁶In the ninth year of Hoshea's reign the king of Assyria captured Samaria and took the people into exile in Assyria. He relocated them in Halah, in Gozan along the Habor River, and in the towns of the Medes.

⁷⁻¹²The exile came about because of sin: The children of Israel sinned against GOD, the GOD who had delivered them from Egypt and the brutal oppression of Pharaoh king of Egypt. They took up with other gods, fell in with the ways of life of the pagan nations GOD had chased off, and went along with whatever their kings did. They did all kinds of things on the sly, things offensive to their GOD, then openly and shamelessly built local sex-and-religion shrines at every possible site. They set up their sex-and-religion symbols at practically every crossroads. Everywhere you looked there was smoke from their pagan offerings to the deities—the identical offerings that had gotten the pagan nations off into exile. They had accumulated a long list of evil actions and GOD was fed up, fed up with their persistent worship of gods carved out of deadwood or shaped out of clay, even though GOD had plainly said, "Don't do this—ever!"

¹³GOD had taken a stand against Israel and Judah, speaking clearly through countless holy prophets and seers time and time again, "Turn away from your evil way of life. Do what I tell you and have been telling you in The Revelation I gave your ancestors and of which I've kept reminding you ever since through my servants the prophets."

¹⁴⁻¹⁵But they wouldn't listen. If anything, they were even more bullheaded than their stubborn ancestors, if that's possible. They were contemptuous of his instructions, the solemn and holy covenant he had made with their ancestors, and of his repeated reminders and warnings. They lived a "nothing" life and became "nothings"—just like the pagan peoples all around them. They were well-warned: GOD said, "Don't!" but they did it anyway.

¹⁶⁻¹⁷They threw out everything GOD, their GOD, had told them, and replaced him with two statue-gods shaped like bull-calves and then a phallic pole for the whore goddess Asherah. They worshiped cosmic forces—sky gods and goddesses—and frequented the sex-and-religion shrines of Baal. They even sank so low as to offer their own sons and daughters as sacrificial burnt offerings! They indulged in all the black arts of magic and sorcery. In short, they prostituted themselves to every kind of evil available to them. And GOD had had enough.

¹⁸⁻²⁰GOD was so thoroughly angry that he got rid of them, got them out of the country for good until only one tribe was left—Judah. (Judah, actually, wasn't much better, for Judah also failed to keep GOD'S commands, falling into the same way of life that Israel had adopted). GOD rejected everyone connected with Israel, made life hard for them, and permitted anyone with a mind to exploit them to do so. And then this final No as he threw them out of his sight.

²¹⁻²³Back at the time that GOD ripped Israel out of their place in the family of David, they had made Jeroboam son of Nebat king. Jeroboam debauched Israel—turned them away from serving GOD and led them into a life of total sin. The children of Israel went along with all the sins that Jeroboam did, never murmured so much as a word of protest. In the end, GOD spoke a final No to Israel and turned his back on them. He had given them fair warning, and plenty of time, through the preaching of all his servants the prophets. Then he exiled Israel from her land to Assyria. And that's where they are now.

[24-25]The king of Assyria brought in people from Babylon, Cuthah, Avva, Hamath, and Sepharvaim, and relocated them in the towns of Samaria, replacing the exiled Israelites. They moved in as if they owned the place and made themselves at home. When the Assyrians first moved in, GOD was just another god to them; they neither honored nor worshiped him. Then GOD sent lions among them and people were mauled and killed.

[26]This message was then sent back to the king of Assyria: "The people you brought in to occupy the towns of Samaria don't know what's expected of them from the god of the land, and now he's sent lions and they're killing people right and left because nobody knows what the god of the land expects of them."

[27]The king of Assyria ordered, "Send back some priests who were taken into exile from there. They can go back and live there and instruct the people in what the god of the land expects of them."

[28]One of the priests who had been exiled from Samaria came back and moved into Bethel. He taught them how to honor and worship GOD.

[29-31]But each people that Assyria had settled went ahead anyway making its own gods and setting them up in the neighborhood sex-and-religion shrines that the citizens of Samaria had left behind—a local custom-made god for each people: for Babylon, Succoth Benoth, for Cuthah, Nergal; for Hamath, Ashima; for Avva, Nibhaz and Tartak; for Sepharvaim, Adrammelech and Anammelech (people burned their children in sacrificial offering to these gods!)

[32-33]They honored and worshiped GOD, but not exclusively—they also appointed all sorts of priests, regardless of qualification, to conduct a variety of rites at the local fertility shrines. They honored and worshiped GOD but they also kept up their devotions to the old gods of the places they had come from.

298

[34-39]And they're still doing it, still worshiping any old god that has nostalgic appeal to them. They don't really worship GOD—they don't take seriously what he says regarding how to behave and what to believe, what he revealed to the children of Jacob whom he named Israel. GOD made a covenant with this people and ordered them, "Don't honor other gods: Don't worship them, don't serve them, don't offer sacrifices to them. Worship GOD, the GOD who delivered you from Egypt in great and personal power. Reverence and fear him. Worship him. Sacrifice to him. And only him! All the things he had written down for you, directing you in what to believe and how to behave—well, do them for as long as you live. And whatever you do, *don't worship other gods*! And the covenant he made with you, don't forget your part in that. *And don't worship other gods!* Worship GOD and GOD only—he's the one who will save you from enemy oppression."

[40-41]But they didn't pay any attention. They kept doing what they'd always done. As it turned out, all the time these people were putting on a front of worshiping GOD they were at the same time involved with their local idols. And they're still doing it. Like father, like son. (2 Kings 17, The Message).[58]

Samaria was a city that was part of Israel during the reign of Hoshea. Hoshea lived in Samaria. Hoshea was a bad king and the Assyrian king attacked the town of Samaria along with the entire country of Israel because Hoshea owed him money. The Assyrian king then relocated the Israelites who were living in Samaria to Halah and the towns of the Medes. Halah was an area in ancient Mesopotamia. Mesopotamia was where Iraq is now, specifically a land that sits between the Tigris and Euphrates rivers. Mesopotamia also encompassed some parts of what we know of today as Syria, Turkey, and Iran. The Israelites were exiled from Samaria to Halah because of the sin they had committed against God by worshiping false gods. The Assyrian king replaced the Israelites of Samaria with pagan peoples from Babylon, Cuthah, Avva, Hamath, and Sepharvaim. The Assyrian king eventually sent Israelite priests to Samaria in order to teach the pagan people there how to worship the true God. Although the pagans

---

[58] The Message Bible Translation is a paraphrased rendition of the Bible.

learned how to worship the true God, they still insisted on worshiping false gods as well. Eventually, these pagan people who lived in Samaria were referred to as Samaritans. The Jews grew to despise them.

Jesus did not consider the Samaritans to be children of God (although they worshiped the true God) because they worshiped false gods along with worshipping the true God. True children of God will only worship the one true God and no other god. Jesus specifically instructed the twelve apostles to first present the gospel to the "lost sheep of Israel" before preaching to the Gentiles and the Samaritans. This is attested to in the following passage of Scripture.

> [1]He called his twelve disciples to him and gave them authority to drive out evil spirits and to heal every disease and sickness.
> [2]These are the names of the twelve apostles: first, Simon (who is called Peter) and his brother Andrew; James son of Zebedee, and his brother John; [3]Philip and Bartholomew; Thomas and Matthew the tax collector; James son of Alphaeus, and Thaddaeus; [4]Simon the Zealot and Judas Iscariot, who betrayed him.
> [5]These twelve Jesus sent out with the following instructions: "Do not go among the Gentiles or enter any town of the Samaritans. [6]Go rather to the lost sheep of Israel. [7]As you go, preach this message: 'The kingdom of heaven is near.' [8]Heal the sick, raise the dead, cleanse those who have leprosy, drive out demons. Freely you have received, freely give. [9]Do not take along any gold or silver or copper in your belts; [10]take no bag for the journey, or extra tunic, or sandals or a staff; for the worker is worth his keep. (Matthew 10:1-10 NIV)

The disciples were instructed to take the good news of the gospel first to the lost Jews before going to the Gentiles or Samaritans with the message. As we have seen earlier, this does not mean that the Gentiles (which included the Samaritans) were not to receive the message of the gospel at all; but simply that the Jews were to receive the gospel first. Jesus himself took the good news of the gospel to a Samaritan woman proving that the gospel was intended to be shared with all people and that it was for anyone who would believe, no matter their background; even the Samaritans. The account of Jesus talking to a Samaritan woman about his message of salvation is found in the following passage of Scripture:

⁴Now he had to go through Samaria. ⁵So he came to a town in Samaria called Sychar, near the plot of ground Jacob had given to his son Joseph. ⁶Jacob's well was there, and Jesus, tired as he was from the journey, sat down by the well. It was about the sixth hour.

⁷When a Samaritan woman came to draw water, Jesus said to her, "Will you give me a drink?" ⁸(His disciples had gone into the town to buy food.)

⁹The Samaritan woman said to him, "You are a Jew and I am a Samaritan woman. How can you ask me for a drink?" (For Jews do not associate with Samaritans).

¹⁰Jesus answered her, "If you know the gift of God and who it is that asks you for a drink, you would have asked him and he would have given you living water."

¹¹Sir," the woman said, "you have nothing to draw with and the well is deep. Where can you get this living water? ¹²Are you greater than our father Jacob, who gave us the well and drank from it himself, as did also his sons and his flocks and herds?"

¹³Jesus answered, "Everyone who drinks this water will be thirsty again, ¹⁴but whoever drinks the water I give him will never thirst. Indeed, the water I give him will become in him a spring of water welling up to eternal life."

¹⁵The woman said to him, "Sir, give me this water so that I won't get thirsty and have to keep coming here to draw water."

¹⁶He told her, "Go, call your husband and come back."
¹⁷"I have no husband," she replied.

Jesus said to her, "You are right when you say you have no husband. ¹⁸The fact is, you have had five husbands, and the man you now have is not your husband. What you have just said is quite true."

¹⁹"Sir," the woman said, "I can see that you are a prophet. ²⁰Our fathers worshiped on this mountain, but you Jews claim that the place where we must worship is in Jerusalem."

²¹Jesus declared, "Believe me, woman, a time is coming when you will worship the Father neither on this mountain nor in Jerusalem.

²²You Samaritans worship what you do not know; we worship what we do know, for salvation is from the

Jews. [23]Yet a time is coming and has now come when the true worshipers will worship the Father in spirit and truth, for they are the kind of worshipers the Father seeks. [24]God is spirit, and his worshipers must worship in spirit and in truth."

[25]The woman said, "I know that Messiah" (called Christ) "is coming. When he comes, he will explain everything to us."

[26]Then Jesus declared, "I who speak to you am he." (John 4:4-26 NIV)

Further along the passage continues:

[39]Many of the Samaritans from that town believed in him because of the woman's testimony, "He told me everything I ever did." [40]So when the Samaritans came to him, they urged him to stay with them, and he stayed two days. [41]And because of his words many more became believers.

[42]They said to the woman, "We no longer believe just because of what you said; now we have heard for ourselves, and we know that this man really is the Savior of the world. (John 4:39-42 NIV)

As indicated earlier, when Jesus expressed that salvation comes from the Jews, what he meant is that it comes from the Jewish line since Jesus himself, was a Jew from the tribal line of Judah.[59] God did not hold back the gift of salvation from the Samaritans. Jesus himself told this particular Samaritan woman who he was and what he represented. He proved to her that he was the Christ by telling her about herself. The woman, in turn, testified of him to other Samaritans and by doing so she ultimately brought them into the knowledge of who Jesus is. Jesus then stayed with the Samaritans two days showing them the way and convincing them that he is the Savior of the world. The Samaritans who heard Jesus and listened to what he said, believed in him, and were saved. If God were a racist then Jesus would have never spoken to the Samaritan woman and the Samaritans would never have had the opportunity for salvation. But Jesus did speak to her and the Samaritans did have the opportunity just as the

---

[59] The Genealogy of Jesus appears in Matthew 1:1-17 along with Luke 3:23-38, see your Bible. During his earthly visitation, Jesus was 100% human and 100% God. This is known as the hypostatic union.

302

Jews did and just as anyone else does who will believe that Jesus is the Son of God that he is God who was made manifest in the flesh, that God raised him from the dead, and that it is only by his name alone that we can be saved. [60]

People of color and Jewish lineage

In America, people of color are not generally thought of as having any kind of Jewish heritage. But when examining the tribe of Joseph, it is very possible that there are people of color who have Jewish ancestry. As mentioned earlier, there are twelve ancient tribes of Israel from which the Jewish nation derives. These tribes are identified in the 49th chapter of the Book of Genesis and are listed as such: Rueben, Simeon, Levi, Judah, Zebulun, Issachar, Dan, Gad, Asher, Naphtali, Joseph, and Benjamin. The tribes represent the descendants of the men who held the tribal names. All twelve men were the sons of Jacob (the son of Isaac who was the son of Abraham) whom God named Israel.

Joseph, from whom one of the twelve tribes originated, was sold into slavery by ten of his brothers due to their jealousy of him that was aroused because of Jacob's favoritism towards Joseph and because of the dreams that Joseph had of one day ruling over his family such as a government official would rule. The historical account of this event is documented in Genesis chapter 37.[61] The brothers (all except Rueben) threw Joseph into a cistern and sold him to Midianite Ishmaelites who in turn sold him to a man named Potiphar. Potiphar was an official captain of the guard to the Egyptian Pharaoh at the time.

During his time in captivity in Egypt, Joseph was able to interpret the dreams of the Pharaoh when no one else could. Because of this, Joseph was able to warn Pharaoh in advance about a famine which would occur in seven years and Pharaoh was consequently able to prepare the country for the famine by storing food away. Pharaoh was so pleased with Joseph's ability to interpret dreams that in order to prepare for the inevitable, he put Joseph in charge of the palace (second to himself). The account of these

---

[60] Then Peter, filled with the Holy Spirit said to them, "Rulers and Elders of the people! If we are being called to account today for an act of kindness shown to a cripple and are asked how he was healed, then know this, you and all the people of Israel: It is by the name of Jesus Christ of Nazareth, whom you crucified but whom God raised from the dead, that this man stands before you healed. He is "'the stone you builders rejected, which has become the capstone.' Salvation is found in no one else, for there is no other name under heaven given to men by which we much be saved. (Acts 4:8-12 NIV)

[61] Genesis chapter 37, see your Bible.

events is documented in Genesis, chapter 41.[62] Genesis 41:41-52 give account as to the beginnings of the tribes of Manasseh and Ephraim; the verses read:

> [41]So Pharaoh said to Joseph, "I hereby put you in charge of the whole land of Egypt." [42]Then Pharaoh took his signet ring from his finger and put it on Joseph's finger. He dressed him in robes of fine linen and put a gold chain around his neck. [43]He had him ride in a chariot as his second-in-command, and men shouted before him, "Make way!" Thus he put him in charge of the whole land of Egypt.
> [44]Then Pharaoh said to Joseph, "I am Pharaoh, but without your word no one will lift hand or foot in all Egypt." [45]Pharaoh gave Joseph the name Zaphenath-Paneah and gave him Asenath daughter of Potiphera, priest of On, to be his wife. And Jospeh went throughout the land of Egypt.
> [46]Joseph was thirty years old when he entered the service of Pharaoh king of Egypt. And Joseph went out from Pharaoh's presence and traveled throughout Egypt. [47]During the seven years of abundance the land produced plentifully. [48]Joseph collected all the food produced in those seven years of abundance in Egypt and stored it in the cities. In each city he put the food grown in the fields surrounding it. [49]Joseph stored up huge quantities of grain, like the sand of the sea; it was so much that he stopped keeping records because it was beyond measure.
> [50]Before the years of famine came, two sons were born to Joseph by Asenath daughter of Potiphera, priest of On. [51]Joseph named his firstborn Manasseh and said, "It is because God has made me forget all my trouble and all my father's household." [52]The second son he named Ephraim and said, "It is because God has made me fruitful in the land of my suffering." (Genesis 41:41-52 NIV)

Joseph had two sons by his wife Asenath; Ephraim and Manasseh. His wife was an Egyptian, not an Israelite. Egypt is a country in North Africa where there are, and have been, even in ancient times, people living there

---

[62] See your Bible.

with varying degrees of skin color; from light to very dark.[63] Therefore many Jews are of African descent since Joseph's wife was African. In addition to this, as discussed earlier, the Scriptures tell us that Moses married an Ethiopian woman. Ethiopia is an African country. Most theologians believe that Moses' Ethiopian wife referred to in the book of Numbers is the same wife that is referred to in the book of Exodus, identified by name as Zipporah. Zipporah bore two sons for Moses; Gershom (Exodus 2:22)[64] and Eliezer (Exodus 18:1-6)[65]. According to 1 Chronicles 23:17,[66] Eliezer had one son named Rehabiah who had many sons. Therefore. Eliezer had many descendants. Gershom had two sons: Shubael (1 Chronicles 23:16)[67] and Jonathan (Judges 18:30).[68] Along with their Jewish ancestry, Gershom and Eliezer were also of African ancestry (because their mother was an Ethiopian) which means that their descendants were also of African ancestry as well.

Eventually Jacob and his eleven sons were reunited with Joseph in Egypt. Jacob blessed both Ephraim and Manasseh, deeming them both Israelites in doing so. The following passage of Scripture gives the account:

> [1]Some time later Joseph was told, "Your father is ill." So he took his two sons Manasseh and Ephraim along with him. [2]When Jacob was told, "Your son Joseph has come to you," Israel rallied his strength and sat up on the bed.
> [3]Jacob said to Joseph, "God Almighty appeared to me at Luz in the land of Canaan, and there he blessed me [4]and said to me, 'I am going to make you fruitful and will increase your numbers. I will make you a community of peoples, and I will give this land as an everlasting possession to your descendants after you.'
> [5]"Now then, your two sons born to you in Egypt before I came to you here will be reckoned as mine: Ephraim and Manasseh will be mine, just as Reuben and Simeon are mine. [6]Any children born to you after them will be

---

[63] Other countries located in North Africa are Algeria, Libya, Morocco, the Sudan, and the Western Sahara. A vast majority of the Africans that were kidnapped and brought to America during the transatlantic slave trade came from West Africa.

[64] See your Bible

[65] See your Bible

[66] See your Bible.

[67] See your Bible

[68] See your Bible.

yours; in the territory they inherit they will be reckoned under the names of their brothers. [7]As I was returning from Paddan, to my sorrow Rachel died in the land of Canaan while we were still on the way, a little distance from Ephrath. So I buried her there beside the road to Ephrath." (that is, Bethlehem).

[8]When Israel saw the sons of Joseph, he asked, "Who are these?"

[9]"They are the sons God has given me here," Joseph said to his father.

Then Israel said, "Bring them to me so I may bless them."

[10]Now Israel's eyes were failing because of old age, and he could hardly see, So Joseph brought his sons close to him, and his father kissed them and embraced them.

[11]Israel said to Joseph, "I never expected to see your face again, and now God has allowed me to see your children too."

[12]Then Joseph removed them from Israel's knees and bowed down with his face to the ground. [13]And Joseph took both of them, Ephraim on his right toward Israel's left hand and Manasseh on his left toward Israel's right hand, and brought them close to him. [14]But Israel reached out his right hand and put it on Ephraim's head, though he was the younger, and crossing his arms, he put his left hand on Manasseh's head, even though Manasseh was the firstborn.

[15]Then he blessed Joseph and said, "May the God before whom my fathers Abraham and Isaac walked, the God who has been my shepherd all my life to this day, [16]the Angel who has delivered me from all harm—may he bless these boys. May they be called by my name and the names of my fathers Abraham and Isaac, and may they increase greatly upon the earth."

[17]When Joseph saw his father placing his right hand on Ephraim's head he was displeased; so he took hold of his father's hand to move it from Ephraim's head to Manasseh's head. [18]Joseph said to him, "No, my father, this one is the firstborn; put your right hand on his head."

[19]But his father refused and said, "I know, my son, I know. He too will become a people, and he too will

become great. Nevertheless, his younger brother will be greater than he, and his descendants will become a group of nations." [20]He blessed them that day and said, "In your name will Israel pronounce this blessing: 'May God make you like Ephraim and Manasseh.'" So he put Ephraim ahead of Manasseh. (Genesis 48: 1-20 NIV)

Although Ephraim and Manasseh were born of an African woman, Jacob (Israel) accepted them as his and they were just as much Israelites as were all of the other Israelites and therefore just as much ethnic Jews as all others. They too were thus, part of the chosen people. The point being; if it were true that the Bible specifically taught that blacks and Jews are inferior to whites, then it would seem that neither Jews nor blacks would be identified in any way as God's chosen. There is no doubt that the Jewish line comes from Israel; the country is named after the man himself. However, when considering Ephraim and Manasseh we see that some of the Jewish line comes from Africa (Ethiopia, Egypt) which gives strong indication that there are many Egyptian and Ethiopian Africans (unarguably people of color) who also come from the lineage of Israel and are therefore also the chosen people of the promise as it pertains to Jewish tribal heritage. There is also therefore no doubt that many black people worldwide who have African ancestors (including black Americans) are unknowingly of Jewish descent.

THE BIBLE WHEN IT COMES TO PREDESTINATION[69]

Through the annals of church history there has been much debate as to the meaning of predestination. The underlying question is whether or not those of us who are saved were predestined to be saved before we were even born. The gist of the argument surrounds the debate over whether or not the gift of salvation has already been promised to people even before a confession of faith in the Lordship and Deity of Jesus Christ has been made.

---

[69] Dodds, Elreta; *Predestination: Did God predestine some people to go to Heaven and others to go to Hell?* Essay written for a 2005 class assignment (Faith Center for Christian Education, Port Huron MI). The majority of the discussion under this heading is quoted from (with revisions) the essay. Copyright 2005. The essay is located on two of this author's Internet blogs: www.predestinations.blogspot.com and www.controversialchristianissues.blogspot.com. Used by permission of the author.

Many theologians believe that God created certain people for salvation and created certain other people for damnation and that those who were created for damnation never had a chance for salvation because they were predestined to be damned the day they were born. They go on to say that there are those who, on the other hand, were predestined for salvation before they were even "born again", before their faith in Jesus Christ became manifest. This is what is referred to as the Calvinist view of predestination. The problem with this view is that many of those who adhere to it often times use it to justify a belief that certain races of people were created for damnation while other races of people were not. The Calvinist view can easily be fit into a racial supremacist way of thinking; which is why we're taking a look at the matter.

The doctrinal teaching of predestination stems from the following two passages of Scripture that are cited below:

> [28] And we know that in all things God works for the good of those who love him, who have been called according to his purpose. [29] For those God foreknew he also predestined to be conformed to the likeness of his Son, that he might be the firstborn among many brothers. [30] And those he called he also justified; those he justified, he also glorified. (Romans 8:28-30 NIV)

> [3] Praise be to the God and Father of our Lord Jesus Christ, who has blessed us in the heavenly realms with every spiritual blessing in Christ. [4] For he chose us in him before the creation of the world to be holy and blameless in his sight. In love [5] he predestined us to be adopted as his sons through Jesus Christ in accordance with his pleasure and will—[6] to the praise of his glorious grace, which he has freely given us in the One he loves. (Ephesians 1:3-6 NIV)

Paul says to the Romans that those who God foreknew, he also predestined to be conformed to the likeness of Jesus and then indicates in his letter to the Ephesians that God has predestined the saved to be adopted as his sons through Jesus Christ. There are two main views that theologians ascribe to when interpreting these two passages of Scripture. One view, mentioned above, is the Calvinist view. The other view is the Arminian view.

The Arminian view says that faith comes before regeneration (being spiritually reborn) and although God predestined those who were called, they were predestined because God is all-knowing so he knew (before he created them) that they would confess a belief in Christ and therefore they were predestined to be saved; not because God created them as saved beings; but because God created them already knowing that they would be saved beings due to the choice they would eventually make. The Arminian view does not give rise to supremacist thinking because the view supports the theological argument that it is *one's choice* whether or not to accept the gift of salvation and go to heaven to be with the Lord Jesus Christ upon physical death.

Those who support the Arminian view use the following verses of Scripture, among others, to support their arguments:

> [8]But what does it say? 'The word is near you; it is in your mouth and in your heart, that is the word of faith we are proclaiming: [9]That if you confess with your mouth, 'Jesus is Lord,' and believe in your heart that God raised him from the dead, you will be saved. [10]For it is with your heart that you believe and are justified, and it is with your mouth that you confess and are saved. [11]As the Scripture says, "Anyone who trusts in him will never be put to shame." [12]For there is no difference between Jew and Gentile—the same Lord is Lord of all and richly blesses all who call on him, [13]for "Everyone who calls on the name of the Lord will be saved." (Romans 10:8-13 NIV)

Then John 3:16-18 quotes Jesus as saying,

> [16]"For God so loved the world that he gave his one and only Son, that whoever believes in him shall not perish but have eternal life. [17]For God did not send his Son into the world to condemn the world, but to save the world through him. [18]Whoever believes in him is not condemned, but whoever does not believe stands condemned already because he has not believed in the name of God's one and only Son." (NIV)[70]

The debate surrounding Calvinism and Arminianism is found in many theological texts, particularly those writings that focus upon Christian

---

[70] The King James Version translates "one and only Son" to the familiar "only begotten Son."

apologetics (studies that defend the Christian faith by means of looking into science, archeological findings, history, logic, language, and ancient culture). In their book entitled, "Handbook of Christian Apologetics,"[71] Christian Apologists and authors Peter Kreeft and Ronald Tacelli tell us that the Calvinist position says that God has certain people slated for hell before they are even conceived in their mother's womb and that they are damned to hell by the will of God himself. Both Kreeft and Tacelli agree that this type of thinking goes against biblical Scripture and they point particularly to Matthew 18:14 which reads:

> In the same way your Father in heaven is not willing that
> any of these little ones should be lost. (NIV)

The Scripture is referring to children. Therefore if God is not willing that children be lost (meaning that he is not willing for children to go to hell) then certainly he would not damn children to hell before they are even born.

The basic disagreement between the two trains of thought has to do with whether or not human beings have free will to express and confess a belief in Jesus or whether or not a confessed belief in Jesus is totally due to God's will. In order to obtain an even clearer understanding of the two differing positions and also to introduce into the discussion how the function of the Holy Spirit is also at the forefront of both arguments, it is important to briefly present further comparisons.

There are five subcomponents to the two different views. The first component has to do with free will. Calvinism teaches that there is nothing that human beings can do to save themselves. Human beings have no free will. If a human being has faith in God it is because God gave him or her that faith. Therefore, the faith did not derive from the believer's heart but the faith, instead, derived from God and was placed in the believer's heart. Arminianism teaches that everyone has free will to believe and confess the Lord Jesus as Savior. The option to accept Christ or not to accept him is available to everyone. The decision whether or not to accept the gift of salvation rests on the person. A person is faced with the decision whether to cooperate with the Holy Spirit (because as Paul has told us, one cannot be saved without adhering to the influence of the Holy Spirit)[72] and

---

[71] *Handbook of Christian Apologetics*, Intervarsity Press, Downers Grove Illinois.
[72] Therefore I tell you that no one who is speaking by the Spirit of God says, "Jesus be cursed," and no one can say, "Jesus is Lord," except by the Holy Spirit. (1 Corinthians 12:3 NIV)

experience regeneration (spiritual rebirth), or whether to reject the word of God and continue to live a sinful life without him.

The second component has to do with the argument of whether or not election is conditional or unconditional. Calvinism ascribes to the persuasion of what is referred to as unconditional election. Unconditional election supposes that a person's receiving of the gift of salvation was an unconditional occurrence on the part of that person. In other words, that person did not have to do anything to receive salvation because God's will was for that person to have the gift of salvation before he or she was born. On the other hand, Arminianism says that salvation is contingent upon the confession and belief of the one who is seeking it. The gift of salvation is available to everyone. But having a gift available and receiving that gift (and making use of it) is two different things. Arminiansim says the gift must be received. Calvinism says the gift is given to the receiver and received without any voluntary acceptance from the receiver.

The third component focuses on atonement.[73] The arguments between the two views are thus: Calvinism says that Christ only came to save those who were already elected to be saved. No one else has a chance, only those who were pre-elected by God. Arminianism says that Christ died for the salvation of everyone. His atonement (his death provided the ultimate living sacrifice to redeem the world of sin) is available to all who will embrace him.

The fourth component has to do with the argument of whether or not the Holy Spirit can be rejected or resisted. Calvinism says that the Holy Spirit calls people to salvation, but only those people whom God has called (predestined) to be saved. Calvinism says that the call is irresistible and therefore, once the person, whom God has already called to be saved, is called, he or she cannot resist the call. Arminianism says that because of the free will that God has given mankind, all people have the choice whether or not to accept the Holy Spirit's invitation to embrace the gift of salvation or reject it.

The fifth and final component has to do with the argument of whether or not salvation can be lost, once obtained. The Calvinist view says that once someone is saved, he or she is always saved, especially since they were predestined to be saved and really didn't have anything to do with the gift of salvation that they have obtained. The Arminian view is split. There are some that support the belief that once a sinner is saved he/she is always

---

[73] Jesus made amends for our sins (atonement) through the shedding of his blood on the cross. Once we believe in Jesus and confess that belief, our sins are forgiven; our sins are atoned for and we are saved.

saved and then there are others who believe that the saved can fall from grace and lose their salvation.

In his book, "The Mystery of the Holy Spirit," renowned Christian apologist R.C. Sproul argues on behalf of the Calvinist viewpoint by stating the following:

> "A monergistic work is a work produced singly, by one person. The prefix *mono*—means one. The word *erg* refers to a unit of work. Words like energy are built upon this root. A synergistic work is one that involves cooperation between two or more persons or things. The prefix *syn*—means 'together with.' I labor this distinction for a reason. It is fair to say that the whole debate between Rome and Martin Luther hung on this single point. At issue was this: Is regeneration a monergistic work of God, or is it a synergistic work that requires cooperation between man and God? When my professor wrote 'Regeneration precedes faith' on the blackboard, he was clearly siding with the monergistic answer. To be sure, after a person is regenerated, that person cooperates by exercising faith and trust. But the first step, the step of regeneration by which a person is quickened to spiritual life, is the work of God and of God alone. The initiative is with God, not with us. The reason we do not cooperate with regenerating grace before it acts upon us and in us is because we cannot. We cannot because we are spiritually dead. We can no more assist the Holy Spirit in the quickening of our souls to spiritual life than Lazarus could help Jesus raise him from the dead. It is probably true that the majority of professing Christians in the world today believe that the order of our salvation is this: Faith precedes regeneration. We are exhorted to choose to be born again. But telling a man to choose rebirth is like exhorting a corpse to choose resurrection. The exhortation falls upon deaf ears."[74]

---

[74] Sproul, R.C., The Mystery of the Holy Spirit, Tyndale House Publishers, Wheaton Illinois, copyright 1990, pgs. 103-10. Used by permission of the publisher.

In the preceding quote, Sproul concludes that the relationship between regeneration and faith can only be one of monergism (produced singularly by one person without the cooperation of another party). He concludes that regeneration is a monergistic occurrence, since in his view, being born again happens without human influence and only by the will of God. He rejects the possibility that regeneration is a synergistic occurrence, involving cooperation between man and God. He concludes that regeneration cannot be synergistic because, as he puts it, those who are spiritually dead cannot make themselves become spiritually alive. But Sproul, (along with other theologians) is either unaware of, or totally neglects a third possibility; and that is that regeneration and faith are simultaneous occurrences. When one confesses a belief in the Lordship of Jesus Christ, regeneration happens instantly, not afterwards…but during. The Holy Spirit is at work instantly, and therefore regeneration can indeed be synergistic.

Sproul says that we cannot cooperate with regenerating grace before it acts upon us because before it acts upon us we are spiritually dead and can no more help the quickening of our souls to spiritual life than Lazarus could help Jesus raise him from the dead. But Sproul leaves out a very important part of the account of Jesus and Lazarus, and that is that Jesus raised Lazarus with a verbal command.[75] In raising Lazarus from the dead, Jesus didn't just stand there and not say anything but instead he commanded Lazarus to "come forth" and upon the command to come forth, Lazarus began making his way out of the tomb. In the account, the exhortation to come forth did not fall upon deaf ears even though Lazarus was physically dead. Instead, the dead man heard the command and responded. Therefore, we can also take this to mean that the spiritually dead can hear as well. They too can hear the spiritual command to "come forth" and get saved; if they choose to listen and respond.

We do not know the exact point at which Lazarus was made alive again but we can safely surmise that it took a conscious effort on Lazarus' part to rise up and leave the tomb at the command of Jesus. There was cooperation between Lazarus and Jesus. Jesus commanded Lazarus to come forth and he did so. In order to leave the tomb, Lazarus would have had to step away from it; just as he did. Lazarus heard the command, obeyed the command, and came forth. He had a choice. He could have ignored Jesus' command and stayed in the tomb. Although Jesus compelled Lazarus to come out; there is no indication that Jesus forced him out. It was still Lazarus' decision whether or not to walk out of the tomb. The opportunity was there but Lazarus had to take it. And so it is

---

[75] John 11:19-45, see your Bible.

with us. God gives us the opportunity to be saved but we must take hold of the opportunity in order for the opportunity to take effect. We must hear the word of God (be open to it; listen) and be willing to step away from the tomb. Lazarus was regenerated immediately upon his acknowledgement of the words of the Lord and his decision to leave the tomb. Regeneration happened in an instant. Lazarus was made alive at the exact moment he began obeying the command,[76] just as we are made alive at the exact moment we confess Christ as Lord and Savior. Lazarus was dead then he heard the word of God and decided to act upon it. If he had not acted upon it; he would have remained in the tomb. God called him; but he had to adhere to the call in order to walk away from death. In the same sense, God calls us; but we must adhere to the call in order to walk away from spiritual death.

When looking at it this way, we can counter the dead man argument by pointing out that a man who is dead in the spirit can indeed experience a rebirth as the result of his faith if we conclude that upon his confession and belief, rebirth takes place at the exact same time that faith is made manifest. Therefore, faith doesn't have to occur before regeneration for regeneration to occur. This train of thought gives greater credibility to the synergistic view of regeneration while at the same time supporting the Arminian view of predestination. When taking into account the possibility of simultaneous occurrence between the regeneration and faith, one does not cancel the other out.

A particularly daunting question comes to mind when entertaining the doctrinal teachings of Calvinism, and that is this: If God made certain people specifically to be doomed to hell then wouldn't we consider the conditions upon which every sin they committed as entrapment? Entrapment is when governing authorities purposely lure someone to do wrong. Then, once the person succumbs to the temptation, they are arrested and thrown in jail. Hell is for those who have unrepentantly practiced sin and have never accepted Jesus as Lord and Savior. But if a person is created to be damned then it would seem that God would not punish him or her for acting in ways that are familiar to the nature of one who is already condemned. However, hell is a punishment and punishments are made for those who are spiritually dead by their own

---

[76] An example of God displaying action at the exact moment of the action of a person is seen in Daniel 4:28-33 when looking at how God punished Nebuchadnezzar due to his pride, before Nebuchadnezzar completed making the prideful statement that he was making (while he was making it). The prideful statement and the initiation of the punishment happened concurrently; at the same time.

314

choice, just as jail is a place for those who are criminals by their own choice and are dead to the mores of society. Immorality is a choice not a calling. And therefore to go to hell is not a calling, but a choice.

There is a simultaneous cause and effect relationship between being reborn and faith and therefore there is indeed something we must do in order to be saved. We must confess and believe that Jesus is Lord (God incarnate). The Calvinist view is a particularly dangerous one. For those who uphold it, it can lead to feelings of superiority, racism, and arrogance. We must keep in mind the declaration Paul made in Romans 10:13 which reads, "For anyone who calls on the name of the Lord will be saved." Anyone includes everyone. And everyone excludes nobody.

CHAPTER SUMMATION

The Bible does not categorize people on the basis of skin color but instead categorizes people first spiritually as to whether or not a person is saved and then on an earthly level as to nationality and familial ancestry. We have also seen that God does not indulge in favoritism of one person over another. However, if God makes a promise, he will keep it, as he did with Abraham. God's promise to Abraham was not favoritism because his promise was made to Abraham as a reward for Abraham's faithfulness and loyalty. When it comes to favoritism, a person is given special privileges, things, or opportunities for no particular reason and no particular purpose; which is the problem with favoritism. The person is simply given preferential treatment because of how he or she looks or because of the material possessions that he or she may have. Scripture teaches us that God does not do this. Not only does Scripture teach us that God does not do this but also that we should not do it as well. Therefore, although the Jews are the chosen people, they do not automatically obtain salvation without confessing the Deity and Lordship of Jesus Christ. In order for them to be assured a place in eternity with God, they too must confess with their mouths that Jesus is Lord and believe in their hearts that God (Father, Son, Holy Ghost) raised him from the dead.

Favoritism is morally wrong. The end result of favoritism is discrimination. A person cannot practice favoritism without inadvertently practicing discrimination along with it. The two go hand in hand. There is no favoritism without discrimination and there is no discrimination without favoritism.

The Bible teaches that there is no person that is humanly superior to another person. The Jew and the Gentile are equal in Christ. One race is no better than the other. As a matter of fact, when studying the subject of race in the Bible, although there are translations that use the word "race" to describe a nation of people; what we see biblically when there is reference to a group of people is not race but instead ancestry, ethnicity, or nationality. God judges nations, empires, and countries, not races of people.

When looking at the issue of slavery we see that there is no truth to the teaching that the Bible teaches that black people are cursed to be slaves. This is a false teaching that has been handed down throughout the ages by those who have sought to misuse the Bible to justify the enslavement of blacks; and in looking at the history of slavery in American there is no getting around the fact that the type of slavery that was imposed upon blacks in early America was wrong due to the fact that men and women were kidnapped from their native land and due to the treacherous way in which the slaves were treated once on American soil. We've seen where it says in the Bible that kidnapping and selling a person was punishable by death. We've also seen that the Bible puts slave trading (kidnapping and selling people) in the same category as murder, patricide, matricide, adultery, and lying. God has regulated the system of slavery to be a humane one. The slave master and the slave are equal in Christ. The master is not superior to the slave. Both have the same creator in heaven and both must ultimately answer to God. Therefore, although whites enslaved blacks during early America; the white slave masters were no better than the black slaves. God is not a respecter of persons.

With regard to the question of the color of God; the color of God, as far as the Bible is concerned, is a non-issue. In the book of Revelation, Jesus has been described symbolically by use of certain colors. His head is described as white, his hair is described as white like wool, and his feet are described as bronze. Are we then to say that Jesus is biracial? Certainly not. This is not what the description is getting at. Instead, Jesus' glorified body is being described symbolically in a vision. The colors represent purity, royalty, and power; not race. Jesus was a Jew. The Jews are a nation of people who are descendants of Abraham. Mary, a Jewish woman, was his biological mother and Joseph was his earthly father. Both Mary and Joseph were Jews. Jesus came from the Jewish tribal line of Judah, a descendant of King David. There is no question that Jesus was Jewish. However, his skin color and hair texture is not known. Whether or not he was a black looking Jew or a white looking Jew, or an Asian looking Jew, or a Jewish looking Jew is not known. The gospels do not say anything about the color of his skin or his physical appearance apparently because it was not important. If it had been important something would have been said about it. He was Jewish and that's it. Any further description of him is conjecture aside from the description of him in Isaiah 53:2b which says,

316

He had no beauty or majesty to attract us to him, nothing
in his appearance that we should desire him. (NIV)

Jesus (God the Son) was manifested in human flesh but was an average
looking man so that those who were attracted to him would be attracted to
him because of what he said and represented and not because of how he
looked. The underlying principle that the Bible is teaching therefore is that
looks don't matter. In general and especially when it comes to those who
are racist, human beings are quick to judge based on appearance. But the
Bible teaches that to do so is not a good thing and that God looks at one's
heart and not his or her outer appearance. We see this clearly when taking
into consideration what the Lord said to Samuel while Samuel was looking
for the next King of Israel amongst Jesse's sons. The Lord God told
Samuel not to look at the candidate's countenance or height and then went
on to say that mankind has a tendency to look at the outside of a person
(skin color, hair texture, clothes, facial features, weight, height, etc) while
God looks at the heart (thoughts and motives).[77] Nowhere in the Bible does
it say that God looks at a person's race in order to make a judgment about
that person. Biblically speaking, how one looks is irrelevant. God does not
judge people by race, and therefore, neither should we.

---

[77] 1 Samuel 16:1-7, see your Bible.

EPILOGUE -- PERSONALIZING THE MESSAGE

Although the Bible, when looking at the original languages of Hebrew, Greek, and Aramaic in which it was written, never mentions race as we define it; and although scientists have proven that there is really no such thing as race, the concept of race is so engrained into cultures worldwide that it is almost impossible to identify oneself without the inclusion of what's deemed as one's racial identity. This is especially true in America, because of the pervading racial prejudices and tensions that still exist on a wide scale.

According to the Bible and according to science, there is really no such thing as race as we know it; however, there is such a thing as race according to most societies in the world. But God categorizes people according to the nation they are from (not according to the color of one's skin), which, in the Bible had to do with which patriarch a person descendent from. Skin color was never an issue. The nation of Israel was composed of twelve tribes (and actually still is although the demarcation of the tribes has been blurred over the centuries) with each tribe representing the descendants of the twelve sons that Jacob (Israel) had, whose father was Isaac, whose father was Abraham. In today's world, one's nationality has more so to do with the country one was born in and/or resides in. Although most countries have a specific concentration of people who belong to one race living there, there is usually some means of allowing people from other countries and races to become citizens. It is the same when we look at things spiritually. The gospel message is available to the Gentile as well as to the Jew and once a Gentile accepts the message of the gospel then he has spiritually become a part of a spiritual nation; the Kingdom of God.

In order to become part of the Kingdom of God, one has to confess the Deity of Christ and believe that Jesus rose from the dead. Therefore any philosophy or doctrine that dissuades persons from embracing the Bible becomes a demonic tool primed to prevent people from realizing the need for salvation and consequently from entering into the Kingdom. The lie that says the Bible condones racism has been, for centuries, one of the tools that have been used to dissuade people from embracing the Bible.

Racism is a sin. It is wrong. Racism, in any form, is immoral and flies in the face of God. The discussions presented in this book have shown this to be so. The Bible teaches against overt and covert discrimination based on the way a person looks (racism and prejudice). Institutional/systematic racism is a type of lookism-discrimination that is hidden and not easily detected, but is revealed when organizations and social institutions that practice institutional racism are pushed to make certain decisions that expose the racism and hypocrisy that is practiced within their confines. The racism is imbedded within the structure of those social institutions.

The only superior person that ever existed in the flesh was Jesus Christ. Jesus Christ is the second person of the Godhead (God the Son) that was manifested as a human being, crucified, and then was resurrected to prove his Deity. And then there is only one superior *being* and that being is God (Father, Son, and Holy Ghost; one God representing himself in three persons). Therefore, to say that a human being, other than Jesus Christ manifested in the flesh, is superior to another human being, is blasphemy against God; for only God is superior. Furthermore, racial discrimination is akin to oppression and favoritism, both of which the Bible clearly identifies and defines as sin. Racial discrimination is also akin to the practice of implementing double standards; a practice which we have seen that the Lord detests.

Not only is racism a sin; but keeping silent about it and not speaking out against it, particularly if the opportunity presents itself within one's own circle, is wrong as well. One of the most somber reasons why racism has been able to sustain itself in America is because the church, as a whole, does not readily speak out against it; this is particularly true with regard to the "white church." This is not to say that there aren't white churches that do speak out against racism, but they are in the minority. In general, the white church is basically silent about the issue, because their leadership is silent. But the only way people will speak out against racism when they have the opportunity to do so is if they are convicted enough morally to take a stand (whether or not they belong to the church). If church leaders ignore the problem and never say anything then that gives parishioners a license towards apathy. But in Christ, there is no Jew or Gentile, which means that there is no black or white, and there certainly is therefore no black church or white church, but just *one* church which is the overall body of believers in Christ.

Unfortunately, in years past, the white Protestant church, in general, supported the Klan. At the expense of their black brothers and sisters in the Lord, white Protestants had convinced themselves that the Klan wasn't really all that bad. We see a similar way of thinking in the mindset of white America today; the general train of thought is that there is still some racism against minorities, but it's not really that much of a problem. It goes without saying that it is only not really that much of a problem to those who are not targeted by it.

To be fair, it is true that there are many people in the dominant group who do speak out against racism and who do join forces to eradicate it; but it can be safely surmised that the dominant group, as a whole, more times than not, due to fear or due to a resistance to give up the privileges and/or benefits they enjoy that results from the preservation of racism, stand by and say nothing, minimize the effect that racism has on minorities, and/or ignore its existence altogether. And to be sure, there are some minorities who do the same. But most minorities today, have found themselves at some point in their lives, the victim of some form of racism (particularly, when it comes to institutional racism) and when they stand up against it, they oftentimes also find themselves being accused of "playing the race card" or of being "hypersensitive" or of "making things worse by bringing up inequities."

The overall message from white America (and surprisingly from some in black America and in other minority "Americas") is that those minorities who point to racial discrimination in the workforce, or in the schools, or within the health care system, or within whatever system they might point it out in, are "whining" and just adding to the problem by saying something about it; after all, it's not really that bad, is it? We've come a long way, haven't we? Yes, we've come a long way but that doesn't mean that we still don't have a ways yet to go. And to say that things are "better" doesn't mean that things are not still bad. Injustice can never really be "better;" only more tolerable than a greater injustice.

The wife that has suffered a black eye and body bruises from the abuse of her husband might be doing "better" than the wife who has to be hospitalized as a result of her husband's abuse; but both scenarios are just as bad. We wouldn't minimize the complaint from the woman with the black eye and hidden bruises simply because her injuries didn't land her in the hospital. When she complains about the abuse she endures that occurs behind closed doors and is hard to see, we wouldn't accuse her of "whining" simply because things between she and her husband used to be a whole lot worse. We wouldn't tell her that by saying something about the abuse that she's being "hypersensitive" and what she should do is just be quiet about it and go out and buy a great looking pair of sunglasses to cover up the madness. But when it comes to the constant abuse of institutional racism that minorities endure, complaints from minorities often times elicit these types of responses from white America. Many whites, not all, but many, are quick to say that blacks are "playing the race card," "whining," and/or are being "hypersensitive."

What is labeled as hypersensitivity is really the *in*sensitivity on the part of the labeler to understand the devastating effect that institutional racism can have on those who are targets of it. Black America keeps taking the sunglasses off and white America keeps insisting that black America put the sunglasses back on.

As a nation, we should not ignore the fact that millions of people in America continue to experience some form of racial discrimination based on the color of their skin, the texture of their hair, the features of their faces, and ultimately the racial category that others put them in. This fact cannot be negated and should not be minimized. But most of all, the Bible should not be misused to misrepresent God's position on the matter.

Because institutional racism lives within every social system of American society but is not easily seen, all Americans, minorities as well as whites, are guilty at some point in their lives of doing something (or not doing something) be it wittingly or unwittingly, to contribute to its sustainability. Despite this, institutional racism is only targeted against minorities in America, not because white Americans are inherently more callous than non-whites as many minorities would like to think, but because whites have enough collective power as a group to exercise institutional racism against another, less powerful, group of people.

Those who are the targets of institutional racism have to fight harder to equally enjoy the privileges and benefits of being an American. If institutional racism exists within all American social institutions (and it appears that it does) then a person's mental, physical, and spiritual well-being, who is the target of such racism, will undoubtedly be affected. This should not be.

As indicated in the Introduction, it is my hope and prayer that this book will help to dispel any misperception that says that the Bible supports racism and discrimination and by doing so will encourage people to accept Jesus Christ as Lord and Savior who otherwise may not have accepted him because of their misgivings surrounding what the Bible says about these matters. It is also my hope and prayer that this book will help some of those who have misrepresented the Bible on these issues for whatever reason to cease in doing so. It is my final hope and prayer that enough has been revealed in this book so that those Americans who read this book who have been silent about, or have minimized the particular evil of institutional racism will realize the magnitude of the problem and speak up against it when the opportunity arises in order to help contribute to paving the road towards guaranteeing that all Americans, regardless of race, ethnicity, or nationality, have *equal* opportunity for life, liberty, and the pursuit of happiness within this great country we call America.

APPENDIX -- THE BASIC BELIEFS OF CHRISTIANITY

To be a Christian means to follow Jesus Christ and to follow Christ means to accept the complete Bible (Old and New Testament) as one's religious source and to specifically embrace the teachings of Jesus Christ and the gospels. The gospels are the first four books of the New Testament (Matthew, Mark, Luke, and John) which give account of Jesus' ministry from beginning to end during the time he was on earth. The gospels document the things that he taught, what he said, and how he said it. The book of Acts and Revelation also document direct messages from Jesus but the messages are post-resurrection after Jesus had ascended back to heaven to sit at the right hand side of the Father.

CHRISTIANS BELIEVE THAT THE BIBLE IS INFALLIBLE AND HAS ABSOLUTE SPIRITUAL AUTHORITY[1]

The Word of God

Christians believe that the Bible is the only religious book that truly represents the word of God. The following passages of Scripture support this belief.

> All scripture is given by inspiration of God, and profitable for doctrine, for reproof, for correction, for instruction in righteousness: (2 Timothy 3:16 NIV)

> [20]Above all, you must understand that no prophecy of Scripture came about by the prophet's own interpretation. [21]For prophecy never had its origin in the will of man, but men spoke from God as they were carried along by the Holy Spirit. (2 Peter 1:20-21 NIV)

---

[1] Dodds, Elreta. The majority of the information in this Appendix is taken directly from *What the Bible Really says about Slavery: This and other information on the issue of Slavery as it applies to History and Religion*. Revised Edition, copyright 2000, Press Toward The Mark Publications. Much of the information is also paraphrased from Josh McDowell's book entitled, *A Ready Defense*, Thomas Nelson Inc., Nashville, Tennessee, copyright 1993.

[44]And he said unto them, These are the words which I spake unto you, while I was yet with you, that all things must be fulfilled, which were written in the law of Moses, and in the prophets, and in the psalms, concerning me. [45]Then opened he their understanding, that they might understand the scriptures, (Luke 24:44-45 KJV. Jesus is speaking in verse 44)

[37]And the Father who sent me has himself testified concerning me. You have never heard his voice nor seen his form, [38]nor does his word dwell in you, for you do not believe the one he sent. [39]You diligently study the Scriptures because you think that by them you possess eternal life. These are the Scriptures that testify about me, [40]yet you refuse to come to me to have life. (John 5:37-40 NIV)

Jesus, the Messiah tells us first hand that what is contained in the Scriptures is what leads to eternal life. He went on to say that those who have written the Scriptures do so as a testimony of him. If then, we understand who Jesus is, we understand what the Bible is. Jesus is God incarnate (discussed later in this Appendix) and he endorsed the Scriptures of the Bible. Therefore, the Bible is God-inspired and is the unadulterated word of God. This is made even more apparent in the following parable spoken by Jesus:

[19]There was a certain rich man, which was clothed in purple and fine linen, and fared sumptuously every day:
[20]And there was a certain beggar named Lazarus, which was laid at his gate, full of sores,
[21]And desiring to be fed with the crumbs which fell from the rich man's table: moreover the dogs came and licked his sores.
[22]And it came to pass, that the beggar died, and was carried by the angels into Abraham's bosom: the rich man also died and was buried:
[23]And in hell he lift up his eyes, being in torments, and seeth Abraham afar off, and Lazarus in his bosom.
[24]And he cried and said, Father Abraham, have mercy on me, and send Lazarus, that he may dip the tip of his finger in water and cool my tongue; for I am tormented in this flame.

²⁵But Abraham said, Son, remember that thou in thy lifetime receivedst thy good things, and likewise Lazarus evil things: But now he is comforted, and thou art tormented.

²⁶And beside all this, between us and you there is a great gulf fixed: so that they which would pass from hence to you cannot; neither can they pass to us, that would come from thence.

²⁷Then he said, I pray thee therefore, father, that thou wouldest send him to my father's house:

²⁸For I have five brethen; that he may testify unto them, lest they also come into this place of torment.

²⁹Abraham saith unto him, They have Moses and the prophets; let them hear them.

³⁰And he said, Nay, father Abraham; but if one went unto them from the dead, they will repent.

³¹And he said unto him, If they hear not Moses and the prophets, neither will they be persuaded, though one rose from the dead. (Luke 16:19-31 KJV. Jesus is speaking in this parable)

In the above Scripture text the phrase, "Abraham's Bosom" is an Old Testament Jewish term that refers to heaven. The phrase, "Moses and the prophets" is referring to the Word of God (the Holy Bible), specifically the Old Testament (theologians have determined that Moses wrote the first five books of the Bible; the remainder of the Old Testament was written, for the most part, by God's prophets). The text tells us that those who absolutely refuse to accept the Bible as the word of God will do so no matter what. If it is not in a person's heart to believe that the Bible is the word of God then they will not believe, despite evidence contrary to their disbelief. Abraham is referred to as "father"² because God promised to make him "a father of many nations" as seen in the book of Genesis chapter 17. It must also be noted that the rich man in the above parable went to hell not because he was rich nor even because he was cruel to Lazarus but because he never accepted the word of God and therefore never worshipped the true God.

---

² A small *f* used for the word *father* refers to a human father whereas a capital *F* used for the word *Father* refers to God, the Father.

The absolute authority of the Scriptures

Christians believe that any other religious book or document that does not agree with what the Bible says is not of God:

> [9]Whoever transgresseth, and abideth not in the doctrine of Christ, hath not God. He that abideth in the doctrine of Christ, he hath both the Father and the Son. (2 John 9 KJV)

> [10]If anyone comes to you and does not bring this teaching, do not take him into your house or welcome him. [11]Anyone who welcomes him shares in his wicked work. (2 John 10-11 NIV)

> [6]I am astonished that you are so quickly deserting the one who called you by the grace of Christ and are turning to a different gospel-- [7]which is really no gospel at all. Evidently some people are throwing you into confusion and are trying to pervert the gospel of Christ. [8]But even if we or an angel from heaven should preach a gospel other than the one we preached to you, let him be eternally condemned! [9]As we have already said, so now I say again: if anybody is preaching to you a gospel other than what you accepted, let him be eternally condemned! (Galatians 1:6-9 NIV. Paul the apostle is speaking here)

> [17]I urge you, brothers, to watch out for those who cause divisions and put obstacles in your way that are contrary to the teaching you have learned. Keep away from them. [18]For such people are not serving our Lord Christ, but their own appetites. By smooth talk and flattery they deceive the minds of naïve people. (Romans 16:17-18 NIV)

> [11]And he gave some apostles; and some, prophets; and some, evangelists; and some, pastors and teachers;
> [12]For the perfecting of the saints, for the work of the ministry, for the edifying of the body of Christ:

[13]Till we all come in the unity of faith, and of the knowledge of the Son of God, unto a perfect man, unto the measure of the stature of the fullness of Christ: [14]That we henceforth be no more children, tossed to and fro, and carried about with every wind of doctrine, by the sleight of men, and cunning craftiness, whereby they lie in wait to deceive; (Ephesians 4:11-14 KJV)

[1]Now the Spirit speaketh expressly, that in the latter times some shall depart from the faith, giving heed to seducing spirits, and doctrines of devils; [2]Speaking lies in hypocrisy; having their conscience seared with a hot iron; (1Timothy 4:1-2 KJV)

[18]For I testify unto every man that heareth the words of the prophecy of this book, If any man shall add unto these things, God shall add unto him the plagues that are written in this book: [19]And if any man shall take away from the words of the book of this prophecy, God shall take away his part out of the book of life, and out of the holy city, and from the things which are written in this book. (Revelation 22:18-19 KJV)

The above Scriptures tell us that any attempt to stray away from, add to, take away from, or pervert the gospel of Jesus Christ is a serious infraction against God. Let's look at a few more Scriptures:

[9]Then shall they deliver you up to be afflicted, and shall kill you: and ye shall be hated of all nations for my name sake. [10]And then shall many be offended, and shall betray one another, and shall hate one another. [11]And many false prophets shall rise, and shall deceive many. [12]And because iniquity shall abound, the love of many shall wax cold. [13] But he that shall endure unto the end, the same shall be saved. [14]And this gospel of the kingdom shall be preached in all the world for a witness unto all nations; and then shall the end come. (Matthew 24:9-14 KJV. Jesus is speaking here.)

Study to shew thyself approved unto God, a workman that needeth not to be ashamed, rightly dividing the word of truth. (2 Timothy 2:15 KJV)

[17]Do not think that I have come to abolish the Law or the Prophets; I have not come to abolish them but to fulfill them. [18]I tell you the truth, until heaven and earth disappear, not the smallest letter, the least stroke of a pen, will by any means disappear from the Law until everything is accomplished. [19]Anyone who breaks one of the least of these commandments and teaches others to do the same will be called least in the kingdom of heaven, but whoever practices and teaches these commands will be called great in the kingdom of heaven. [20]For I tell you that unless your righteousness surpasses that of the Pharisees and the teachers of the law, you will certainly not enter the kingdom of heaven. (Matthew 5:17-20 NIV. Jesus is speaking here)

Evidences that support the Bible as being the Word of God

- *Authorship*

The Bible was written by more than forty authors, in three different languages (Hebrew, Aramaic, and Greek), in different years and centuries, and on three different continents (Asia, Africa, and Europe). Many of the authors never met one another. Despite this, the Bible is in total agreement with itself. No author contradicts another author. This, alone, is a miracle when we think of the diversity of man. In this day and time, if we were to ask forty people, who speak different languages, to write an essay on the same subject over a period of years, without conferring with one another, it would stand to reason that not all forty would agree with one another in their writings. The Old Testament was written between 1400 B.C. and 400 B.C. (approximately a 1000 years). Following this was a period of 400 years where no biblical text was written (the silent years). Most theologians believe that the New Testament was written between A.D. 45 and A.D. 95 (some believe it was written before A.D. 70). Now, just think how remarkable it is that all the authors of the Bible agreed with one another, especially since the Bible was written over a time span of roughly 1500 years. Their literary congeniality certainly could not have happened by chance. There had to have been a common factor, a person directing them in their writings. That person was God.

327

- ***Circulation***

Out of all the books ever written, the Bible has been the most circulated and published worldwide and throughout history. No other book has been translated into as many languages as the Bible has. This is not an accident but rather, has taken place by Divine will.

- ***History***

No other book in history has been as vehemently attacked as the Bible has. Withstanding historical attempts to destroy, ban, and outlaw the Bible, it has survived. Not only has the Bible survived attempts to destroy it but it has also prevailed in spite of the lack of technology during the eras in which it was written. In copying the Bible, the Jewish scribes counted every word and paragraph to make certain that they were precisely copying the text.

- ***Prophecies***

Regardless of world scrutiny and doubt, many prophecies of the Bible have materialized. When taking the 1948 Palestinian restoration of Israel as a nation for an example, we see that the Old Testament prophet Ezekiel predicted this restoration (just one of many biblical predictions concerning Israel) when he spoke to the Jews by saying,

> [8]After many days you will be summoned; in the latter years you will come into the land that is restored from the sword, whose inhabitants have been gathered from many nations to the mountains of Israel which had been a continual waste; but its people were brought out from the nations, and they are living securely, all of them. (Ezekiel 38:8 NASB)

Before 1948 there were many people, including some Christian scholars, who shed doubt on the biblical prophecies that spoke of the restoration of Israel as a nation in Palestine (many declare that Palestine and Israel are one in the same). Despite this, the biblical prophecy prevailed as did (and will) many other biblical prophecies.

Christ himself gave credence to the Scriptures. Let's take a look:

> [44]And he said unto them, These are the words which I spake unto you, while I was yet with you, that all things must be fulfilled, which were written in the law of Moses, and in the prophets, and in the psalms, concerning me. [45]Then opened he their understanding, that they might understand the scriptures. (Luke 24:44-45 KJV)

The first 39 books of the Bible comprise the Old Testament, while the remaining 27 books make up the New Testament. There are 66 books in all. The Old Testament books are the books that were written by Moses and the prophets before the coming of Jesus Christ. The New Testament books are the books written by the apostles and their assistants after the advent of Christ.

As indicated earlier, Moses wrote the first five books of the Old Testament and the prophets of God wrote the rest of the Old Testament books. The prophets responsible for writing the Old Testament were Isaiah, Hosea, Joel, Jeremiah, Nahum, Habakkuk, Zephaniah, Ezekiel, Daniel, David, Samuel, Solomon, and others. Jesus was very specific when referring to the writings of the Old Testament. His reference to Old Testament writings also made for his endorsement of them.

Disciples were students and followers of Jesus. Jesus chose twelve specific men from among his many disciples. These twelve were the apostles. They had a specific calling. The word *apostle* itself comes from the Greek word *apostolos* meaning messenger or ambassador and specifically means *to be sent* on behalf of another. The apostles were to act as personal representatives of the living Christ. It was their job to begin to spread the gospel worldwide and to establish churches in the cities that they visited. They were sent into the world on behalf of and as personal representatives of God manifested in the flesh: Jesus Christ. The following verses of Scripture bring light to this:

> [13]When morning came, he called his disciples to him and chose twelve of them, whom he also designated apostles: [14]Simon (whom he named Peter), his brother Andrew, James, John Philip, Bartholomew, [15]Matthew, Thomas, James son of Alphaeus, Simon who was called the Zealot, Judas son of James, and Judas Iscariot, who became a traitor. Luke 6:13-16 NIV)

The apostles, with some exception, wrote the majority of the New Testament. Not all of the apostles wrote New Testament books. Mark who was an assistant to Peter wrote the gospel of Mark. Luke who was an assistant to Paul wrote the gospel of Luke. Paul became an apostle when during his traveling near the city of Damascus, the Lord spoke to him from heaven and he was converted (Acts 22)[3]. Paul's apostleship thus began and he suffered greatly for the namesake of the Lord. Paul authored more New Testament books than any other New Testament author.

The books of the New Testament are referred to as Scripture just as the books of the Old Testament. Jesus endorsed the writings of the prophets and apostles as Scripture. As pointed to earlier, 2 Timothy 3:16 teaches that all Scripture is inspired by God. Jesus is the second person of the Godhead (explained later in this Appendix) and therefore the inspiration given the prophets and apostles to write what they wrote, came from him (as well as from the Father and the Holy Spirit; one God represented in three persons). The apostles may also be considered prophets because, with the writing of the New Testament, *to prophesy* developed a broader meaning; it not only refers to those who *foretell* future spiritual things but also refers to those who preach the gospel of Christ as well (those who *tell forth the* message). Jesus' endorsement of the Scriptures is revealed in the verses of Scripture below:

> Jesus answered and said unto them, Ye do err, not knowing the scriptures, nor the power of God. (Matthew 22:29 KJV)

> [25]And He said to them, "O foolish men and slow of heart to believe in all that the prophets have spoken!
> [26]"Was it not necessary for the Christ to suffer these things and to enter into His glory?"
> [27]Then beginning with Moses and with all the prophets, He explained to them the things concerning Himself in all the Scriptures. (Luke 24:25-27 NASB)

Since Jesus is God, then his support and endorsement of the biblical Scriptures give evidence to the Bible as being the word of God.

---

[3] See your Bible.

- *Archeology*

Not once has an archeological finding contradicted the Bible. As a matter of fact, archaeological discoveries have given more credibility to the authenticity of the Bible. For example, the existence of the nation of Hittites recorded in Genesis of the Old Testament was once doubted. The Hittites were thought to be a mythological nation of people since the Bible is the only book in history that mentions them. However, archaeological findings now give evidence that an ancient nation of Hittite people did in fact exist and had existed for more than twelve hundred years. This discovery not only stunned many opponents of the Bible but also astonished many archaeologists as well.

CHRISTIANS BELIEVE IN JESUS CHRIST AS LORD AS SAVIOR

To be saved means that when one dies one will go to heaven to live with the Lord and will be saved from an afterlife of eternal damnation in hell. Salvation is the gift of eternal life in God's eternal kingdom. The Bible teaches that Jesus Christ is the only person that ever walked the face of the earth who has the power to save souls and that those who believe in Jesus Christ as Lord and Savior will go to heaven when they die. The Bible teaches that there is no other way to heaven. The following passages of Scripture support these beliefs.

> [9]If you confess with your mouth that Jesus is Lord and believe in your heart that God raised him from the dead, you will be saved. [10]For it is by believing in your heart that you are made right with God, and it is by confessing with your mouth that you are saved. [11]As the Scriptures tell us, "Anyone who trusts in him will never be disgraced." [12]Jew and Gentile are the same in this respect. They have the same Lord, who gives generously to all who call on him. [13]For "everyone who calls on the name of the Lord will be saved." (Romans 10:9-13 NLT)

> [14]Jesus answered, "I am the way, the truth, and the life. No one comes to the Father, except through me." (John 14:6 NIV)

> [16]For God so loved the world, that he gave his only begotten Son, that whosoever believeth in him should not perish, but have everlasting life. [17]For God sent not

his Son into the world to condemn the world; but that the world through him might be saved. [18]He that believeth on him is not condemned: but he that believeth not is condemned already, because he hath not believed in the name of the only begotten Son of God. (John 3:16-18 KJV)

[32]Whosoever therefore shall confess me before men, him will I confess also before my Father which is in heaven. [33]But whosoever shall deny me before men, him will I also deny before my father which is in heaven. (Matthew 10:32-33 KJV. Jesus is speaking here)

[9]We accept man's testimony, but God's testimony is greater because it is the testimony of God, which he has given about his Son. [10]Anyone who believes in the Son of God has this testimony in his heart. Anyone who does not believe God has made him out to be a liar, because he has not believed the testimony God has given about his Son. [11]And this is the testimony: God has given us eternal life, and this life is in his Son. [12]He who has the Son has life; he who does not have the Son of God does not have life. (1 John 5:9-12 NIV)

[8]Then Peter, filled with the Holy Spirit, said to them: "Rulers and elders of the people! [9]If we are being called to account today for an act of kindness shown to a cripple and are asked how he was healed, [10]then know this, you and all the people of Israel: It is by the name of Jesus Christ of Nazareth, whom you crucified but whom God raised from the dead, that this man stands before you healed. [11]He is "'the stone you builders rejected, which has become the capstone.' [12]Salvation is found in no one else, for there is no other name under heaven given to men by which we must be saved." (Acts 4:8-12 NIV)

[43]Stop grumbling among yourselves," Jesus answered. [44]No one can come to me unless the Father who sent me draws him, and I will raise him up at the last day. [45]It is written in the Prophets: 'They will all be taught by God. Everyone who listens to the Father and learns from him

comes to me. [46]No one has seen the Father except the one who is from God; only he has seen the Father. [47]I tell you the truth, he who believes has everlasting life. [48]I am the bread of life. (John 6:43-48 NIV)

CHRISTIANS BELIEVE IN THE DIETY OF CHRIST

Christians believe that there is one God who exists and represents himself in three persons: The Father, The Son, and The Holy Ghost. This description of God is what Christians refer to as the "Trinity." However, the word *Trinity* is not found in the Bible and is merely used as a semantic tool for explaining the Godhead (Father, Son, Holy Ghost). The second person of the Trinity, The Son, was manifest as a man (Jesus Christ). Christians believe that Jesus Christ is God incarnate. These beliefs are supported by biblical Scripture.

It might also seem as if there is a contradiction here since the preceding Scriptures under the preceding heading refer to Jesus as the *Son of God*. However, there is no contradiction when one considers the meaning of certain words and phrases during biblical times. *The New Treasury of Scripture Knowledge* edited by Jerome Smith states that the word "begotten", as applied to Jesus and as understood in the Greek, is biblically defined as one who is unique to the family from which he comes and the only one of his kind. In other words, there is no one else like him. Smith explains that at the time that Jesus was with the Father before his manifestation into the flesh (his preexistence) he was God's unique Son and that he has always been God's unique Son. Smith references Isaiah 9:6 that speaks of Jesus prophetically in the following way:

> For to us a child is born, to us a son is given, and the government will be on his shoulders. And he will be called Wonderful Counselor, Mighty God, Everlasting Father, Prince of Peace. (NIV)

The Son that is given, that the Old Testament prophet Isaiah is referring to in the above Scripture, is Jesus Christ. Jesus was and is the literal Son of God. God is our spiritual Father. With this understanding, one can see how Jesus can be the Son of God as well as God in the flesh. Now, we will look at some Scriptures that support the belief that Jesus himself is God:

> And without controversy great is the mystery of godliness: God was manifest in the flesh, justified in the

333

Spirit, seen of angels, preached unto the Gentiles, believed on in the world, received up into glory. (1 Tim 3:16 KJV)

The above Scripture tells us that God was manifested in the flesh. When coupled with the following two verses of Scripture below, it becomes plain that Jesus is whom the above Scripture is referring to.

[1]In the beginning was the Word, and the Word was with God, and the Word was God. [2]The same was in the beginning with God. [3]All things were made by him; and without him was not any thing made that was made. [4]In him was life; and the life was the light of men. [5]And the light shineth in darkness; and the darkness comprehended it not. (John 1:1-5 KJV)

[14]And the Word was made flesh, and dwelt among us, (and we beheld his glory, the glory as of the only begotten of the Father,) full of grace and truth. (John 1:14 KJV)

John 1:14 identifies the only begotten as the Word made flesh that dwelt among us. Jesus is identified as God's only begotten. The Word is identified as God. Therefore, if Jesus is the only begotten, and the only begotten is the Word and the Word is God, then Jesus is God.

Jesus is the Word that the above Scriptures speak of. The Word was God. The Word was with God in the beginning and became flesh. Jesus is the only person spoken of in the Bible as God in the flesh. Therefore, Jesus is part/personage of the Godhead; the second personage to be exact (Father, *Son*, and Holy Ghost) and was with God in the beginning. Let's look further.

[10]Ye are my witnesses, saith the LORD, and my servant whom I have chosen: that ye may know and believe me, and understand that I am he: before me there was no God formed, neither shall there be after me. [11]I, even I am the LORD and beside me there is no saviour. [12]I have declared, and have saved, and I have shewed, when there was no strange god among you: therefore ye are my witnesses, saith the LORD, that I am God. (Isaiah 43: 10-12 KJV)

334

There is no savior besides God. Jesus is identified throughout the Bible as Lord and Savior. Therefore, Jesus must not only be God but a person of God as well, since the Savior was manifest as a man and sacrificed himself for the sins of the world. The following Scripture reference points this out even further:

> [1]God, after he spoke long ago to the fathers in the prophets in many portions and in many ways, [2]in these last days has spoken to us in His Son, whom He appointed heir of all things, through whom also He made the world. [3]And He is the radiance of His glory and the exact representation of His nature, and upholds all things by the word of His power. When He had made purification of sins, He sat down at the right hand of the Majesty on high; [4]having become as much better than the angels, as He has inherited a more excellent name than they. [5]For to which of the angels did He ever say,
>
> "YOU ARE MY SON,
> TODAY I HAVE BEGOTTEN YOU"?
> And again,
> "I WILL BE A FATHER TO HIM,
> AND HE SHALL BE A SON TO ME"?
> [6]And when He again brings the first-born into the world, He says,
> "AND LET ALL THE ANGELS OF GOD WORSHIP HIM."
> [7]And of the angels He says,
> "WHO MAKES HIS ANGELS WINDS,
> AND HIS MINISTERS A FLAME OF FIRE."
> [8]But of the Son He says,
> "YOUR THRONE, O GOD, IS FOREVER AND EVER, AND THE RIGHTEOUS SCEPTER IS THE SCEPTER OF HIS KINGDOM. (Hebrews 1:1-8 NASB)

In the preceding verses of Scripture, God refers to Jesus as God as evidenced in verse 8. The angels are even commanded to worship him (verse 6). Moreover, Jesus Christ has identified himself as God as attested to in the following passages of Scripture:

> [6]Jesus answered, "I am the way and the truth and the life. No one comes to the Father except through me. [7]If you

335

really knew me, you would know my Father as well. From now on, you do know him and have seen him." [8]Philip said, "Lord, show us the Father and that will be enough for us." [9]Jesus answered: 'Don't you know me, Philip, even after I have been among you such a long time? Anyone who has seen me has seen the Father. How can you say, 'Show us the Father'? (John 14:6-9 NIV)

Jesus does not mince words. He specifically said that those who have seen him have seen God the Father. This is so because Jesus is part of the Godhead. The three personages of the Godhead (Father, Son, and Holy Spirit) are all part of one God. Jesus brings the point home even further by saying the following:

> I and the Father are one. (John 10:30, NIV. Jesus is speaking here).

Jesus, himself, says that He and the Father are one, meaning that there is a special union between the Father and Jesus. Both parties make up the Godhead. This union is further established when examining the following:

> [10]And we pray this in order that you may live a life worthy of the Lord and may please him in every way: bearing fruit in every good work, growing in the knowledge of God, [11]being strengthened with all power according to his glorious might so that you may have great endurance and patience, and joyfully [12]giving thanks to the Father, who has qualified you to share in the inheritance of the saints in the kingdom of light. [13]For he has rescued us from the dominion of darkness and brought us into the Kingdom of the Son he loves, [14]in whom we have redemption, the forgiveness of sins. [15]He is the image of the invisible God, the firstborn over all creation. [16]For by him all things were created: things in heaven and on earth, visible and invisible, whether thrones or powers or rulers or authorities; all things were created by him and for him. [17]He is before all things, and in him all things hold together. [18]And he is the head of the body, the church; he is the beginning and the firstborn from among the dead, so that in everything he might have the supremacy. [19]For God was pleased to have all his fullness dwell in him, [20]and

through him to reconcile to himself all things, whether things on earth or things in heaven, by making peace through his blood, shed on the cross. (Colossians 1:10-20 NIV)

Verse 16 says that by Jesus, all things were created. Therefore Jesus must be God because Genesis 1:1 tells us that "in the beginning God created the heavens and the earth." The fullness of God dwells in Jesus.

In the Old Testament, we see that God identified himself by name, that name being I AM THAT I AM. This is not only a name but an identity as well. God is the great I AM. He is the one who is, always was, and always will be. The Scriptures below give the account of God identifying himself:

[13]And Moses said unto God, Behold, when I come unto the children of Israel, and shall say unto them, The God of your fathers hath sent me unto you; and they shall say to me, What is his name? What shall I say unto them? [14]And God said unto Moses, I AM THAT I AM: and he said, Thus shalt thou say unto the children of Israel, I AM hath sent me unto you. (Exodus 3:13-14 KJV)

There is no question that God's name is I AM. The Jews accepted God's identity and name as I AM. Jesus identified himself as I AM[4] as evidenced by the following conversation some of the Jews had with Jesus:

[48]The Jews answered him, "Aren't we right in saying you are a Samaritan and demon possessed?"
[49]"I am not possessed by a demon," said Jesus, "but I honor my Father and you dishonor me. [50]I am not seeking glory for myself; but there is one who seeks it, and he is the judge. [51]I tell you the truth, if anyone keeps my word, he will never see death."
[52]At this the Jews exclaimed, "Now we know that you are demon-possessed! Abraham died and so did the prophets, yet you say that if anyone keeps your word, he will never taste death. [53]Are you greater than our father Abraham? He died, and so did the prophets. Who do you think you are?"

---

[4] Jesus' name as "I AM" appears in all capital letters in the Amplified version of the Bible.

[54]Jesus replied, "If I glorify myself, my glory means nothing. My Father, whom you claim as your God, is the one who glorifies me. [55]Though you do not know him, I know him. If I said I did not, I would be a liar like you, but I do know him and keep his word. [56]Your father Abraham rejoiced at the thought of seeing my day; he saw it and was glad,"

[57]You are not yet fifty years old," the Jews said to him, "and you have seen Abraham!"

[58]"I tell you the truth," Jesus answered, "before Abraham was born, I am!" [59]At this, they picked up stones to stone him, but Jesus hid himself, slipping away from the temple grounds. (John 8:48-59 NIV)

The Jews wanted to Kill Jesus because he identified himself as I AM and by doing so he was making himself equal with God. Let's look further:

[1]After these things there was a feast of the Jews, and Jesus went up to Jerusalem.

[2]Now there is in Jerusalem by the sheep gate a pool, which is called in Hebrew Bethesda, having five porticoes.

[3]In these lay a multitude of those who were sick, blind, lame, and withered, [waiting for the moving of the waters;

[4]for an angel of the Lord went down at certain seasons into the pool, and stirred up the water; whoever then first, after the stirring up of the water, stepped in was made well from whatever disease with which he was afflicted.]

[5]And a certain man was there, who had been thirty-eight years in his sickness.

[6]When Jesus saw him lying there, and knew that he had already been a long time in that condition, He said to him, "Do you wish to get well?"

[7]The sick man answered Him, "Sir, I have no man to put me into the pool when the water is stirred up, but while I am coming, another steps down before me."

[8]Jesus said to him, "Get up, pick up your pallet, and walk."

[9]Immediately the man became well, and picked up his pallet and began to walk.

Now it was the Sabbath on that day.

[10]So the Jews were saying to the man who was cured, "It is the Sabbath, and it is not permissible for you to carry your pallet."

[11]But he answered them, 'He who made me well was the one who said to me, "Take up your pallet and walk."'

[12]They asked him, "Who is the man who said to you, 'Take up your pallet, and walk'?"

[13]But the man who was healed did not know who it was; for Jesus had slipped away while there was a crowd in that place.

[14]Afterward Jesus found him in the temple, and said to him, "Behold, you have become well; do not sin anymore, so that nothing worse happens to you."

[15]The man went away, and told the Jews that it was Jesus who had made him well.

[16]For this reason the Jews were persecuting Jesus, because He was doing these things on the Sabbath.

[17]But He answered them, "My Father is working until now, and I Myself am working."

[18]For this cause therefore the Jews were seeking all the more to kill Him, because He not only was breaking the Sabbath, but also was calling God His own Father, making Himself equal with God. (John 5:1-18 NASB)

Each time Jesus equated himself with God, the Jews wanted to kill him. The Jews believed that Jesus was breaking the Sabbath day rules and that only God had the option to work on the Sabbath day. However, Jesus had already taught that he had not come to abolish the law but to fulfill it (Matthew 5:17).[5] Therefore, as explained earlier in Chapter 7, the Sabbath day laws were fulfilled by Christ's coming and literal rest was no longer needed since believers in Christ automatically enter God's perpetual rest (Hebrews 3:7-19 through 4:1-11)[6].

The fact that Jesus identifies himself as God is evidence, in Christendom, of his deity because he is the only person in history who has ever claimed to be God who stood up to the test. According to the Scriptures, Jesus walked on water, healed the lame and blind, prophesied about his own death, raised Lazarus from the dead, quieted the storm,

---

[5] It reads, *Do not think that I have come to abolish the Law or the Prophets; I have not come to abolish them but to fulfill them.* (NIV)

[6] See your Bible.

walked through doors, resurrected from the dead exactly when he said he would, and the list goes on. There have been many men who have claimed to be God but none can match what Jesus did to prove it.

The Bible informs us that Jesus came to the earth as God in human form and gave himself as a living sacrifice for the redemption of our sins. During Old Testament times, before the coming of Christ, an unblemished lamb was one of the animals that God instructed his people to offer to him (by way of bringing the sacrifice to the priests) as a living sacrifice for their sins. When Jesus came, he took the place of the actual unblemished lamb and became the figurative unblemished Lamb of God. Because of this, animal sacrifice had become a shadow of things to come (it is no longer necessary). After the coming of Jesus there was no more need for animal sacrifices for the redemption of sin. Jesus became our sin offering. He sacrificed himself for our sins and is the Lamb of God. The following passage of Scripture clarifies this:

> [18]For you know that it was not with perishable things such as silver or gold that you were redeemed from the empty way of life handed down to you from your forefathers, [19]but with the precious blood of Christ, a lamb without blemish or defect. [20]He was chosen before the creation of the world, but was revealed in these last times for your sake. [21]Through him you believe in God, who raised him from the dead and glorified him, and so your faith and hope are in God. (1Peter 1:18-21 NIV)

God raised Jesus Christ from the dead. The ultimate confirmation of the Deity of Jesus Christ is his resurrection. The resurrection of Christ is the basis on which the Christian faith rests (1 Corinthians chapter 15).[7] Jesus predicted his own death and resurrection. He said he would raise himself up from the dead. Romans 10:9 teaches us that *God* raised Jesus from the dead. Therefore since Jesus raised himself up from the dead and God is identified as raising Jesus from the dead, then Jesus must be God. The following passage of Scripture gives the account in which Jesus told the Jews that if they destroyed him, he'd raise himself up from the dead in three days:

> [18]Then the Jews demanded of him, "What miraculous sign can you show us to prove your authority to do all this?"

---

[7] See your Bible.

¹⁹Jesus answered them, "Destroy this temple, and I will raise it again in three days."
²⁰The Jews replied, "It has taken forty-six years to build this temple, and you are going to raise it in three days?" ²¹But the temple he had spoken of was his body. ²²After he was raised from the dead, his disciples recalled what he had said. Then they believed the Scripture and the words that Jesus had spoken.
²³Now while he was in Jerusalem at the Passover Feast, many people saw the miraculous signs he was doing and believed in his name. (John 2: 17-23 NIV)

Then Romans 10:9 reads as follows:

⁹If you confess with your mouth that Jesus is Lord and believe in your heart that God raised him from the dead, you will be saved. (NLT)

It was the power of God (The Father, the Son, and the Holy Ghost) that raised Jesus from the dead. Although others have been raised from the dead (e.g. Lazarus), Jesus is the only person whoever lived who predicted exactly when he would be raised from the dead ("Destroy this temple, and I will raise it again in *three* days.") This is strong biblical proof that Jesus is God.

Evidences that support the belief that Jesus is God

- **His birth and his Name**

The Scriptures tell us that Jesus was conceived and born of the Virgin Mary by the Holy Spirit and the power of the Most High. This in itself is a miracle. To get a better understanding of this, we will take a look at the historical account:

²⁶In the sixth month, God sent the angel Gabriel to Nazareth, a town in Galilee, ²⁷to a virgin pledged to be married to a man named Joseph, a descendant of David. The virgin's name was Mary. ²⁸The angel went to her and said, "Greetings, you who are highly favored! The Lord is with you."
²⁹Mary was greatly troubled at his words and wondered what kind of greeting this might be. ³⁰But the angel said

341

to her, "Do not be afraid, Mary, you have found favor with God. [31]You will be with child and give birth to a son, and you are to give him the name Jesus. [32]He will be great and will be called the Son of the Most High. The Lord God will give him the throne of his father David, [33]and he will reign over the house of Jacob forever; his kingdom will never end."

[34]"How will this be, "Mary asked the angel, "since I am a virgin?"

[35]The angel answered, "The Holy Spirit will come upon you, and the power of the Most High will overshadow you. So the holy one to be born will be called the Son of God. (Luke 1:26-35 NIV)

Mary was told to give her son the name Jesus, which in Hebrew is Yeshua and means "salvation." The account tells us that Jesus is the literal Son of God. Jesus is the only literal Son of God who ever was and ever will be. Those of us who are in Christ are also referred to as sons of God but on a spiritual level, not on a literal physical level. Since Jesus is the literal Son of God, then he is just as much God as he was human. Isaiah 7:14 prophesied that the Messiah would be born of a virgin. It says:

[14]Therefore the Lord himself will give you a sign: The virgin will be with child and will give birth to a son, and will call him Immanuel. (NIV)

"Immanuel" means "God with us." When the prophet Isaiah indicated that Jesus will be called Immanuel he was literally saying that Jesus would be *referred* to as God. This was not to mean that the Messiah's actual name would be Immanuel but that people would refer to him as "God with us." Matthew 1:18-25 reveals that the prophecy was fulfilled. It says:

[18]This is how the birth of Jesus Christ came about: His mother Mary was pledged to be married to Joseph, but before they came together, she was found to be with child through the Holy Spirit. [19]Because Joseph her husband was a righteous man and did not want to expose her to public disgrace, he had in mind to divorce her quietly.

[20]But after he had considered this, an angel of the Lord appeared to him in a dream and said, "Joseph son of David, do not be afraid to take Mary home as your wife,

342

because what is conceived in her is from the Holy Spirit. [21]She will give birth to a son, and you are to give him the name Jesus, because he will save his people from their sins." [22]All this took place to fulfill what the Lord had said through the prophet: [23]"The virgin will be with child and will give birth to a son, and they will call him Immanuel" which means, "God with us." [24]When Joseph woke up, he did what the angel of the Lord had commanded him and took Mary home as his wife. [25]But he had no union with her until she gave birth to a son. And he gave him the name Jesus. (NIV)

Many critics of the Bible have spoken against the account of Jesus' conception by arguing their view that something like this is virtually impossible. Some have even perverted the gospel by saying that the Holy Spirit had sex with Mary. However, the Scriptures say no such thing. The Scriptures tell us that the Holy Spirit came upon Mary and that she was overshadowed by the power of the Most High, not that she had sex with the Holy Spirit.

Although we can be sure that virgin-birth skeptics lived during the time of Jesus' birth, no skepticism surrounding Jesus' birth is expressed in the Bible. For that matter, no ancient historical book expresses any skepticism of the account of Jesus' conception either. The conditions surrounding Jesus' conception were well accepted by ancient peoples despite the seemingly impossibility of it all. In addition, medical technology has proven that it is no longer necessary for a woman to have sex to become pregnant. Man's process of in vitro fertilization is a medical procedure whereby a woman is impregnated without having sex. Now, if man can do it.... why can't God?

- *The Messianic prophecies*

The Old Testament prophets predicted (prophesied) that a Messiah would come. They gave over three hundred predictions concerning his coming. At the time of their predictions the Messiah (Jesus) had not yet come. The prophets predicted how the Messiah would come, what would happen to him when he came, his genealogy, how he would die, and so forth. There are sixty specifically distinctive Old Testament messianic prophecies which include prophecies that indicate that the Messiah would be born of a virgin, come from the tribe of Judah, be born in Bethlehem, be called Lord, be called Immanuel (God with us), teach in parables, be

343

resurrected, be betrayed by a "friend" (Judas), be sold for thirty pieces of silver, be beaten and crucified, be buried in a rich man's tomb, perform many miracles, preach the Word of God, and so on.

Josh McDowell explains this very well in the following quote:

> In the Old Testament there are sixty major messianic prophecies and approximately 270 ramifications that were fulfilled in one person, Jesus Christ. It is helpful to look at all these predictions fulfilled in Christ as His 'address.' You've probably never realized how important the details of your name and address are - and yet these details set you apart from the five billion other people who also inhabit this planet. With even greater detail, God wrote an address in history to single out His Son, the Messiah, the Savior of mankind, from anyone who has ever lived in history - past, present, or future. The specifics of this address can be found in the Old Testament, a document written over a period of a thousand years, which contains more than three hundred references to His coming. Using the science of probability, we find the chances of just forty-eight of these prophecies being fulfilled in one person to be right at one in 10^{157} (a one followed by 157 zeros!).[8]

Now, 10 to the first power is the multiplication of one ten and equals ten. 10 to the tenth power (10^{10}) is the multiplication of ten tens and would look like this: 10 x 10 x 10 x 10 x 10 x 10 x 10 x 10 x 10 x 10 equaling 10, 000, 000, 000 (ten billion). Therefore, one in ten to the one hundred and fifty seventh power (10^{157}) looks like this: 1 in 10,000,000,000,000,000, 000,000,000,000,000,000,000,000,000,000,000000,000,000,000,000, 000,000,000,000,000,000,000,000,000,000,000,000000,000,000,000, 000,000,000,000,000,000,000,000,000,000,000,000.

God gave the prophets their foreknowledge concerning Jesus Christ in order that they may impart to others those factors that would identify him. For those who may be skeptical regarding the time period in which the prophecies where written, McDowell goes on to say:

---

[8]Reprinted by permission. (*A Ready Defense*), Josh McDowell, copyright 1993, Thomas Nelson Inc. Nashville, Tennessee, all right reserved. p. 210

The task of matching up God's address with one man is further complicated by the fact that all the prophecies of the Messiah were made at least 400 years before He was to appear. Some might disagree and say that these prophecies were written down after the time of Christ and fabricated to coincide with His life. This might sound feasible until you realize that the Septuagint, the Greek translation of the Hebrew Old Testament, was translated around 150-200 B.C. This Greek translation shows that there was at least a two-hundred-year gap between the prophecies being recorded and their fulfillment in Christ. Certainly God was writing an address in history that only the Messiah could fulfill. Approximately forty major claims to be the Jewish Messiah have been made by men. Only one—Jesus Christ—appealed to fulfilled prophecy to substantiate His claims, and only His credentials back up those claims.[9]

We will briefly take a more in-depth look at some of these messianic prophecies. Micah 5:2 predicted that the Messiah would be born in Bethlehem. It reads,

But you, Bethlehem Ephrathah, though you are small among the clans of Judah, out of you will come for me one who will be ruler over Israel, whose origins are from of old, from ancient times. (NIV)

Matthew 2:1-2 reveals that the prophecy was fulfilled. It says,

After Jesus was born in Bethlehem in Judea, during the time of King Herod, Magi from the east came to Jerusalem [2]and asked, "Where is the one who has been born king of the Jews? We saw his star in the east and have come to worship him. (NIV)

---

[9] Reprinted by permission. (*A Ready Defense*), Josh McDowell, copyright 1993, Thomas Nelson Inc. Nashville, Tennessee, all right reserved. p. 211

Not only would the Messiah be God but Deuteronomy 18:18 predicted that the Messiah would be a prophet as well. It says,

> ^{18}I will raise up for them a prophet like you from among their brothers; I will put my words in his mouth, and he will tell them everything I command him. (NIV, God is speaking here)

Matthew 21:11 reveals that the prophecy was fulfilled. It says,

> The crowds answered, "This is Jesus, the prophet from Nazareth in Galilee." (NIV)

Isaiah 40:3 predicted that the coming of the Messiah would be preceded by a messenger who would tell of him. It reads,

> The voice of one calling:
> "In the desert prepare
> the way for the Lord
> make straight in the wilderness
> a highway for our God. (NIV).

Matthew 3:1-3 reveals that this prophecy was fulfilled. It reads,

> ^{1}In those days John the Baptist came, preaching in the Desert of Judea ^{2}and saying, "Repent, for the kingdom of heaven is near."
> ^{3}This is he who was spoken of through the prophet Isaiah: "A voice of one calling in the desert, 'Prepare the way for the Lord, make straight paths for him.' (NIV)

Psalm 105:1-5 teaches us that the Lord is able to bless with wonderful acts and work many miracles. It reads:

> ^{1}Give thanks to the LORD, call on his name; make known among the nations what he has done. ^{2}Sing to him, sing praise to him; tell of all his wonderful acts. ^{3}Glory in his holy name; let the hearts of those who seek the LORD rejoice. ^{4}Look to the LORD and his strength; seek his face always. ^{5}Remember the wonders he has

done, his miracles, and the judgments he pronounced, (NIV)

Matthew 9:35 reveals that Jesus worked many miracles during his earthly ministry. It reads:

> [35]Jesus went through all the towns and villages, teaching in their synagogues, preaching the good news of the kingdom and healing every disease and sickness. (NIV)

Psalm 16:9-10 predicts the resurrection of Christ. It reads:

> [9]Therefore my heart is glad and my tongue rejoices; my body also will rest secure,
> [10]because you will not abandon me to the grave, nor will you let your Holy One see decay. (NIV)

In this psalm, David was speaking to God through lyrics. Not only does David (the psalmist) predict the resurrection of Christ but Jesus predicted his own death and resurrection which we saw earlier in John 2:18-22, which reads:

> [18]Then the Jews demanded of him, "What miraculous sign can you show us to prove your authority to do all this?"
> [19]Jesus answered them, "Destroy this temple, and I will raise it again in three days."
> [20]The Jews replied, "It has taken forty-six years to build this temple, and you are going to raise it in three days?"
> [21]But the temple he had spoken of was his body. [22]After he was raised from the dead, his disciples recalled what he had said. Then they believed the Scripture and the words that Jesus had spoken. (NIV)

Luke 24:1-8 speaks more on the fulfilling of the resurrection prophecy. It reads:

> [1]On the first day of the week, very early in the morning, the women took the spices they had prepared and went to the tomb. [2]They found the stone rolled away from the tomb, [3]but when they entered, they did not find the body of the Lord Jesus. [4]While they were wondering about

this, suddenly two men in clothes that gleamed like lightning stood beside them. [5]In their fright the women bowed down with their faces to the ground, but the men said to them, "Why do you look for the living among the dead? [6]He is not here; he has risen! Remember how he told you, while he was still with you in Galilee: [7]'The Son of Man must be delivered into the hands of sinful men, be crucified and on the third day be raised again.'" [8]Then they remembered his words. (NIV)

Just as the psalmist predicted, the body of Jesus never saw decay. Jesus was raised in a body three days after he was crucified and walked the earth for forty days before ascending to heaven.[10] His body therefore never decayed.

The prophecies that have been spoken of here only scratch the surface of the number of messianic prophecies contained in the Old Testament. Some of the other prophecies are as follows: That the Messiah would have a ministry in Galilee, preach to many, be rejected by Jews and Gentiles alike, be betrayed by a friend (Judas Iscariot), be sold for thirty pieces of silver, endure humiliation and torture in the form of whippings, be crucified, be pierced by the sword, and be buried in a rich man's tomb.

No one other than Jesus Christ has fulfilled all of the messianic prophecies. This is an historical fact. As previously stated, the probability of one man fulfilling just forty-eight of the prophecies is one in ten to the one hundred and fifty seventh power. This number is so large that seemingly there are no words to describe it. Therefore when looking at the fulfillment of messianic prophecies, the only logical conclusion we can arrive at is that Jesus is God, our Messiah, our Lord and our Savior.

- **Other historical documents**

There are many non-biblical historical accounts as to the life of Jesus. These accounts correlate with the historical accounts in the Bible. One example of this is seen in the complete works of the historian, Flavius

---

[10] "In my former book, Theophilus, I wrote about all that Jesus began to do and teach until the day he was taken up to heaven, after giving instructions through the Holy Spirit to the apostles he had chosen. After his suffering, he showed himself to these men and gave many convincing proofs that he was alive. He appeared to them over a period of forty days and spoke about the kingdom of God." (Acts 1:1-3 NIV). [Luke is speaking here].

Josephus who was born A.D. 37. The life of Jesus is included in his writings and his writings correlate with biblical accounts.

- ### *Risk of execution*

Anyone claiming to be God in the days of Jesus was risking execution. The Jews saw Jesus' claim to be God as blasphemous. Jesus continued with his claims to be God despite the fact that he knew that he would be put to death in a most painful and agonizing way because of his claims. If Jesus was not God then, as Josh McDowell has said, he must have been suffering from delusions.[11] In looking at our wide source of apologetic information, common sense would tell us that the probability of Jesus being God is substantially higher than the probability of him suffering from delusions. If Jesus was suffering from delusions, then all of his disciples, all of the apostles, everyone who believed in him, everyone he healed, and everyone who saw the risen Christ would have had to be suffering from delusions as well; and not only delusions but hallucinations;[12] and the same delusions and hallucinations at that!

- ### *Martyrdom*

Many men and women have been martyrs for Christ. Martyrdom for the sake of Christ continues today. The historical account of the horrific deaths that most of the apostles met, points at the dedication and commitment of those martyred for Christ in ancient times, as the following quote attests to:

> Though the facts are cloudy, here is one suggested list of how the apostles met their deaths: Peter, crucified at Rome, head downward. James, beheaded at Jerusalem (Acts 12:2). John, plunged into a boiling cauldron during persecution under Emperor Domitian, from which he was miraculously saved, later to be banished to the Isle of Patmos (where he wrote the Book of Revelation), from which he was returned to Ephesus where he died a natural death. Andrew, crucified at Patras, Greece on an

---

[11] A delusion is a false belief.
[12] To hallucinate is to see something that isn't really there (visual hallucination), hear something that really hasn't really been spoken (auditory hallucination), smell an odor that isn't really there (olfactory hallucination), or feel something touching one's person that isn't really there (tactile hallucination)

X-shaped cross that now bears his name. Philip, hanged, crucified, or stoned in Asia Minor. Bartholomew, flayed alive and beheaded in Armenia. Matthew, slain with a sword in Ethiopia. Thomas, his body run through with a lance in India. James the Less, thrown from a tower in Jerusalem, stoned, and clubbed, from which he recovered, then later sawed into pieces. Judas (Thaddaeus/Labbaeus), shot to death with arrows in Mesopotamia. Simon the Zealot, fatally attacked by a mob near the Persian Gulf. Judas Iscariot, a suicide.[13]

As we see from the above quote, Judas Iscariot (the disciple who betrayed Jesus by handing him over to the Romans for thirty pieces of silver) committed suicide. He was not a martyr, but instead a betrayer. However, his suicide indicates that he may have been aware of the atrocity he had committed. The other apostles (martyrs indeed) died dreadful deaths as well, as did thousands of others in that time for the sake of Christ. Those who died for the namesake of Christ were Christian martyrs. History shows us that most martyrs have died for factual causes.

- *Miracles and healings*

Jesus claimed to be God and he backed up his claim by working profound miracles and healings as documented throughout the gospels of Matthew, Mark, Luke, and John. The greatest miracle of all was his resurrection along with his prediction of his resurrection before it happened.[14] There is no other account of any other person in history who performed as many miracles as did Jesus. Reaction to this is aptly described in the following quotation from Josh McDowell in his book, *A Ready Defense*, which reads:

Who you decide Jesus Christ is must not be an idle, intellectual exercise. You cannot put Him on the shelf as a great moral teacher. That is not a valid option. He is either a liar, a lunatic, or Lord and God. You must make a choice.[15]

---

[13] Flynn, Leslie B., *The Twelve,* Wheaton Illinois, Victory Books, 1988. Fair use.
[14] John 2:18-22, quoted under the following subheading
[15] [15]Reprinted by permission. (*A Ready Defense*), Josh McDowell, copyright 1993, Thomas Nelson Inc. Nashville, Tennessee, all rights reserved, p. 245

McDowell goes on to indicate that the evidence strongly points to Jesus Christ as Lord and Savior and that those who reject Christ and are resistant to accepting the evidence of Jesus as Lord are resistant because there are certain moral responsibilities that go along with accepting Jesus and they are not willing to live the moral life necessary that it takes to sincerely follow him.

CHRISTIANS BELIEVE IN THE RESURRECTION OF JESUS CHRIST

Christians believe that Jesus Christ is the only person ever to walk the earth who has been resurrected from the dead never to die again. His resurrection and the circumstances surrounding it prove his Deity. As discussed earlier, Jesus predicted his own resurrection. Let's look at it again:

> [18]Then the Jews demanded of him, "What miraculous sign can you show us to prove your authority to do all this?"
> [19]Jesus answered them, "Destroy this temple, and I will raise it again in three days."
> [20]The Jews replied, "It has taken forty-six years to build this temple, and you are going to raise it in three days?" [21]But the temple he had spoken of was his body. [22]After he was raised from the dead, his disciples recalled what he had said. Then they believed the Scripture and the words that Jesus had spoken. (John 2:18-22 NIV)

As revealed in the preceding verses of Scripture Jesus predicted his own death and resurrection. Let's continue....

> [1]Now upon the first day of the week, very early in the morning, they came unto the sepulchre, bringing the spices which they had prepared, and certain others with them.
> [2]And they found the stone rolled away from the sepulchre.
> [3]And they entered in, and found not the body of the Lord Jesus.

351

> [4]And it came to pass, as they were much perplexed thereabout, behold two men stood by them in shining garments:
> [5]And as they were afraid, and bowed down their faces to the earth, they said unto them, Why seek ye the living among the dead?
> [6]He is not here, but is risen: remember how he spake unto you when he was yet in Galilee,
> [7]Saying, The Son of man must be delivered into the hands of sinful men, and be crucified, and the third day rise again.
> [8]And they remembered his words, [9]And returned from the sepulchre, and told all these things unto the eleven, and to all the rest. (Luke 24:1-9 KJV)

The first people to witness the empty tomb of Jesus were women who had come to the tomb with prepared spices. The women went to the apostles to tell them that they had been approached by angels who told them that Jesus had risen.

Jesus appeared unto many people (including the apostles) in his resurrected body. The following verses of Scripture give account of this:

> [1]Now, brothers, I want to remind you of the gospel I preached to you, which you received and on which you have taken your stand. [2]By this gospel you are saved, if you hold firmly to the word I preached to you. Otherwise, you have believed in vain.
> [3]For what I received I passed on to you as of first importance: that Christ died for our sins according to the Scriptures, [4]that he was buried, that he was raised on the third day according to the Scriptures, [5]and that he appeared to Peter, and then to the Twelve. [6]After that, he appeared to more than five hundred of the brothers at the same time, most of whom are still living though some have fallen asleep. (1 Corinthians 15:1-6 NIV)

Paul is speaking here and has indicated that Jesus had literally been seen by hundreds of people after his resurrection. The following passage of Scripture gives the account of one of the apostles who wouldn't believe that Jesus had resurrected from the dead until he could see him up close and see the actual wound marks of the nailing and piercing. The passage reads:

[24]Now Thomas (called Didymus), one of the Twelve, was not with the disciples when Jesus came. [25]So the other disciples told him, "We have seen the Lord!" But he said to them, "Unless I see the nail marks in his hands and put my finger where the nails were, and put my hand into his side, I will not believe it."
[26]A week later his disciples were in the house again, and Thomas was with them. Though the doors were locked, Jesus came and stood among them and said, "Peace be with you!" [27]Then he said to Thomas, "Put your finger here; see my hands. Reach out your hand and put it into my side. Stop doubting and believe." [28]Thomas said to him, "My Lord and my God!"
[29]Then Jesus told him, "Because you have seen me, you have believed; blessed are those who have not seen and yet have believed."
[30]Jesus did many other miraculous signs in the presence of his disciples, which are not recorded in this book. [31]But these are written that you may believe that Jesus is the Christ, the Son of God, and that by believing you may have life in his name. (John 20:24-31 NIV)

Thomas believed only after he had seen the risen Jesus for himself. However, those who believe that Jesus was resurrected, but have not seen Jesus with their own eyes, are blessed indeed because their belief is based on faith. After his resurrection, Jesus did not die again but was instead, after a period of time, taken up into heaven to sit at the right hand of God, which was his place before the beginning of time. The following passage of Scripture documents Jesus' ascension.

[19]After the Lord Jesus had spoken to them, he was taken up into heaven and he sat at the right hand of God. [20]Then the disciples went out and preached everywhere, and the Lord worked with them and confirmed his word by the signs that accompanied it. (Mark 16:19-20 NIV)

The Lord was still working with the disciples after his ascension, and he still works with Christians today. The entire Christian faith rests upon the fact that Jesus resurrected from the dead, as the following passage of Scripture attest to:

> [12]Now if Christ be preached that he rose from the dead,
> how say some among you that there is no resurrection of
> the dead? [13]But if there be no resurrection of the dead,
> then Christ is not risen: [14]And if Christ be not risen, then
> is our preaching vain, and your faith is also vain.
> (1 Corinthians 15:12-14 KJV)

The resurrection of Jesus Christ is the single historical event that justifies belief in Christ as God incarnate. Jesus predicted his own death and resurrection. He knew that he would rise from the dead exactly three days after his death. After his resurrection, he showed himself to people and eventually ascended into heaven in front of witnesses. No one else in the history of the world has done all of this.

Evidences giving support that Jesus was resurrected and sits at the right hand side of the Father

- #### *The resurrection cannot be disproved*

There is absolutely no question that a man named Jesus walked the earth some two thousand years ago, claimed to be God, was crucified for his claims, died, was buried in a tomb, and resurrected from the dead. The most adamant critics of Christianity believe this to be so. But most critics of the Bible do not accept the resurrection of Jesus Christ. The irony of this is that these critics will accept complete biographical accounts of any other historical figure but when it comes to Jesus Christ they begin to pick and choose what and what not to believe, especially when looking at the issue of the resurrection. The resurrection of Jesus Christ is part of the complete account of the historicity of Jesus and no one has ever been able to disprove that it actually occurred. We must either accept the complete biblical account or reject it. There is no "in-between." It is all or nothing.

There have been many attempts to disclaim the resurrection of Jesus Christ. Many skeptics have said that the disciples stole the body. Others have said that Jesus never really died. Still, some have said that another man was buried in his place. Whatever the arguments, no one has ever successfully disproved that three days after Jesus was buried his body was not found in the tomb. The body simply wasn't there. The historical account of Jesus' burial discredits any argument that says that his body wasn't buried. It was. The resurrection of Jesus Christ has never been disproved because there is no evidence against it.

The biblical account tells us that when Jesus was buried, the Roman Guards were ordered to stand guard at the tomb. As another security precaution, a huge stone was placed at the opening of the tomb and a Roman seal was placed on the stone. The reason for the extra security centered on Jesus' own prediction that he would rise from the dead three days after his death. The chief priests and the Pharisees did not believe that Jesus would actually resurrect from the dead but instead believed that his body would be stolen in an attempt to make it look as if he had risen. The extra security was issued in support of their assumptions.

Any of the Roman Guard who fell asleep at his post would be beaten and burned. In the face of such a penalty one would think that the Roman Guard would have made certain that Jesus' body stayed buried in the tomb. However, the Roman Guard didn't because they couldn't. No man can fight the power of God.

When considering the history of the Roman Guard we know that there had to at least be sixteen men guarding the tomb the night the Guard kept watch over Jesus' tomb. Despite all of these precautions, the biblical historical account tells us that an angel of God descended from heaven causing an earthquake and that this angel moved the stone from in front of the tomb and sat on it (Matthew 28:2).[16] The Scriptures go on to inform us that the soldiers who were guarding the tomb were petrified with fear and became virtually comatose. When the soldiers awoke from their stupor the body of Jesus was gone. They went into the city to explain the occurrence to the chief priests. The elders told the soldiers to say that the disciples came and stole the body. The soldiers did as they were instructed and many of the Jews believed this lie. However, it is very unlikely that all of the soldiers guarding the tomb would have fallen asleep at their posts knowing the punishment that awaited them if they did so. They were to guard the tomb "with their lives." There could be no other explanation for their inability to perform such a simple task as guarding the tomb other than the fact that the soldiers fell into a deep sleep and Jesus was actually resurrected just as the biblical account says he was. The entire account of Jesus' execution and resurrection can be found in the gospel of Matthew 26:62-66 coupled with Matthew Chapters 27 and 28.[17]

- *Hundreds of eyewitness accounts*

There were many eyewitness accounts of the miracles that Jesus

---

[16] It reads, *There was a violent earthquake, for an angel of the Lord came down from heaven and, going to the tomb, rolled back the stone and sat on it.* (NIV)
[17] See Your Bible.

performed[18] and of his bodily appearance after his resurrection.[19] If the miracles and resurrection never occurred then each eyewitness had to have purposely lied or had to have been simultaneously suffering identical auditory and visual hallucinations which would lead to delusions. Two people may experience a similar hallucination but the possibility of the same two people experiencing the *exact same* hallucination is extremely remote and becomes even more remote when looking at the possibility of those same two people experiencing the exact same hallucination at the exact same time. However, this is inadvertently what people are saying when they deny the resurrection of Christ. The eyewitnesses had no reason to lie about what they saw. As a matter of fact, they would have had more reason to deny what they saw, since at the time, a confession of faith in Christ most often meant certain death. One must either believe in the resurrection of Jesus Christ or ignore all the evidences that support it.

CHRISTIANS BELIEVE IN THE DOCTRINE OF THE "TRINITY"

Christians believe that there is one God that represents himself in three persons: The Father, the Son and the Holy Ghost. These three persons/personages of God are separate in office but equal in Godliness:

> [26]And God said, Let us make man in our image, after our likeness: and let them have dominion over the fish of the sea, and over the fowl of the air, and over the cattle, and over all the earth, and over every creeping thing that creepeth upon the earth. [27]So God created man in his own image, in the image of God created he him; male and female created he them. (Genesis 1:26-27 KJV)

Verse 26 says that God said "Let *us* make man in *our* image." Verse 27 tells us that *God* created man in *his* own image." The words "us" and "our" denote plurality while the words "God" and "his" are singular. Therefore God must be a singular being[20] who represents himself plurally in three different persons those being the Father, the Son and the Holy Ghost.

---

[18] The Gospels document most of the miracles that Jesus performed and the book of Acts documents the miracles that the apostles performed through the power of Jesus' name and the Holy Spirit.

[19]After that he appeared to more than 500 brothers at the same time, most of whom are still living, though some have fallen asleep. (1 Corinthians 15:6 NIV)

[20] God is spirit, and his worshippers must worship in spirit and in truth. (John 4:24 NIV)

> [18]And Jesus came and spake unto them, saying, All power is given unto me in heaven and in earth. [19]Go ye therefore, and teach all nations, baptizing them in the name of the Father, and of the Son, and of the Holy Ghost: (Matthew 28:18-19)

Jesus himself mandated that believers be baptized in the name of the Father, Son, and Holy Ghost. However, he never alluded to more than one God. Therefore, all three must be personages of the Godhead working together as one. Baptism symbolizes rebirth. When we are physically born we come through water (the water from the mother's placenta). Immersion into water and then out of it during a baptism is symbolic of a baby's immersion from water during birth. Jesus has commanded those who confess a belief in him and who follow him to be baptized which symbolizes a rebirth or new birth into the kingdom of God. The person is "born again" through water (and through his confession of Christ) but this time he is on his way to a heavenly existence instead of on his way to just an earthly one. The new believer gets baptized as a confirmation of his or her belief.

CHRISTIANS BELIEVE THAT GOD HAS A NAME

God has identified himself by name. Let's take a look:

> [13]And Moses said unto God, Behold, when I come unto the children of Israel, and shall say unto them, The God of your fathers hath sent me unto you; and they shall say to me, What is his name? What shall I say unto them?
> [14]And God said unto Moses, I AM THAT I AM: and he said, Thus shalt thou say unto the children of Israel, I AM hath sent me unto you. (Exodus 3:13-14 KJV)

As mentioned earlier, when Moses asked, God revealed his name to Moses. God's name is I AM THAT I AM. This is not only a name but an identity as well. God is the great I AM: The one who is, always was, and will always be. God's name is represented in Hebrew by four consonants: YHWH. The written Hebrew language does not use vowels. When reading a Hebrew document, the reader must mentally supply the vowels himself. When examining the ancient Hebrew language, scholars agree that the correct pronunciation of YHWH is Yahweh. Exodus 20:7 teaches us that the name of God should never be used in vain. In other words, God's name should never be used haphazardly, but instead only in sacred matters of prayer, worship, prophecy (which includes preaching), teaching, praise, and when giving honor. Blasphemy, in Old Testament law (Leviticus 24:16), was punishable by death. Blasphemy in the Old Testament was defined as the improper use of God's name and is deemed the unforgivable sin. Using God's name in a disrespectful way is therefore blasphemous. The New Testament widened the definition by indicating that attributing the works of God to another besides God is blasphemous as well.

In order to avoid the possibility of mistakenly or unintentionally using God's name in vain, the Hebrews did not use it at all. Instead they used the word "Adonai" to take the place of YHWH. Adonai is the Hebrew word for LORD. Consequently, God is referred to as LORD in the majority of the Old Testament Scriptures. Thus, the Hebrew word for LORD (Adonai) became a substitute for the name YHWH. Even when coming across the written name YHWH in any form of literature the Hebrews (Jews) would automatically substitute it for Adonai. After a while, the correct way to pronounce YHWH was forgotten. Because of this, the Jewish scholars of the Middle ages devised reading aids in which, when writing Hebrew, certain symbols were placed beside consonants. These symbols indicated which vowels to use. The vowels for Adonai were placed with the name YHWH. This was done to remind the reader to substitute the word Adonai for YHWH. However, many biblical readers of the Middle ages did not know that the vowels from the word Adonai placed with the name YHWH, was the writer's way of simply reminding his reading audience to use Adonai instead of YHWH. Consequently, many readers fused the consonants YHWH with the vowels of Adonai together. By doing this, they began to pronounce what was literally written which is what translates into the English language as the word *Jehovah:* a name for God that was never really used by the ancient Jews.

Just as the Jews substituted the word Adonai for YHWH, non-Jewish people substituted the Greek word "kurios" for the name YHWH. Kurios is the Greek word for Lord. The New Testament was written in Greek. The writers of the New Testament respected the tradition of the Jews thereby following in their footsteps when it came to the writing and usage of God's name: YHWH. In most of the New Testament writings, God is called Lord (Kurios). Jesus is called Lord (Kurios) as well.

This brings us back to the biblical teaching that Jesus is God. Jesus himself claimed to be God. Let's take another look:

> [58]Jesus said unto them, Verily, verily, I say unto you, Before Abraham was, I am. [59]Then took they up stones to cast at him: but Jesus hid himself, and went out of the

temple, going through the midst of them, and so passed
by. (John 8:58-59 KJV).

"I am" is the shortened version of Gods name: I AM THAT I AM. As
discussed earlier, the Jews set about to stone Jesus because they realized
that by referring to himself as "I am," Jesus was referring to himself as
God. Those who attempted to stone Jesus were responding to Old
Testament Mosaic Law that says the following:

> [16]Moreover, the one who blasphemes the name of the
> Lord shall surely be put to death; all the congregation
> shall certainly stone him. The alien as well as the native,
> when he blasphemes the Name, shall be put to death.
> (Leviticus 24:16 NASB)

The Jews set out to stone Jesus because they believed that he was
breaking the portion of the Law that speaks against blasphemy. But Jesus
was not blaspheming because he was indeed God, as he was claiming to
be. Jesus eluded the Jews' attempts to stone him. It was not yet time for
Jesus to die and the prophecy of Jesus' death was to be fulfilled by
crucifixion, not by stoning. Jesus did not try to defend himself when the
Jews attempted to stone him for blasphemy. There is no biblical account
that he ever took back his claim to be God and his claim to have existed
before Abraham (the father of the Jews) did. There is no doubt that Jesus
was claiming to be God and he proved his Deity with his resurrection.

God was also called The God of the Fathers and often times the word
El was used as a generic term for God. Those who worshipped the true
God as well as those who worshipped false gods used the generic term El
when referring to God. In the Bible El is frequently used as a replacement
term for Yahweh and is also used in combination with adjectives, which
describe the character of God. Let's take a look:

> [2]God spoke further to Moses and said to him, "I am
> the LORD; [3]and I appeared to Abraham; Isaac, and
> Jacob, as God Almighty, but by My name, LORD, I
> did not make Myself known to them. (Exodus 6:2-3
> NASB)

God Almighty translates as El-Shaddai in the Hebrew language.
Abraham, Isaac, and Jacob knew God as El-Shaddai. God is Almighty. No
one or nothing is more powerful than God is. Let's look further:

> [14]The Lord thundered from heaven,
> and the most High uttered his voice.
> (2 Samuel 22: 14 KJV)

The Most High is translated as El-Elyon in the Hebrew. The term also means the exalted one. No one or nothing has more authority in heaven and on earth than God. Acts 7:49[21] tells us that heaven is God's throne and that the earth is his footstool. God is the ultimate supreme authority.

> [33]And Abraham planted a grove in
> Beersheba and called there on the
> name of the LORD, the everlasting
> God. (Genesis 21:33)

El-Olam is the term used for God Everlasting. God is an eternal God. God will exist for eternity. There also is no time when God did not exist. In the book of Revelation, God refers to himself as the Alpha and Omega, the beginning and the end. This in itself attests to his everlasting nature. God's everlasting nature is also depicted when he is defined as the Ancient of Days in Daniel 7:9. Ancient of Days is a symbolic figurative title for God, which helps us to look at God as an ancient being.

Elohim denotes a plurality of God. This plurality has to do with the nature of God and in no-way signifies the possibility of more than one God. As stated before, there is one God who represents himself in three persons: Father, Son, and Holy Ghost.

There are additions to God's actual name Yahweh which describe some of the attributes of God. Yahweh-Jireh (Jehovah-Jireh) means that the Lord will provide. Yahweh-Nissi (Jehovah-Nissi) means that the Lord is our banner or battle cry. Yahweh-Mekaddesh (Jehovah-Mekaddesh) means that the Lord is one who sanctifies. To sanctify means to set apart from others. Those who are in Christ and worship Yahweh through Christ are set apart from others. Yahweh-Shalom (Jehovah-Shalom) means that God is a God of peace. Yahweh-Sabaoth (Jehovah-Sabaoth) means *God Almighty* or *Lord of Hosts*. The 23rd Psalms, written by King David, begins by describing the Lord as his shepherd, which translates into the Hebrew as Yahweh-Rohi. By using the word *shepherd*, David was saying that God is our protector. David also describes God in the book of Psalms as a person of refuge, a shield, and a fortress.

In the New Testament, Jesus referred to himself as God as well as referring to the Father as God. Jesus often times spoke of the Father when

---

[21] See your Bible.

the disciples asked him certain questions. Jesus called God "Father" but at times used the word *Abba* which is the less formal rendering of the Greek word for Father and is similar to the word *Daddy* in the English language. Mark 14:36 gives us the historical account of Jesus praying to God in Gethsemane in which he addresses God the Father as Abba (Daddy). The apostle Paul indicates in Galatians 4:6 that those of us who are in Christ may address God informally by calling him "Abba" (Daddy).

CHRISTIANS BELIEVE THAT SATAN IS REAL

Before Satan became Satan, he was Lucifer. As discussed earlier in chapter 6, Lucifer was a beautiful angel assigned to cover the glory of God. However, there came a time when Lucifer wanted to overthrow God and become God himself. Because of this, a war was waged in Heaven between Lucifer and Michael, the archangel. Satan in the Greek means *adversary.* Lucifer rebelled against God and therefore became his adversary, his enemy. The Scriptures indicate that from then, therefore, he was referred to as Satan. Satan and his army of angels, a third of the angelic hosts, were defeated and thrown out of Heaven. When Satan was ousted from heaven he took a portion of the angelic heavenly hosts with him who are now referred to as demons. Not only is Satan God's enemy but he became man's enemy also. Satan wanted to be like God and became rebellious. This is when God banished him from heaven. Just as Satan tricked Eve in the Garden of Eden, he continues today to try to trick us today in order to turn us against God and tempt us to sin. Satan would rather that we worship him instead of God. Let's look at some Scriptures that support this view of Satan:

> [12]How art thou fallen from heaven, O Lucifer, son of the morning! how art thou cut down to the ground, which didst weaken the nations!
> [13]For thou hast said in thine heart, I will ascend into heaven, I will exalt my throne above the stars of God: I will sit also upon the mount of the congregation, in the sides of the North:
> [14]I will ascend above the heights of the clouds; I will be like the most High.
> [15]Yet thou shall be brought down to hell, to the sides of the pit. (Isaiah 14:12-15 KJV)

Satan, who was once named Lucifer by God, which in the Hebrew means "day star" or "angel of light" decided that he wanted to be God and attempted to dethrone God. Instead, Lucifer was thrown out of heaven. Let's look further.

> [11]The word of the Lord came to me; [12]"Son of man, take up a lament concerning the king of Tyre and say to him: 'This is what the Sovereign Lord says: You were the model of perfection, Full of wisdom and perfect in beauty.
> [13]You were in Eden, the garden of God; every precious stone adorned you: ruby, topaz and emerald, chrysolite, onyx and jasper, sapphire, turquoise and beryl. Your settings and mountings were made of gold; On the day you were created they were prepared.
> [14]You were anointed as a guardian cherub, for so I ordained you. You were on the holy mount of God; You walked among the fiery stones.
> [15]You were blameless in your ways from the day you were created till wickedness was found in you.
> [16]Through your widespread trade you were filled with violence, and you sinned. So I drove you in disgrace from the mount of God, And I expelled you, O guardian cherub, From among the fiery stones.
> [17]Your heart became proud on account of your beauty, and you corrupted your wisdom because of your splendor. So I threw you to the earth; I made a spectacle of you before kings, (Ezekiel 28:11-17 NIV)

The King of Tyre refers to the historical king of Tyre who was Ithobalus II. Scholars agree that Lucifer is the supernatural king of Tyre. Therefore, there is a double reference. Statements that could refer to the human being are actually referring to the historical king while statements contrary to human characteristics are speaking of Lucifer. With this understanding the passage is made clearer.

The verses of Scripture also talk about Lucifer's perfect beauty and how various precious stones adorned his supernatural body. Satan is a cherub which is a certain rank order (or kind) of angel. Verse 15 tells us that Lucifer's ways were perfect until sin was found in him. Satan lost his honorable title of Lucifer and was exiled from heaven. The following passage of Scripture documents the war in heaven that took place between Michael and Satan and their angelic armies along with them:

362

⁷And there was war in heaven. Michael and his angels fought against the dragon, and the dragon and his angels fought back. ⁸But he was not strong enough, and they lost their place in heaven. ⁹The great dragon was hurled down—that ancient serpent called the devil, or Satan, who leads the whole world astray. He was hurled to the earth, and his angels with him. (Revelation 12:7-9 NIV)

The Scriptures tell us that Satan didn't leave heaven quietly. God had the righteous angels (Michael and his angels) to fight against the dragon (Satan) and his angels. Satan and his angels (demons) were thrown out of heaven by means of war. They were hurled down to earth. Since Satan did not succeed in overthrowing God, he now aims to spiritually overthrow man by tempting man to sin, do evil, and turn against God. The Scripture tells us that Satan leads the whole world astray. He roams "back and forth" in the earth looking to see whom he may tempt (devour) as attested to in the following passage of Scripture.

Be sober, be vigilant; because your adversary the devil, as a roaring lion, walketh about, seeking whom he may devour: (1 Peter 5:8 KJV)

As stated before, the word "Satan" means adversary. So whenever the Bible speaks of the devil, it is talking about Satan. As discussed previously in chapter 7, Jesus taught that there are children of God and that there are children of the devil. The following passage of Scripture reveals this:

³⁶Then Jesus sent the multitude away, and went into the house: and his disciples came unto him, saying, declare unto us the parable of the tares of the field.
³⁷He answered and said unto them, He that soweth the good seed is the Son of man;
³⁸The field is the world; the good seed are the children of the kingdom; but the tares are the children of the wicked one;
³⁹The enemy that sowed them is the devil; the harvest is the end of the world; and the reapers are the angels.
⁴⁰As therefore the tares are gathered and burned in the fire; so shall it be in the end of this world. (Matthew 13:36-40)

Jesus identifies the enemy that sowed the tares (weeds) as the devil, Satan himself. He that soweth the good seed is identified as the Son of man (Jesus). The good seed is described as the children of the Kingdom (children of God). However, the tares are identified as the children of the wicked one (children of the devil). Those who confess a heartfelt belief in Jesus Christ as Lord and Savior, and live so accordingly, are children of God.

BIBLIOGRAPHY AND ADDITIONAL SOURCES

BIBLE TRANSLATIONS

Barker, L. Kenneth; NIV Study Bible, 10th Anniversary Edition, Zondervan Publishing Company; Grand Rapids Michigan copyright© 1995.[1]

Contemporary English Version Copyright © 1995 by American Bible Society. (CEV)

1611 King James Version, (KJV)

The Message, Copyright © by Eugene H. Peterson 1993, 1994, 1995, 1996, 2000, 2001, 2002. NavPress Publishing Group.

New American Standard Bible®, Copyright © 1960, 1962, 1963, 1968, 1971, 1972, 1973, 1975, 1977, 1995 by the Lockman Foundation (NASB)

New King James Version. Copyright © 1982 by Thomas Nelson, Inc. (NKJV)

New Living Translation, copyright 1996, 2004. Tyndale House Publishers, Inc., Wheaton, Illinois (NLT)

New International Version®, NIV®, Copyright©1973, 1978, 1984 by Biblica, Inc.™, Zondervan, (NIV)

Today's New International Version® TNIV, Copyright ©2001, 2005 by Biblica Inc.™ Zondervan. (TNIV)

BOOKS

Branch, Taylor; *Parting The Waters: America in the King Years* 1954-63, A Touchstone Book, Rockefeller Center, New York NY, Published by Simon & Schuster Inc., New York, NY, copyright ©1988

Butler, Trent C., General Editor; *Holman Bible Dictionary*, Holman Bible Publishers; Nashville Tennessee; copyright ©1991, Homan Bible Publishers

Diagnostic and Statistical Manual of Mental Disorders, Fourth Edition, Text Revision, (copyright 2000) American Psychiatric Association

Dodds, Elreta, *What The Bible Really says about Slavery*, Revised Edition; Press Toward The Mark Publications, Detroit Michigan, copyright© 2000, Third Printing

Etcoff, Nancy, *Survival of the Prettiest: The Science of Beauty*, First Anchor Books Edition, Division of Random House Inc, July 2000, New York; copyright 1999

Flynn, Leslie B., *The Twelve,* Wheaton Illinois, Victory Books, copyright ©1988.

Ham, Ken and Wieland, Carl; *One Blood: The Biblical Answer to Racism,* by Ken Ham; Carl Wieland; and Don Batten. First printing 1999, sixth printing 2002, copyright 1999, Master Books Inc., (a division of New Leaf Press) Green Forest Arizona, copyright 1999.

Healy, Joseph F. *Diversity and Society, Race, Ethnicity, and Gender*, Pine Forge Press, Thousand Oaks California, copyright ©2004, Sage Publications Inc.

Kennedy, Stetson; *Jim Crow Guide: The Way it Was*, Florida Atlantic University Press, Boca Raton Florida, Third Printing, Copyright © 1992

Knowles, Louis L. and Prewitt, Kenneth. *Institutional Racism in America.* Prentice-Hall Inc., Englewood Cliffs, New Jersey, A Spectrum Book. Copyright ©1969

Kozol, Jonathan. *The Shame of the Nation: The Restoration of Apartheid Schooling in America*, Three Rivers Press, an imprint of the Crown Publishing Group, a division of Random House, Inc, New York, copyright ©2005

King, Martin Luther (Foreword), *The State of Black America* 2009, National Urban League copyright ©2009

Kreeft, Peter and Tacellis, Ronald; *Handbook of Christian Apologetics,* InterVaristy Press, Downers Grove, Illinois 60515, copyright ©1994

Lopez, Ian F. Haney, *White by Law: The Legal Construction of Race*, New York University Press, New York and London, copyright ©1996

Meeks, Kenneth, *Driving While Black*, Broadway Books, New York, NY, copyright ©2000

McDowell, Josh; *A Ready Defense*, Thomas Nelson Publishers Inc. Nashville, Tennessee; copyright © 1993

McKissic, William Dwight Sr., *Beyond Roots: In Search of Blacks in the Bible;* Woodbury, NJ: Renaissance Productions, Inc., copyright ©1990

Smiley, Tavis (Introduction), *The Covenant with Black America*, Third World Press, Chicago Illinois, Copyright ©2006

366

Smith, Jerome H., *Treasury of Scripture Knowledge*; Thomas Nelson Publishers; Nashville Tennessee, Copyright© 1992

Sproul, R.C., *The Mystery of the Holy Spirit,* Tyndale House Publishers, Wheaton Illinois, copyright © 1990

Walters, Jerome, One *Aryan Nation under God: How Religious Extremists Use the Bible to Justify Their Actions*, Sourcebooks Inc., Naperville Illinois, Copyright© 2001

Washington, Harriet A. *Medical Apartheid*, Harlem Moon Broadway Books, New York NY. copyright© 2006, Hardcover originally published by Doubleday, 2006.

OTHER SOURCES

Jim Casey Youth Opportunities Initiative, Racial Disproportionality in the Child Welfare System, copyright©2003, St. Louis Missouri, data for the Fact Sheet come from Dorothy Roberts, Racial Disproportionality in the U.S. Child Welfare System, Annie E. Casey Foundation, 2002, Jennifer Clark, unpublished paper, 2002; CWLA, Child Abuse and Neglect: A Look at the States, 2000.

Clark, Adam. Commentary. 1830 Public Domain

MAGAZINE ARTICLES

Allen, Mike, *Living too Much in the Bubble?* Time Magazine, Cover Title: *System Failure: An Investigation into what went so wrong in New Orleans*, Time Inc., Rockefeller Center, New York NY copyright September 19, 2005

Cloud, John; *Mopping New Orleans,* Time Magazine, Cover Title: *System Failure: An Investigation into what went so wrong in New Orleans*, Time Inc., Rockefeller Center, New York NY copyright September 19, 2005

Scott, Ginger; *Fade to Black: The Disappearance of the Black Model*, Ebony Fashion Fair Magazine, Johnson Publishing Company, Chicago Illinois, copyright© 2008

Time Magazine, *4 Places where the System Broke Down*, Cover Title: *System Failure: An Investigation into what went so wrong in New Orleans*,Time Inc., Rockefeller Center, New York NY copyright September 19, 2005

Thomas, Cathy Booth, and Padgett, Tim; *Life Among the Ruins,* Time Magazine, Cover Title: *System Failure: An Investigation into what went so wrong in New Orleans*,Time Inc., Rockefeller Center, New York NY copyright September 19, 2005

GOVERNMENT SOURCES

Arizona Senate Bill 1070
United States of America, Plaintiff v State of Arizona; and Janice K. Brewer, Governor of the State of Arizona, in her Official Capacity; case 2:10-cv-10413-NVW Document 1 Filed 07-06-10, pgs. 2-3. Government document.

Constitution, United States

United States Senate Resolution 39, June 13, 2005

United States General Accounting Office, Washington D.C. 20458, *Better Targeting of Airline Passengers for Personal Searches could produce Better Results*, A report to the Honorable Richard J. Durbin of the United States Senate, March 17, 2000 from the United States General Accounting Office, U.S. Customs Service, Government Document http://www.gao.gov/new.items/gg00038.pdf

http://www.dol.gov/oasam/programs/history/reich/reports/ceiling.pdf
(Glass Ceiling report)

http://digitalcommons.ilr.cornell.edu/cgi/viewcontent.cgi?article=1117&context=k ey_workplace (Glass Ceiling Commission Recommendation)

http://www.ourdocuments.gov/doc.php?doc=100&page=transcript (actual voting rights act)

http://www.thecre.com/fedlaw/legal6/eo10925.htm (Kennedy's Executive Order 10925, Affirmative Action)

(United States General Accounting Office), Washington D.C. 20458, A report to the Honorable Richard J. Durbin of the United States Senate, March 17, 2000 from the United States General Accounting Office, U.S. Customs Service: *Better Targeting of Airline Passengers for Personal Searches could produce Better Results*, Government Document.
http://www.gao.gov/new.items/gg00038.pdf

INTERNET ARTICLES AND ESSAYS

Ayres, Ian and Jonathan Borowsky, *A Study of Racially Disparate outcomes in the Los Angeles Police Department,* written for the ACLU, October 27, 2008 (taken from an Internet article by TChris entitled *Racial Profiling in the LAPD,* Talk Left, the Politics of Crime, Internet site, Section Civil Liberties, http://www.talkleft.com/story/2008/10/27/14266/187

Barlow, Kimberly L., *Retail Racism Studied*, University of Pittsburg, University Times, Volume 40, number 5, October 25, 2007
http://mac10.umc.pitt.edu/u/FMPro?-db=ustory&-lay=a&-format=d.html&storyid=7788&-Find

Dodds, Elreta; *Predestination: Did God predestine some people to go to Heaven and others to go to Hell?* Essay written for a 2005 class assignment (Faith Center for Christian Education, Port Huron MI). Copyright 2005. www.predestinations.blogspot.com
www.controversialchristianissues.blogspot.com.

Fauci, Cara A.*, Racism and Health Care in America: Legal Responses to Racial Disparities in the Allocation of Kidneys*, Boston College Third World Law 2000-2001 Journal, Volume 21, pages 35-68, Student Publications. Copyright©2001 by Boston College Law School, Reprinted from 21 B.C. Third World L.J. 37 (2001) http://www.bc.edu/bc_org/avp/law/lwsch/journals/bctwj/21_1/02_TXT.htm

Gibson, Robert A., *The Negro Holocaust: Lynching and Race Riots in the United States,* 1880-1950, Yale-New Haven Teachers Institute, Yale Station, New Haven Connecticut, 1979 Volume II.
http://www.yale.edu/ynhti/curriculum/units/1979/2/79.02.04.x.html

Hoffman, Matthew; *"Electoral College Dropouts,"* http://www.thenation.com. http://www.thenation.com. http://www.thenation/article/electoral-college-dropouts June 17, 1999 issue of The Nation. Copyright©1999

Jones, Ernestine F.*, Public Policies and Practices in Child Welfare Systems that Affect Life Options for Children of Color*, Joint Center for Political and Economic Studies, Washington D.C., www.joingcenters.org, copyright 2006, http://www.jointcenter.org/hpi/files/manual/public%20Policies%20andPercent20P ractices%20inPercent20Child%20Welfare.pdf

Kopp, Carol, The *Bridge to Gretna: Why did Police block desperate Refugees from New Orleans,* Gretna Louisiana December 18, 2005 copyright MMV, CBS World Wide Incorporated, CBS News/60 Minutes website. http://www.cbsnews.com/stories/2005/12/15/60minutes/main1129440.shtml

McIntosh, Dr. Peggy, *White Privilege and Male Privilege: A Personal Account of Coming to see Correspondences through Work in Women's Studies.* Center for Research on Women, Wellesley College, MA, copyright ©1988.
http://www.case.edu/president/aaction/UnpackingTheKnapsack.pdf

Ongunbayo, Modupe, article: *Death Threats against Oba*ma, Newswatch, online magazine, Sunday November 23, 2008
http://www.newswatchngr.com/index.php?=com_content&task=view&id=297&it em=41option / www.newswatch.com

369

Race, Ethnicity, and the Criminal Justice System, American Sociological Association, Department of Research and Development, http://www.asanet.org/galleries/Research/ASARaceCrime.pdf

Rivera, Amaad, *An Unstable Foundation and Racism in the Structure*, July 5, 2007; TomasPaine.common sense
http://www.tompaine.com/articles/2007/07/05/an_unstable_foundation_and_racis m_in_the_structure.php

Sorensen, Sandy, *What Color is Toxic Waste?* Internet Article, United Church of Christ,http://www.ucc.org/ucnews/octnov07/what-color-is-toxic-waste.html, October – November 2007, October 1, 2007

Thomas-Lester, Avis; *A Senate Apology for History on Lynching*, The Washington Post, Washington D.C. Copyright © June 14, 2005

Vedantam, Shankar; *Racial Disparities found in Pinpointing Mental Illness*, The Washington Post, Washington D.C. Copyright © June 28, 2005.

Watson, Jamal; *Katrina shows Racial Divide in America*, The Sun, New York, NY
http://www.nysun.com/new-york/katrina-shows-racial-divide-in-america/19696/

Wing, Bob.,*"White Power in Election 2000,"* Colorlines: The National News Magazine on Race and Politics, Spring 2001, copyright ©2001, online www.colorlines.com/article.php?ID=127&p=2

DOCUMENTARIES

Lee, Spike; When the Levees Broke: Requiem in Four Acts, Spike Lee Films, Documentary, copyright ©2006, HBO Documentary, DVD[1]

OTHER INTERNET SOURCES

http://www.ameasite.org/loving.asp
Timeline of the American Civil Rights Movement

http://en.wikipedia.org/wiki/Interstate_Commerce_Act
(Interstate Commerce Commission)
http://www.woolworthwalk.com/diner/index.html

http://www.ags.uci.edu/~skaufman/teaching/win2001ch4.htm
(Emmett Till)

---

[1] Any profanity spoken in this film is not sanction by this author.

Freedom riders
http://en.wikipedia.org/wiki/Freedom_ride

http://www.olemiss.edu/depts/english/ms-writers/dir/meredith_james/
(James Meredith)

http://www.ourdocuments.gov/doc.php?flash=true&doc=97&page=transcript
(The Civil Rights Act of 1954)

http://www.now.org/nnt/08-95/affirmhs.html (Affirmative Action)

http://en.wikipedia.org/wiki/Selma_to_Montgomery_marches
(The Selma Marches)

http://www.liu.edu/cwis/cwp/library/african/2000/lynching.htm
(Lynching in America, a History not known by many)

http://www.washingtonpost.com/wp
dyn/content/article/2005/06/13/AR2005061301720.html "A Senate Apology for
History on Lynching; vote condemns past failure to act, by Avis Thomas-Lester;
Washington Post; June 14, 2005 page A12

http://landrieu.senate.gov/releases/06/2006801C52.html
(Offshore oil and gas revenue sharing bill

http://landrieu.senate.gov/releases/06/2006C09513.html
(Dominican Landrieu, offshore oil)

http://neworleans.about.com/od/governmentcivicissues/a/levees.htm (Levees)

http://www.pbs.org/wgbh/amex/flood/timeline/timeline2.html
(Great flood of 1927)

http://www.squidoo.com/FiveBlackPresidentsoftheUSA
(Presidents allegedly black)

http://en.wikipedia.org/wiki/Montgomery_Bus_Boycott
(Montgomery Bus Boycott)

http://en.wikipedia.org/wiki/Congress_of_Racial_Equality
(Congress of Racial Equality)

http://en.wikipedia.org/wiki/March_on_Washington_for_Jobs_and_Freedom
(March on Washington)
http://www.apologeticspress.org/articles/2607

http://felonvoting.procon.org/viewresource.asp?resourceID=286 (Voting laws in each state as it pertains to felons)

http://www.declareyourself.com/voting_faq/state_by_state_info_2.html (Voting laws per state)

Noble Prize.org http://nobelprize.org/nobel_prizes/peace/laureates/1964/king-bio.html (Rev. Dr. Martin Luther King Jr., Noble Prize)

http://en.wikipedia.org/wiki/Pace_v._Alabama (Pace vs. Alabama)

http://en.wikipedia.org/wiki/F.W._Woolworth_Company (Woolworths)

http://www.digitalhistory.uh.edu/database/article_display_printable.cfm?HHID=3 63 (Woolworths sit-in)

http://www.spartacus.schoolnet.co.uk/USAsitin.htm (Woolworth sit-in)

http://library.thinkquest.org/C004391F/mississippi_riot1.htm (James Meredith, Mississippi riot)

http://en.wikipedia.org/wiki/16th_Street_Baptist_Church_bombing (Sixteenth Street Baptist Church)

http://en.wikipedia.org/wiki/March_on_Washington (March on Washington)

http://www.cmgww.com/historic/malcolm/about/bio.htm (Malcolm X Official Website)

http://en.wikipedia.org/wiki/Malcolm_X (Malcolm X)

http://en.wikipedia.org/wiki/Literacy_test (literacy tests)

http://www.sourcewatch.org/index.php?title=Voting_Rights_Act_of1965 (States that were guilty of disenfranchising blacks the right to vote)

http://en.wikipedia.org/wiki/Michael_Donald (Michael Donald: the last lynching in America)

http://en.wikipedia.org/wiki/James_Byrd_Jr. (James Bryd, 1998 racially motivated hate crime murder)

http://www.talkleft.com/story/2008/10/27/14266/187 (Racial profiling, LAPD)

http://www.aclu.org/racialjustice/racialprofiling/15788prs20020801.html
(Customs, Racial profiling)

Predatory Lending and the Mortgage Crisis: A Modern Example of Structural Racism.
http://www.eraseracismny.org/html/library/housing/resources/published_reports/P redatory_lending_mortgage_crisis.pdf referenced from Wilhelmina A. Leigh and Danielle Ruff, Joint Center for Political and Economic Studies #1, *African American and Homeownership, Separate and Unequal*, 1940 to 2006 (November 2007)

http://en.wikipedia.org/wiki/Hurricane_Katrina (Hurricane Katrina)

http://en.wikipedia.org/wiki/Environmental_racism (Environmental racism)

http://www.hurricanekatrinarelief.com/faqs.html#What%20category%20hurricane %20was%20Katrina (Hurricane Katrina)

http://en.wikipedia.org/wiki/Hurricane_Katrina (Hurricane Katrina)

http://en.wikipedia.org/wiki/Great_Mississippi_Flood_of_1927 (Flood of 1927)

http://katrinacoverage.com/2005/09/26/superdome-convention-center-death-toll-exaggerated.html (Hurricane Katrina, Superdome)

http://www.cbsnews.com/stories/2005/12/15/60minutes/main1129440.shtml
(Bridge to Gretna)

http://en.wikipedia.org/wiki/Russel_L._Honor%C3%A9
(Lieutenant Russel Honore)

http://en.wikipedia.org/wiki/Dike (Levee)

http://en.wikipedia.org/wiki/Redlining (Redlining)

http://www.thisnation.com/congress-facts.html (Congress, facts)

http://en.wikipedia.org/wiki/United_States_House_of_Representatives (House of Representatives)
http://en.wikipedia.org/wiki/United_States_Congress (Congress)

http://www.archives.gov/federal-register/electoral-college/2008/dates.html
(Electoral College)

http://www.fairvote.org/?page=964 (Electoral College; faithless electors)

http://www.270towin.com/blog/electoral-college/what-happens-if-there-is-a-tie-in-the-electoral-college (Tie in the Electoral College)

http://en.wikipedia.org/wiki/United_States_House_of_Representatives (House of Representatives)

http://en.wikipedia.org/wiki/District_of_Columbia_voting_rights (D.C. voting rights)

http://en.wikipedia.org/wiki/George_Wallace
http://www.counterpunch.org/wing02062009.html (George Wallace)

http://thomas.loc.gov/home/lawsmade.toc.html (How American laws are made)

http://en.wikipedia.org/wiki/United_States_Senate (U.S. Senate)

http://en.wikipedia.org/wiki/Executive_Order_9066 (Executive Order 9066)

http://en.wikipedia.org/wiki/P._B._S._Pinchback

http://en.wikipedia.org/wiki/Deval_Patrick (Deval Patrick)

http://www.newswatchngr.com/index2.php?option=com_content&do_pdf=1&id=297 (Death threats against the President)

http://www.bodhipaksa.com/archives/more-than-500-death-threats-against-obama (Death threats against the President)

http://en.wikipedia.org/wiki/Rush_Limbaugh (Rush Limbaugh)

http://en.wikipedia.org/wiki/White_flight (White Flight)

http://www.cogwriter.com/samaritan.htm (Samaritans)

www.biblegateway.com

http://members.tnns.net/wordweb/mans2.htm

http://net.bible.org/verse.php?book=Sos&chapter=1&verse=5 (Song of Solomon, tents made of the hair of black goats) http://www.guardian.co.uk/world/2010/jan/04/barack-obama-effigy-hanged-georgia (Hung in Effigy)

http://www.washingtonpost.com/wp-dyn/content/article/2009/10/15/AR2009101501992.html
(Crack and powder cocaine)

http://www.ehow.com/about_5098213_history-hair-relaxers.html (History of hair relaxers)

http://www.eraseracismny.org/html/library/housing/resources/published_reports/Predatory_lending_mortgage_crisis.pdf (Predatory lending)

http://www.inmotionmagazine.com/aahist.html (Affirmative Action)

http://www.infoplease.com/spot/affirmative1.html (Affirmative action)

http://www.education.vic.gov.au/hrweb/divequity/eeo/eeoact.htm
(Equal Opportunity Act 1995)

http://www.dol.gov/oasam/programs/history/reich/reports/ceiling1.pdf
(Glass Ceiling)

http://www.ethnicmajority.com/glass_ceiling.htm (Glass Ceiling, report from the Ethnic Majority)

http://www.case.edu/president/aaction/UnpackingTheKnapsack.pdf
(White privilege.)

http://www.gilderlehrman.org/collection/doc_print.php?doc_id=115 (The first 13th Amendment)

http://www.washingtonpost.com/wp-dyn/articles/A61428-2004Nov18.html
(Death of Bobby Frank Cherry)

http://www.stephensizer.com/2009/08/where-is-the-promised-land/
(Promised Land)

http://www.urbandictionary.com/define.php?term=Horizontal%20Racism
(horizontal racism)
United Nations, International Convention on the Elimination of all forms of Racism, New York New York, 1966.

ACLU Releases Report on Racial Profiling in Louisiana
http://www.aclu.org/racialjustice/racialprofiling/36358prs20080806.html,
www. Aclu.org

National Poverty Center, Poverty in the United States Frequently Asked
Questions, The University of Michigan, Gerald R. Ford School of Public Policy,
copyright, 2006 Regents of the University of Michigan, http://www/npc.umich.edu/poverty/

*Predatory Lending and the Mortgage Crisis: A Modern Example of Structural
Racism.*http://www.eraseracismny.org/html/library/housing/resources/published_r
eports/Predatory_lending_mortgage_crisis.pdf

The History of Affirmative Action Policies, Americans for a Fair Chance,
Washington D.C. http://www.inmotionmagazine.com/aahist.html, published in *In
Motion Magazine*, October 12, 2003. Online resource.

President John F. Kennedy, Executive Order 10925, 1961, taken from Internet
resource http://www.thecre.com/fedlaw/legal6/eo10925.htm Government
document.

Glass Ceiling Commission, *Good for Business: Making full use of the Nation's
Human Capital, The Environmental Scan,* A Fact-Finding Report of the Glass
Ceiling Commission, Washington D.D. 1995. Government document.

The Ethnic Majority, website (www. EthnicMajority.com) founded by Clifford
Tong in 2002. Tong is the CEO of Diverse Strategies, a management consulting
firm.

NAME INDEX

378

NAME INDEX

SUBJECT INDEX